MW00562265

Realism and Representation

Science and Literature

A series edited by George Levine

Realism and Representation

Essays on the Problem of Realism in Relation to Science, Literature, and Culture

Edited by
GEORGE LEVINE

The University of Wisconsin Press

The University of Wisconsin Press
114 North Murray Street
Madison, Wisconsin 53715

3 Henrietta Street
London WC2E 8LU, England

5 4 3 2 1

Printed in the United States of America

An earlier version of chapter 2 appeared in *New Orleans Review* 18 (1991): 76–85.

Chapter 12 appeared in an earlier version, in various sections of Part One of *Sequel to History: Postmodernism and the Crisis of Representational Time* (Princeton: Princeton University Press, 1992), copyright © 1992 Elizabeth Deeds Ermarth.

An earlier version of chapter 14 appeared in *History of the Human Sciences* vol. 3, no. 2 (June 1990).

Library of Congress Cataloging-in-Publication Data
Realism and representation: essays on the problem of realism in relation to science, literature and culture / edited by George Levine.
348 p. cm.—(Science and literature)
Papers originally presented at the Conference on Realism and Representation in Nov. 1989.
Includes bibliographical references and index.
ISBN 0-299-13630-2 ISBN 0-299-13634-5
1. Realism in literature. 2. Naturalism in literature. 3. Mimesis in literature. 4. Literature and science. 5. Literature—Philosophy. I. Levine, George Lewis. II. Series.
PN56.R3R36 1992
809′.912—dc20 92-26774

For Aaron, newly, wonderfully real

Contents

Illustrations

Preface

The essays gathered here—except for the Introduction—were originally written for the conference on Realism and Representation, which took place from 10 to 12 November 1989 at Rutgers University. I have tried to keep signs of the conference visible in many of the papers to give a sense of the moment and of the possibilities of dialogue that the occasion provided. Nevertheless, most of the essays are at least partially revised, and at least partially in response to that dialogue. For this volume, the entire program has been rearranged. Thus the unpredictability of the occasion has been swapped for a greater coherence and thematic consistency and development. There is still, of course, a certain tentativeness and, dare we say it, indeterminacy about the arguments as a whole, and this is appropriate both to the diversity of opinion represented and to the nature of the subject. The contributions of Richard Rorty and Bruce Robbins (in Rorty's case, substantially revised and extended) were delivered first as commentaries. Rorty's additional remarks on Robert Scholes's essay were written after Scholes added his afterword to his own essay (in response to developments in the conference). While it has not been possible to keep all the very useful formal responses in the conference for this volume, Rorty's and Robbins' remain—Rorty's because it is indispensable for an understanding of the major philosophical arguments, and Robbins' because it was almost universally perceived to be a turning point in the debates, a shift from epistemological to social historical dimensions. There has been no possibility of incorporating much of the discussion from the floor, but the organization of the materials, along with the comments of Rorty and Robbins, reflects something of the conference's main directions.

While it is the custom in collections of this sort to attempt to impose artificial unity by providing a summary of each essay in the preface or introduction, I have decided to ignore this convention. I will have occasion in my introductory essay to discuss certain important points raised by conference participants, but I do not believe that any summaries of the essays I might provide would do much for them or for a fair representation of the intricacies of the play of ideas and arguments that constitute the real value of the conference and of this volume. The essays speak for themselves without further homogenization for the purposes of the editor's project.

The volume is organized to move from direct confrontation with epistemological issues (framed in the discourse of science), to (in the middle sections) a series of attempts to think about the relations of literature and science side by side, with particular reference to questions of interpretation, epistemological authority, realism, and representation. While the penultimate section deals with modernism and mere chronology would suggest it ought to be the final one, the logic of the conference and of the implicit argument of this volume required that the essays treating questions of realism in sociological and historical context conclude it. The final section thus provides a series of historical test cases, as it were, considerations of how science operates in culture, and, by implication, what its modes of operation tell us about questions of realism.

The conference was made possible by the generous support of Rutgers University, through the Center for the Critical Analysis of Contemporary Culture, which I have been honored to direct since its inception more than five years ago. And it received important support from the History of Science Society, Douglass College, Rutgers College, the Rutgers College Honors Program, and the Rutgers University Graduate School. Since what happened at the conference lies behind what appears in the book, it is important to notice the invaluable contributions of a great many people at Rutgers. In particular, I want to thank Beryle Chandler, who is the guiding spirit of the Center and of all its activities. For more than half a year, Alan Rauch was the conference coordinator, and his help was not only logistical but intellectual as well. Now at the Georgia Institute of Technology, he is continuing his work on the relations of science and literature in the same remarkable spirit with which he worked on the conference. Jonathan Smith, who was completing a dissertation on Victorian science at Columbia and teaching courses at Rutgers, volunteered assistance and was extraordinary in the time, intelligence, and energy he gave to the conference. In addition, I want to thank Stuart Peterfreund for very useful suggestions about the structure and content of this volume.

But most of all I want to thank Jennifer Rose. As the person responsible for every detail of the conference, she performed remarkably, with a dedication and perfectionism that all the participants valued almost as much as I did. The work she did so well for the conference she has continued with this volume. Neither the conference nor the volume would have been possible without her. I am grateful not only for the quality of her work, her initiative and imagination, but for her loyalty, good humor, and friendship.

Part 1

Introduction

CHAPTER 1

Looking for the Real: Epistemology in Science and Culture

GEORGE LEVINE

Yes, once again, realism rears its hydra head. One reviewer of a proposal for the conference which formed the basis for this volume responded with alarming lack of sympathy: "MEGO," he or she contemptuously wrote, "My Eyes Glaze Over." The hostility of that response reflects, in a paradoxical way, the urgency of the ostensibly tired subject. Of course, thinkers have been wrestling since Plato with the problem of the real[1]—with whether we can ever know it, ever even have access to it, whether there is any possibility of discovering it apart from its representation (which may fully constitute it), whether the very idea of representation does not falsely presuppose the reality it displaces. The questions go on well beyond. For many, perhaps for MEGO, the question seems "unreal," unrelated at all to the reality with which everyone has no choice but to be engaged.

The results of all this debate have not—it is probably unnecessary to point out—been decisive. In response to millennia of inconclusiveness, Richard Rorty's influential *Philosophy and the Mirror of Nature* (1979) staked out forcefully a position he calls pragmatist that has been widely admired, particularly by nonphilosophers of a literary-theoretical bent, and intensely derided by many philosophers: the tradition of philosophy that focuses on the relation between language and reality must be abandoned. Philosophy has become a futile and pointless exercise. Rorty is certainly not the first philosopher to deny the "correspondence" theory of truth or to reject, as a consequence, the conception of representation (the province of epistemology). Representation, on this account, implies a foundational self as agent. The self employs language to represent a foundational reality that exists outside of language; representation (language) becomes a "third thing." Representation, moreover, implies that some correspondence between language and nonverbal reality can be established.[2]

To suggest something of the complication of the question of "realism," one should note that Rorty's philosophically subversive and relativist position is not inevitably antirealist. *Belief* in the real is almost beside the point. As Rorty puts it, "To deny the power to 'describe' reality is not to deny reality,"[3] but it is to place any particular assertion within the frame of contingency—of history and chance. He insists that

> we need to make a distinction between the claim that the world is out there and the claim that truth is out there. To say that the world is out there, that it is not our creation, is to say, with common sense, that most things in space and time are the effects of causes which do not include human mental states. To say that truth is not out there is simply to say that where there are no sentences there is no truth, that sentences are elements of human languages, and that human languages are human creations. . . . The world is out there, but descriptions of the world are not.
> (Rorty, *Contingency* 5)

That language is not, as he puts it, "transparent to the real" (Rorty, *Mirror of Nature* 368) has important consequences for the way we think about reality. That is, it entails that all "descriptions" of reality, all governing assumptions about it, are arbitrary. They must be recognized not as fixed and stable formulations of a prelinguistic real but as part of a continuing and—from Rorty's point of view—liberating "conversation" in which all reality claims are implicated in particular social, political, and historical moments and must be considered as part of a fully human, not merely "rational" or intellectual, activity.

Ironically, as many otherwise sympathetic critics of Rorty's radical subversion and deconstruction of epistemology and foundationalism have argued, he tends, in effect, to leave things pretty much where they were. From my point of view, the crucial philosophical question addressed to his account is how it can explain "change." Languages, as Rorty explains it, simply change; one way of talking comes to displace another, as for example the Copernican view of the world became more convenient than the Ptolemaic. The change in language constitutes the change in knowledge, or at least in the nature of the truth claims we are ready to make; and that change comes without agency and without traditionally conceived logical force. It is only a matter of whether the new language seems to be a more efficient tool than the language it displaces. Rorty feels no responsibility to explain such changes further.

It is a further irony that even in the professional discipline of philosophy things have continued to be as they were: epistemology remains focal, even in debates about Rorty's position. So it may well be that the impatient MEGO acquired glazed eyes from having heard too much of a debate that seems to have had no "real" consequences except the profusion of debate. Further quibbling and nit-picking about reality and representation when there is real work to be done constitute a kind of professional gibberish; even Rorty's suggestion that we drop epistemology should be dropped. Let's get real.[4]

It is, perhaps, a final irony that Rorty's denial of the correspondence theory of truth and of the value of epistemology and his insistence on the futility of our pursuit of the fundamental (and implicitly metaphysical) questions of philosophy lead him to reject not realism so much as the entire realism/antirealism debate. Were it not that Rorty was himself an invaluable participant in the conference and in this volume, one might even have made him a good candidate for the otherwise anonymous MEGO. Rorty's opposition to the debate should suggest that his important position in this volume does not quite represent the position of the volume itself, the very shape of which, with its opening emphasis on philosophical issues, implies some resistance to the commonsensical suggestion that we get real. The debate here is not merely between realists and antirealists over the old, inescapably metaphysical issues. But those issues are present, and in ways that—as Rorty's own remarks make clear—are not entirely satisfactory to him.

It might be useful here to invoke Hilary Putnam, whose disagreements with Rorty can suggest something of why philosophical arguments, against the grain of some poststructuralist thinking, are still worth having after all. Putnam—an antifoundationalist like Rorty—argues that foundationalism was not "a *basis*" of Western culture but merely a reflection upon it. Its failure, therefore, does not have the profound consequences for philosophy, daily life, politics, and culture that Rorty seems to assume. As Putnam puts it,

> I hope that philosophical reflection may be of some real cultural value; but I do not think it has been the pedestal on which the culture rested, and I do not think our reaction to the failure of a philosophical project—even a project as central as "metaphysics"—should be to abandon ways of talking and thinking which have practical and spiritual weight. . . . That a controversy is "futile" does not mean that the rival pictures are unimportant. Indeed, to reject a controversy without examining the pictures involved is almost always just a way of *defending* one of those pictures (usually the one that claims to be "antimetaphysical"). In short, I think philosophy is both more important and less important than Rorty does. It is not a pedestal on which we rest (or have rested until Rorty). Yet the illusions

that philosophy spins are illusions that belong to the nature of human life itself, and that need to be illuminated. Just saying "That's a pseudo-issue" is not of itself therapeutic; it is an aggressive form of the metaphysical disease itself.

(*Realism with a Human Face* 20)

Putnam, in effect, accuses Rorty of being "metaphysical" in the very directness of Rorty's refusal of metaphysics and foundationalism. Such an accusation is not inconsistent with other critiques of poststructuralism's tendency to infer relativism from the failure of foundationalism. Rom Harré, for example, interestingly argues that skeptics about the possibility of true scientific description of reality are guilty of the "fallacy of high redefinition," a view that since science can never produce indisputable or *totally* adequate results, total skepticism about it is justifiable.[5] Again, Larry Laudan, in his dialogue against relativism, has one of his speakers accuse the relativist of "infallibilism," another version, I believe, of Harré's fallacy of high redefinition. Since relativists require an absolute proof if they are to accept any truth statement, they in effect hold scientists and realists to a much more demanding standard of proof than the "probability" that actually guides them. The only resistance to total skepticism becomes absolute proof.[6] Putnam's point about the way metaphysics is implicit in the rejection of realism seems confirmed here.

Of course, Putnam says, "philosophical problems are unsolvable; but as Stanley Cavell once remarked, 'there are better and worse ways of thinking of them' " (*Realism with a Human Face* 19). The demand that the discussion "lead somewhere" smacks of a teleology that the critique rejects. I do not, in any case, expect that the realism/antirealism issue will be "settled"—and certainly not here—but I, and most of the contributors to this volume, share with Rorty at least his sense of the value of the conversation. In this respect, in the commitment to better or worse discussion, to the value of the discussion itself, Putnam and Rorty may be closer together than they allow. (In fact, Rorty's and Putnam's positions are close enough in so many respects that Putnam has to spend a lot of time explaining how, indeed, he differs from Rorty.) But the commitment to final solutions, even from the point of view of many kinds of realism, has deadly implications.

Thus, although Rorty occupies a crucial position in this volume, having the privilege of final commentary on several of the epistemologically oriented essays, his analysis of them takes its place not as "authoritative" but as part of the conversation. Representation—a category disbarred from Rorty's world where "correspondence" between word and thing is a chimerical idea—figures importantly throughout the volume and not simply as object of critique. Representation, whether demystified or af firmed, becomes one of the most fruitful subjects of study. Moreover, the implicit relativism of Rorty's position is not the inevitable consequence of some of the constructivist work included here, and the relativist position, ostensibly so closely allied to constructivism and critiques of realism, comes under particular scrutiny from the perspective of history and philosophy of science. Again, the project of epistemology, which has been, historically, to clear the debris of limited perspective from the establishment of authoritative knowledge, is not at an end. The debris surely cannot be cleared away, but understanding what its effects are and what it is remains necessary. Epistemology is a discipline that has always threatened to subvert itself by undercutting the possibility of its goal of authoritative knowledge, and always revives. Even Rorty's anti-epistemological arguments are, of course, epistemological.

The epistemological problems have led, in this volume, to a heavier emphasis on representation than on reality. Open as the Realism and Representation conference was to alternative points of view, its bias, like that of this volume, was certainly antirealist, though in a variety of ways, and always with a concern to take into account the fundamental problems for any antirealist philosophy of science. Overall, strong realism is not represented here, except in the arguments of Paisley Livingston and, perhaps implicitly, in Paul Churchland's essentially asymptotic understanding of how the mechanism of the mind processes information about the real. Whether the essays are philosophical or historical, they tend to accept or argue explicitly for some form of constructivism. But constructivism and realism are not necessarily incompatible either.[7]

In any case, the point of the volume is not to argue out the philosophical issues, important as these are, nor is it to build a case for constructivism, which at this late date in the history of philosophy and the developments in literary study probably needs no additional defenders: rather, it is to begin to find ways toward a more direct engagement of literary and scientific perspectives on the very complex problems of "realism" and "representation." Speaking allegorically and reductively, I can say that the point of this volume and of the conference is to break down the absoluteness of the relativist/antirealist positions of the literary camp and the objectivist/realist positions of the scientific one. Of course, few people on either side are "absolute" in their positions, but at this critical moment it is clear that the constructivist arguments, often with inadequately thought out consequences, are winning among the literary; and that in response to those arguments, scientists are holding firmly to their "realism."

The achievements of each are badly misunderstood by the other; they need to take account of each other. Much of this volume is concerned explicitly with the relations between science and literature, then, not only because of the intrinsic importance of these relations but because of the way they bring to prominence the fundamental issues involved in the realism and representation debate and call into question their own dominant assumptions. "Scientific realism" has a large body of literature surrounding it, a literature that is often directly relevant to the dominant discourses of critical theory, but normally not considered.[8] Rorty's strong refusal to see science as anything but one among many competing languages is a position widely accepted in the humanities, but it requires much more examination than it usually gets.[9] In this volume, Paisley Livingston argues for the importance of "scientific realism" to literary scholarship—the heuristic spur it gives to finding rational grounds for disagreement, to believing in the possibility of something like "discoveries." Science raises immediately questions not necessarily raised by other intellectual disciplines: how to account for its "success"; whether it is possible to deny the "rationality" of its methods and descriptions of the natural world; whether the precision of its applications in the world does not argue for the precise correspondence of its language to an extraverbal reality; whether concepts of "representation" are adequate to the sorts of nonverbal interventions science must make.[10]

One question of very great importance to the debates about realism, with all their moral and political freight, is whether there is a mode of knowledge in which ontology precedes epistemology, and a form of acquiring knowledge that does not depend on language. Science is clearly the place to look. In his defense of science against the radical skepticism of poststructuralist thought, Rom Harré argues that "existence is prior to theory, and that while no ontology for science could be absolute, nevertheless ontologies (realized in referential practices) are always, at any moment, less revisable than their associated belief-systems." He argues, further, that

> "science" is not a logically coherent body of knowledge in the strict, unforgiving sense of the philosophers' high redefinition, but a cluster of material and cognitive *practices*. . . . Science is an activity: it is something people *do*. Some, but not all of that doing is thinking, and a yet more minor part of it is producing discourses in which the results of making those material manipulations and doing that thinking are recorded. Perhaps a second "philosophers' fallacy," ancestor of the fallacy of high redefinition, is to mistake the discourse and its properties for the practice of which it is a partial and rhetorically distorted representation. I take the problem of *scientific* knowledge to be tackled by the work of philosophers making explicit the tacit skills, both conceptual and practical, of the scientific community.
> (*Varieties of Realism* 8)

Despite MEGO, the issues, especially as they emerge from the confrontation of scientific activity with antifoundationalist discourse, need rehearsing: feelings are intense, and, ironically, assumptions tend to be unexamined, even by those who insist that self-consciousness is a condition of knowledge. On both sides of the divide there are oversimplifications and failures of understanding. On the literary side, which I occupy, one often finds a complacent and dogmatic antirealism that rather comfortably underestimates science as imaginative and intellectual achievement and immediately connects a commitment to constructivism to antirealism and relativism. At the same time, as we have seen, it fails to recognize or come to terms with its own strong metaphysical implications. The tendency to argue as though "constructivism" allowed for the reduction of all languages, including scientific languages, to various disguises for ideology often threatens to turn debate into ideological posturing. (It would be dangerous to ignore the fact, however, that the valuable insistence on recognizing the ideological implications of ostensibly apolitical intellectual procedures and achievements has become a target of conservative critics of current practices in higher education, all too ready to oversimplify.)

The intensity of the divisions is evident anywhere the issues are broached. To fill out my little allegory, I will indulge here in some anecdotes that should illuminate the origin and purposes of this volume. One of the initiating events was a casual conversation with a brilliant, positivistically oriented sociologist friend of mine: if, he said, you want to argue publicly for the importance of empirical validation and make claims for its authority on the grounds of "objectivity," you're going to be called a fascist. When he told me this, he did not have the supporting evidence of another story I had just heard: a distinguished colleague of mine, whose "credentials" in current debates on ethnography are unquestionable, found himself beleaguered after a lecture in which he used the word "objectivity" without criticism. So violent was the revulsion from the word that it was impossible to discuss the subject of the talk any longer, and my colleague could manage only defensive and credential-asserting strategies until the session mercifully ended. He then went into a deep period of soul-searching about whether he was, by invoking objectivity, actually guilty of the moral and social crimes of which he had been accused. The sociologist, far less sympathetic to poststructuralist constructivism than my ethnographical colleague, is, to be sure, occasionally given to heightened rhetoric—but there is plenty of evidence (if I may use the word here) that there is something to what he said. It was disturbing.

The views that all facts are theory laden, that all argument is "interested," that all knowledge is culturally constructed, that all reality is mediated by representation, are dominant in literary theory and criticism, in sociology of science, and in some areas of philosophy of science. The exposure of the hidden political, social, and gender implications of "facts" and "objectivity" and rigorous procedures of verification has been one of the most exciting and valuable activities of modern intellectuals. But these views need not lead in the directions in which they are normally and all too easily taken these days—to relativism and, some argue, anti-intellectualism. Larry Laudan, who is also not a realist, makes the point angrily:

> The displacement of the idea that facts and evidence matter by the idea that everything boils down to subjective interests and perspectives is—second only to American political campaigns—the most prominent and pernicious manifestation of anti-intellectualism in our time.
>
> (*Science and Relativism* x)

One need not be "conservative" to find something important in such criticisms. Within this volume, several of the essayists who are most strongly antifoundational and most skeptical of traditional metaphysical realist claims firmly resist the kind of relativism that would undercut science, or transform it into just another (if more worrying) fiction. Problems with pure constructivism have been recognized by critics fundamentally sympathetic to it. Donna Haraway is perhaps the most striking example. One of the most outspoken and "postmodern" critics of science, a historian who has devoted much of her career to exposing the political and social factors that determine scientific activity, Haraway has argued forcefully that the idea of "objectivity" has been used to naturalize what is socially constructed and to deny the experience and knowledge of women by disguising its male face behind claims for universality. Nevertheless, she says, "the further I get in describing the radical social constructivist program and a particular version of postmodernism, coupled with the acid tools of critical discourse in the human sciences, the more nervous I get."[11] The nervousness results in part from the enforced recognition that the tools she has found work not only on hostile objects but on oneself. One hasn't a leg to stand on.

Feminist theory of science has interestingly moderated the radical forms of relativism and critiques of objectivity while sustaining strong critiques of the way in which objectivity has been mystified, and scientific detachment wrenched from the reality of laboratory and national politics. The costs of the pure and "acid" critique can be high if it is not conducted with precision and if its "objects" are not precisely discriminated. The unmasking of objectivity led for feminists, says Haraway, to "one more excuse for not learning any Post-Newtonian physics and one more reason to drop the old feminist self-help practices of repairing our own cars. They're just texts anyway, so let the boys have them back"

("Situated Knowledges" 578). Perhaps in part because of this kind of danger, Evelyn Keller has sought to preserve an idea of objectivity as "the pursuit of a maximally authentic, and hence maximally reliable, understanding of the world around oneself." But just as Haraway attempts to preserve something of what is thrown out with the idea of objectivity by defining a "situated knowledge," Keller has discriminated two kinds of objectivity—"dynamic" and "static"—only the latter of which is damagingly mystifying.[12] Helen Longino, at work on a similar project, supports what she calls "contextual empiricism." Arguing that all knowledge is context dependent, Longino insists nevertheless on the possibility of "objectivity," as long as that objectivity is understood (in a rather Rortyan way, I would think) as defined within the context of a scientific community whose values are embedded in the very methods it endorses.[13] Keller, Haraway, Longino, and my positivist sociologist would, I am sure, agree on very little. But the implications of their critiques made it clear to me that the questions I have been talking about are not at all abstract, remote, or, at this stage, glaze-inducing. Debunking objectivity has its dangers if it is not accompanied by an effort to recuperate what is valuable in the concept. Clearly, doing that matters to the way people will act in the world—fixing their own cars, recognizing and resisting unjustified authority, studying genetic structures, or denigrating the possibility of knowledge itself—as well as to how they write essays in philosophical journals.

Another impulse to create this volume came from my experience of "the other side," where I have been struck by the deep, even visceral hostility of most working scientists and almost all of the philosophers whom I know personally to the forms of antirealism implicit in much poststructuralist thought. Even Haraway's feminist defense of the necessity for allowing some form of objectivity through the construction of what she calls "situated knowledge" would likely be disturbing to them.[14] Feminist projects are perceived to be "extrinsic" to scientific activity and thus irrelevant to its rigorously impersonal procedures. Feminism, for most practicing scientists, even the women scientists I know, feels like any strong constructivism: for them, constructivism simply fails to take account of the objectivity essential to science. When human interests enter, scientific authority is undermined.

From the point of view of working scientists, discussions of feminist philosophy of science seem irrelevant to the practice of science; indeed, for most of them, any philosophy of science is likely to be at best vaguely interesting. At worst it is the conduit through which such unscientific or antiscientific thinking as that of Thomas Kuhn and the sociologists of science and the feminist critics deliver their disruptive messages. The scientists' hostility to deconstruction, which is often taken as the dominant form of antirealism for literary critics and which has made serious incursions into history and the social sciences, is particularly violent—at least verbally violent.

My experience with a rather distinguished astrophysicist, whom I see perhaps three or four times a year at parties, is not, I believe, untypical. He invariably rushes up to me on these occasions, passion burning in his eyes, and *demands* to know whether, if you pushed a deconstructionist from a high tower, he could deconstruct the fall and not be smashed to bits. Is the theoretical—in more ways than one—victim going to fall? And is he going to fall at a speed my astrophysicist will be able to predict? Murderous smiles accompany the question, and the astrophysicist is never satisfied when I tell him (a) every deconstructionist I know would do everything possible to avoid being thrown off a high tower, and (b) I don't know what the question has to do with deconstruction. Although I usually don't get this far, I might at my next encounter invoke Rorty's argument that denying that truth is anything but the property of sentences does not entail denying the existence of a "reality" that is what it is without regard for human interests.

"Reality" itself is at stake here. What can be the point of a theory that insists that there is nothing outside the text if its practitioners believe in reality enough not to walk through walls or allow themselves to be pushed off towers? If science does not describe the real, then why do deconstructionists believe its descriptions and predictions? As I have already suggested in mentioning the arguments of Harré and Putnam and Laudan, it doesn't take a deconstructionist to raise questions about the ontological status of scientific descriptions. Philosophers of science who are not "antirealists" (in the sense of rejecting the aspiration of science to describe the "real") often are forced to conclude that science simply has not made the case that it is in fact describing reality.[15] Since science succeeds, the common sense position goes, science is true, or at least approximately true. But this, as Larry Laudan argues, is a traditional fallacy: "exhibition that a theory had some true consequences left entirely open the truth-status of the theory. . . . false theories, as well as true ones, could have true consequences." (Leplin, *Scientific Realism* 242). One of the most prominent positivists on the contemporary scene, Bas C. van Fraassen, resists the sort of reality claims my astrophysicist implicitly makes. He allows for the "empirical adequacy" of scientific theories. "We can take it to be the aim of science to produce a literally true story about the world, or simply to produce accounts that are empirically adequate." Van Fraassen will settle for the latter, and argues that "theories need not be true to be good" (Leplin, *Scientific Realism* 251).

To pursue the philosophical debates much further would be to complicate the issues in ways not directly relevant to this volume. Nevertheless, I want to suggest briefly here that in the disciplinary divisions that determine the shape of the debate, antirealist philosophers of science tend to take a rather different view from that of antirealist literary theorists. As Arthur Fine argues, in what I take to be one of the most sensible and valuable contributions to the argument, the real differences between antirealist philosophers of science and realist philosophers of science are actually rather slight, and by examining that slight difference, Fine moves on to an important new position in the debates. Realist and antirealist "must both accept the certified results of science," he says, in the same way that they accept "homely" truths. The difference is in what they "add onto the core position." What the realist adds is only "a desk-thumping, foot-stamping shout of 'Really!' "[16] In other words, the realist is no more committed to the validity of the scientific idea than is the antirealist, only he wants to claim ontological status for the world that science imagines.

Fine begins, then, with what might be called a commonsense position—the one my astrophysicist friend thinks he is defending from the antirealists; he comfortably accepts currently acceptable scientific procedures and discoveries in the same way as he accepts the homely truths of ordinary life while not committing himself to ontological claims. He calls this position the "natural ontological attitude." One might wonder how much fun he is having with "natural," but the position in any case remains both relaxed and sensible. It avoids the absurdities that my astrophysicist apparently sees in poststructuralist critiques and skepticism, and it reasonably accounts for the way the deconstructionist can both refuse to be pushed off the tower and make antirealist claims at the same time. Without accepting the realist baggage of belief in the asymptotic progress of scientific knowledge, and without the vague satisfaction that comes with believing that science can achieve more than van Fraassen's "empirical adequacy," Fine can accept the hardheaded and objectivist stances of science while keeping his faith in its validity constrained by the particular results of particular investigations.

His is not, then, a realist position, but it is not fully compatible with "literary" antirealism either. But unless the primary function of antirealism is the disturbance of conventional ways of thinking, there is no reason it shouldn't be compatible. Antirealism, even literary antirealism, depends on a sense of the impossibility of unmediated knowledge; it does not require a refusal to accept the conditions of "homely" truths. Fine's natural ontological attitude gives us a leg to stand on while refusing to give away the game to realist imaginations of perspective-neutral facts, or to the dangerous reification of such facts into the "natural." As Fine describes it, "the natural ontological attitude" is neither realist nor antirealist:

> NOA sanctions ordinary referential semantics and commits us, via truth, to the existence of the individuals, properties, relations, processes, and so forth referred to by the scientific statements that we accept as true. Our belief in their existence will be just as strong (or weak) as our belief in the truth of the bit of science involved, and degrees of belief here, presumably, will be tutored by ordinary relations of confirmation and evidential support, subject to the usual scientific canons.
>
> (*Shaky Game* 130–31)

While this might seem, like Rorty's more radical arguments, to leave us exactly where we have begun, it actually leaves us in a better position to argue for change. "Ordinary referential semantics" may seem, like the now abjured realism, mere acquiescence in what is; but ordinary referential semantics allow for challenges to the ideal of objectivity, for example, that are not self-refuting, as relativist arguments must always be. They allow precisely grounded particular arguments about the perspectival distortions and biases of particular truth claims. Ordinary referential semantics, accepted on Fine's "homely" terms, do not entail reification, essentialism, or a rejection of the view that knowledge is "constructed." But they make far more difficult a facile constructivism that implies that since all knowledge is constructed, all knowledge can be changed immediately—or with an appropriate amount of table thumping. As I understand Fine's position, it can be useful only if it is supplemented by hard work in every particular case, by careful accumulation of empirical evidence organized within self-consciously elaborated structures of thought and worked out through agreed upon procedures.

Nobody from the literary side of these debates has, so far as I know, given much thought to Fine's views; they are, after all, philosophy, and they are also, apparently, proscience. Fine simply is having nothing of the infallibilism and high redefinition that have characterized much poststructuralist language-oriented theory. On the other hand, his complex form of nonrealism has made little impression on practicing scientists either, for they tend to respond to philosophy only when it obviously impinges on or threatens their own work. Scientists are no more comfortable with the "proscience" scientifically sophisticated theories of philosophers like Laudan and van Fraassen and Fine than they are with antirealist literary theoreticians, and the degree of their discomfort can be measured by the anger with which they greet antirealist arguments.

Clearly, there is more at stake here than a philosophical position. After a lecture to a general audience in which I was outlining some of these issues, I responded to a question about how such thinking might affect the actual practice of science by assuring the questioner that neither I nor people like me made decisions about funding science projects. A scientific voice from the front row shouted, "Thank God!" This hasn't to do with philosophy.

The disciplinary divisions are almost absolute. Scientists don't talk to philosophers of science; philosophers of science don't talk to literary theorists; literary theorists—while implying their right through the study of language and discourse to tread on everyone's turf—seem not to talk to anybody but like-minded theorists. Indeed, it is one of the ironies of the contemporary scene and another impetus for this volume that antirealist philosophy of science is almost as little attended to by antirealist humanist theorists as by the scientists themselves.

Evelyn Keller identifies two noncommunicating levels of discourse about science,

> one an increasingly radical critique that fails to account for the effectiveness of science, and the other a justification that draws confidence from that effectiveness to maintain a traditional, and essentially unchanged, philosophy of science. What is needed is a way of thinking and talking about science that can make sense of these two very different perspectives—that can credit the realities they each reflect and yet account for their differences in perception.
>
> (*Reflections* 6)

Can we, as Helen Longino asks, "develop an analysis of scientific knowledge that reconciles the objectivity of science with its social construction"? (While I doubt that many will agree with me, I believe that Fine comes close to such a reconciliation.) That reconciliation within science needs to be achieved also between science and those committed now to a deep critique of objectivity and to constructivism.

The contributors to this volume, of course, have their own agendas (and did not have the opportunity to hear my own quasi-philosophical comments, which were written after all their essays were in); but I have brought them together here because I believe that Longino and Haraway and Keller's project is a crucial one for the intellectual and, indeed, the political integrity of the projects of literary theory and of science itself. This volume was inspired, then, by an increasingly urgent sense of profound intellectual barriers that must be broken down. The questions, as they shape themselves in contemporary literary critical theory, in the social sciences, in philosophy, and in philosophy of science are not only abstract and theoretical, although crucial philosophical issues are at stake. The fears of the scientist who was relieved that people like me don't determine who gets scientific grants provide just one example of the practical importance of these debates.

It is because the essays in this volume do not follow the curve of the arguments on which I have been concentrating that I have tried here to focus on the more abstract forms of the debate as they are worked out in philosophy. The epistemological issues remain important but they need to be seen within a larger historical and social context: they do not get argued out in a vacuum, and philosophy is not the only form in which "realism" gets debated. If the philosophical argument that all knowledge is "interested" has any validity, the realist/antirealist debates need to be understood in terms of "interest," too. Philosophy of science and the discoveries of quantum mechanics have reinforced the view that there is no point outside the fray from which the whole battle may be perceived and understood and resolved. "Quantum theory," as P. W. Bridgman put it many years ago, "forces us to realize that we cannot have information without acquiring that information by some method, and that the story is not complete until we have told both what we know and how we know it."[17]

Self-evidently, the important feminist historians and philosophers I have cited have a large moral and political investment in the issues and see that investment as part of the epistemological question. But epistemology has almost always been also a form of ethics, from Plato and his cave, through Bacon, who saw knowledge as possible only after "self-humiliation," to our modern philosophers. Putnam sees Rorty, for example, as aspiring to be "a doctor to the modern soul" (*Realism with a Human Face* 20). Harré's defense of science is overtly moral: science builds on its own ideal community, in which "trust" is a condition of knowledge. Philosophers less directly concerned with ethics or politics are equally implicated in the social fabric: to defend "realism" or attack it is almost always to ally oneself with a whole set of related and nonphilosophical conditions.

The conference, in a sense, grew impatient with epistemology divorced from this social context. It might be fair to say, even of a group of participants preponderantly constructivist, that they, and their auditors, were eager to get closer to "reality," in a perhaps nonphilosophical sense. They wanted to engage with the "interests" not quite expressed in the philosophical discussions, to see what the debates about realism meant within culture and society. The question is how one makes the apparent transition from epistemology to cultural practice. For many scientists, as I have suggested, that transition marks an absolute demarcation: science is rational and ordered and objective; cultural practice has nothing to do with the internal practices of science. History of science on these terms reduces to a history of rational procedures by which scientific discoveries are made. Anything more implies a radical subversion of the scientific project.

The battle about realism, then, gets fought in the very description of scientific projects. Although in this volume only Simon Schaffer might be directly allied to the arguments of the "strong program" of sociology of science, all the historical work represented here (and this, of course, is no accident) is constructivist. The question of whether the constructivism implies, as believers in the "strong program" might contend, that the explanation of the acceptance of scientific beliefs is *entirely* context dependent and regardless of intrinsic properties is part of what is at stake, even among constructivists themselves. For very few of the participants at the conference was the object the radical subversion of science. That is because while the issues that impelled the conference as they impel this volume are, in the not so long run, moral, social, political issues, nobody assumed that to engage with moral issues was to subvert science.

The question is how to work out the relation between the abstract issues of philosophy and theory and the way we live and have lived. That connection, Putnam himself has argued in a book primarily philosophical, lies in the necessary connection of any philosophical enterprise with "values." The impossibility of any grounding of knowledge or truth even in the notion of "being a standard of a culture" (a Rortyan ostensibly relativist conception) leads Putnam back to fundamental and, it may be, unanalyzable values: "without the cognitive values of coherence, simplicity, and instrumental efficacy, we have no world and no facts, not even facts about the world." These cognitive values are part of "our historic holistic conception of human flourishing," and, "like every activity that rises above the mere following of inclination or obsession, is guided by our idea of the good" (*Realism with a Human Face* 139).

This argument remains at a very high level of abstraction, of course, yet it pushes epistemology back toward an engagement with human values, where, because it always depended so much on trust, self-effacement, honesty, it had begun. Putnam's position may be eccentric in the world of professional philosophy (it is not at all eccentric in feminist theory of science), but the determination to reengage philosophical debate with "human flourishing" is a crucial move in putting science and philosophy back into culture where, in fact, they have always been, but from which their professional practice has artificially separated them.

"Realism" and "Representation" are terms that imply social engagement. Epistemological preoccupations with the impossibilities of achieving a position outside interest, a "God's-Eye View," has led to a kind of paralysis of knowledge—a refusal to trust or believe in empirical evidence. In response to this phenomenon, Marshall Sahlins has, in conversation, suggested that postmodern ethnology suffers from "epistemological hypochondria," that it is so preoccupied with the impossibilities of effacing the knowing subject in the interests of direct access to the cultures being studied that it can't any longer get around to studying those cultures at all. This volume, with all its preoccupation with the limits of perception and the necessity of self-referentiality, insists with Putnam and Sahlins that knowledge, in a meaningful sense, is possible. And in its last essays, it moves from theory to cultural/historical analysis of the way "knowledge" gets itself authorized.

As I have already suggested, the immediate problem is that the ostensible implications of studies that treat the history of science from the perspective of society rather than from the perspective of its own internally accepted methods seem to be subversive of true scientific knowledge because they are radically relativist. But, as Harriet Ritvo wrote to me after the conference, the charges of "relativism" were off the mark and deeply disturbing to her and other panelists. "It never occurred to me," she wrote,

> that the fundamental question I ask when I think about the scientific practice of several centuries ago is: was (or could it have been) right? why or why not? Instead, I mean to ask, why did it come out the way it did? That is, I think I am essentially asking a question about the culture that produced science and not about the science itself.

Ritvo's procedures suggest only that there is nothing natural or logically inevitable about the establishment of scientific truths at any historical moment. They have to win their way and they can do so only if they can be understood as somehow consonant with the values and dominant assumptions of the culture at large and, particularly, of those elements within the culture who exercise the greatest power. She wants to know how the culture operated, how science maneuvered within culture. For her, as she puts it, "theory is not anterior to practice." As we read her work and that of Ludmilla Jordanova and Simon Schaffer in this volume, we can see that theory is woven fully into the practice.

Simon Schaffer provides a historical example of the process in a remarkable treatment of the politics of Newtonianism. "Questions of trust and legitimacy," says Schaffer, "are hard to separate from questions of adequacy and reference." The real is established culturally, and the history of its establishment is effaced in scientific discourse. Studies of the kind Schaffer and Ritvo and Jordanova pursue push the theoretical issues into the arena of history and culture. Of course, here too, interpretation is critical, and the epistemological problems do not go away. But such histories depend also on careful empirical study. If all the facts narrated are, as the philosophers tell us, theory laden, they remain, nevertheless, indispensable to useful arguments about how science works. There are, as Putnam and Cavell argue, "better and worse theories."

Theory enters history. And with that entry—as Bruce Robbins discussed it in his mid-conference commentary—the conference and this volume turned. Robbins takes one crucial step by suggesting how the realism debate might be translated from the epistemological to the social. He pushes the question of realism into another tradition entirely, one in which socially oriented critics like Lukács, Raymond Williams, and Fredric Jameson elaborate the notion of reality beyond the immediate, sensible experience into the very structures that underlie social life and action. Robbins carefully disentangles this imagination of realism from the naive realism that is the straw man of most recent literary arguments. "Every time a text is triumphantly shown to transcend realism," he argues, "the demonstration is only partly about the text; it is also a pious exercise in disciplinary self-corroboration, a demonstration that the discipline of literary criticism is justified in its distinctness and autonomy."

In making this argument, Robbins implicitly justifies the whole enterprise of this volume. He suggests how the science/literature dichotomy often works to allow literature to trivialize itself by denying any cognitive content. The attempt to see science and literature as equivalent modes of discourse can be a move not to transform science into a fiction but to transform literature into a cognitive mode. Both science and literature, on this reading, turn out to establish their ground not on some intrinsic, pure, "professional" way of knowing, but on social consensus. This, of course, is arguable: and Putnam, with all his commitment to the moral significance of philosophy, would deny the "consensus" theory of truth as itself being ungrounded and subject to its own critique.

But Robbins' insistence on the way that truth-building is a social process is a move toward the reconciliation of perspectives as divergent as that of Harré, Rorty, Schaffer, and Scholes. Science, as Harré and Longino, among many others, have argued, is a social activity, dependent even in its most specialized knowledge claims on community. It is for this reason that this volume concludes with the essays of Ritvo, Jordanova, and Schaffer, all of whom address the question of realism indirectly, from the perspective of cultural history rather than of philosophy. Schaffer provides the most extensive and detailed historical study, showing how even so ostensibly fundamental a worldview as Newton's had to win its way by a complex process of social and political establishment of "trust" in those who supported that view. Ritvo, Jordanova, Schaffer, and Robbins all participate in a complex recognition of the ways in which social and political issues are always involved in questions of knowledge. It is not clear whether all would agree that there is nevertheless a possibility, eloquently affirmed at the end of Robbins' arguments and based on comments by S. P. Mohanty, that it is possible to "develop a set of general criteria which would have interpretive validity" in contested areas.

Not that we have developed such criteria. But the possibility can be realized only if we work through the realism/representation debate and across the disciplinary divides that keep us rather too complacent about the strength of our positions. The essays gathered here are, of course, preliminary to a generally successful reconciliation between our antimetaphysical, antifoundational rejection of realism and representation, and our continuing social and political and moral need to find ways to overcome epistemological hypochondria and, with a steady eye on the complicated social and historical details, establish mutually satisfactory criteria for rational and humane discourse.

NOTES

1. In this Introduction, I cannot begin to suggest the range of debate over "realism." For the most part, I will be concentrating on the way the issue has been formulated around "scientific realism" in recent decades. But even the bibliography of recent philosophical excursions into realism would be very long. For a fair overview of the various positions within philosophy of science, see Jarrett Leplin, ed., *Scientific Realism* (Berkeley: University of California Press, 1984). Leplin's introduction makes a point of real import to my arguments here: "Like the Equal Rights Movement, scientific realism is a majority position whose advocates are so divided as to appear a minority" (1). Another important collection, which centers around the arguments of Bas van Fraassen, is Paul M. Churchland and Clifford A. Hooker, eds., *Images of Science* (Chicago: University of Chicago Press, 1985). The career of Hilary Putnam, which has swerved from forms of antirealism to a position he calls "internal realism," provides an important example of major philosophical work on the subject and of the complications and difficulties of either a strong realism or relativism. See, for example, Hilary Putnam, "Why There Isn't a Ready Made World," *Synthese* 51 (1982): 141–67; "Three Kinds of Scientific Realism," *Philosophical Quarterly* 32 (1982): 194–200; "What is Realism," in Leplin 140–53; *Realism and Reason* (Cambridge: Cambridge University Press, 1983); *The Many Faces of Realism* (LaSalle, Ill.: Open Court, 1987); and, most recently, *Realism with a Human Face* (Cambridge: Harvard University Press, 1990). I would also recommend, as a difficult but fascinating rethinking of the issues, Roy Bhaskar, *Reclaiming Reality: A Critical Introduction to Contemporary Philosophy* (London: Verso Books, 1989). Bhaskar works outside the dominant traditions of Anglo-American philosophy, arguing for the possibility of an ontology not dependent upon epistemology, and for what he calls a "critical" or "transcendental realism" in the interests of a revitalized socialism.

2. For an interesting example of Rorty's direct discussion of this issue, see "Texts and Lumps," *New Literary History* 18 (1985): 1–16, in which he con-

siders the relation between literature and science. Among other things, Rorty argues the likelihood that we have greater access to human reality than to the natural world by way of science. In *Contingency, Irony, and Solidarity* (Cambridge: Cambridge University Press, 1989) Rorty provides one of his clearest expositions of his antifoundational argument against correspondence, against the idea that language is a "medium": "Think of the term 'mind' or 'language' not as the name of a medium between self and reality but simply as a flag which signals the desirability of using a certain vocabulary when trying to cope with certain kinds of organisms" (15).

3. Richard Rorty, *Philosophy and the Mirror of Nature* (Princeton: Princeton University Press, 1979), 375.

4. T-shirts with "Get Real" slogans were sold at the "Realism and Representation" conference on which this volume is based. It may be of interest to readers to know that while there are still quite a few of these available, all the shirts with the alternative slogan, "No Reality Without Representation," sold out immediately.

5. Harré describes the fallacy in this way: "By their defining, even only tacitly, such cognitive phenomena as scientific knowledge in terms of truth and falsity, the demands placed on a community which has the task of accumulating some of 'it' are set in such a way that 'it' can never be achieved. 'Look,' shouts the triumphant sceptic, 'you haven't given us what we want by way of knowledge, so scientists haven't made any progress at all!' " *Varieties of Realism: A Rationale for the Natural Sciences* (Blackwell, 1986), 7. Harré goes on to identify another overreaction based in too high metaphysical expectations—"logical essentialism": "that there could never be good reasons for a scientific belief does not show that there aren't any good reasons. It does show that the concept of 'good reason,' as it is used by the scientific and to any extent by the lay community, does not yield to an explicatory analysis in logicist terms."

6. See Larry Laudan, *Science and Relativism: Some Key Controversies in the Philosophy of Science* (Chicago: University of Chicago Press, 1990), 86.

7. Any thorough philosophical treatment of the subject—which this volume does not aspire to be—would require a full disentangling of these concepts. "Realism" takes many forms as does "antirealism." (See the catalogue of kinds of realism in the first pages of Leplin, for a useful beginning.) Constructivism does not necessarily entail "relativism," and antirelativist positions can also be antirealist. The categories cross and recross. Larry Laudan, who has written impressively against realism, writes ferociously against relativism, as in his dialogue among positivist, realist, relativist, and pragmatist. Roy Bhaskar, who calls himself a "transcendental" or "critical" realist, can also be seen as a constructivist. Churchland, in his *Scientific Realism and the Plasticity of Mind* (Cambridge: Cambridge University Press, 1979), while arguing for a more refined, more mechanically precise understanding of perceptual processes, of "epistemic engines," recognizes—like any good constructivist—that all perceptions are theory laden. His realism points only to better theory, the "best theory available" (35). Putnam is both realist and relativist, on his own accounting: "The key to working out the program of preserving commonsense realism while avoiding the absurdities and

antinomies of metaphysical realism in all its familiar varieties (Brand X: Materialism; Brand Y: Subjective idealism; Brand Z: Dualism . . .) is something I have called *internal realism.* I should have called it pragmatic realism! Internal realism is, at bottom, just the insistence that realism is *not* incompatible with conceptual relativity. One can be both a realist and a conceptual relativist" (*The Many Faces of Realism* 17).

8. The most ambitious and interesting study of this question is Paisley Livingston, *Literary Knowledge: Humanistic Inquiry and the Philosophy of Science* (Ithaca: Cornell University Press, 1988). Livingston presents forcefully the arguments for scientific realism, particularly the work of Richard N. Boyd, most of whose writing appears in philosophical papers in journals. See, for example, "Metaphor and Theory Change," in *Metaphor and Thought,* ed. Andrew Ortony (Cambridge: Cambridge University Press, 1979), and "On the Current Status of the Issue of Scientific Realism," *Erkenntnis* 19 (1983): 45–90.

9. I have myself supported that position in *One Culture: Essays in Science and Literature* (Madison: University of Wisconsin Press, 1987); but I have tried to qualify it in "Why Science Isn't Literature: The Importance of Differences," *Annals of Scholarship* nos. 3/4 (1991): 365–379. I survey some of the literature and the possibilities of connection between scientific realism and literary theory and criticism in "Scientific Realism and Literary Representation," *Raritan* 10 (1991): 18–39.

10. The most satisfying discussion of the question of whether verbal representation adequately accounts for the activities of science can be found in Hacking, *Representing and Intervening: Introductory Topics in the Philosophy of Natural Science* (Cambridge: Cambridge University Press, 1983): "Maybe there are two quite distinct mythical origins of the idea of 'reality.' One is the reality of representation, the other, the idea of what affects us and what we can affect. Scientific realism is commonly discussed under the heading of representation. Let us now discuss it under the heading of intervention. My conclusion is obvious, even trifling. We shall count as real what we can use to intervene in the world to affect something else, or what the world can use to affect us" (146). The "material" condition of science, as apart from its verbal expression, is a matter of increasing concern among philosophers of science. That condition should also provide something of a test case for literary theorists whose emphasis is language and representation. Some of the most interesting work in this area is now being done by Peter Galison. See his "History, Philosophy, and the Central Metaphor," *Science in Context* 2 (Spring 1988): 197–211. See also *How Experiments End* (Chicago: University of Chicago Press, 1987). The book begins: "Despite the slogan that science advances through experiments, virtually the entire literature of the history of science concerns theory" (ix). Galison goes on to argue that while "experiments begin and end in a matrix of beliefs," scientific discovery depends on "the context of real laboratory life," which works by neither "capricious discovery" nor "rule-governed justification" (277).

11. Donna Haraway, "Situated Knowledges: The Science Question in Feminism as a Site of Discourse on the Privilege of Partial Perspective," *Feminist Studies* 14 (1988): 577.

12. Evelyn Fox Keller, *Reflections on Gender and Science* (New Haven: Yale University Press, 1985), 116–17.

13. Helen Longino, *Science as Social Knowledge: Values and Objectivity in Scientific Inquiry* (Princeton: Princeton University Press, 1990), see esp. 219ff.

14. Haraway's prophetic mode is more obviously provocative than that of other strong feminist critics of science. Her project as described above is paralleled—as I have suggested—by the work of Evelyn Fox Keller. The most sustained attempts at thinking through not only a feminist orientation in science but a feminist epistemology and method have been by Sandra Harding. See, in particular, her *The Science Question in Feminism* (Ithaca: Cornell University Press, 1986). In an interesting survey of feminist critiques of science, Clifford Geertz, attempting not to be unsympathetic to the feminist project but clearly convinced that current scientific method cannot be improved by a gender critique, formulates the tension much as Keller does, but with the evident assumption that feminism and the activities of science are not compatible and that Keller's desire for a way of thinking and talking that would reconcile them is probably a fantasy. He asks how the tension can be resolved between "the moral impulses of feminism, the determination to correct gender-based injustice and secure for women the direction of their lives, and the knowledge-seeking ones of science, the no-less-impassioned effort to understand the world as it, free of wishing, 'really is.' " "A Lab of One's Own," *New York Review of Books* 37 (8 Nov. 1990): 23.

15. A perhaps typical, moderate, case is made by Nicholas Rescher in *Scientific Realism* (Dordrecht: D. Reidel, 1986). Rescher rejects both instrumentalism and a hard scientific realism that argues for the real existence of theoretical entities. He carefully tries to show that the history of science fails to reveal that science's truth assertions can ever be taken to describe the real adequately. It is a condition of science that its truth assertions will be overturned by future science. On the other hand, he argues that science attempts to find out "what is really going on in the world" (36), and that "the intention to describe the world is a crucial aspect of the goal-structure of science" (37). But we are entitled only to believe that "we can know something about" the world; "We can acquire (a substantial volume of) accurate information about the nature of the real" (154).

16. Arthur Fine, *The Shaky Game: Einstein, Realism and Quantum Theory* (Chicago: University of Chicago Press, 1986), 129.

17. P. W. Bridgman, "Quo Vadis," *Daedalus* 87 (Winter 1958): 89. Of course, the Heisenberg uncertainty principle is regularly invoked by contemporary critics, one of the few aspects of philosophy of science to attract respectful attention in contemporary theory. It has, indeed, become a cliché.

Part 2

Epistemology: Science and Reality

CHAPTER 2

Constrained Constructivism: Locating Scientific Inquiry in the Theater of Representation

N. KATHERINE HAYLES

The Theater of Representation

One of the important developments in science studies has been the increased awareness that scientific inquiries are social and ideological constructions. Donna Haraway's explorations of primatology, Shapin and Schaffer's investigations into the sociology of Boyle's laboratory, and Bruno Latour's study of "black boxes" in science are only a few of the seminal analyses that have challenged accounts of how science is done.[1] So extensive and successful have these critiques been that it now seems the aspect of science most in need of explanation is its power to arrive at apparently ahistorical and transcultural generalizations. Given that science is socially constructed, how can we explain, as Michel Serres puts it, that "entropy increases in a closed system, regardless of the latitude and whatever the ruling class."[2]

A clue can be found in a curious lacuna that occurs when this question is discussed within the philosophy of science. There the debate has been constructed as a division between the realists and the antirealists. Both sides grant that there is something called observables, and that these observables have an instrumental efficacy in the world. You tighten a loose battery cable, and the car starts where it would not before. But they disagree as to whether or not the observables relate to entities that exist in reality as such. The realists say there really is an electrical current that flows, while the antirealists want to weaken or deny this claim. The lacuna occurs in the anthropomorphic grounding that underlies the idea of observables. Without being explicit about it, both sides mean observable from a human perspective. This assumption has important implications.

Consider a frog's visual cortex. Studies indicate that objects at rest elict little or no neural response in a frog's brain.[3] Maximum response is elicted by small objects in rapid, erratic motion—say, a fly buzzing by. Large objects evoke a qualitatively different response than small ones. This arrangement makes sense from a frog's perspective, because it allows the frog to discriminate prey from nonprey, and prey from predators that want to eat it. Now imagine that a frog is presented with Newton's laws of motion. The first law, you recall, says that an object at rest remains so unless acted upon by a force. Encoded into the formulation is the assumption that the object stays the same; the new element is the force. This presupposition, so obvious from a human point of view, would be almost unthinkable from a frog's perspective, since for the frog moving objects are processed in an entirely different way than stationary ones. Newton's first law further states, as a corollary, that an object moving in a straight line continues to move so unless compelled to change by forces acting upon it. The proposition would certainly not follow as a corollary for the frog, for variation of motion rather than continuation counts in his perceptual scheme. Moreover, it ignores the *size* of the object, which from a frog's point of view is crucial to how information about movement is processed.

My point is not that humans know what frogs cannot fathom. The scientists who did the frog research put it well: their work "shows that the [frog's] eye speaks to the brain in a language already highly organized and interpreted instead of transmitting some more or less accurate copy of the distribution of light upon the receptors" ("What the Frog's Eye Tells" 1950). This and other studies conclusively demonstrate that there can be no perception without a perceiver.[4] Our so-called observables are permeated at every level by assumptions located specifically in how humans process information from their environments.

Observing with instruments rather than with unaided human perception does not rescue us from our anthropomorphism, for the instruments we design and build are just those that would be conceptualized by someone with our sensory equipment. Instruments extend and refine human perceptions, but they do not escape the assumptions encoded within the human sensorium. Add the profound influence of acculturation upon cognitive processing, and it becomes clear that observables really mean observations made by humans located at specific times and places and living in specific cultures. In short, we are always already within the theater of representation. Everything we perceive, think, or do is always already a representation, not reality as such.

Yet representation may be too passive a concept to account for the complexities involved. Research by Walter Freeman and Christine Skarda on the olfactory bulb of rabbits indicates that perceptual processing is context-dependent as well as species-specific.[5] Rabbits continually sniff; these sniffs take in molecules of odorants that fall on the cilia of receptor cells in the nose, which in turn are connected to mitral cells in the olfactory bulb of the cortex. When the odors are neutral, oscillatory bursts of neural activity appear that can be reliably identified as characteristic of a given animal. When the animal sniffs an odor that he has been conditioned to recognize as significant, a different pattern appears. Then the burst is amplified in a cascading effect that brings together selectively coactivated neurons in a nerve cell assembly. This amplification happens very fast, within milliseconds. At certain critical thresholds, further changes take place that affect the entire global area of the olfactory bulb. The data demonstrate that perception is not a passive response to stimuli but an active process of self-organization that depends on prior learning and specific contexts. "Perception begins *within* the organism with internally generated neural activity," Skarda writes ("Understanding Perception" 52). "What happens within the brain is about interaction" (53).

Although the data vary with individual animals and between species, additional experiments on the visual cortex of the monkey and the somatosensory cortex of a human subject indicate that the active, self-organizing nature of perception applies in these cases as well.[6] On this basis, Skarda and Freeman have argued that neuroscience should give up the concept of representation (which Skarda calls "representationalism"), because it encourages the fallacy that perception passively mirrors the external world. Representation in this sense happens only when an observer enters the scene. It is the *experimenter's* viewpoint, Skarda writes, which "requires that conclusions be drawn about what the observed activity patterns represent to the subject" ("Understanding Perception" 57). From this vantage, our anthropomorphism has led us not only to universalize our species-specific perspective into a vision of an autonomously existing reality but also to falsify the nature of our own perceptual processing.

The point is telling. I am not willing, however, to relinquish a term as central to literary discourse as representation. I want to introduce another way of formulating it that will make representation a dynamic process rather than a static mirroring. Suppose we think about the reality "out there" as an unmediated flux. The term emphasizes that it does not exist in any of the usual conceptual terms we might construct (such as reality, the universe, the world, etc.) until it is processed by an observer. It interacts with and comes into consciousness through self-organizing, transformative processes that include sensory and cognitive components. These processes I will call the cusp.

On one side of the cusp is the flux, inherently unknowable and unreachable by any sentient being. On the other side are the constructed concepts that for us comprise the world. Thinking only about the outside of the cusp leads to the impression that we can access reality directly and formulate its workings through abstract laws that are universally true. Thinking only about the inside leads to solipsism and radical subjectivism. The hardest thing in the world is to ride the cusp, to keep in the foreground of consciousness both the active transformations through which we experience the world and the flux that interacts with and helps to shape those transformations. For as soon as the thought forms, we become aware of the paradox: what we imagine is not the cusp itself, but the representation of it that is in our conceptual realm.

The reflexive mirroring that enfolds cusp into concept shows how we can be trapped within the prison house of language. This inherent reflexivity was part of what Derrida had in mind when he proclaimed, "There is no outside to the text."[7] As long as positive assertions are made, there is indeed no way out of the reflexive loop, no way to conceptualize the cusp without always already falling short of what the conceptualization attempts to represent. Negation, however, is a more complex and ambiguous function. In negation, possibilities for articulation exist that can elude the reflexive mirroring that would encapsulate us within textuality and nothing but textuality. This elusive negativity authorizes a position that grants the full weight of the constructivist argument but draws back from saying anything goes. Such a position is necessary if science is to retain its distinctive characteristic as an inquiry into the nature of the physical world, while also rightfully being recognized as an arena of social discourse and cultural practice. Central to it are contexts, consistency, and constraints. Their interaction allows the cusp to be posited and its relation to elusive negativity explored.

Riding the Cusp: What We Remember, What We Forget

This afternoon Hunter and I went for a walk. Hunter is a handsome, medium-sized dog, half beagle and half hound. Hunting rabbits is bred into his genes, and there are a lot of rabbits where we live. It is not uncommon for a rabbit to run across the road in front of us. He sees it, I see that he sees it, he sees that I see he sees it. Having lived with Hunter for over ten years, I know that I have about two seconds to convince him to remain at heel rather than run after the rabbit. I also know that the outcome will depend in part on how authoritative my voice is, how close the rabbit, how intense the scent and how bad his arthritis. Most of the time I succeed in convincing him not to run; occasionally I fail. In either case, complex communications take place between us about an external reality that we both perceive and that affects our actions. How does this happen?

No doubt Hunter processes the world in a very different way than I do, from the limited color range he experiences to the vastly richer role scent plays in his universe. Despite these differences, we are able to communicate because we share a context that remains largely consistent from day to day. I do not perceive the world as he does, but my perception of his perception stays relatively constant. I know the kinds of things that excite his attention and what his probable responses will be, just as he knows mine. When the rabbit runs across our path, we each react within our different sensory realms to a stimulus that catalyzes our responses, which are also conditioned by past experiences with the world and each other. This consistency allows for the shorthand "Hunter sees the rabbit," although on reflection I am aware that "rabbit" is an anthropomorphic concept that Hunter does not share with me in anything like the same sense another human being could. The unmediated flux impinges on him, impinges on me; I see the rabbit and Hunter's response in my way, he sees the rabbit and my response in his. We both know that we are responding to an event we hold in common, as well as to a context that includes memories of similar events we have shared.

The temptation to forget the complexities of this account and abstract to the shorthand is very strong. From such abstraction comes the belief that nature operates according to laws that are universally and impartially true. What is the harm in moving to the abstraction? The implications become clear when we look at what it leaves out of account. Gone from view are the species-specific position and processing of the observer; the context that conditions observation, even before conscious thought forms; and the dynamic, interactive nature of the encounter. In such a pared-down account, it is easy to believe that reality is static and directly accessible, chance and unpredictability are aberrations, and interaction is nothing more than an additive combination of individual factors, each of which can be articulated and analyzed separate from the others.

This is, of course, the world of classical physics. It continues to have a vigorous existence in popular culture as well as in the presuppositions of many practicing scientists. When the TV camera, accompanied by Carl Sagan's voice-over, zooms through the galaxy to explore the latest advances in cosmology, these presuppositions are visually and verbally encoded into an implied viewpoint that seems to be unfettered by limitations of context and free from any particular mode of sensory processing. As a representation, this simulacrum figures representation itself as an inert mirroring of a timeless, objective reality.

Perhaps its most pernicious aspect is the implicit denial of itself as a representation. The denial is all the more troubling because of the ideological implications encoded within it. Among those who have explored these implications are Evelyn Fox Keller, who points out the relation between an "objective" attitude, the masculine orientation of science, and the construction of the world as an object for domination and control; Ilya Prigogine and Isabelle Stengers, who relate the appeal of a timeless realm to a fear of emotional involvement and death; Nancy Cartwright, who demonstrates that the idea of scientific "laws" always derives from the act of analysis and never intrinsically from the situation itself; and Michel Serres, who reminds us that deviations from idealized, abstract forms are not exceptions but the noise that constitutes the world.[8] These critiques can be seen as acts of recovery, attempts to excavate from an abstracted shorthand the complexities that unite subject and object in a dynamic, interactive, ongoing process of perception and social construction.

A model of representation that declines the leap to abstraction figures itself as species-specific, culturally determined, and context-dependent. Emphasizing instrumental efficacy rather than precision, it assumes local interactions rather than positive correspondences that hold universally. It engages in a rhetoric of "good enough," indexing its conclusions to the context in which implied judgments about adequacy are made. Yet it also recognizes that within the domains specified by these parameters, enough consistencies obtain in the processing and in the flux to make recognition reliable and relatively stable.

Since the claim for consistency separates this position from strict social construction, it is worth exploring more fully. Central to this claim is the idea of constraints. By ruling out some possibilities—by negating articulations—constraints enable scientific inquiry to tell us something about reality and not only about ourselves. Consider how conceptions of gravity have changed over the last three hundred years. In the Newtonian paradigm, gravity is conceived very differently than in the general theory of relativity. For Newton, gravity resulted from the mutual attraction between masses; for Einstein, from the curvature of space. One might imagine still other kinds of explanations, for example a Native American belief that objects fall to earth because the spirit of Mother Earth calls out to kindred spirits in other bodies. No matter how gravity is conceived, no viable model could predict that when someone steps off a cliff on earth, she will remain suspended in midair. This possibility is ruled out by the nature of physical reality. Although the constraints that lead to this result are interpreted differently in different paradigms, they operate universally to eliminate certain configurations from the range of possible answers. Gravity, like any other concept, is always and inevitably a representation. Yet within the representations we construct, some are ruled out by constraints, others are not.

The power of constraints to enable these distinctions depends upon a certain invariability in their operation. For example, the present limit on silicon technology is a function of how fast electrons move through the semiconductor. One could argue that "electron" is a social construction, as are "semiconductor" and "silicon." Nevertheless, there is an unavoidable limit inherent in this constraint, and it will manifest itself in whatever representation is used, provided it is relevant to the representational construct. Suppose that the first atomic theories had developed using the concept of waves rather than particles. Then we would probably talk not about electrons and semiconductors but about indices of resistance and patterns of refraction. There would still be a limit, however, on how fast messages could be conveyed using silicon materials. If both sets of representations were available, one could demonstrate that the limit expressed through one representation is isomorphic with the limit expressed in the other.

Note that I am not saying constraints tell us what reality is. This they cannot do. But they can tell us which representations are consistent with reality, and which are not. By enabling this distinction, constraints play an extremely significant role in scientific research, especially when the representations presented for disconfirmation are constrained so strongly that only one is possible. The art of scientific experimentation consists largely of arranging situations so the relevant constraints operate in this fashion. No doubt there are always other representations, unknown and perhaps for us unimaginable, that are also consistent with reality. The representations we present for falsification are limited by what we can imagine, which is to say, by the prevailing modes of representation within our culture, history, and species. But within this range, constraints can operate to select some as consistent with reality, others as not. We cannot see reality in its positivity. We can only feel it through isomorphic constraints operating upon competing local representations.

The term I propose for the position I have been urging is constrained constructivism. The positive identities of our concepts derive from representation, which gives them form and content. Constraints delineate ranges of possibility within which representations are viable. Constrained constructivism points to the interplay between representation and constraints. Neither cut free from reality nor existing independent of human perception, the world as constrained constructivism sees it is the result of active and complex engagements between reality and human beings. Constrained constructivism invites—indeed cries out for—cultural readings of science, since the representations presented for disconfirmation have everything to do with prevailing cultural and disciplinary assumptions. At the same time, not all representations will be viable. It is possible to distinguish between them on the basis of what is really there.

Are constraints not themselves representations? If so, how is the claim for their invariability justified? With these questions, the distance between articulation and cusp threatens to collapse, cutting off the connections that interactively put us in touch with the unmediated flux. To answer them and elaborate the dynamic figure of representation, I return to the crucial difference between *congruence* and *consistency.* Congruence implies one-to-one correspondence. In Euclidean geometry, one can test for congruence by putting one triangle on top of another and seeing whether they match. If the area and shape of one exactly fits those of the other, congruence is achieved; any deviation indicates that they are not congruent. Congruence thus falls within the binary logic of true/false. Consistency, by contrast, cannot adequately be accounted for in a two-valued logic. In addition to true and false, two other positions—let us call them not-true and not-false—are necessary. The introduction of these two values reveals an important asymmetry between affirmation and negation. From this asymmetry emerges a sense of the relation between language and representation that steps outside the reductive dichotomies of the realist/antirealist debate.

The Semiotic Square and Elusive Negativity

Mapping the four positions mentioned above onto a semiotic square will make explicit the multiple connections and disjunctions that constitute their interactions. A. J. Greimas introduced the semiotic square as a way to represent the possibilities for signification in any semiotic system.[9] These possibilities, although very rich, are not infinite. They are created through the interaction of what Greimas called "semiotic constraints"—deep structures that enable meaning to emerge by restricting articulations to certain axes of signification. Ronald Schleifer has interpreted and expanded on Greimas' construction of the semiotic square, and the discussion that follows is indebted to his work as well as to Greimas.[10]

If we grant that we are always already within the theater of representation, it follows that no unambiguous or necessary connection can be forged between reality and our representations. Whatever the unmediated flux is, it remains unknowable by the finite subject. Representations arise in response to such historically specific factors as prevailing disciplinary paradigms and cultural assumptions, as well as such species-specific factors as the human sensorium and neurophysiology. Observations are culturally conditioned and anthropomorphically determined. We can never know how our representations coincide with the flux, for we can never achieve a standpoint outside them. Consequently, the true position cannot be occupied because we cannot verify congruence.

The false position, however, can be occupied. Within the range of representations available at a given time we can ask, "Is this representation *consistent* with the aspects of reality under interrogation?" If the answer is affirmative, we still know only our representations, not the flux itself. But if it is negative, we know that the representation does not adequately account for our interaction with the flux in a way that is meaningful to us in that context. The asymmetry revealed by this analysis should not be confused with Popper's doctrine of falsification.[11] Understanding that theories could not be verified, Popper nevertheless maintained congruence as a conceptual possibility. The problem for him was that congruence was empirically based and so always liable to exceptions that might appear in the future. In the scheme articulated here, future exceptions do not play a privileged role in explaining why congruence cannot be achieved. Even if by some fiat we could be sure that no future exceptions would exist, the most we could say is that a model is consistent with reality as it is experienced by someone with our sensory equipment and previous contextual experience. Congruence cannot be achieved because it implies perception without a perceiver.

The four positions are mapped onto a modified semiotic square as shown in Figure 2.1. The horizontal relation between the two top positions, false and true, is constructed through a contrary relation that makes them mutually exclusive alternatives. What is true cannot be false, and what is false cannot be true. The bottom two positions, not-true and not-false, are in a more complex relation. Not-false, designated as the more restrictive, is occupied by models found to be consistent with the flux as it is interactively experienced. Not-true is occupied by models which have been imperfectly tested or not tested at all; these I call unknown. Between the negated categories of not-false and not-true, two kinds of oppositions are in play. One is a polarity between negation and affirmation (false/true), the other between indefinite and definite (unknown/consistent). This ambiguity folds together the ability to negate exclusion

(inconsistent) False ←--------→ True (unoccupied)

overlap

(unknown) Not-True ←-----→ Not-False (consistent)

Figure 2.1. The semiotic square and binary/fourfold logic

with the ability to specify. In doing so, it opens an escape hatch from the prison house of language.

The entanglement of negation with specificity can be explored through the linguistic concepts of modality and marking. Traditionally defined, a modality is a statement containing a predicate that is affirmed or denied by other qualifications. The modern definition expands a modality into any statement about another statement. Nonmodal articulations appear as mere statements of fact. In this sense they are unmarked, allowing for a reading that does not take the speaker's position into account. In general unmarked terms are those which have been naturalized by cultural assumptions and so rendered transparent. "Man" is an unmarked noun, "woman" a marked one; "as old as" is an unmarked phrase, "as young as" a marked one. In modality the marking is accomplished by the qualifying phrase that calls attention to the statement's swerve from facticity. Affirmation and negation are nonmodal; denial and assertion are modal. When the president's press secretary says, "The rumor is false (or true)," he has negated (or affirmed) it. When he says, "I say that the rumor is false (or true)," he has denied (or asserted) it. Denial *implies* negation while subtly differing from it, just as assertion *implies* affirmation without exactly being affirmation.

As their compound form signals, not-true and not-false are marked terms. Realism tends to elide the differences indicated by these markings, assimilating not-false into true and not-true into false. When a scientific textbook states, "All the matter in the universe was once contracted to a very small area," the difference between the model and the reality tends to disappear, as do the position and processing of the observer for whom the statement makes sense. Far from eliding markings, the semiotic square displays them along the vertical axis. Expanding the binary dichotomy of realism to the quadrangle of semiotics, this distance-as-difference reminds us that articulations emerge from particular people speaking at specific times and places, with all of the species-specific processing and culturally conditioned expectations that implies. The vertical axis thus separates as well as implicates, as shown in the schematic in Figure 2.2.

Beyond the marking that not-true and not-false share is the additional negativity inhering in not-true. Located at the lower left corner of the square, it occupies the space that on a Cartesian grid represents the negative of both axes. The negative of a negative, it is the position most resistant to assimilation into the transparencies of nonmodal statements. Fredric Jameson calls it "the place of novelty and of paradoxical emergence," noting that it is "the most critical position and the one that remains open or empty for the longest time."[12]

The implications of its excess negativity can be unpacked by again referring to modality. It is possible to negate a modality, creating as it were a double marking. The press secretary may say, "I cannot say that the rumor is false (or true)," in which case the status of the rumor remains indeterminate. This situation corresponds to a residue within the not-true position that cannot be articulated—models that we cannot conceive because they are alien to our mode of processing the world. Not coincidentally, it also points to the reason why we cannot say a model is congruent with reality. Because we can never achieve a viewpoint outside our viewpoint, "unknown" overlaps with and implies "unknowable."

Schleifer has argued that this kind of ambiguous negation is characteristic of scientific theories and art forms that elude either/or categorization, particularly quantum mechanics and literary modernism.[13] Shoshana Felman has called it "radical negativity," which "belongs neither to *negation*, nor to *opposition*, nor to *correction* . . . —it belongs precisely to *scandal*."[14] Calling this scandal the "outside of the alternative" because it emerges from a "negativity that is neither negative or positive" (141–42), she suggests that it opens the way to reconceive referentiality (76–77). In my terms, it allows the question of reference to be reintroduced without giving up the insights won by the new sociology of science when it bracketed reference.

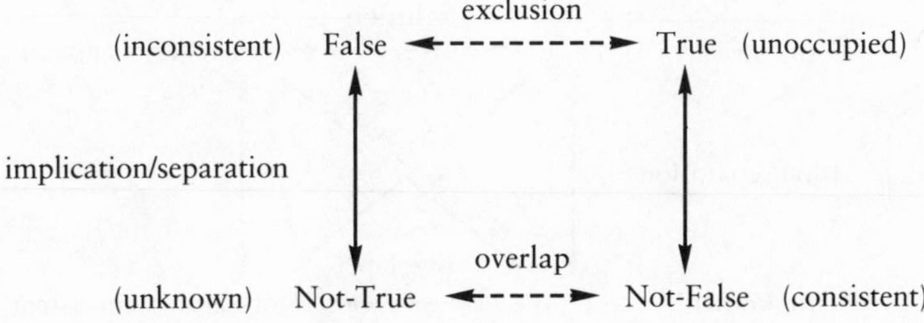

Figure 2.2. The semiotic square and modality/nonmodality

The relation of constraints to representation can now be articulated more precisely. When constraints become representations, they necessarily assume a positive cognitive content that moves them from the cusp into the theater. When I say, "The total entropy of a closed system never decreases," I am expressing a representation of a constraint. Representations of this kind operate along the diagonal that connects inconsistent and consistent models. At the cusp, the interactions expressed by these representations have no positive content. The inability of language to specify these interactions as such is itself expressed by the elusive negativity that exists within the not-true position. The diagonal connecting true and not-true reveals their common concern with the limits of representation. At the positive ("true") end of the diagonal, the limits imply that we cannot speak the truth. At the negative ("not-true") end, they paradoxically perform the positive function of gesturing toward that which cannot be spoken. Elusive negativity, precisely because of its doubly negative position, opens onto the flux that cannot be represented in itself.

The complete semiotic square can now be given. (Fig. 2.3). It is no accident that the semiotic constraints generating the semiotic square bring the not-true position into view. Language structures how we conceptualize any representation, including mathematical and scientific ones. But language is not all there is. Elusive negativity reveals a synergy between physical and semiotic constraints that brings language in touch with the world. Physical constraints, by their consistency, allude to a reality beyond themselves that they cannot speak; semiotic constraints, by generating excess negativity, encode this allusion into language. There is a correspondence between language and our world, but it is not the mysterious harmony Einstein posited when he said that the mystery of the universe is that it is understandable. Neither is it the self-reflexivity of a world created through language and nothing but language. Our interactions with the flux are always richer and more ambiguous than language can represent. Elusive negativity, acknowledging this gap, gestures

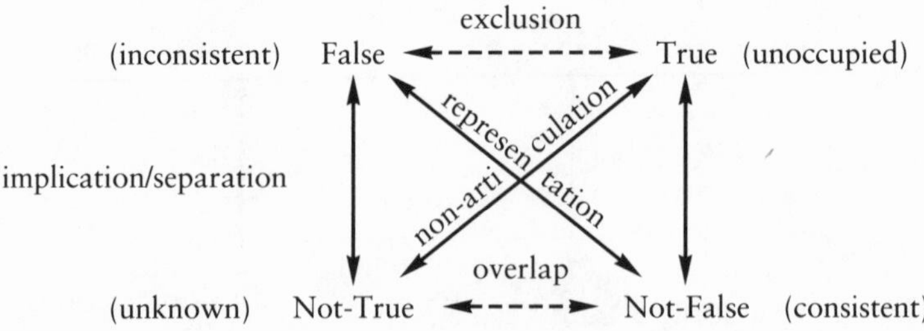

Figure 2.3. The semiotic square and the limits of representation

toward this richness and so provides a place within semiotic systems to signify the unspeakable—to signify the cusp.

Making Connections: The Language of Metaphorics

To posit a model for scientific inquiry is to presuppose or evoke a correlative view of language. A realistic model calls for and is reinforced by the assumption that language is a transparent medium transmitting ideas directly from one mind to another; a positivist model produces and is produced by attempts to formalize language into theory and observation components; a social constructivist model is associated with a nonreferential view of language that sees discourse operating through relations of sameness and difference. These correspondences are not accidental. They must obtain in any coherent account of scientific inquiry, for inquiry is constituted as such only when it enters the social arena of discourse. Like other representations of scientific inquiry, constrained constructivism corresponds to a particular view of language. The view of language correlative with it can be found within the emerging field of metaphorics. The difference between a representation consistent with reality and one that depicts reality is the difference between a metaphor and a description. Constrained constructivism thus implies that all theories are metaphoric, just as all language is. Metaphorics, defined as the systematic study of metaphoric networks as constitutive of meaning production, presents a view of scientific inquiry that enriches and implies the figure of representation presented here.

Since Max Black's influential analysis of metaphor, it has become customary to emphasize the power of metaphor to create new understanding.[15] According to this argument, metaphors not only express similarities between disparate concepts; they also set up complex currents of interaction that change how the terms brought into relation are understood.[16] A similar argument is adopted by Lakoff and Johnson in *Metaphors We Live By.*[17] Like Black, Lakoff and Johnson are concerned with systems of associated commonplaces that infuse into each other when two terms are brought into metaphoric interplay. Their emphasis falls on ordinary metaphors which, precisely because they do not surprise, reveal presuppositions deeply embedded within the culture.

In Arbib and Hesse's *The Construction of Reality,* metaphorics is explicitly connected with scientific inquiry.[18] They argue that perception takes place through schema which operate through relational similarities and differences. The category "dog" has as its reference not some Platonic idea that captures the essence of dog, but a network of individual perceptions that form a group, albeit one fuzzy at the edges. In their account, the tension between similarity and difference characteristic of metaphor, far from being a special subset of language usage, is fundamental to how language works. The "loose bagginess" of the metaphoric relation allows for constantly changing configurations within metaphoric networks; these changes in turn correlate in a systematic fashion with shifts in paradigms. "Scientific revolutions," Arbib and Hesse write, "are, in fact, metaphoric revolutions, and theoretical explanation should be seen as metaphoric redescription of the domain of phenomena" (156).

In James J. Bono's account, metaphorics allows cultural presuppositions to be articulated together with scientific discourse systems.[19] Bono argues that metaphor functions "as both the site and means for exchanges among not only words or phrases, but also theories, frameworks, and most significantly, discourses" (73). He envisions interactive, synchronic networks of metaphors that span disciplinary boundaries, in which traces of metaphors inherited diachronically from disciplinary traditions interfere and intersect with other metaphoric systems within the culture. Meaning production in this account can never be contained within a scientific field alone. Rather, it depends upon and emerges from resonances and interferences between inter- and extrascientific networks of metaphors that engage one another at highly specific sites.

Constrained constructivism matches these views of scientific language with an interactive, dynamic, locally situated model of representation. Recognizing that scientific theories operate within the theater of representation, it emphasizes that meaning production is socially and linguistically constructed. The elusive negativity that is a consequence of taking consistency rather than congruence as a standard for correctness reveals ambiguities intrinsic to any account of scientific models. These ambiguities ensure fluidity in language, thus reinforcing the claim that scientific revolutions are effected through metaphoric redescription. Finally, the transformative nature of interactions at the cusp makes the model context-dependent as well as species-specific, encouraging the idea that specific exchanges take place at local sites. Constrained constructivism thus presents a figure of representation that itself can be a metaphor for the inquiries of metaphorics.

Situated Knowledge: No Outside But a Boundary

Constrained constructivism puts limits on Derrida's aphorism that there is no outside to the text. Although there may be no outside that we can know, *there is a boundary.* The consequences that flow from positing a boundary or cusp rescue scientific inquiry from solipsism and radical subjectivism. At the same time, constrained constructivism acknowledges that we cannot have direct, unmediated access to reality. There is much to be said on why this acknowledgment is felt as an intolerable limitation by some realists. In "Situated Knowledges: The Science Question in Feminism as a Site of Discourse on the Privilege of Partial Perspective," Donna Haraway alludes to the ideology embedded within an omniscient viewpoint when she calls it a "god trick."[20] Objectivity is associated with a view from everywhere, and hence from nowhere—a view with no limitations and hence no connections to humans located at specific places and times.[21] That it is a power trip is undeniable. That this power has frequently been misused is also undeniable. The illusion that one can achieve an omniscient vantage point, and the coercive practices associated with this illusion, have been so thoroughly deconstructed that they do not need further comment here. The liberatory spirit with which the critiques of objectivity were undertaken has been realized in the valuable contributions they have made to our understanding of how ideology and scientific objectivity mutually reinforce each other.

But in the process, objectivity of any kind has gotten a bad name. I think this is a mistake, for the possibility of distinguishing a theory consistent with reality from one that is not can also be liberating. If there is no way to tell whether the claim that blacks and women have inferior brains is a less accurate account of reality than the claim that they do not, we have lost a valuable asset in the fight for liberation. George Levine eloquently made this point when he argued for the need to break out of coterie politics and strive for a faithful account of reality.[22] Donna Haraway also recognizes this possibility when she calls for a paradoxical, noninnocent stance that will recognize limited objectivity at the same time that it continues to deconstruct all claims to omniscient knowledge. The problem she wrestles with is underscored by Levine as the central issue of the contemporary sociology of knowledge: "how to have *simultaneously* an account of radical historical contingency for all knowledge claims and knowing subjects, a critical practice for recognizing our own 'semiotic technologies' for making meanings, *and* a no-nonsense commitment to faithful accounts of a 'real' world, one that can be partially shared and that is friendly to earthwide projects of finite freedom, adequate material abundance, modest meaning in suffering, and limited happiness" ("Situated Knowledges" 579).

Haraway's solution is to emphasize that every perspective is partial, all knowledges situated. She tackles the difficult task she sets herself by continuing the vision metaphor but insisting that it is partial and contingent rather than full and unlimited. I am fully in sympathy with her project, and I think that she has articulated the central problem that a feminist sociology of knowledge faces. I am concerned, however, that the idea of partial vision can be easily misconstrued. It can be taken to suggest that part of our vision sees things as they really are, while only part is obscured. Whatever our vision is, this is not the case; we see things whole, not in parts. An alternative approach is to follow the lead of Merleau-Ponty when he suggests that situatedness, far from being a barrier to knowledge, enables it.[23] Given that we are not God, we can come in touch with the universe only through particular sets of sensory apparatus located within specific cultures and times. Constrained constructivism has this double edge: while it implies relativism, it also indicates an active construction of a reality *that is meaningful to us* through the dynamic interplay between us and the world. Renouncing omniscience and coercive power, it gains connectedness and human meaning.

NOTES

In writing this essay, I have benefited from conversations and correspondence with F. C. McGrath, Ronald Schleifer, Walter Freeman, Evelyn Keller, and James Bono. George Levine and Gillian Beer gave helpful encouragement and guidance.

1. Donna Haraway, "Animal Sociology and a Natural Economy of the Body Politic, I and II," *Signs* 4 (1978): 21–60; Steven Shapin and Simon Schaffer, *Leviathan and the Air Pump: Hobbes, Boyle, and the Experimental Life* (Princeton: Princeton University Press, 1985); Bruno Latour, *Science in Action: How to Follow Scientists and Engineers through Society* (Milton Keynes: Open University Press, 1987).

2. Michel Serres, *Hermes: Literature, Science, Philosophy,* ed. Josué V. Harari and David F. Bell (Baltimore: Johns Hopkins University Press, 1982), 106.

3. J. Y. Lettvin, H. R. Maturana, W. S. McCulloch, and W. H. Pitts, "What the Frog's Eye Tells the Frog's Brain," *Proceedings of the Institute for Radio Engineers* 47 (1959): 1940–51.

4. For a summary of visual mechanisms in different species, see *Models of the Visual Cortex,* ed. David Rose and Vernon G. Dobson (New York: John Wiley and Sons, 1985).

5. Christine A. Skarda, "Understanding Perception: Self-Organizing Neural Dynamics," *La Nuova Critica* 9–10 (1989): 49–60. See also Walter Freeman and Christine Skarda, "Mind/Body Science: Neuroscience on Philosophy of Mind," in *John Searle and His Critics,* ed. E. LePore and R. van Gulick (London: Blackwell, 1988); and "Representations: Who Needs Them?" *Proceedings of the Third Conference on the Neurobiology of Learning and Memory* (forthcoming).

6. Walter Freeman, private communication.

7. Jacques Derrida, *Dissemination,* trans. Barbara Johnson (Chicago: University of Chicago Press, 1981).

8. Evelyn Fox Keller, *Reflections on Gender and Science* (New Haven: Yale University Press, 1985); Ilya Prigogine and Isabelle Stengers, *Order Out of Chaos: Man's New Dialogue with Nature* (New York: Bantam, 1984); Nancy

Cartwright, *How the Laws of Physics Lie* (New York: Oxford University Press, 1983); and Michel Serres, *Hermes.*

9. A. J. Greimas, "The Interaction of Semiotic Constraints," *On Meaning: Selected Writings in Semiotic Theory,* trans. Paul J. Perron and Frank H. Collins (Minneapolis: University of Minnesota Press, 1987), 48–62.

10. Ronald Schleifer, *A. J. Greimas and the Nature of Meaning: Linguistics, Semiotics and Discourse Theory* (London: Croom Helm, 1987), 22–55.

11. Karl L. Popper, *Conjectures and Refutations: The Growth of Scientific Knowledge,* 2d ed. (New York: Basic Books, 1965).

12. Fredric Jameson, Foreword, *On Meaning* xvi.

13. Ronald Schleifer, "Analogy and Example: Heisenberg, Negation, and the Language of Quantum Mechanics," MS. See also Ronald Schleifer, *Rheteric and Death: The Language of Modernism and Postmodern Discourse Theory* (Champaign: University of Illinois Press, 1990).

14. Shoshana Felman, *The Literary Speech Act: Don Juan with J. L. Austin, or Seduction in Two Languages,* trans. Catherine Porter (Ithaca: Cornell University Press, 1983), 141–42.

15. Max Black, *Models and Metaphors* (Ithaca: Cornell University Press, 1962). See also "More about Metaphor," in *Metaphor and Thought* ed. Andrew Ortony (Cambridge: Cambridge University Press, 1979), 19–43.

16. Paul Ricoeur emphasizes the torque that metaphors put on terms in *Interpretation Theory: Discourse and the Surplus of Meaning* (Fort Worth: Texas Christian University Press, 1976).

17. George Lakoff and Mark Johnson, *Metaphors We Live By* (Chicago: University of Chicago Press, 1980).

18. Michael A. Arbib and Mary B. Hesse, *The Construction of Reality* (Cambridge: Cambridge University Press, 1986), 147–70.

19. James J. Bono, "Science, Discourse, and Literature: The Role/Rule of Metaphor in Science," in *Literature and Science: Theory and Practice,* ed. Stuart Peterfreund (Boston: Northeastern University Press, 1990), 59–89.

20. Donna Haraway, "Situated Knowledges: The Science Question in Feminism as a Site of Discourse on the Privilege of Partial Perspective," *Feminist Studies* 14 (1988): 575–99.

21. For a different (and more realist) position on how subjectivity and objectivity can be integrated, see Thomas Nagel, *The View from Nowhere* (New York: Oxford University Press, 1986).

22. George Levine, Plenary Address at the Society for Literature and Science Society Conference, September 1988.

23. Maurice Merleau-Ponty, *The Phenomenology of Perception* (London: Routledge & Kegan Paul, 1962).

CHAPTER 3

On the Problem of Truth and the Immensity of Conceptual Space

PAUL M. CHURCHLAND

I will come back to our focal topics of truth, representation, conceptual change, and objectivity toward the last third of this essay. Those issues are usually discussed within a framework of beliefs about the basic nature of cognition, and I want to set the stage by outlining an *alternative* conception of what cognition is. It is a conception of cognition that derives from recent work in cognitive neurobiology, connectionist artificial intelligence (AI), and parallel distributed processing research in psychology.

It is of interest because its basic kinematics and dynamics for cognitive activity are radically different from the kinematics and dynamics with which we are so familiar. Common sense and traditional AI and psychology all agree that the basic kinematic element in cognition is the belief, or sentence, or proposition. Our current cognitive state is relevantly represented by the set of beliefs we hold, the set of sentences to which we are committed. And the dynamics of cognition, on this view, concerns the inferences that reason requires one to draw from accepted sentences to further sentences. Fresh observation sentences can confirm or refute old theories; new theories can be embraced because they explain old puzzles; discovered contradictions can force deletions and adjustments among our beliefs; and so forth. In these ways does the set of accepted sentences, or perhaps the probabilities that we assign to them, *change* over time.

So far the tradition. But here I want to argue for a new conception of what cognitive activity is, and for a very simple reason. The conception I have just described to you is almost certainly *false*, as a description of what cognitive activity is in creatures generally, and even in humans specifically. I am not going to try to *convince* you of the new view. That sort of thing takes a good deal of time, and the next several years will take care of that anyway, because lovely results keep flowing out of this new approach. I will let that process take care of itself. My principal aim is rather to make it intelligible and just a little appealing to you. I hope to pull you in a little, so that you can then say, "So that's what it's all about."

But why is it interesting? There are many reasons, but the ones I will discuss here concern some consequences it has for the notion of truth, and for the process of pursuing truth over individual and historical times. But I will come to these consequences after I have put you in the picture.

I begin by drawing your attention to Figure 3.1, because I have found it extremely helpful in locating people in the relevant conceptual space. What we have here is a cartoon sketch of one of the initial pathways in

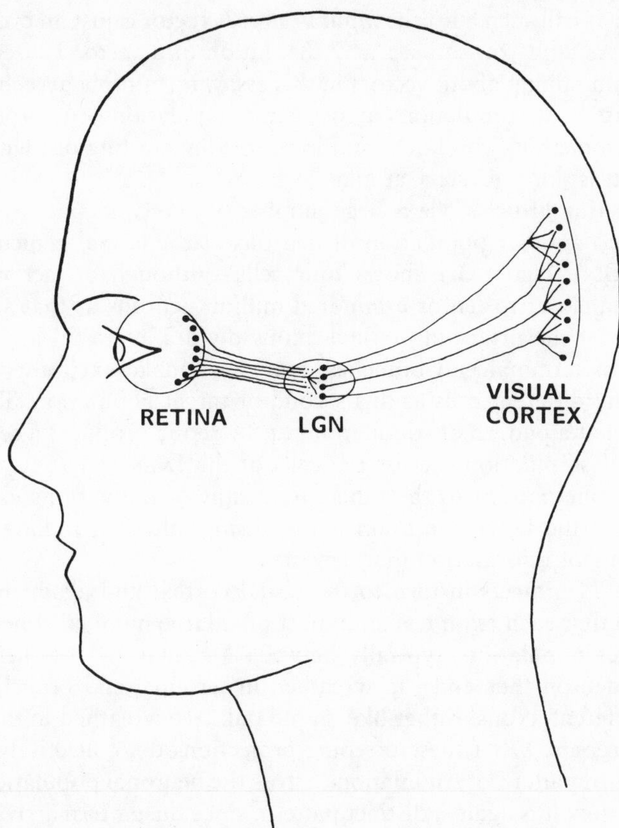

Figure 3.1. Pattern-to-pattern transformations in the primary visual pathway

the brain. Of course, projections go from the back of the brain to a zillion other places in the brain as well, but if you draw too many, it just looks like spaghetti, so I have drawn just three stages here for reasons that will become clear presently. This diagram has two virtues. First, it exploits the fact that you already have no problem appreciating how a *pattern of stimulations* across your retina can *represent* the world. Any particular scene you might be viewing will produce a characteristic pattern of stimulations across the cells of the retina. You have about a hundred million cells on each retina, though I have drawn only eight retinal cells in Figure 3.1. But the point is clear enough: we can specify any pattern of retinal stimulation by a unique list of numbers—decimal numbers between zero and one, say—each one telling us by what fraction of maximum its corresponding cell is stimulated.

Theorists call such a list the *input vector.* A vector is just an ordered list of numbers, and you can see why the notion of a vector is useful here. When I am talking about vectors in this essay, it is simply as a shorthand for a pattern of stimulations across some population of neurons. Your retina is something you know and love, so I am starting out with something that is not a mystery at all.

Your retina *projects,* via a large number of axons, its pattern of stimulations to another population of neurons at the lateral geniculate nucleus (LGN). Figure 3.1 shows four cells—although in fact you have something closer to ten or a hundred million neurons at that site—and each one of the projecting retinal axons divides at its tip into a large number of terminal end branches, and these make excitatory contact with many different cells at this second or target population. The basic result is that a pattern of stimulations at the retina produces a secondary pattern of stimulations across the cells of the LGN. There is a change from the one pattern to the other: by means of the various excitatory contacts at the LGN, the brain is processing, filtering, pulling out the special bits of information that it wants.

The LGN projects in turn to the visual cortex, and again the axons divide so that each axon has an impact on a large number of neurons at this target population, typically between 10^3 and 10^4 of them. Each cortical neuron thus ends up wreathed in terminal end branches from many different axons, rather like an old oak tree wreathed in thousands of ivy creepers. What these creeping projections do, collectively, is produce a third pattern of stimulations across the neuronal population at the visual cortex. It is again a distinct pattern, since the pattern arriving from the LGN goes through millions of those little terminal connections, called *synapses,* which vary widely in their conductivity. The arriving pattern is thus transformed as it acts on the target population: it produces a new pattern of stimulations across the cortical neurons. What we have then is a device for transforming a complex pattern at the sensory periphery into a series of different patterns at subsequent layers of neurons.

In aid of what? we might ask. Consider Figure 3.2. This is a model, and it is useful because it represents the salient features of the process discussed above. You may think of the bottom layer of cells as the sensory periphery, and the middle and top layers as representing the LGN and the visual cortex, respectively. You will notice the synaptic connections at the tip of each axonal end branch, represented by small bars, and you will notice that some of them are rather bigger than others. That means that any stimulation arriving at such a synapse will have a large effect on the receiving cell. The same stimulation arriving at a small synapse will have only a small effect on the receiving cell. You may think of these as gates of varying sizes. Depending on what overall configuration of gates mediates the incoming pattern of stimulations, we get a specific *transformation* effected between the vector conveyed upward toward the middle layer, and the vector (= pattern of stimulations) that finally results across the middle-layer neurons themselves.

You can think of the neurons, by the way, as humming to themselves, and to each other. For they emit pulses along their axons with a frequency varying between zero and perhaps 500 Hz. With a high level of activation

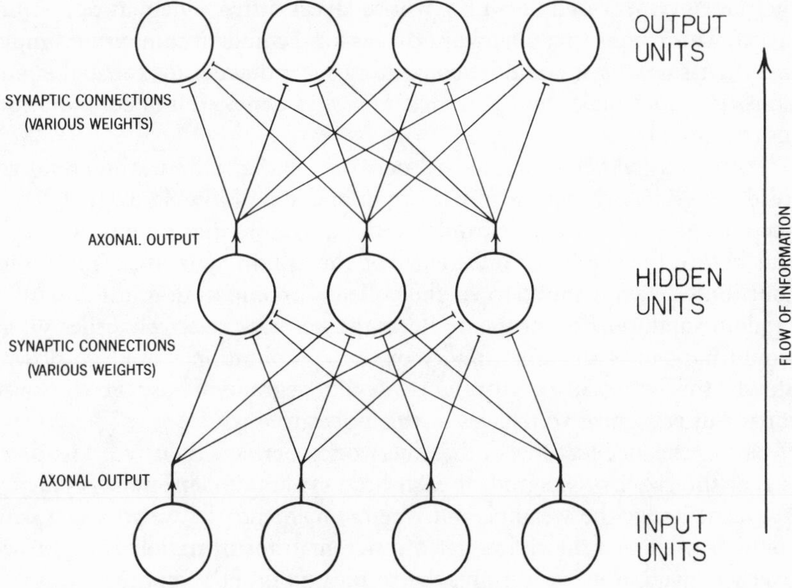

Figure 3.2. A simple network

a cell is humming a high note; with low activation, a low note. So you have a sort of barbershop quartet humming away at the bottom layer, and a musical chord is sent upward toward the middle layer where it is transformed by the synapses into a different chord struck at the middle layer. The same process occurs at the next layer, where yet a third chord of notes ends up being hummed across the output cells. The parts of the brain, then, are humming to each other in something like the language of complex musical chords.

Of course, the chords struck in the brain are typically not the simple three-to-four-element creatures we encounter in music. Networks can be very, very large, and you have already seen from the example of the retina that the musical chord at the human visual periphery has something like a hundred million notes in it! So it is a very complex representation. In fact, we can make neural networks as large as you like—each horizontal layer in Figure 3.2 could be extended to the left and right out to 100 million cells or larger. And an interesting feature is displayed in pattern transformers of this kind. This much larger computer—it computes a function, it does a transformation from a large input vector to a large output vector—will compute its more complex function just as swiftly as the tiny network of Figure 3.2 computes its much simpler function. Indeed, the speed of computation is *independent* of the cell population at each layer. All that matters is the *distance* between layers, and that can be the same even for two networks whose layers differ widely in cell population. This means that a network of this kind could be computing simple one-digit sums, or it could be computing second-order differential equations. It would make no difference. It would complete the computation just as quickly.

There is a further virtue of this network configuration. You could go inside the network with a tiny shotgun and start blowing away its connections at random, and it would *continue* computing more or less as it had before the damage. Since each of the zillion synaptic connections contributes such a tiny part of the collective computation, the loss of a random small portion of them affects the network relatively little. What would happen is that the *quality* of the computation would go down. Slowly the network's performance would degrade. Those of you over forty will recognize yourselves in this portrait.

One of the nice features of these networks, perhaps their nicest feature, is that the size or "weight" of each little synaptic connection is *plastic*. You can change the weights, and when you change the weights to a new configuration of values, you get a different transformation effected between a given input vector and the resulting output vector. You can toy with those weights until you get any transformation you want. In fact, a recent result shows that, for any input-output transformation whatsoever (as long as it is an "effectively computable function," for those of you who know or care what that is), there exists a three-layer network of the kind you have just seen, with a suitable configuration of synaptic weights, that will approximate that input-output function to any degree of accuracy desired.

This is a universality result, for neural networks, analogous to the Universal Turing Machine result that so excited people in AI several decades ago. It means, not to put too fine an edge on the point, that they can do *anything*. They just have to be big enough, and have the right configuration of weights.

That problem—how to find the right configuration of weights—was solved by David Rumelhart and others about 1980. But as the story has been related to me, nobody realized at the time that the solution was a genuine solution. Rumelhart invented the "back-propagation algorithm," but Geoffrey Hinton, his colleague, looked at it and said, "That's not going to work; it's going to get stuck in false configurations all the time." So they more or less put it on the shelf for four years. After it had sat there for a good while, Rumelhart pulled it down one day to try to solve a weight-configuration problem that had resisted other methods. It worked beautifully. So they tried it on other problems. And it worked again. They discovered empirically that it only rarely got stuck in unhappy configurations.

The back-propagation learning algorithm works as follows. It repeatedly changes the synaptic weights of the student network by tiny increments, so that the weights slowly approach the configuration that makes the network do what you want. This is best illustrated with a real example, to which I now move (see Fig. 3.3).

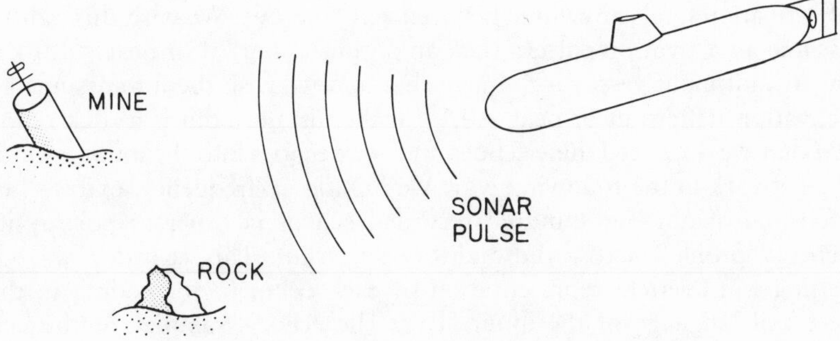

Figure 3.3. A discrimination problem: mines versus rocks

Suppose we want to train a network to do the following kind of transformation. We are going to feed it, as input vectors, vector codings for two kinds of sonar echoes that are returned to us from two kinds of objects. One kind is a dangerous explosive mine with a proximity fuse, and you don't wish to let your submarine get near those. The other is a benign submarine rock, which items litter the ocean bottom naturally. You'd like to be able to distinguish between those by sonar, but the problem is that sonar echoes from mines (of which there are many different shapes and sizes) and sonar echoes from rocks (of which there are many different shapes and sizes) sound pretty much the *same* to the human ear. They are almost impossible to distinguish.

It turns out that after a long tour of duty, sonar operators can, rather like "baby-chicken sexers," start to sense the difference, with perhaps 60 percent accuracy. But that is not good enough to risk your $10 billion Trident submarine in mine-laden waters. So we need another way of doing this. (I must say that there is no military enthusiasm behind this example. I choose it because it is salient, gripping, and because someone has actually done a study of just this problem. So I can give you a real example of network learning.)

We can solve the problem in the following way. Put fifty different mines down on the ocean bottom in various positions, bounce sonar signals off them, and record the returning echoes. You will then have fifty examples of mine echoes. Do the same with fifty rocks, so you have fifty different rock echoes on tape as well. You would like to train the network to discriminate between them. So you proceed as follows.

We construct a network that has essentially the same structure as those you have already seen. It has a few more units at the input layer because it has to code a more complex input stimulus. And it has only two output units because we just want it to tell us whether the sonar echo is returned from a mine or from a rock (see Fig. 3.4). Let those two units be capable of activation levels anywhere between zero and one. We wish this pair to assume an activation pattern (i.e., an output vector) at or near <1,0> if the distant input vector is a mine echo, and we wish them to assume an activation pattern at or near <0,1> if the distant input is a rock echo.

What we do is feed mine echoes and rock echoes into the input layer of the network in the following way. We first do a "frequency analysis" of each one of our one hundred recorded echoes in order to portray its "energy profile" across the auditory spectrum. This is just a way of getting a numerical representation of each echo, fit for coding in the vectorial language of the input layer. The echo is sampled at thirteen different spectral points, because we have thirteen input units.

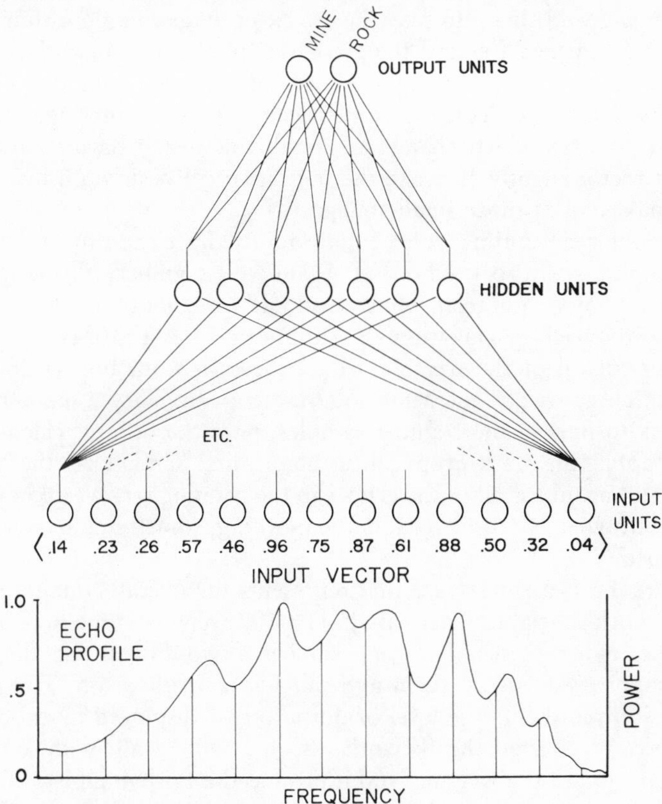

Figure 3.4. Perceptual recognition with a large network

At the outset of the training session, we set all of the network's synaptic weights at small random values, because we really do not have any idea of how we *should* set them to solve the discrimination problem. We then enter a suitably coded mine echo at the input, and let it propagate through the network. What do we get at the output layer? We get gibberish, of course, because we set the weights at random.

Suppose the output vector was, say, <.6,.5>. That is not what we wanted—we wanted <1,0>, because we entered a *mine* echo. We always know which of the two codings we want, because they are our echoes, after all. We have them all labeled. This allows us to compare what we got to what we wanted, and thus get an *error vector* for each trial: in this case it is (<1,0> minus <.6,.5> =) <.4,−.5>.

Now we can bring into play the "back-propagation algorithm" that I mentioned earlier. We feed the error vector into the algorithm, and it calculates a set of small changes for each of the many synaptic weights in the network. Each change is very specific. The back-propagation algorithm calculates which change, up or down, would have produced an output vector slightly closer to the output vector desired on this trial. It then makes all of those small changes.

With the weights thus incrementally adjusted, we enter the next echo in our training set: a rock echo, say. Again we get gibberish. But again we subtract what-we-got from what-we-should-have-got to get the error vector, and the back-propagation algorithm calculates a further set of small changes for all of the weights. This process is both boring and time-consuming, so we give the whole job over to an auxiliary computer whose job it is to feed in the training samples, note the output, calculate the error, apply the back-propagation algorithm, and adjust the weights again and again for all of the echoes in the training set. We go home and sleep. But when we come back in the morning, something marvelous has happened.

Figure 3.5 is a state-space that represents the overall configuration of the network's weights. There are in fact 102 weights in the network, but since I cannot represent 102 dimensions in a two-dimensional diagram, I have suppressed 100 of them and put just 2 of them on. The vertical dimension represents the level of output error displayed by the student network. We started the network off, you will recall, with a random configuration of the weights, and it produced a fairly high level of error. But in the course of the evening, the system has responded to each of these errors, and has progressively adjusted its weights so as to slide down an "error gradient." It comes to rest at an error minimum, a place where the resulting output errors are close to zero for all of the training echoes.

The result is a network that will successfully distinguish all of the mine echoes from all of the rock echoes. That is moderately amazing, and there was no guarantee that it would succeed in this, because we were not entirely sure that there was a systematic difference between the two kinds of echoes. But there was, and the network managed to lock onto it—to become tuned to that complex and subtle difference—in the course of training. It has another nice feature. It will now generalize to new rock echoes and mine echoes. Go get some more, ones the network has never heard before, and it will discriminate them correctly also.

But how does it do this? We have made a little artificial brain. We have trained it up to solve a subtle problem. But we have no idea how it does it. It is now as mysterious to us as the biological brain we were theorizing

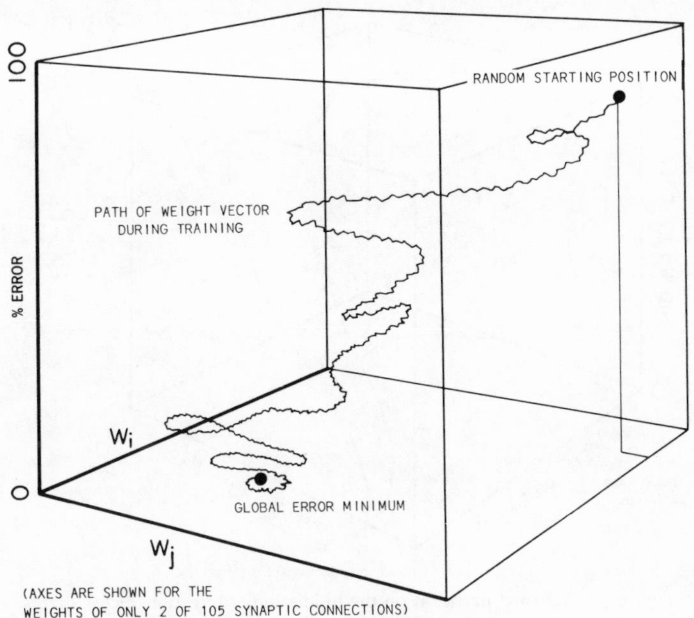

Figure 3.5. Learning: gradient descent in weight/error space

about to begin with! What can we say by way of answering these questions? Notice that we have an advantage in the case of artificial networks. We do not have to go in there with a microelectrode and stick a tiny probe into a single fragile cell, thence to ponder the significance of its lonely voice in the short period before it dies from our invasion. Rather, we can read out the simultaneous levels of activation of every unit in the network at any stage of its processing during any cognitive feat whatever. We can find out what it is doing.

When you do that, you discover that something marvelous has happened at the level of the hidden units. Let me now present to you a different space (see Fig. 3.6). The earlier space I showed you represented the space of possible configurations of synaptic weights, the "weight space." That space is important, but this new space represents something different. It represents the possible patterns of activation or stimulation across the hidden units. (They are called "hidden units" because they are hidden away between the inputs and the outputs.) These patterns of activation are again like musical chords, as we discussed earlier. In the mine-rock network, the hidden-unit chord will have seven elements. But

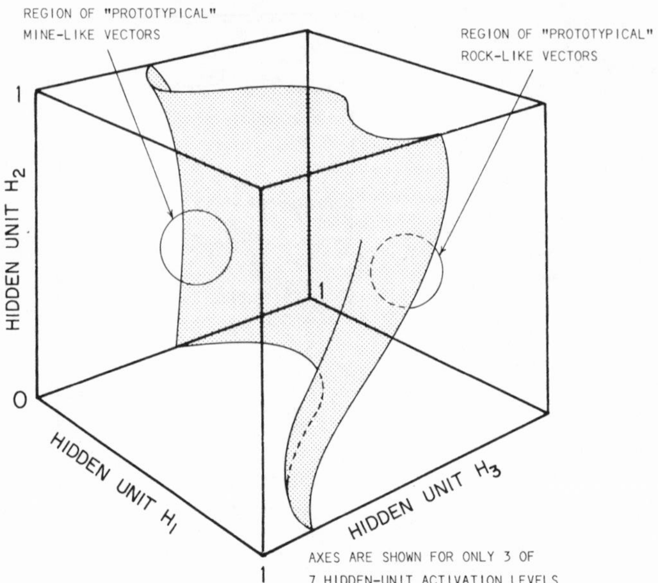

Figure 3.6. Learned partition on the hidden-unit activation-vector space

since I cannot represent seven dimensions on a two-dimensional surface, I will suppress four of them and settle for representing three. Each axis represents the level of activation of a specific hidden unit. So any given point in that space will represent a specific combination, pattern, or vector of activation levels across that population of cells.

What has happened in the course of training is this. The synaptic weights have assumed a configuration that does something to the activation space: it *partitions* it roughly across the middle. There is now a curtain, as it were, across this space of possible activation patterns. Specifically, all of the minelike echoes produce a hidden-unit activation pattern somewhere in the left-hand volume of the space, and all of the rocklike echoes produce a pattern somewhere in the right-hand volume of that space. More intriguing still, there is in the middle of each subvolume a prototypical "hot spot" such that, if one enters into the network a clearly typical or five-star example of a mine echo (or rock echo), it gets coded in the appropriate central or "preferred" region.

Finally, there is a "similarity gradient" within each subvolume, grading off from the prototypical hot spot and toward the curtain, which represents the "surface of indecision" between the two alternatives to which the network has been trained. Input vectors judged as "similar" by the network will get coded at closely proximate places in this space, and dissimilar ones at distal places. (If something gets coded on the curtain itself, then the network does not know what it is: it will "throw up its hands" and give you something like a <.5,.5> vector at the output layer.)

The network is sensitive to such similarities, even to the point of responding correctly to "degraded" inputs. If we enter an input vector that is, say, just the left half of a prototypical mine-echo vector, the network will say, "I know what that is: it's a mine," because its prior learning has generated those prototypical hot spots that function like *attractors*. Almost anything you enter, if it vaguely resembles either a mine or a rock, tends to be drawn toward those two hot spots, so far as its hidden-unit coding is concerned.

Thus the basics of neural networks. Now we must address the human case. The partitions across the activation space are very important. You can think of this space as the network's "conceptual space." In the course of training it has developed a specific "conceptual scheme," a binary scheme: it has exactly two categories. It represents prototypes; it has similarity gradients; and it will even do *ampliative inference*. If you give it a degraded or a partial input, it will say, in effect, "I think I know what that is," and it will give you a response at the output layer that is surprisingly accurate most of the time.

The mine-rock network does a binary discrimination, but we can train networks to make many more discriminations than that. Sejnowski and Rosenberg, for example, trained a rather large network, called NETtalk, to take graphemes as input and give phonemes as output. In effect, it was trained to *read aloud* from arbitrary written text. This is an interesting task, because there are 79 phonemes in English, but only 26 letters, which means that there is ambiguity in how most letters should be sounded. The system has to learn which of several phonemes is the appropriate transform for some input grapheme relative to the larger context in which it occurs on this occasion (*c* is soft in *city*, hard in *cat*, something else again in *cello*, and so forth).

NETtalk was trained in the same fashion as the mine-rock network: by the back-propagation algorithm working with a large corpus of proper word-to-sound examples. After the network had been successfully trained to read aloud, its creators asked, "How is it doing this?!" After all, it has learned, in effect, the highly irregular set of "rules" that govern the pronunciation of standard English spelling. They analyzed the behavior of the hidden units during each of the 79 possible grapheme-to-phoneme transforms, and they discovered that the space of possible activation patterns had been partitioned into an intricate hierarchy. It displayed a primary division into two subspaces: one in which all *consonant* transforms were coded, and the other in which all *vowel* transforms were coded. And within each space there were many subspaces, one for each of the altogether 79 possible transforms. Further, these finer partitions were tightly organized within the space according to their relative similarities: for example, the coding vector for the *s*-to"zzz" transform, as in *busy*, was right next to the coding vector for the *s*-to-"sss" transform, as in "sissy" (see Fig. 3.7). So here we have a network making a 79-ary discrimination, using a conceptual space that has been intricately and hierarchically organized in the course of learning.

I am leading you up by stages here, because I want ultimately to get to networks of the complexity of *you*. In this regard I should mention briefly that we can train networks to solve sensorimotor problems as well. Figure 3.8*a* shows a schematic crab that locates external objects by triangulation with its two eyes, and then reaches for them with a two-jointed arm. I have trained up a simple network, portrayed in 3.8*b*, to take a pair of eye angles as input and deliver a pair of joint angles as output, such that the tip of the crab's arm reaches for the triangulation point of the eyes, wherever that happens to be. In this way it can grab whatever it sees. Such problems are far from trivial, especially with more complex animals, but you can see roughly how networks can deal with them, and I want now to move to something else.

Consider ambiguous perceptual figures (see Fig. 3.9*a*). Here is a case where you can activate one of two different prototype vectors within your brain—prototypes developed during prior learning—and thus see a given object in two quite different ways: as a duck, or as a rabbit. The old woman / young woman (3.9*b*) is another familiar case. How do neural networks recreate this sort of phenomenon?

Take a network of the kind I showed you before, but this time give it what are called "recurrent pathways" (see Fig. 3.10). Adding recurrency brings many interesting features to a network, but in this context it permits the following. Depending on your "state of mind" at the third layer of Figure 3.10, information will be sent down to the hidden units, information that will shape or shade the way in which the bottom-most input vector impacts the hidden layer. You can thus look at the duck-rabbit figure and direct yourself, "See it as a duck," and you do; or, "See it as a rabbit," and you do. What is going on here (I hereby hypothesize) is that recurrent pathways are doing that job for you.

The required wiring is there. Recurrent pathways are not just common, they are the rule throughout the brain. The LGN, for example, which projects to the visual cortex, receives about ten times as many axons *from* the visual cortex as it sends there. Why is there so much effort spent on

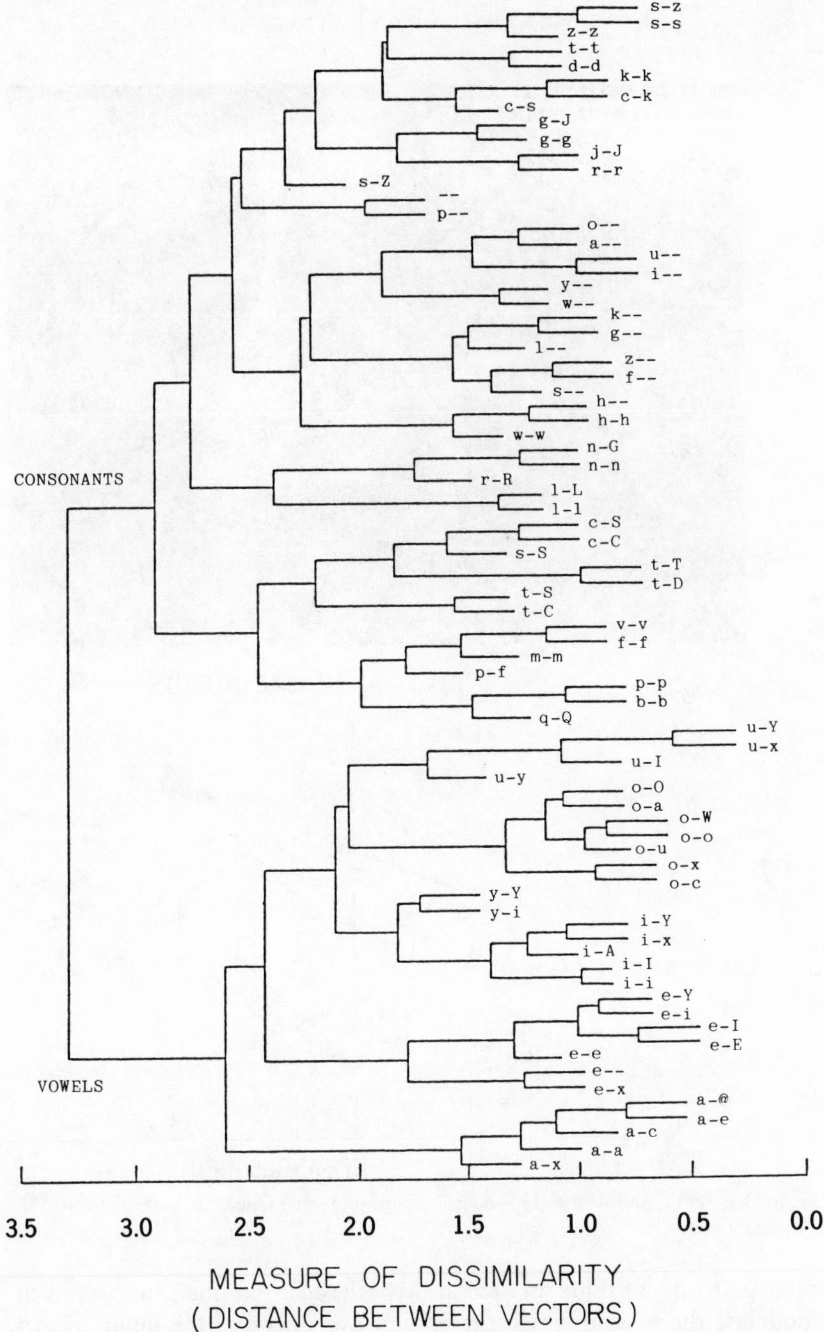

Figure 3.7. Learned hierarchy of partitions on NET talk's hidden-unit activation-vector space

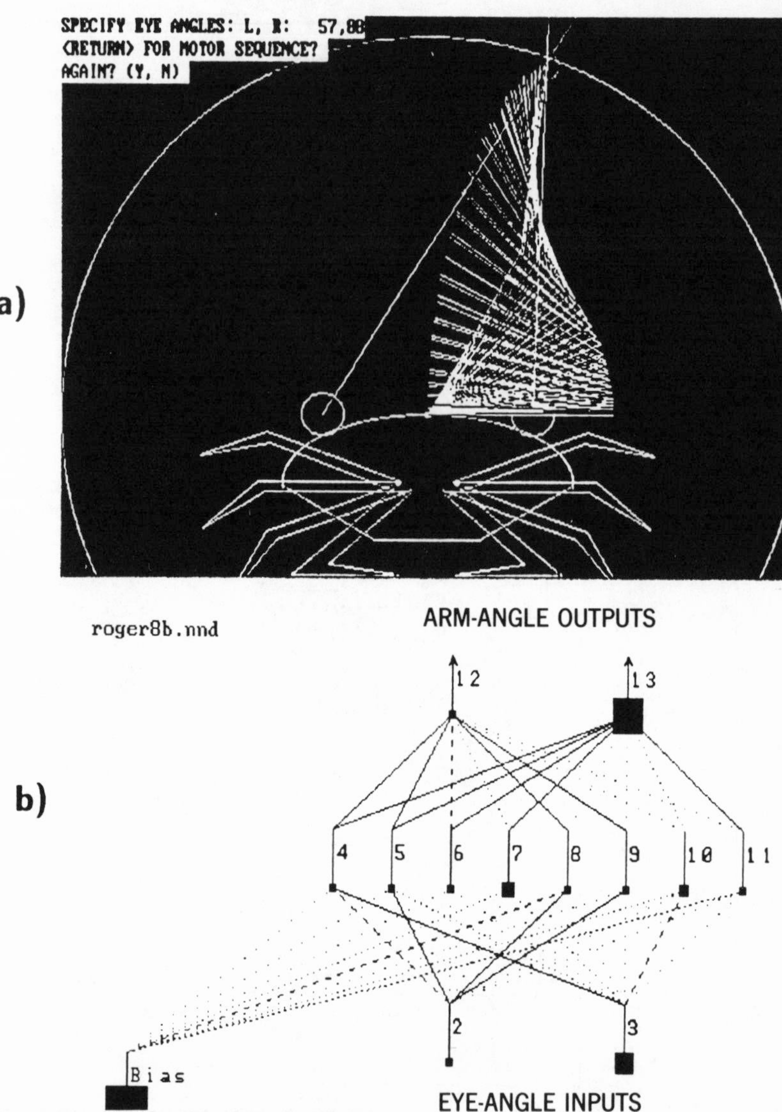

Figure 3.8. Sensorimotor (eye-claw) coordination for a schematic crab, as implemented in a neural network

these pathways? I think an obvious hypothesis is that their function is to modulate the way in which the earlier layers process the input vectors arriving from the sensory periphery. This makes us, by the way, genuine dynamical systems, because once you kick the network into operation you can shut down the peripheral inputs and the system will wind away

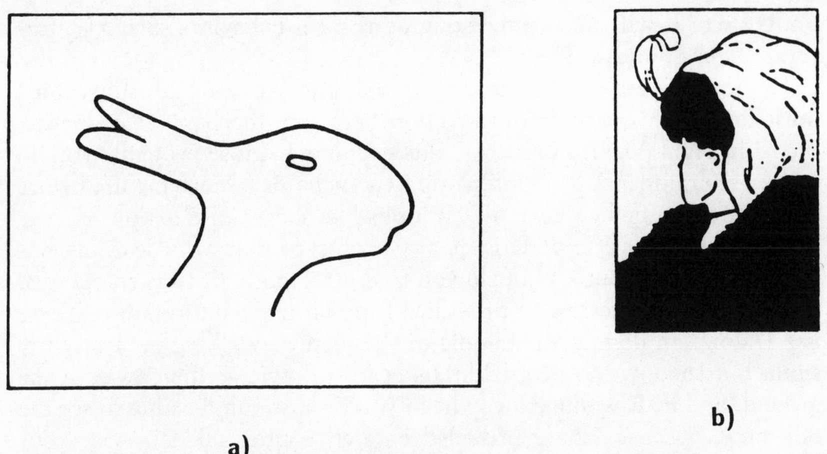

Figure 3.9. Ambiguous figures: (*a*) duck/rabbit; (*b*) old woman/young woman

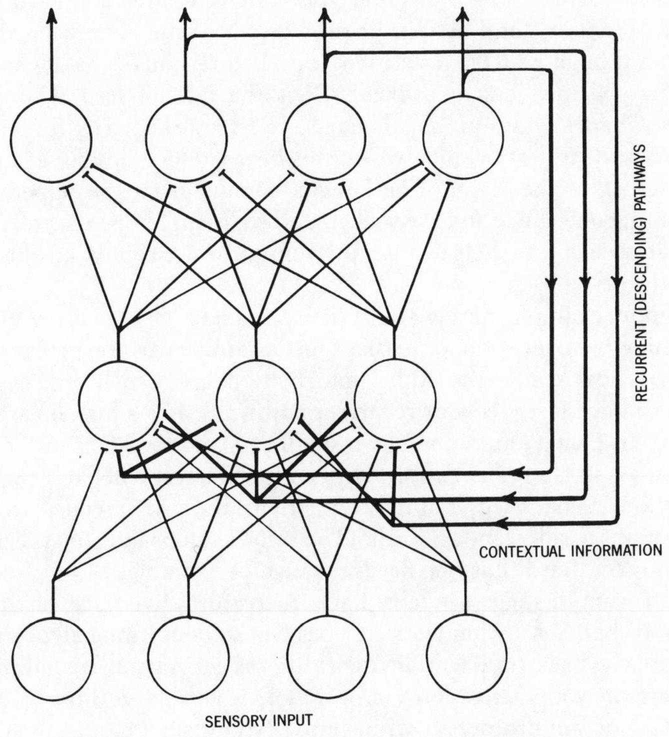

Figure. 3.10. A recurrent network: pathways for self-modulation

on its own. It will show interesting dynamical behaviors such as bifurcation, chaos, and so forth.

The following pictures introduce a new dimension of difficulty. But I must first give you some misdirection here. See the baseball game depicted in Figure 3.11*a*. I give you this example because probably you do not see anything in 3.11*a*, unless you have seen this famous picture before (it is not a baseball game at all). It looks like sheer noise to you. Here is a case where you do *not* activate any prototype that prior learning has produced in you. But I will help you to do it. Figure 3.11*a* is a degraded input which requires me to provide a little bit more information. There is a Dalmatian dog, in the middle of the picture, walking on a brightly sunlit but shadow-mottled field. His head is down, sniffing away at the ground, and he is walking away from you. You should be able to see the dog now, because I have provided enough contextual data that your recurrent pathways could nudge your hidden units in the direction of your "spotted dog" prototype vector, close enough so that the noisy input of 3.11*a* finally fell into that waiting attractor.

Now observe the snowy mountain in Figure 3.11*b*—this is misdirection again, of course. I got this one from a book written a long time ago by N. R. Hanson,[1] and he tells at the bottom of the page what this is. (But even though he tells, it was ten years before I finally saw what was there. So you may find it difficult.) It is the face of Jesus Christ. Or perhaps Charles Manson, as someone once remarked. His forehead is cropped at the top of the picture, but his bearded face can be seen in the upper center of the frame. The light is coming from the upper right, illuminating one cheek and eye socket, and so forth. I hope that recurrent information has now helped the initial input to activate your "bearded man" prototype vector.

One more example, harder still. What is in Figure 3.11*c*? Probably you get nothing but confusion, or perhaps just a smiling cartoon face near the top. Here now comes the added information, to be delivered to your relevant hidden layer by your recurrent pathways: it is a man on a horse. The horse is facing left, with its two small ears and long face just visible. Below this is its chest and two front legs. Now the rest will likely pop into recognition: its back legs and tail to the right, the two extended feet and bent arm of the rider, and so forth. (The rider remains indistinct. Perhaps this one is too hard. But one needs a range of examples.)

What I want to suggest here is that—in creatures like mice, or cats, or coyotes, or humans—what learning does, via some learning algorithm or other (not the back-propagation algorithm), is generate a large library of partitions on your activation-vector space, a *very* large library. These partitions contain prototypes with similarity gradients falling away. You

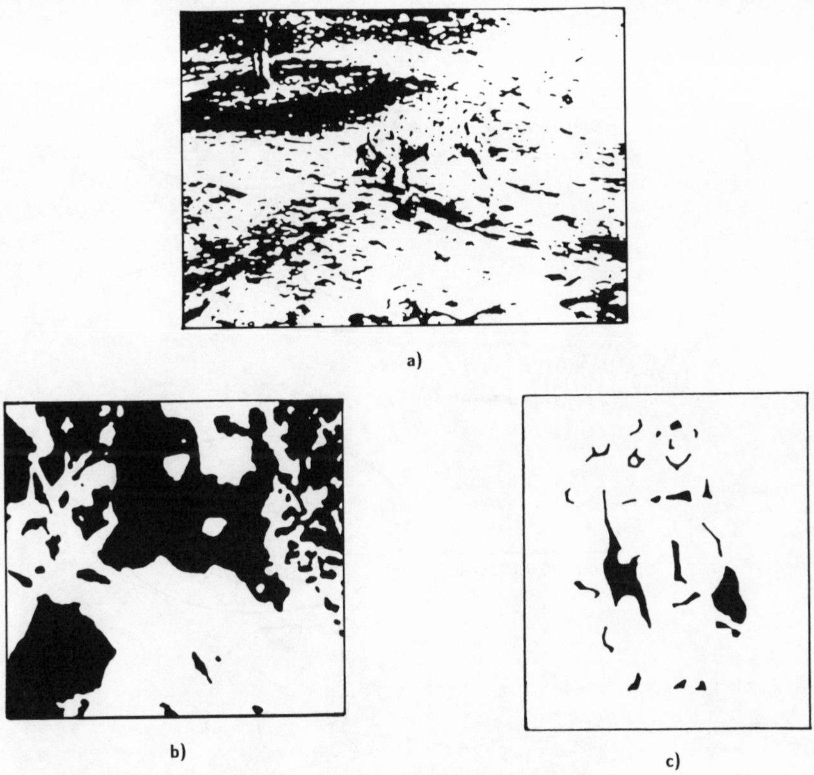

Figure 3.11. Degraded perceptual inputs

can think of these prototypes as dynamical *attractors* into which various stimuli, even degraded ones, will tend to "fall." At bottom, this is how you recognize the objects and situations in the world.

Obviously this needs a lot of expansion if I am to account for the kind of cognitive complexities we display. Let me make a start on that in the following way. What are the neuronal resources we are playing with? There are at least 10^{11} neurons in the brain. If you think of a standard three-story colonial-style academic's house filled from basement to rafters with grains of sand, then that is the number of neurons you possess. The relative proportions of grain-to-house and neuron-to-head are about the same.

If we suppose that the brain divides itself into roughly 1,000 distinct subsystems, each devoted to processing some proprietary type of information, then each such subsystem will have something like 10^8 neurons in it. This means that you can represent things in that subsystem with a

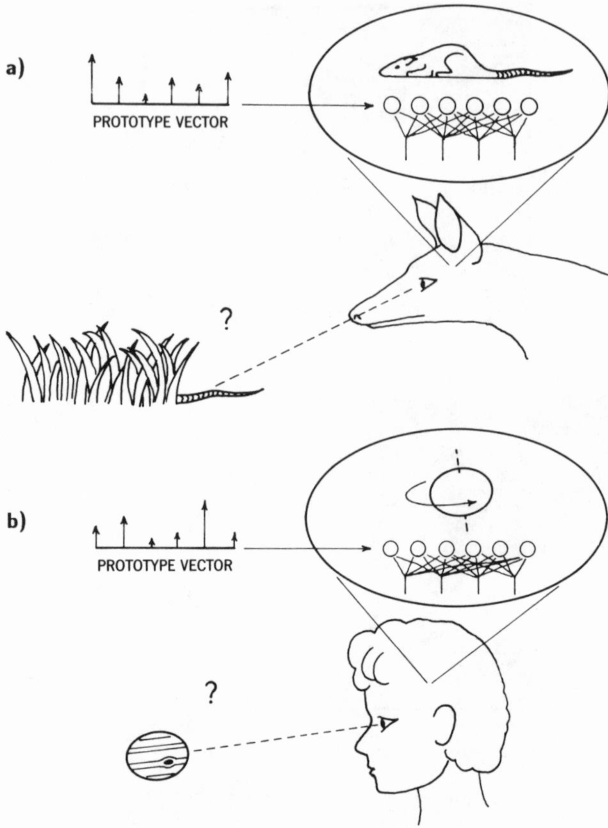

Figure 3.12. Vector completion/prototype activation in well-trained networks: (*a*) coyote recognizing a desert rat; (*b*) astronomer recognizing a rotating plastic body

vector that contains 10^8 (100 million) elements. That vector is big enough to represent the contents of an *entire book* with one fleeting pattern. So the representational resources here are very rich indeed, rich enough, evidently, to represent things as complex as . . . a stellar collapse. It does not have to be something simple like "mine echo," or "soft *c*." Such a large vector can represent cell meiosis, or oceanic rift, or harmonic oscillator, or economic depression, or any complex theoretical notion you choose. We have the resources to represent, vectorially, phenomena as complex as these quite easily. We have more than enough resources to do it.

All right, suppose that we do. What then? Then we can give a theory of perceptual recognition, and explanatory understanding, and abductive inference that counts all three as instances of the same thing: *prototype activation*. In Figure 3.12*a* we have a well-trained coyote who espies a little tail sticking out from a tuft of desert grass, and what gets activated there is his "desert rat" vector. Notice that this involves an *ampliative* inference: the coyote might be mistaken. The tail could be the tail of a poisonous snake, in which case the coyote is in for a surprise. Networks can make mistakes.

For a human case (Fig. 3.12*b*) we have Margaret Burbidge, say, looking through a telescope at the planet Jupiter and noticing that its figure is not a perfect sphere but rather an oblate spheroid. She is a well-trained network, and so the "rotating plastic body" vector gets activated straightaway. Rotating plastic bodies are of course typically deformed in the fashion at issue, so she has an understanding of what is going on. Again the activation is ampliative, since the prototype vector portrays information beyond what the input vector strictly guarantees, but we have seen that this is typical of the behavior of trained networks. They exploit information gleaned from past encounters with the world to "fill out" current inputs in prototypical ways.

I wish to present this as a general theory of explanation, or more precisely, of explanatory understanding, but space does not allow me to argue for it properly here. I conclude this topic with a summary diagram that I hope will stick with you (see Fig. 3.13). Here we have Sir Isaac looking at the moon, which activates a prototype vector that very few people commanded at the time. Isaac was just about the only one. The vector in question is the "motion compounded of a rectilinear, inertial component plus a centripetal, accelerated component" vector. Such a motion will be elliptical and earth-focused, and the moon's puzzling motion is thus apprehended in an explanatory fashion.

Thus, explanatory understanding (or misunderstanding) consists in the activation of a prototype vector. This works for mundane cases as well, as when you look up from your morning newspaper and realize at a glance why one end of the kitchen is *filled with smoke:* THE TOAST IS BURNING! That is a case of explanatory understanding and it is impressive just how quickly we can get it. We do not have to search through the zillions of beliefs that we have and pull up exactly the relevant law that says, "When toast is left in the toaster for more than *n* minutes, then. . .," and then laboriously deduce some appropriate conclusion from the local initial conditions. We do not do anything remotely like that. We do not have time.

It is significant just how quickly we do get the right take on such situations, typically in half a second or less. This makes perfect sense on the prototype activation model of explanatory understanding. For there are roughly ten layers of hidden units in the hierarchy that reaches from

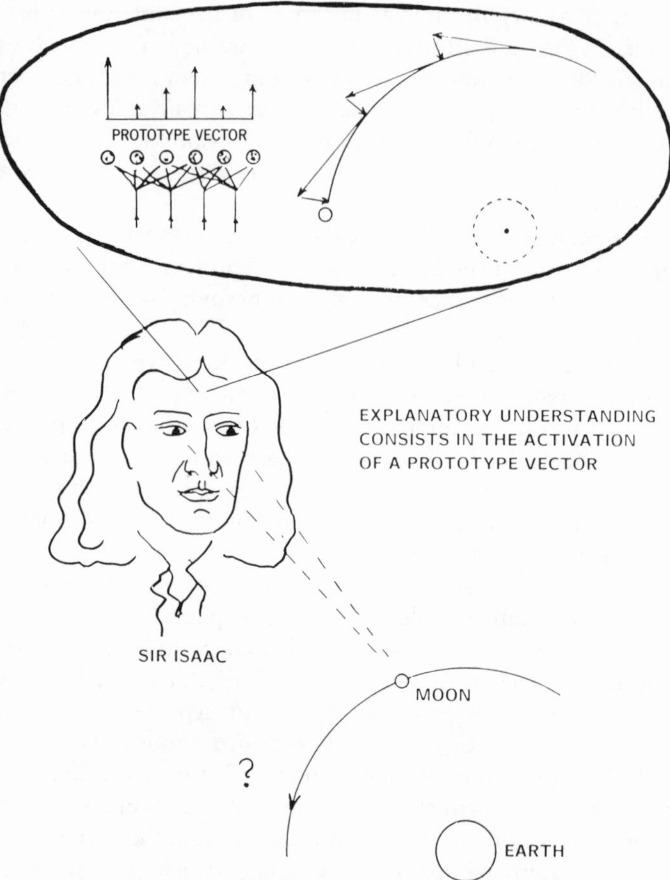

Figure 3.13. Explanatory understanding consists in the activation of a previously learned prototype vector

the retina to the output layer of the visual cortex in the human brain. Conduction time between the layers averages about 20 milliseconds. So the throughput time for the whole stack is about 200 milliseconds. Such a system, therefore, can reach explanatory understanding in as little as a fifth of a second (although it may take longer if the input is confusing and various recurrent nudgings have to be tried). Our swift comprehension of complex situations is therefore not at all surprising.

I return now to the question of truth. It connects with the preceding fairly quickly. The principal mode of *representation* that humans and all animals use, on the neurocomputational view, is not the sentence or the propositional attitude. It is the activation vector across a large population of neurons. And the principal mode of *computation* is not the inference from one sentence or belief to another; it is the swift transformation of one activation vector into another by means of a matrix of synaptic connections. Gaining knowledge consists in configuring your synaptic weights so that your network performs the transformations that you want, the ones that help you find your toothbrush in the morning, find your way to school, pass your algebra test, make yourself dinner, play the flute, find yourself a mate, and all of the things that make for a functional life.

Truth may be a virtue of sentences, but it is not obviously a virtue of activation vectors, or of weight configurations. These latter invite a more pragmatic dimension of evaluation, since their cognitive role is to facilitate useful anticipations of the future and useful sensorimotor coordinations. One is tempted to think of the hidden-unit partitions as "corresponding" in some way to the structure of the world, or to some part of it. But there are many ways of "corresponding" to the world, and it is not obvious that we can here demand the uniqueness that the classical notion of truth implies.

A conceptual framework is a partition across your activation spaces, or rather a set of partitions, and these can be dramatically complex, especially in the case of a brain as large as yours. Let us pursue the possibilities here. How many neurons in the brain? 10^{11}. How many connections per neuron? At least 10^3. So the total number of synaptic connections in the brain is at least 10^{14}. That is a very large number, and it is nice because we get to exploit the combinatorics of 10^{14} weighted elements, each of which can be set at . . . what? Let us say ten different values. There have to be at least two: the connection weight has to be either big or small. And probably there are no more than 100 functionally distinct values for any given weight. I guess 10 here in order to do some easy arithmetic.

How many different synaptic-weight configurations are possible for the human brain? Remember, it is the weight configurations that dictate the activation-space partitions and the resulting input-output function, so we are asking after the number of possible conceptual frameworks or functional accommodations with the world possible for the human brain. The relevant calculation is simple. There are 10 possible weights for the first connection, times 10 for the second connection, times 10 for the third, and so on through all of the 10^{14} connections. The total number of distinct configurations, therefore, is 10 to the 10^{14}th power, or $10^{100,000,000,000,000}$.

How big is this number? For comparison, recall that the total number of elementary particles in the physical universe, photons included, is only about 10^{87}. Alternatively, pick a unit of space, a cubic meter, say. That is a size you can get your arms around. How many cubic meters in the astronomical cosmos? Only about 10^{80}. Physical space may be large: it is astronomically large. But conceptual space is larger still. It is superastronomical.

But as soon as I have said this, an objection arises. One might say, "Look, Paul. It is not true that changing the value of one synaptic connection will produce in me a (significantly) different conceptual scheme. In fact, you told us earlier that one could go into a network with a shotgun and blow away large numbers of its connections entirely, and yet have only a minor or a negligible effect on its activity." This is correct. The alternatives calculated above count only as "just barely discriminable" alternatives, not *significantly* different conceptual alternatives.

Very well, how many *significantly* different conceptual alternatives are possible for a human-sized network? That is hard to say, given the vagueness of the term "significant." But we can do a very rough estimate in fixing a lower bound. Consider the baby artificial networks like those I discussed at the outset: the mine-rock net, NETtalk, and others like that. These typically contain fewer than 1,000 units, usually much fewer, closer to 100. The reason they do not contain more is that it takes too long to train them if they are much larger.

However, if we limit ourselves to networks of 1,000 units and roughly 10^6 connections (the number of connections tends to be roughly the square of the number of units), it must be said that these easily admit of thousands of "significantly different" conceptual partitions and functional properties. There are people on both coasts and up and down the Midwest who are training up small nets to perform all sorts of wonderful things, such as compose music, or convert graphemes into phonemes, or distinguish mines from rocks, or scrutinize loan applications to ferret out the deadbeats, or discriminate plastique explosives in airplane luggage, or play backgammon, or coordinate jointed limbs, or recognize the curvature of surfaces, or discriminate valid inferences in the propositional calculus, or perform stereo vision, and so on. The number of significantly different partitions imposed on essentially the same physical network resource is already into four figures and is still climbing. And this variety is achieved in a network with no more than 10 to the 10^6 distinct possible weight configurations.

How then do *our* combinatorial resources compare with those of a baby network? Ours are greater by a factor of (10 to the 10^{14}) over (10 to the 10^6), which is equal to a factor of $10^{99,999,999,000,000}$. That is still a spectacularly large number, and we have to multiply it by at least 1,000, which was our lower-bound measure of the significant conceptual variety possible for a baby network. The resulting lower limit for our own conceptual diversity is therefore $10^{99,999,999,000,003}$. Rounding down, for the sake of being conservative, we still get $10^{10,000,000,000,000}$ significantly different conceptual alternatives possible for the human brain. Correcting for our initially inflated estimate still leaves us with a superastronomical space of conceptual possibilities.

Consider further. Suppose you had the talent to change every one of your synaptic weights to some desired new value, that is, to adopt an interestingly different conceptual scheme, every 100 msec. That is, ten times a second. So, bingo, you are Mozart. Bingo, you are Attila the Hun. Bingo, you are Virginia Woolf. Bingo, you are Einstein. And so forth. And you did this for your whole life. How many different frameworks would you go through? You have about 10^8 seconds in a lifetime, and you would streak through 10 schemes every second. So you would traverse a total of 10^9 different schemes during your lifetime.

But recall from the next-to-last paragraph just how much space you are trying to explore. Even at the breakneck pace described, you will have explored only an infinitesimal portion of the vast conceptual space available. Evidently, exploring conceptual space with the resources we have, even if accelerated in implausible ways, is going to be about as effective as exploring the astronomical universe with nothing more than one's own two feet. It is just too large to hope to explore all of it. (Of course we can still *explore* it. And we do.)

Notice further that conceptual space will be even larger for any creature with more neurons and more synaptic connections than we have. And since there is no theoretical limit to how large a brain might be—we can always add more units—there is therefore no limit, in principle, to the size of conceptual space. It is infinite. For a given network, there is always a finite space. And for a larger network, there is a yet larger finite space for it to explore. And so on. But this progression goes on indefinitely.

From which I draw the following conclusion. It is not a demonstration, strictly, but rather an interesting possibility. Perhaps there is no unique point in human weight space, nor perhaps in any other weight space, that yields the One True Theory of Everything. In fact, when we are contemplating conceptual variety and conceptual spaces on this scale—spaces, moreover, that are indefinitely extendible—the idea that there is a single, Uniquely Correct account of the universe starts to look . . . well, silly. Perhaps theories or conceptual frameworks just get better and better, ad infinitum . . . That would be nice. It means we need never stop having fun.

And it also means that the cognitive adventure may be rather more like the evolutionary adventure—the *biological* adventure—than we first imagined. Rather than a convergence toward a Unique Truth, perhaps we confront an indefinitely fecund radiation. Recall that the idea of a convergence toward perfection, or toward God, was common in early discussions of biological evolution also. But this is inconsistent with Darwin's message that there is nothing teleological about the process. It is not converging on any point. It is a process of blind *radiation*, nudged by endless contingencies. And it is being snipped here and there by sundry teeth and claws. So selection is going on. But it is a process of blind radiation to explore the many niches that are there. From the model of this paper, it rather looks as if the same thing is true of our individual and collective cognitive activity. This theme is not novel with me. Thomas Kuhn[2] and Donald Campbell[3] have been pushing it for years. But it is evident that the recent developments in computational neurobiology provide a new dimension of support for their general point of view.

Now all of this tends to put me into the same bag with the various people who are beating on the realists and trashing objectivity and so forth, and I fear that the preceding reflections may distress some of my colleagues at the conference. For I fear that I was invited here in the hope that I would Stand Up for Truth. As you see from the preceding, I feel somewhat chary of doing so. But I would like to stand up for something that may be close to it.

We have learned something that we did not know in our early history: that there is no *largest number.* The sequence of natural numbers forms an infinite set. There is no Biggest Number. Children often have a difficult time getting hold of this, at first. They think there must be a biggest number, and they are a bit surprised to learn that there is no such number. But no one has ever exclaimed, with alarm, "Oh my god, there's no biggest number! And so we can no longer tell whether any number is bigger than another number, because we cannot tell whether it is *closer* to the Biggest Number. How terrible this is!"

Such a worry would be confused. We can still tell whether any number is bigger than another number, even though there is no Biggest Number from which to measure their relative distance. Similarly, we can still tell whether one theory is better than another, without appeal to the respective proximities they might bear to a Unique Truth. In fact, the difference in performance is *usually* dramatic, even though there is no Best Theory. And the differences between them, in their anticipatory and coordinative properties, will be as objective as anything can be. What is free to vary is our interest in which particular anticipatory and coordinative properties to pursue.

Altogether, then, the conception of cognition portrayed here today invites, I think, the following view. First, it invites a humility with regard to our current conceptual achievements. Considering the space we are exploring and the little journey we have already had, we cannot have achieved *very* much, relative to what is possible. Second, what is *possible* starts to look pretty good. There must be a lot of cognitive fun left to be had, and lots of rewards to be discovered. And finally, the idea that, cognitively speaking, things can just get better and better and better, ad infinitum, may be a more effective draw to continued intellectual activity than the idea of a Final Resting Place could ever be.

NOTES

This paper is a lightly edited transcription of a recording of my informal conference presentation.

1. N. R. Hanson, *Patterns of Discovery* (Cambridge: Cambridge University Press, 1958).
2. Thomas Kuhn, *The Structure of Scientific Revolutions* (Chicago: University of Chicago Press, 1962).
3. Donald Campbell, "Evolutionary Epistemology," in P. Schilpp, *The Philosophy of Karl Popper* (La Salle: Open Court, 1974).

Part 3

Epistemology: Science and Literature

CHAPTER 4

Interpretation in Science and in the Arts

BAS C. VAN FRAASSEN AND JILL SIGMAN

Both the natural sciences and the fine arts, throughout their respective histories, have widely been characterized as representational; that is, as activities whose primary goal is representation. By exploring the criteria for representation, we propose to show how even in supposedly simple cases of representational works of art and scientific theories we must inevitably admit that interpretation plays a crucial role. Admitting this role for interpretation brings to light how representation can be incomplete or even sabotaged in these works. This leads to the question of whether there can be criteria for interpretation beyond the basic criteria for representation. We will first turn to art, where these issues more commonly arise, and then show parallels in the philosophy of science.

Art as Representation

Today the idea that art is representational is met at once with examples of apparently nonrepresentational art, which are (at least prima facie or putatively) counterexamples to that theory. This reaction allows, however, that art may have been representational in the past, before these new developments established themselves as art. Certainly the view of art as representation has been widely held; perhaps it is indeed the first to be voiced in Western philosophy. Plato's discussion of art in general, and more specifically of poetry, in the *Republic* stands as a paradigm example.[1] That such a view of art was dominant also (or still) during the Renaissance is evident, for example, in Vasari's survey of Italian art from the thirteenth to the sixteenth century. He writes, "painting is nothing more than the simple portrayal of all things alive in nature by means of design and color as nature herself produces them."[2] But is this theory of art actually as simple as it seems? Let us begin to answer this question by examining representation in what appears to be the most straightforward case. In Plato's example of a painting of a bed, the painting is related to the real bed in the same way the real bed is related to the Form. Whether or not he is oversimplifying his theory of Forms here, it is clear that the painting represents the bed in the following way. Suppose it is merely a line drawing; then the drawing is the projection of a solid geometric figure, from a certain perspective, onto a plane figure on the canvas. Logically speaking, such a geometric relation could also hold accidentally between a solid and some lines "drawn" in sand by rivulets of water. Such an accidental matching would not be a case of representation, so the representational relationship must be one that is established intentionally.[3] Furthermore, it has been shown (particularly by Gombrich) that even in this simple case the viewer must learn how to "read" the picture—the use of projection is a convention for *coding* the data selected for representation.

In sum, representation of an object involves producing another object which is intentionally related to the first by a certain coding convention which determines what counts as similar in the right way. With regard to this last point Plato discusses the examples of coding visual aspects of the object in painting, auditory aspects in music and song, and aspects of every sort by means of words in poetry. These points apply equally to nonartistic, nontheoretical examples of representation, such as a snake-like symbol indicating a bump in the road.

The First and Second Criteria of Faithful Representation

Although there are many ways to evaluate any particular representation (is it beautiful? does it have socially redeeming features?), the first criterion is accuracy, the criterion most closely related to the aim of representation. But even accuracy is not as simple as it seems. In the case of a subject-predicate statement, accuracy of description may be a straight yes/no matter—it is true or it is false. In Aristotle's words, to be true is to say of what is, that it is, and of what is not, that it is not. But a representation which is not a simple verbal description cannot easily be judged by this standard. First of all, in such a case, accuracy with respect to what is depicted is no longer a two-valued variable, but a matter of degree. And second, what is depicted is invariably selected from what could be depicted. Somehow, completeness—how much is included, and how much is left out—needs to be distinguished from accuracy in a narrower sense, namely, as fit between what is shown and the part or aspect selected for depiction.[4]

To illustrate this, let us ask of a line drawing of a bed whether it is accurate. It does have the shape required, which makes it a projection of the relevant three-dimensional solid on the two-dimensional page—but not exactly, of course, not perfectly. This in fact makes the drawing seem fairly adequate. But it does not have the same dimensions as the bed; presumably the artist did not select size as a characteristic to be depicted. The narrowest criterion of adequacy for representation concerns the first point. It is the criterion applied if we say that a nose was drawn too large, a chin too round, the hair too wavy. We assume in that case that the artist did mean to (or was supposed to) get those proportions right. In other words, this criterion of accuracy is indeed in some sense the most basic criterion, but it presupposes a context, in which the question of selectivity is already regarded as settled.[5]

But how is the selectivity itself to be evaluated? In general, selectivity in narration or depiction lends itself to deception (or misdirection) of several distinct sorts.[6] It is after all possible to give an appearance of completeness when the depiction is but partial, and to select perversely with respect to interest and value even when accurate. On the other hand, selection may be of what is of special value, discarding the "irrelevant," "unimportant," or "inessential."[7] That is, if we look at the work with interests or values already at hand, selectivity can be the focus of criticism. The criterion applied, however, cannot be called something simple like "accuracy"—completeness as such is clearly unattainable, so it is only completeness in some respect that can be required. In addition, it is clear that values which have nothing to do with geometric projection or matching of colors must be operative here, and they may well vary from case to case, context to context.

So even at the most basic level, the concept of representation has a curious complexity. For when something is offered as representation, it is subject to two basic criteria—the first, though straightforward enough, presupposing as given the selection of features rendered (hence only contextually applicable), the other importing some value ("from outside," so to say) to determine the features to be selected.

But now is that all? These points apply equally to any sort of representation, such as for example a census report. The census taker tries to include every person in his domain of responsibility, selects only certain respects to which to attend, for instance age and income, and then represents those accurately by writing the correct numerals on paper. The selection could be criticized, but only on the basis of a judgment of what information matters (to us, for our purposes, in this particular year, etc.), and then the accuracy criticized on the basis of whether the numerals written denote the correct numbers. But of course there must be more to representation in art—and also, as we shall see further on, in science.

Representation *as* versus Representation *of*

Today we have many examples of art that purports not to be representation at all, and these obviously lead us to question the idea that art is representation, or that its aim is representation. More interesting is the question of whether *even* in the case of art that seems explicitly representational, it is an adequate view of art to regard it simply in that way. Certainly we have many examples of art works that represent, such as paintings of the adoration of the mystical lamb, of an angel's annunciation to Mary, of a woman with a swan who was a god, of the Emperor Napoleon, of several men and women having lunch on the grass. They depict something, they are depictions *of* something. But is that the main point, is that the crucial thing to say about them?

These paintings are not merely depictions *of* this, that, or the other; unlike a census report, they do not only select some items and then simply encode them—they represent their subject *as* something. The adoring are represented as devout, the women as undaunted, demure, aghast, or resisting, the men as arrogant or vulnerable. The question we want to raise here is: can the idea of *representation as thus or so* be conceptually accommodated under that of *representation of this or that?*

At first sight, it seems so. To represent the men as arrogant would seem to be simply a matter of selecting certain characteristics for representation—their hair color, their posture, and also their arrogance. In just the same way, the census taker selects annual income and age among the characteristics to enter in his or her report on the individual. But we shall argue that this is not the case, and consequently that the view of art as representation is seriously undermined. Certainly the form of words is preserved: we say "*representation* of the men as arrogant." Certainly also, the importance or extent of the involvement of representation in art is not denied: it is not possible to have a representation as thus or so, except in the sense of having a representation *of* something as thus or so. But we will try to show that when attention is directed to how art (and also science) represents *as*, interpretation takes on a crucial role, at various levels, and the pristine simplicity of the idea of mere representation, in the paradigmatic sense of a geometric projection, is altogether lost.

With this conclusion, we can arrive at an understanding of how failure of representation and even sabotage of the project of representation can also play a legitimate role in art. That would be inconceivable, even self-contradictory, if our concept of art were simply that of a mode of representation.

Consider for a moment that painting of a luncheon on the grass. Let us agree, if only for the sake of argument, that the men are represented as arrogant. How is this achieved? Perhaps we have in this painting an exact representation—a certain geometric solid has been precisely projected onto the two-dimensional canvas, and the colors-as-seen have been correctly filled into the corresponding areas, up to a certain varying level of detail—of just those aspects which the painter selected for depiction. But what of the arrogance? Unfortunately, *being* arrogant is not equatable with having any one particular set of physical characteristics, and *looking* arrogant is not universally equatable with any set of visual characteristics describable in terms of shape and color. So how exactly have the men been represented as arrogant?

Could it be that there is a particular representational code, such as a lifted eyebrow to indicate skepticism, which here conveys the arrogance? Does this painting perhaps belong to an artistic tradition which uses a highly elaborate set of apparently naturalistic details as symbols with recognizable iconographies, as in the religious art of the Renaissance? Are these men shown in a conventional posture of arrogance, in the way that in medieval religious art men and women are depicted in conventional postures of sorrow, supplication, anger, and so forth? The answer would seem to be *no* to all these questions.

Of course, the artist could not depict the men as arrogant if they could not, in similar circumstances, convey their arrogance to us via some set of depictable characteristics. But "arrogant" (like, e.g., "complacent," "offended," "friendly," "hypocritical") is an adjective of interpretation. Whether or not a certain action, posture, or facial expression counts as arrogance depends on the whole social, cultural, and historical context in which it appears. How does all that get into this plane figure filled with colors?

It doesn't. The artist succeeds not by accuracy of represented details that univocally express arrogance, but by creating or provoking the relevant impression in the viewer/reader addressed.[8] To represent the men as arrogant, the artist must enable us to see those depicted men in the depicted situation as arrogant—from within our culture, at a certain point in time, and with our specific history. Success in this respect, however, rests not only on what he does or shows. For if he did the same thing with another audience or public (who encounters the work in a different social, cultural, or historical context) the resulting interpretation could be markedly different. This is seen readily in the case of the plays of Jean

Cocteau. For example, in *Orphée* the deliberate choice of words carries additional connotations in certain social sectors, which affect the interpretation of the work.[9] Some conventional signs may be involved in interpretation, but for most attitudes and emotions—which tend after all to take on ever new complexities—there are no such blatantly recognizable signs as the lifted eyebrow and clenched fist.

What succeeds as coding clearly varies tremendously from one context to another, and may not rely on conventions that are at all widespread. Equally, cues offered by the artist may not be recognizable in the viewer's own context. Quite frequently, in trying to interpret a work the viewer needs to look to the context in which it was created, focusing on the actual process of creation (the available materials and techniques, for example, if it is a work of visual art), or social, political, intellectual, or historical influences. A clear example is Carl Schorske's examination of the works of Gustav Klimt in terms of the intellectual and political climate in fin-de-siècle Vienna.[10] For his interpretation of Klimt's mural *Philosophy (Das Wissen,* the first of a series of three murals commissioned in 1894 for the new University of Vienna), Schorske draws upon Wagner, Schopenhauer, and Nietzsche, figures admired by the intellectual circles to which Klimt belonged. Most striking is the assertion that we can possibly identify the philosophic priestess at the bottom of the painting as Nietzsche's drunken poetess in *Thus Spoke Zarathustra.* Schorske sees her as "affirming the World of Will," clearly enough an extrapolation from Nietzsche's philosophy. Such a reading can derive its support only from an examination of the actual historical context; while clearly not uniquely forced even there, it cannot be even plausibly advanced independent of that context.

Thus there is no uniqueness and no context independence of interpretation with regard to a given artistic representation. It is similarly, and not independently, the case that when we view other people in the context of ordinary life, there is no certainty that our interpretation matches either what is really going on or what we were intended to make of it. That is an unavoidable consequence of the irreducibility of the psychological to the physical, mental activity to behavior, mind to body. The mere idea of representation is too poor to tell the story of representational art, because it is too poor to tell the story of perceptual experience itself.[11]

Selectivity thus plays an additionally crucial role in representation, as we must now conceive it. It is not just that the artist happens to think some elements or aspects of his subject more worthy of note than others. To evoke an interpretative response, attention must be drawn to selected aspects, by hiding or omitting others. The role played by selectivity in representational art is derivative from the role it plays in all other communication, explicit or implicit, conscious or subliminal.[12]

Before continuing the argument, we should emphasize that the conclusion we are drawing here is very modest. There may well be reasons for taking it further than this. At this point, however, there are still three alternatives:

a. pure or mere representation of something—e.g., the representation of a colored cube as a colored cube, by faithful reproduction (via a known code) of some of its features (such as by geometric projection yielding a plane figure, with matching colors filled in), or the numerical encoding of age and income of the population in a census;
b. representation with a conventionally dictated interpretation—e.g., the representation of a person as skeptical by drawing a face with raised eyebrows, as evil or good by accompanying horns or halo;
c. interpretative representation, which succeeds by evoking from a public which encounters it in a certain cultural/historical context a reaction which classifies the work as a representation of its subject as having attributes predicated by certain adjectives of interpretation.

The stronger position which one might take would be to insist that *(a)* is at best a limiting case of *(b)*, and *(b)* a limiting case of *(c)*, which describes a continuum of cases which can only be arbitrarily subdivided. A still stronger position results if one then adds that not only is there a continuum here, but that no case is pure, no limiting cases can really exist. That would entail that there is no representation free of interpretation, in any nontrivial sense—not even census reports, architects' blueprints, or police artists' composite drawings. It would mean that explicitly accepted and recognized coding conventions never suffice to determine or dictate the meaning uniquely.[13]

We are not taking such a strong position at this point, because it is not needed for our argument. As long as there are clear cases of *(c)* which are not instances of *(a)* or *(b)*, our point will stand. For if that is so, it will not be tenable to say that art *is* merely a species of representation, but only that it involves representation, and in addition crucially involves interpretation which is not uniquely determined by the character of the representation. Moreover, the basis we have advanced for this comes not from recent developments in art but rather from reflection on art of a quite traditional, "representationalist" sort. The problem with the concept of art as representation is not that we have admitted examples of "nonrepresentational" art. There have in any case always been works that would be difficult to classify as pure, deliberate, single-minded attempts at accurate representation. In how many respects, for example, is El Greco's Christ like any man one could possibly expect to encounter in the Temple court? The problem is rather that representation as such is too poor, too meager a concept to allow us to say much about any art at all.

Ultimately, we shall argue that we are now in a position to see how it can be crucial to art to defeat the purposes of representation, to violate the criteria which would apply if representation were the aim. But first let us consider to what extent our argument thus far could equally apply to views of science.

The Parallel Case for Science

Art, we have argued, is at least not simply representation of something, but crucially involves interpretation. But what of science? Does science perhaps have as aim exactly the faithful representation which art cannot or does not mean to achieve? Its medium is language, and the body of science is a body of information, a putative description of what there is in the world, and even of what the world as a whole is like. The criterion of accuracy divides again into two, as we saw for representation in general: it is easy enough to say something true, impossible to say all that is true about a given subject. Selectivity in science is deliberate, purposeful, and subject to evaluation as well. We ask not only if a given science provides accurate information about the aspects it has selected for attention, but whether it has selected well, whether it answers all or many of the *important* questions. Just as before, such evaluation draws on values current or imposed in its context, for what is important in the welter of data that assails us is not "written on the face of" the data, nor is it yet another datum among them.

There have certainly been a succession of views of science, of the sort typically labeled scientific realism, which take the aim of science to be correct description, or more generally representation, of what there is. However there have been major shifts in even these views due to revolutionary upheavals in science in recent times. Compare the following sentiment from the middle of the nineteenth century:

> Now there do exist among us doctrines of solid and acknowledged certainty, and truths of which the discovery has been received with universal applause. These constitute what we commonly term *Science* . . .[14]

with even a very conservative form of scientific realism in our century:

> Science aims at a literally true account of the physical world, and its success is to be reckoned by its progress toward achieving that aim.[15]

The difference between the first and second is not with respect to truth as defining aim—the difference lies instead in the erosion of certainty, with its concordant disentangling of the two concepts of truth and of certainty. The end in view is still truth, but this does not imply that we can have even potential certainty that this end has been attained. The two concepts are now (by scientific realists in the mid-twentieth century) seen as logically independent.

In the light of our discussion of representation, we can compare this sort of view of science with a contrary view. On such realist views as the above, science too is seen as simply representation. Recalling the amendments which were necessary for the view of art as representation, we arrive at the contrary view, that even when science produces a representation of some part or aspect of the world, interpretation is also involved, and indeed, enters at several different levels. It is easy to imagine how a relatively conservative philosopher of science might respond: "Precision, accuracy, univocity, invulnerability to deconstruction or alternative interpretation are evidently the very hallmarks of rigor in the sciences—which is perhaps, if you are right, the very reason why scientific texts won't be literary texts as well, and why science is not art." But let us scrutinize the sort of representation science provides.

Newton represented the solar system, accurately in many respects—the respects which he selected for thematic presentation—but he represented it *as* (what we now call) a Newtonian mechanical system. Obviously he abstracted from the facts, but does this consist—when perfectly successful—simply in deletion of certain aspects, the ones not selected for representation? If so, abstraction can presumably introduce no inaccuracy or falsehood—what it produces is the truth remaining after we ignore some of the truth to be found. But this irenic account of what Newton did—what he called his induction, his rigorous derivation from the phenomena—is too simple and too comforting, too good to be true.

How the solar system appears to Newton's God, how it appears in the view from nowhere, is not how it appears to us. Attending to what does appear and has appeared to us, can we apply the interpretative adjective "Newtonian"? Newton showed us that we could, by constructing a mathematical model and showing that it provided an adequate representation of the solar system. God created the world, Newton represented it as a Newtonian mechanical system, and we saw that it was good. Later Einstein represented it as a relativistic mechanical system, and again we saw that it was good—this time even better. The conclusion to draw is that the phenomena, to the extent Newton knew them, admitted his sort of representation—allowed being represented as a Newtonian system—but did not dictate that. They could equally be represented as an Einsteinian, relativistic system. We can draw a parallel here to the work of a portrait painter: he or she represents the subjects as arrogant, or as complacent, and the fact is that their comportment, as displayed to him, allowed both interpretations.

But someone might object: a serious disanalogy between science and art can be pressed here, after admitting to a minor analogy. By viewing the works of, for example, the Impressionists or the Fauves, we might become enabled to see nature, and humanity, in a new way. Analogously, Newton showed us how to see nature in a new way. Certainly, the new way of seeing involves the application of an interpretative attribute—the fact is only that the phenomena (how nature has appeared to us) *admit* of being classified as the appearances of Newtonian systems. Newton was wrong only in thinking that the interpretation was unique. Quite possibly Einstein's models do not fit the recorded phenomena prior to 1700 any better than do Newton's. The fact remains that since they are a feasible alternative, the phenomena did not compel Newton's interpretation uniquely.

This admitted analogy—so the objection would go—must be followed by a much more important disanalogy. The viewer may react to the painting by seeing the men on the grass as arrogant or as complacent—the painting represents them as admitting both interpretative responses. This does not deny that if there was or had been a real situation as original, that way of painting it was not compelled but only allowed or *admitted* along with other alternative possible renderings. Thus there are two levels at which nonunivocal interpretation enters the scenario. With regard to science, the real situation corresponds to the solar system, the way the situation appeared to the painter corresponds to the recorded celestial phenomena (the data), and the painting corresponds to Newton's model. So science, like art, interprets the phenomena, and not in a uniquely compelled way. But one might object that science itself does not admit of alternative rival interpretations. While there is ambiguity in the painting, and crucially so, there is no ambiguity in the scientific model. And so while the literary text is an open text, the scientific text remains closed.

But the history of science puts the lie to this story, and in successively more radical ways. Gravitation, the only force treated successfully by Newton himself, is a *central force*, with the center supplied by the gravitating mass. In the eighteenth century, it was taken as a principle of mechanical modeling that all forces in nature are central forces. Was this an addition to Newton's science? We must first reflect on this question itself and ask what kind of answer it requires. Does it ask whether Newton deliberately omitted the principle from the principles of mechanics, or whether he indicated it tacitly, so that it was there for him but as a principle which had not risen to the level of explicit formulation? All Newton's models are of the type admitted in the eighteenth century; it is as if he already had that principle as well. But "as if" is all we can say. Should we instead take Newton's science to be defined solely by what was explicitly stated? But in that case all the Newtonians would appear to have misunderstood Newton's mechanics. For, to take one example, Laplace only formulated the common understanding when he used the dramatic device of an omniscient genie to convey that the Newtonian world picture is entirely *deterministic*. But if we look only to explicitly formulated principles, we must say that this science was not deterministic. The law of conservation of energy was not recognized as an independent and needed addition until the nineteenth century—perhaps partly because nonconservative systems had not been sufficiently well conceptualized—and the science implicitly allowed for indeterminism before that was done.

What retrenchment could come next? Newton managed to create in this audience (the physicists and educated lay public of the modern era) the impression of total determinism with such force that their own view of science began to include it as a criterion—the *telos* of science is representation *as* deterministic. The task of science is not finished till that is done—and of course, except for details, it has been done; that is the implicit conviction of the nineteenth century, in the most visible quarters. It was not shared by all, Charles Sanders Peirce being an honorable exception, for example, and indeed it was compelled neither by the phenomena, nor by the science, nor by its success. Science itself admitted of different interpretations at each stage, even if at each stage one interpretation seemed to be dominant.[16]

The admission of alternative interpretations is spectacularly visible in philosophy of physics today, with respect to quantum mechanics. The basic tension, which had to cause vacillation and hence suspicion that the theory cannot have a satisfactory interpretation, was perhaps first made fully explicit in Wheeler's commentary on Everett.[17] On the one hand quantum mechanics is putatively the fundamental science, in principle encompassing all sciences as parts, and in principle affording a complete description of the world. On the other hand, much of it developed in the form of a theory of partial systems—systems studied in relation to an environment, in terms of input from and output to that environment. The question is then whether the title of Davies' book *The Quantum Mechanics of Open Systems* really describes the entire theory (with every aspect of an environment being potentially part of a described system, which will itself however always be described as open to an environment), merely a subtheory, or a proper extension of the theory. Interpretations of quantum mechanics presently available differ on this question; and even when they agree, they differ in other significant ways.

So in science too we find interpretation at two different levels: the theory represents the phenomena *as* thus or so, and that representation itself is subject to more than one tenable but significantly different interpretation. As in art, we find the persons involved (those who create the work, those who peruse or appreciate it) often unconscious of the non-uniqueness of their interpretations and of the creative element in their response as readers. The texts of science too are open texts.

Interpretation and the Specter of Ambiguity

We have argued so far for the rather modest (today perhaps not even very novel) contention that, both in science and in art, representation on canvas or page does not uniquely dictate how we are to understand it. We should now inquire into the role and importance of the multiplicity of interpretations which the work admits. Is this to be taken as a defect, an obstacle which the artist and/or scientist strives to overcome? Does the artist's or scientist's success consist in blinding us to all but a very narrow range of interpretations, and thus determining our interpretative reactions? Or is there rather a special value or virtue to be found through this interpretational multiplicity? We shall again focus solely on art for the time being; we shall then return to the question whether the case for science is parallel.

Before looking at specific examples, let us carefully distinguish two possible attributes of a text or work of art that both suggest multiplicity of interpretation. The first is *openness* (as in "open text") and the second *ambiguity,* narrowly construed. A work is open if (or to the extent that) it does not dictate its own interpretation. The closed text is the paradigm of bad literature: the text tells us that the heroine is in love, that her sighs are sighs of sadness and unselfish devotion, that her joy is untainted with misgivings. We are not allowed to remain puzzled for long if she throws a tantrum or an axe; all is explained. The reader is not guided so comfortably in his reading of, for example, *Madame Bovary* or *Strait Is the Gate.* As a minimum, the openness consists exactly in leaving open a number of interpretations, of different ways to view the action as manifesting character, purpose, and emotion.

But of course that is not all there is to it, since that minimum could also be achieved by quite ordinary vagueness. The work draws our attention in some definite ways to certain of the interpretations logically left open, thus giving them some degree of privilege, making them salient or at least fmore salient than the others. If the reader/viewer simply interprets the work in one definite way, unconsciously closing all the gaps left open, then the viewing experience is not subjectively different from that evoked by a closed work. The value of the openness, and of the presence of alternatives in interpretation, is then lost. In the open work, the openness must be exploited, and that can be achieved only through a selective privileging of certain interpretations. But typically the process goes a step farther, and we have not merely openness to interpretation, limited in one way or other, but a tension or conflict between the interpretations which saliently present themselves. That is ambiguity (in the narrow sense indicated above, for which we reserve this term here), an effect which goes beyond the presence of alternative interpretations. It consists in the tension, the conflict between interpretations which are made salient in such a way as to undermine each other, to prevent the irenic embrace of one or other of them for any length of time.

In the case of both qualities (though especially in the latter) it is very clear that the work in some way flouts the aims of representation as such. Openness means deliberate incompleteness, deliberate absence of answers to questions which selection of represented detail did bring to the fore, and even deliberate salient making of alternative possible answers, as if to taunt the understanding, to challenge it to creativity of its own. Ambiguity means even more: it is sabotage of any possible effort to eliminate the openness, to remove the equivocation, or to settle on a single picture to the exclusion of others. If these features of works of art do indeed contribute crucially to their value or attractiveness as works of art, then it seems that the value of art consists partly in something that conflicts with the criteria of representation.

Let us take Klimt's striking painting *The Kiss* (1907–8) as an example of a work of which our experience is consistently and overwhelmingly characterized by the apprehension of ambiguities, or tensions between seemingly contradictory features (see Fig. 4.1). The scene is both wonderfully enchanting and somehow sinister, and while there is something open and carefree about it, it seems also clandestine, our viewing almost voyeuristic. This is very much the result of the ambiguity in the subject matter of the painting, for it is unclear even what exactly the viewer is witnessing. On one level the description seems simple: a man and a woman, kneeling, embrace. But is it an act of extreme intimacy and tenderness, or of violence and victimization, a moment of pleasure or pain? The woman's tilted head, closed eyes, and arching hands suggest a sort of ecstasy, but perhaps equally repulsion. Does she hold her left arm folded close to her body, her hand resting on the man's, to draw him closer to her, or to protect herself, poised to pull his hand away from her face? And

Figure 4.1. *The Kiss* (1907–8), by Gustav Klimt, courtesy of the Öesterreichische Galerie, Vienna

do his large hands express coercion and force, or do they deny their apparent strength in an act of gentleness? The expression on the woman's face, as well as the position of the two bodies, also enhances this ambiguity.

The couple's position in relation to its environment is ambiguous as well. Are they as steady as the organic form encapsulating them would have us believe, or are they about to fall, as suggested by their somewhat precarious position on the edge of a rather unusual cliff? The environment is, on one hand, rather abstract; the figures are seen on a fairly homogeneous, partially metallic ground, covered with gold flecks and mottled gold rectangular forms. Yet the cliff which supports them, covered with flowers and vines, is relatively naturalistic and organic in contrast to this otherworldly space. Even the passage of time is affected by this contrast. The static patterning gives the scene an air of eternity, while the seemingly momentary curling under of the woman's toes brings the viewer back to a reality in which time is passing and the scene he sees cannot last.

It might be objected that we chose as example a work in which the subject itself has a certain ambiguity—perhaps as if we attempted to show the importance of ambiguity to literature as such by pointing to ambiguous statements and behavior on the part of characters. But the picture is also spatially ambiguous, for the dense decoration of the cliff, the abstract metallic background, and the extensive patterning incorporated into the couple's bodies strongly suggest a two-dimensional space, while the more conventionally naturalistic way in which selected parts of the figures are painted creates the illusion of three dimensions. Such an effect is achieved through differences in the way contrasting areas are painted. The patterned areas are relatively finely divided and painted homogeneously within divisions so as to detract from the brushwork (see, most obviously, the black rectangular patches on the man's robe), while areas depicting flesh are more continuous but mottled, and painted with a mixture of colors (close study of the woman's shoulder reveals the presence of greenish brushstrokes in the overall reddish flesh tone). The juxtaposition of these areas—for example, the woman's shoulder and arm broken by the overlay of her dress and the man's garment—make the contrast still more striking. Three-dimensional areas seem to emerge and recede back into the planar surface because of such strategic breaks in their continuity.

There are additional tensions in the two-dimensional patterning, for the outlines of the figures and the amoebalike form engulfing them are markedly organic, whereas the geometrical pattern elements seem extremely inorganic. Although the patterns themselves are painted in an inorganic style, they depict, in part, organic things. What begin as rectangles and spirals resemble flowers and eyes on the garment of the woman, and become, further down the composition, more clearly recognizable as flowers and vines. The differentiation of forms is unclear: human forms seem to emerge and melt back into the more abstract forms, and in what we perceive as a whole we sometimes see autonomous or separate parts. There is a sense of unity but also of division; are we to resolve this image into one unit or its composite parts?

These numerous tensions contribute to a general ambiguity in the realism of the painting. It seems both naturalistic and otherworldly, establishing a reality we recognize through subject matter and to some degree the depiction of it, but then challenging it with incongruous characteristics—elements that do not seem to fit into this reality but are recognized as magical or fantastic, somehow out of keeping with the interpretation which this "realism" suggests.

The question remains whether such tensions, which appear to play a dominant role in our experience of this work, are crucial to art as a whole. The sort of analysis we have just applied to bring out these ambiguities can however be extended to other works, to uncovering tensions in more technical or abstract ways. To maintain some continuity, we should choose another representation of a person, for instance, *Frauenkopf—Blauschwarzes Haar* (Woman's Head—Blue-black Hair), a watercolor by Emil Nolde, executed in 1910, shortly after Klimt's *Kiss*. The watercolor and ink wash face does not exhibit the more blatant stylistic variation of Klimt's work, but grows more intriguing the longer it is viewed. If we ask what it is that is initially so attractive about this image, the answer is not the ambiguity of realistic representation, although the image is by no means overwhelmingly realistic in the conventional sense. Instead, the strength of the heavy black ink lines that form the woman's face and hair seems to be the most appealing feature of the work, and the very lines of the eyebrows, nose, and chin are somehow attractive in both their confidence and contour. Upon further consideration, one realizes that the patches of yellow and aqua wash that shade the face also pull the viewer toward the image, especially as complemented by the touches of rose-colored wash at the eyes, nose, and mouth. But what is it about these particular configurations of ink on paper that makes them so appealing? Is it simply the lines, and shapes, and colors that have such appeal, devoid of the subject matter they depict?

Let us focus on a particularly interesting area of the composition in the upper right corner. The tousle of hair that falls lightly over the woman's face is composed of strong overlapping lines of blue and black ink, featuring an especially attractive thick line (presumably a curl or lock of hair) that stands apart to the right of the others. Its separation from the larger mass of hair is highlighted by the presence of white (absence of

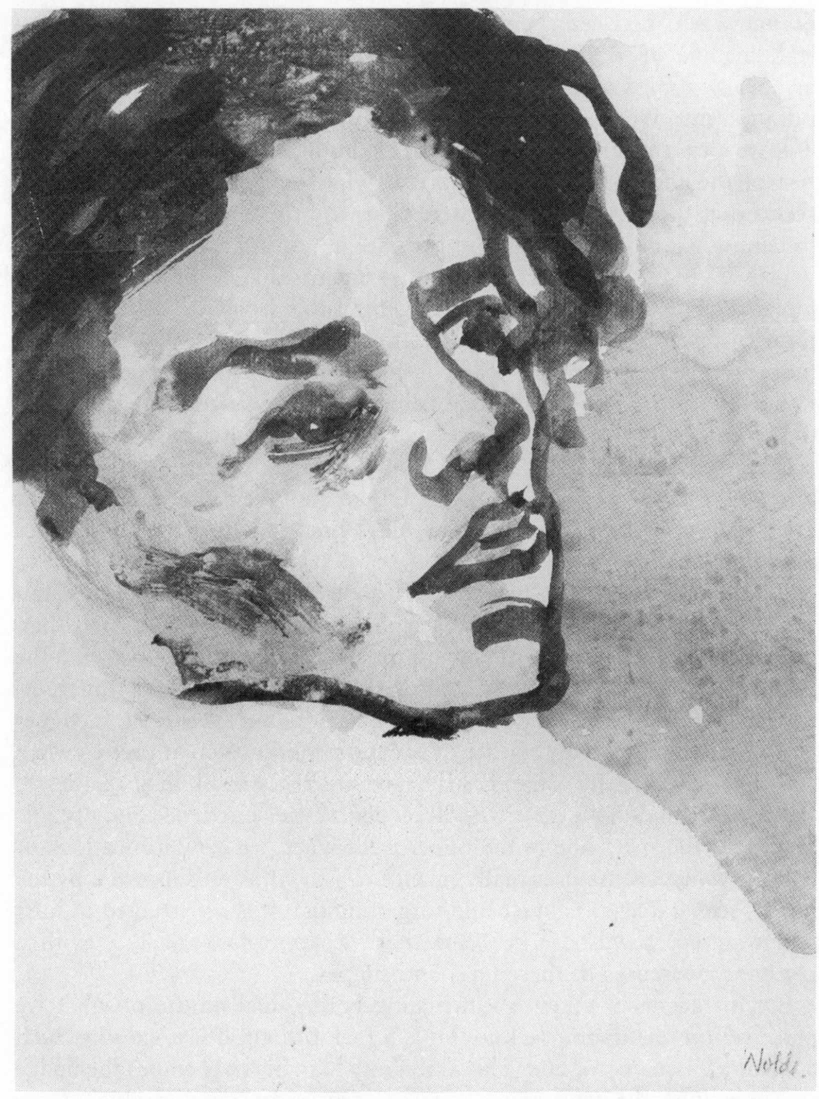

Figure 4.2. *Frauenkopf—Blauschwarzes Haar* (1910), by Emil Nolde, reproduced by permission of Christian Kunze.

orange wash) between them. Granted this area, and especially the outstanding line, are particularly compelling. But are they compelling simply as lines and mass alone, or does their attraction result from their incorporation into the image, their role as representing hair?

If we view this area of the paper in isolation, so that its relation to the rest of the image is unacknowledged, what happens to these lines? It seems that they are still quite interesting, and to some degree compel us to continue looking at them. But they are not as interesting as they were when viewed in the context of the entire image. That is not to say that the image as a whole is more interesting than this isolated patch of it (although indeed it may be), but that this particular area itself becomes more interesting given knowledge of the rest of the image, or rather when imbued with the representational value that knowledge and recognition of the image provide. Thus, these lines, intriguing in themselves, become even more intriguing when viewed as hair. And in like manner, the yellow and blue patches of color on the face take on added interest when they are not only surrounding thick blue-black lines but also shading the face of a woman.

Do we then, however, just look at these things for their representational value? Does the context overshadow the components such that, because the face is more interesting than the isolated lines, we like the lines better, knowing in theory that they are there, but never quite perceiving them as lines? This is a difficult question, but since what intrigues us about the lines when they are in isolation continues to attract us when they are viewed in the context of the face, we might think that we are still aware of them *as lines,* that we still recognize the confidence and organic quality of the stray line in the upper right when we view it as a lock of hair. Anyway, are we ever really taken in by the illusion suggested by the image, seeing it as a real face and forgetting that it is constructed of lines and watercolor washes? It seems that we appreciate the face with a constant awareness of these lines and shapes.

But in fact what seems so intriguing is this dual nature of what we perceive; on one hand, we know it is a lock of hair, but it exhibits such a wonderful quality of line. This ambiguity may be what makes the image so appealing—the tension between the representational quality of the image and the blatant admission of its construction, the ambiguity between line *as line* and line as the subject it represents (in this case, line as hair). The first thing to attract us about the drawing, already admitting recognition of the representational image, was the quality of line, which suggests, by contrast, the apprehension of line *as line.* Thus the ambiguity was actually present, even in that first impression of the image as appealing by virtue of its lines.

Could Ambiguity Have Value in Science?

As our examples show, contemplation of a work of art consists to some extent in becoming more aware of the openness and the ambiguities, and these can contribute crucially to its value. Indeed, we tentatively advance the stronger thesis that this ambiguity is crucial to aesthetic value in general, and not just in certain examples. But what about science? The argument in the section before last purports to establish at least the pervasive openness of science to interpretation. On the one hand, what science gives us is a representation of the phenomena which involves interpretation, since its character is not uniquely determined (but rather, as we say, "underdetermined") by the data. On the other hand, the scientific theory is itself an open text, subject to diverging interpretations—what the theory represents the phenomena *as* is itself not a hard datum. Here even important alternatives are often present without coming fully to light in the awareness of those involved, and when some do come to light, they are largely ignored in the day-to-day engagement of the working scientist. But in retrospect such interpretational elements—such as that Newtonian mechanics was regarded as an essentially deterministic theory, and temporal relations as absolute rather than relative—are seen to have thoroughly constrained scientific thinking.

But in the case of art we have seen something more: not only the openness of the work, but awareness of the openness of the work, and not only openness to alternative interpretations, but the conflicts and tensions between these interpretations can contribute crucially to the value of the work. Isn't it true that in science the admissibility of alternative interpretations creates the demand to settle on one of them? Even more, doesn't the appearance of ambiguity, of any tension between ways of taking a theory, create quite urgently the demand to resolve and eliminate that ambiguity? In other words, aren't those features which we have argued to be of value in art just defects when they are found in science?

Recent history of physics includes a famous negative answer to these questions, namely Bohr's views on complementarity. But that answer does not any longer enjoy the high regard it once had. Scientists educated in classical physics had two sorts of pictures, two sorts of models, which were mutually exclusive: the wave picture and the particle picture. Different processes were modeled in these two different ways, and no process could be of both sorts. For a while in the twentieth century, scientists were using both sorts of pictures for the same processes, though in connection with different experimental setups. Sometimes the behavior of light, for example, admitted representation as a wave in a medium and sometimes it admitted representation as a stream of particles. Bohr's quite revolutionary idea was that this could be accepted as a normal and satisfactory state of affairs, that a theory could simply offer two families of models, with some prescription about when to switch from one to the other. The idea was workable only, however, if that prescription itself was not equivocal, and hence only if the scientist's apparatus could be exempted from this, and could be said to have a univocal description. But the only univocal description available was that of classical physics, which unfortunately predicted wrongly even at the macroscopic level of the apparatus. Today there seems little hope of reinstituting complementarity as the key to interpretation of physics.

It seems to us that for the philosopher there nevertheless remains an important question: Are these ambiguities found in science, its openness to interpretation, valuable? The disanalogy with art will remain if all we've done is to point out defects in the scientific practice of obtaining a univocal interpretation both of phenomena and of theory. However, the question of value should be subdivided into two. First we ask whether ambiguity and openness have been of value to science in practice, or instead hampered its progress. Then we must ask how different philosophical views rule on whether ambiguity and openness are defects, or alternatively, can be valuable to science.

As to the first question, no philosopher should prejudge the history, sociology, or psychology of science. At every point in the history we see both blindness and insight, and the two are inseparable. The insight that Newtonian mechanics lent itself to being the mainstay of a deterministic worldview blinded the Enlightenment to the possibilities of indeterminism. Prima facie, at least both that insight and its correlate blindness are to be credited with inspiring the spirit of research which led to the triumphs, and *also* to the phenomenal limits, of classical physics. But then the previously unseen alternatives—the previously undetected gaps, vaguenesses, and ambiguities—became visible as it was realized that science did already have resources to begin the study of discontinuity and chance in nature.

As to the second question, we must admit that a naive scientific realism would entail that ambiguity, vagueness, and gaps are all defects. The latter two spell incompleteness of achievement with respect to the literally true story of the world. The first also obstructs, sabotages, such achievement as it drives thought into several different directions at once—the aimed-for achievement continues only with the elimination of conflicting interpretations. But what if the empirical predictions remain invariant under all ways of resolving the ambiguity (all ways of opting for one interpretative completion over its rivals)? Then empiricism sees no defect. Indeed, the only way to truly enhance the understanding of science, for the empiricist, is not to resolve such ambiguity, but to find out in how many different ways it could be resolved. Each tenable interpretation will throw new light on the theory, by showing that this is how the world could be as the theory describes it; all such new light is valuable. And since each of those ways of seeing the world is potentially a good way to respond to new phenomena as yet unexpected or even unimagined, they are not to be chosen among, but valued and appreciated. Indeed, the tensions created by ambiguity, like the paradoxes about infinity and infinitesimals that plagued modern mathematics, may well be the crucial clues to creative development.

Are There Criteria for Interpretation?

Our inquiry into the criteria for representation led us to interpretation, and the inadequacy of views of art or science as (simply) representation. But does the admission of interpretation lead us into a mire of pluralism? What are the criteria proper to interpretation, if any? We have some idea of what is a faithful representation—as well as of the difficulties inherent in that idea—but what makes for a good or better interpretation? First of all, are there basic, minimal criteria (such as those relating to accuracy and selectivity in the case of representation), and if so, are there ways of assessing interpretation that go beyond those minimal ones?

Suppose someone offers an interpretation of a work of art, a text, or a scientific theory. At first sight, it must always be a valid question whether this is an admissible interpretation at all. If it is, there must be further valid questions, surely, about how good it is as interpretation, and whether it is better or worse than its alternatives. It is possible that such questions can arise meaningfully only in very rich contexts, if only because an interpretation makes no sense if divorced from its cultural, social, and historical context. In that case we must inquire also into the extent to which values "from outside" enter into such evaluation, in the sense in which that is so already for evaluations of the artist's selectivity.

Let us for a moment consider the alternative. Suppose that there are no objective or publicly valid criteria to be applied to interpretation, and that judgments of admissibility as interpretation, and of how good an interpretation is (as interpretation of the work in question), are only a matter of personal taste. What, in effect, is the critic or reader then doing? His reaction to the work has in that case the character of a psychological subject's reactions to a Rorschach test. No one investigates whether there are geometric or color correspondences between the blot and things mentioned—mother, blood, sunburst, spider—in the subject's response. That response is investigated only in its own right as a clue to the subject's mood disorders. The question whether the response was an interpretation *admitted* by the inkblot does not arise. But to do the same with a painting, a poem, or the text of Einstein's "On the Electrodynamics of Moving Bodies" is to miss the point.

But what sort of criteria can there be? A familiar and obvious interpretation occurs when we read *The Pilgrim's Progress* as an allegory of the spiritual life. This reading implies in the first place that the text is a representation of a journey. Here we are surely at a level where no more is involved than conventional coding, the dictionary meanings of the words. Similarly, the interpretation of a certain painting suggested by its title, *The Adoration of the Mystical Lamb* (the Ghent Altarpiece), implies in the first place that it is a representation of a lamb surrounded by people. Again, no more than conventional coding need be appealed to here; no creative viewer/reader response is called for beyond that to be expected from a minimally educated person in our culture. If now someone were to offer an interpretation of that painting as one of Leda and the Swan, we expect to be able to criticize it on this very basic level. If this interpretation implies that the painting is or includes a representation of Leda and of a swan, then we can say: even the criteria for representation rule out that interpretation. Questions about the value of the interpretation would be moot, for the work is not even a representation of what it is said (implied) to represent.

What this suggests is that there are indeed minimal criteria of interpretation, but they are the criteria already for representation.[18] We can make the parallel point for science, both with regard to its interpretation of the phenomena, and with regard to interpretations of theories. As example of the first, suppose that someone proposes an explanation of why the sky is blue. It should be possible to answer: "That is lovely as an explanation, it is original, coherent, unifying, intellectually exciting—but the phenomena do not admit that interpretation." The theory may have every internal or cultural value imaginable, and not fit the data. In that way science—conceived of as interpretation of the phenomena—submits to public criteria. As example of the second, if someone, for example Sir Karl Popper, offers an interpretation of quantum mechanics, we can say: "How wonderful! What a cosmic, inspiring vision of the world, and how intellectually satisfying! But the 'no-hidden-variable' theorems show that any theory which does admit your interpretation will make predictions at odds with those of quantum mechanics. Therefore *that* theory does not admit your interpretation." The point is that quantum theory does not even count as a representation of Popper's world, at the very basic level of accuracy with respect to the empirical phenomena.

The question is, however, what sort of criteria could come into play beyond this? What we should like to be able to say about an interpretation includes that it gives us real, new insight into the work in question. We have a sense of discovery, of seeing what was there all along, but had not been discerned before the interpretation was offered. This suggests a relation between the work and its interpretation which is objectively there, and yet goes beyond the very minimal sort of adequacy described above.

We have no substantial answer to offer to this question. But perhaps it is possible at least to remove an assumption which, if tacitly held, may certainly obstruct the inquiry. That is the assumption that insofar as a response to a work cannot be evaluated in terms of its relation to the work itself (or more liberally, *to* the work *in* the publicly accessible cultural and historical context), it is either arbitrary or of idiosyncratic or autobiographical interest only. The threat of the nihilistic possibility, that the critic's response is, beyond the most minimal level of adequacy, no different after all from free association to a Rorschach blot, may just come from the assumption that there is nothing else for it to be.

There are certainly philosophies of art which are at odds with that assumption. Consider for example Collingwood's view that the work of art, properly speaking, is the artist's imaginative construction. He may have created this by or through the production of a material work—and that production will have shown every sign of being a problem-solving activity, as the artist tries to "get it right"—but what was created cannot be identified with the resulting object, score, single performance, or written text. The audience—or reader—response consists then also in an imaginative construction, evoked by the material work (which functions therefore always as language does paradigmatically). In that case, the beholder is a "secondary" artist, so to speak, who creates a work of imagination related to the real work of art. The important question is not how accurate a reproduction of the artist's own imaginative construction results, but how valuable the product at second remove is in its own right. The great artist facilitates, evokes, guides our lives of the imagination, in which we too should hope to be more creative than docile.

Reader-response theories of literature obviously come to mind here as well. The literary text—unlike the cartoon or genre novel—is an open text, which does not dictate or normatively dominate the reading. We should add that in order not to quibble but take advantage of the new distinctions so allowed, we must acknowledge that the artist brings into being much more than the original "work of art proper"—the material work is the temporally persisting focus of a sequence of imaginative creations, which can alternately be viewed as a single imaginative work evolving through centuries, liberated from the confines of any one individual mind, including the artist's. The weight placed on criteria relating an interpretation to its reference's (original) structure is therefore not written in stone; it is itself a theoretical bias brought to this problem area.

Let us close by looking again into a possible parallel at the level of scientific theorizing. In the case of Newton, there was the original work of imagination, completed by the writing of the *Principia*. Since then there have been countless such works evoked in response, from the amateur who looks again at the moon after laboriously working through Newton's elegant solution to the two-body problem, through the teachers who expressed their understanding of Newton's work conditioned by their own philosophical and scientific milieu, to the great Laplace, Lagrange, Hamilton . . ., whose readings progressively transformed the science. Taking for granted (for just a moment longer) that we can very simply divide such a theory as Hamilton's into the part which exactly duplicates the *Principia* and a novel remainder, it is clear that our evaluation is not at all restricted to the former. We can criticize or laud the addition, but do so in its own right, not merely because it has no clear pedigree in the original. Again, although representation of the original is not what is at issue, the criteria are not independent of questions of representation. There is a question clearly whether, even if all future phenomena admit classification as Newtonian systems, Hamilton's modeling will prove as fortunate. It is debatable whether Hamilton thought he had merely rewritten Newton's theory in alternative formalism. If so, it appears he was more creative than he himself appreciated—the new way of seeing things was essentially novel. But with respect to other sorts of criteria, the verdict is by no means "everyone to his taste"; Hamilton's theory is required to be good physics.

How does this discussion reflect back on art? Parallels are more evident for some arts than for others. How would Vasari, Walter Pater, John Berger, and Northrop Frye each read the others' work on painting? Their mutual critique would not disappear in bland harmony, once each had noticed every detail the others point out! Even more remarkable is the transformation of literature as it appears through successive critics' pens; an extreme example is perhaps J. Hillis Miller's deconstructionist reading of Crabbe's "The Parting Hour" as compared with readings of forty or fifty years before. Even if the written text were to remain letter by letter the same, this constant is only the focus of an evolving multiplicity of interpretations. Those interpretations are evaluated, but only partly in terms of literal faithfulness to the text. Other criteria are not logically independent of questions of representation, but extend beyond it. Does the interpretation in question enable other readers, in our culture, to read the work fruitfully, or even without strain? Can I really read *Hamlet* as Freudian case history without ending in amusement at Freudian pretensions? The communal judgment that the interpretation is strained, forced, malapropos, or egregious will typically seem to be made in terms of fidelity to the original text, but will largely get its bite from expectations of the role this reading or staging could play in the evolving tradition of interpretative responses focused on this work.

What we have suggested here, in effect, is that the problem of evaluation of interpretations of a work of art or of science is to be subsumed under the problem of evaluation of art and of science themselves. Without being able to say what the criteria are for interpretation, beyond the most basic ones (for accuracy and completeness of representation), we suggest that there are such criteria, and that they are essentially the same as for the initial creative activity.

NOTES

1. In book 2 (373b), the *mimêtai* include painters, musicians, poets, actors, and choral dancers; the discussion in book 10 (596e–603a) starts with the painter (compared with the carpenter, but at three removes from truth [597d, 602c]), concentrates on the poet, and ends with an analysis of the ways in which song, music, and dance are suited for mimesis. Of course, this was by way of setting for Plato's critique of poetry as a snare and deception, to be banished from the republic. But the core of his polemic, the view of art as representation, is explicitly shared by Aristotle's *Poetics,* although the prosaic Aristotle wrote it to refute the poet Plato's rejection of that art (see *Poetics* 1449b 25–28).
2. Cited in E. H. Gombrich, *Art and Illusion* (Princeton: Princeton University Press, 1960), 12.
3. We recognize that the word *representation* is commonly used also in a wider sense, in which someone might be said to produce a representation accidentally or unintentionally. We limit ourselves to discussing representation in the narrower sense here outlined. If one person unintentionally produces an object in which someone else spots a striking similarity to George Washington, for example, and the second person displays the object as a portrait, then the first person has not represented Washington (as we use "represent") but the second person may have succeeded in doing so.
4. Henceforth the word *accuracy,* when unqualified, will be used in the narrower sense here explained.
5. For both accuracy and selectivity, one could ask whether the limiting case is in fact possible, that is, perfect accuracy of depiction with respect to some selected feature, or total completeness of selection of features for depiction. The existence or possibility of the limiting case, however, is not required for evaluation of more and less to be possible. For example, there is no longest distance; however, the possibility of comparing distances gives the concept of distance its legitimacy.

6. This too can be illustrated by Plato's discussion; see *Republic* 2.378a, 396c–d; 10.598a–b, 605a–b (in view of 604): the person is analyzed as having various parts, some more and some less noble; the imitative poet tends to select the less noble parts for representation.

7. Aristotle appears to make the role of a certain selectivity crucial to his defense of poetry: "poetry is a more philosophical and serious business than history; for poetry speaks more of universals, history of particulars" (*Poetics* 145lb, 8–9). By showing selectively and variously what can happen and what will happen "according to probability or necessity," the poet can represent universal patterns in human history and human affairs, while the historian, so much less selectively, portrays particular happenstance.

8. As noted in section 1, we are discussing intentional representation, the case in which the artist tries to carry out his intention to represent the subject in a certain way, and perhaps succeeds. It is not to be assumed either that this is what makes his activity art, or that the value of the work of art depends on success in this respect. We are here inquiring into just what is involved in those cases in which art does involve (intentional) representation.

9. "In the context of a largely homosexual audience, at one level, the play can become a kind of private experience during which some groups understand allusions of which others are unaware: from a certain point of view, misogyny becomes the center of the work (women destroy the creator Orpheus, women attempt to destroy the artist's inspiration). . . ." Lydia Crowson, *The Esthetic of Jean Cocteau* (Hanover, N.H.: University Press of New England, 1978), 54.

10. Carl E. Schorske, *Fin-de-Siècle Vienna: Politics and Culture* (New York: Vintage Books, 1981).

11. This, of course, is an area of philosophy of mind in which issues have been hotly contested of late. See Lynne Rudder Baker, *Saving Belief* (Princeton: Princeton University Press, 1987), and Hilary Putnam, *Representation and Reality,* especially his chapter "Why Functionalism Didn't Work."

12. Note well the layered structure of levels here at which interpretation enters. The artist represents some men on the grass. He may succeed in getting us to see the painting as a representation of those men as arrogant—as well as (or in some way *through*) getting us to interpret as arrogant the way those men comport themselves. In other words, the viewer must be provoked into interpreting what he sees as (a material object which is) *a representation that represents its subject matter as* thus or so.

13. In the philosophy of science we have such a strong position concerning the language of science in the denial (e.g., Sellars, Feyerabend) that there even could exist a pure, not theory-infected hygienic observation language. This is now widely accepted.

14. William Whewell, "On the Nature and Conditions of Inductive Science," in J. J. Kockelmans, ed., *Philosophy of Science—The Historical Background* (New York: Free Press, 1968), 51.

15. Jarrett Leplin, ed., *Scientific Realism* (Berkeley: University of California Press, 1984), 2 (from the editor's Introduction).

16. "Seemed," because the remaining incompleteness in the interpretation was of course (if there was such dominance) not perceived. We should also add that the incompleteness is different at different historical stages. Perhaps after the addition of the conservation laws, mechanics as officially codified (say, around 1890) was deterministic. The diverging axiomatizations of classical mechanics that appeared over the next hundred years show, however, that the treatment of mass had still been left ambiguous. Those who took Mach's and Hertz's monographs on mechanics seriously could have perceived this already then, but this sort of awareness grows slowly.

17. Contrasting one specific formulation of these two ways of viewing quantum mechanics, John Wheeler wrote, "Our conclusions can be stated very briefly: (1) The conceptual scheme of 'relative state' quantum mechanics is completely different from the conceptual scheme of the conventional 'external observation' form of quantum mechanics and (2) The conclusions from the new treatment correspond completely in familiar cases to the conclusions from the usual analysis." *Review of Modern Physics* 29 (1957): 463–65. This contrast is not essentially bound up with the specific account (by Everett) on which Wheeler was commenting.

18. This point is not affected if we think that there is no sharp division, but only a continuum of representations, with more and less by way of involved interpretation—or, on the other side of the coin, a continuum of interpretations from the minimal case of geometric projection to elaborate and sophisticated reader response. It is after all possible to make meaningful, nonarbitrary divisions in a continuum; and indeed, most predicates do exactly that.

CHAPTER 5

Meaningful Projects

RICHARD W. MILLER

Many contemporary literary theorists are united in protesting against a certain authoritarian view of literary reading. According to the authoritarian view, the right way to read a work of literature is to identify what the author meant to say while discerning the formal skill (or clumsiness) with which the author used words to say it. This view is authoritarian in at least three ways. Only one way of reading is supposed to be right. Also, if the one way goes well, the interaction between reader and text is controlled by an external fact, what the author intended. (This way of reading is submissive.) Finally, the view is advanced as the only coherent understanding of what could count as interpreting a work of literature and assessing its literary value. An attempt to disagree about these tasks would be a sign of ignorance or unreason, not just of a different commitment or location in a different tradition. The liberating impulse is to reject all of these claims.

As the protesters are well aware, the authoritarian view is a stereotype, which few influential theorists (if any) would advocate literally and in every detail. Still, the authoritarian view has enormous influence, to which many readers succumb in the readings they give and, above all, in the options they neglect. For example, the authorized task of figuring out what someone intends to convey by a literary work largely consists of discovering unifying intentions that eliminate apparent inconsistencies and irrelevancies. So if one is influenced by the authoritarian assumptions, one ignores self-undermining or inconsequentially shifting readings.

As usual, I agree with the anti-authoritarians. I have been freed by them and helped in my reading. My subject is the ways in which recent Anglo-American philosophy helps these appeals for literary freedom, and the ways in which it doesn't. I will begin with an essay in frustration. The investigations of realism made possible by the death of positivist philosophy of science have not established premises for an argument from scientific to literary freedom. In particular, anti-authoritarians are sometimes tempted by this appeal to morals supposed to be derivable from that long torment, the death of positivism: "the rational goal of scientific theorizing is not the true description of an external reality, and the scientific justification of theories always depends on background principles subject to rational dissent; so the same must be true of literary theory, which could not be more concerned with external facts than science is, or more constrained by reason and evidence." I think that the premises of this argument, the morals drawn from the death of positivism, are wrong, though not all wrong. In scientific theorizing, rational inquirers are often in a position to make tentative claims as to approximate truth—though sometimes they are not and sometimes this is not the point of their uses of theories. When someone is in a position to make a scientific truth-claim, sometimes there is no relevant possibility of rational dissent—but sometimes there is: it all depends on the content of the claim and the nature of the evidence and argument. Scientific inquiry displays all possible relations to the goal of truth and the constraints of reason and evidence. Which parts of science are the right analogues for literary theory will depend on the specific goals and arguments relevant to literary reading. So no appeal to a general analogy with science will help.

When I clarify my antipositivist morals and use examples to make them more plausible, their uselessness for arguments from analogy will be obvious enough. But these morals drawn from the death of positivism *are* helpful in a very different way, by motivating a new approach to content, i.e., to the limits of genuine disagreement and agreement. Current theories of meaning that rule on such issues would rule out some of the mixed verdicts according to which a truth-claim is justified even though the claimant ought to acknowledge that dissent would not depend on unreason or ignorance of relevant data. According to those theories, what supports such radical difference in response creates a difference in meaning, so that there is no genuine dissent, just a changing of the subject. (Because the mixed verdict is so often the right assessment of moral judgments, I will have much to say about the moral realism dispute as well as the scientific one.)

My main endeavor will be to develop an approach to content that explains how the mixed verdicts are possible. In this account, the limits to content are set by strategic reasoning about the most effective use of words in common projects of social learning. I'll conclude by employing that account in defending an anti-authoritarian view of what a genuine literary reading could be. If these arguments are right, then current philosophical debates over realism are most useful to literary theorists when they generate fruitful puzzles about meaning, truth, and justification—i.e., what's useful is the fruit of those puzzles, not general characterizations of truth and justification in science.

The Emptiness of "Realism"

In Anglo-American philosophy these days, the hottest topics concerning truth and justification (perhaps, the hottest topics, period) are the disputes over scientific realism and the analogous position about moral judgment, moral realism. One reason it is hard to learn from Anglo-American philosophy is that these topics are ill formed. In each case, a variety of questions are in dispute, and the answers to each question are naturally assessed as realist or as antirealist. Yet, applied to the same hypothesis or judgment in science or morality, the correct answer to one question can be realist, to another antirealist. It is better to let the questions speak for themselves.

The Scopes of Reason

One question that might be posed is whether a hypothesis might be asserted by one person, denied by another, when each is rationally responding to the same evidence. According to positivism, a principal ghost at our smorgasbord, the answer was always "no." Any rational inquirer's response to the data had to be justifiable as a dictate of a single canon of general principles valid in all fields at all times, which no rational person could reject. For reasons of space and in expectation of general agreement, I will simply assume that this demand should be abandoned. Read without the pressure of the positivist demand, the history of science does seem to include actual cases of such rational discord. Maxwell took the data to support the hypothesis that the movement of one charge would produce movement in another, with a regular time delay, by producing stress in an intervening massless medium. His justification relied on the principle that "the propagation in time" must be "either the flight of a material substance in space or the propagation of a condition of motion or stress in a medium already existing in space."[1] Neumann, responding to the same data, took them to support the hypothesis that the movement of the first charge acts on the other at a distance and with a delay, with no relevant change in intervening matter. Potential was the primary causal factor in his explanatory framework; this factor was not attributed to further underlying forces or ascribed to matter.[2] Because of the difference in frameworks, each theorist seems rational, though their evidence was the same.

To put the matter more generally—the justification of a theoretical hypothesis (some of us would add, the justification of any hypothesis, even a mere empirical generalization) is an inference from the best explanation of the data. But rational inquirers cannot and need not dispense with topic-specific background principles as means to sift through alternative explanations, in pursuit of the best. Sometimes these indispensable bases for justification will differ from rational inquirer to rational inquirer, even when they share all available relevant evidence.

Of course, in science, people hope to end such disagreements through reason and further evidence, a process that ended the dispute between Maxwell and Neumann, in which both sides proved to be wrong. However, there may be cases, even in the physical sciences, in which all the relevant observable facts there ever will be would lead to contrary hypotheses, justified in frameworks, actually employed, which are reasonable in light of all that evidence. Contrary cosmological hypotheses have been rationally advanced in the past. Perhaps such contrariety would persist in light of all the data. Even more clearly, this might be the case in the social sciences. Rational differences about the explanation of the coming of the U.S. Civil War have been grounded—and perhaps they always will be—on different assumptions about the importance of people's reasons, as opposed to their objective interests, in the causation of their conduct and belief.

Still, it always seems to be a rational hope, in science, that more evidence will overcome disagreement among rational inquirers. In the other great field for the "realism" controversy, moral judgment, this comfort is not always available. Even when he contemplates inequalities among Greek males of equal potential, Aristotle thinks that a constitution under which everyone flourishes to a substantial extent is worse than one in which a handful flourish to a higher degree at the cost of stultifying drudgery for the rest. Unlike his subordination of women and "natural slaves," this elitism does not depend on false biology or any premise that he would have to abandon in the face of evidence if he were rational. No doubt he would have judged differently if he had settled ultimate questions of good and bad with equal concern and respect for all affected. But he would have rejected our more egalitarian ways of moral learning as sentimental departures from appropriate concern for the highest activities. This rejection may be misguided, but it would not depend on unreasonableness or ignorance of modern data.

So far, the questions about rational disagreement have concerned frameworks for inquiry that people actually employ. In science and morality, we are not normally concerned to achieve a higher form of universality than acceptability to all actual rational inquirers if they possessed all relevant data. In much (probably not all) of science, much (perhaps less) of morality, and almost all ordinary inquiry into gross features of middle-sized earthly objects, frameworks are similar enough to yield this kind of rational determinability. Of course, our rational beliefs in these spheres must often be tentative and approximate. Still, discounting frameworks that fail tests which they themselves impose, we are often justified in a tentative belief that the totality of evidence would not make it rational to reject our judgment as fundamentally wrong in any framework that an actual investigator employs. So the view of reason that I have outlined so far does not provide a quick argument by analogy in favor of widespread liberation in literature. It simply yields advice to become clearer on the various specific principles in use in rational, informed investigations of literature.

Nonetheless, one further question might seem to yield a prospect of limitless rational dissent. Isn't there always a possible framework, perhaps not actually employed but still reasonable in light of all the data, whose employment would make it possible to dissent without unreason or ignorance of data? If so, any limit to rational conclusions about nature (or morality) is just the result of what traditions, convictions, and choices happen to arise. Surely this will be true of conclusions about literary works as well.

Consider such well-hedged banalities as these: in normal contexts and in the absence of special arguments for rival explanations, if a person screams, that is evidence that she is in pain; if a procedure makes features that are visible in a blurry way to unaided sight clearly and distinctly visible, that is evidence that the same procedure reveals real phenomena when it seems to make the wholly invisible visible. Someone with the experiences that are normal for human beings who nonetheless rejects such truisms would show a failure to grasp the concepts involved. In other words, someone departing from the corresponding practices of inference is either responding unreasonably or addressing himself to something other than the content of the standard assertion. Either he is not genuinely rational or he is not genuinely disagreeing. Like the rules in the canon that the positivists sought, such truisms set limits to rational dissent. Unlike the hoped-for canonical rules, the truisms are specific in subject matter, and are not independent of relevant experience. Such truisms together with all relevant evidence compel tentative belief in most of the gross findings about middle-sized earthly objects with which technical science begins. Similar arguments, appealing to often extraordinary evidence, would seem to compel tentative belief in at least some technical science. Think of the role of truisms concerning the blurry and the distinct in the seventeenth-century case for microbes, or the role of inferences made by almost every baby in establishing the principle of inertia.[3]

The Force of Reason and the Practice of Moral Judgment

In moral inquiry, the limits to dissent are more complex. They illustrate a fact that I will exploit in more detail in my eventual view of content, namely, that the possibility of rational dissent can depend on the inquirers' goals and practices.

One can imagine a possible monster, a moral nihilist who grasps moral concepts but regards all moral judgments as false. He grasps the concepts of right and wrong, good and evil because he understands on what bases we employ them—rather as an atheist might understand how the Catholic church applies the term "saint." Still, he does not locate acts in a moral spectrum with obligations at one end, wrongful acts at another, and morally indifferent acts in between. He thinks there are no moral properties. Nonetheless, he can use the usual moral terms as labels for the nonmoral properties in virtue of which the moral ones are supposed to be possessed. So he can explain the data as well as we. His denial that there are moral properties or moral facts is reasonable in light of relevant evidence.

However, if we turn from the dissenter from all moral judgment and look at dissenting moral judges instead, moral inquiry looks like scientific inquiry, with possible rational dissent importantly constrained by specific truisms. If someone has gravely, intentionally harmed another person, this is grounds for supposing the act is wrong in the absence of certain special circumstances. Though these circumstances are diverse in every actual framework and differ as between some frameworks, no one could be rationally engaged in moral judgment if he did not grasp the relevance of grave harm to wrong or if he took certain circumstances as making an act all right. In order to enjoy a transient skittish thrill, Caligula is said to have invited guests on board a ship, ordered them thrown over the sides, and had them beaten off with oars and boathooks until they drowned. "Why is that reason to believe that the emperor did wrong?" is a frank expression of a failure to grasp the subject of the moral judgment, if it is not a coy expression of the nihilist denial that there is such a subject.

The limits of dissent in moral inquiry will be specially revealing because they are a first indication of the role of concerns and practices. Limits to disagreement may bind only when people are engaged in a practice of judgment. And this engagement may require that relevant people have appropriate concerns. If the nihilist, who understands our practices of inference so well, were to share our concerns for others, taking their well-being, integrity, and suffering to be reasons for choice in the ways we do, then his verbal rejection of all our moral judgments would be merely verbal, not nihilism but confusion. By the same token, the rationality of his position is made plain by imagining someone who utterly lacks concern for others, someone for whom it would not be a reason to push a button that it would relieve excruciating pain in another with no cost whatever to the button pusher. Such radical lack of concern, combined with the nihilist's grasp of our practices and his verbal rejection of all moral judgments, makes his nihilism genuine. Yet it is mere wishful thinking to suppose that reason and evidence are incompatible, in principle, with so cold a heart.

The moral nihilist's rationality does not merely depend on his unconcern. It depends on concern in others. For he is a semantic parasite whose capacity to grasp what moral terms mean consists in an understanding of how they are used by those who actually arrive at moral conclusions. If the practice to which he alluded were not a practice in which anyone at all employed other-directed concerns as reasons for choice, his parasitism would fail. He would not be talking about wrongness and rightness in denying that anything is right or wrong or in between. (Perhaps an individual can utterly fail to care about others and still make moral judgments. In the sentences that she uses, accepts, and rejects, she will be closer to our practice than the nihilist. Still, she too will be a semantic parasite, since her engagement with the content of morality will depend on participation in practices shared with others who do care.)

Rational, informed nihilism, in the sense of a wholesale rejection with no specific argument to support it, is possible in the moral realm but not in the realm of basic talk about matter. (Of course, specific arguments for wholesale rejection are offered in both realms. I find them wanting for familiar reasons, but their study would lead far afield.) It might seem that the combination of the one possibility with the other impossibility must be due to the fact that moral judgments depend on desire and, unlike basic material object talk, are not genuine beliefs. But really the only distinction needed to make sense of the different degrees of freedom is the obvious one, that moral inquiry depends on inquiry into basic facts about people and things. The latter realm is so basic that someone dispensing with it would lack the means to be a semantic parasite. Someone who did not arrive at any conclusion about people or things, even if licensed by the basic truisms, could not understand how others reached such conclusions and, so, could not grasp their concepts well enough to reject their beliefs.

Detecting Truth

The anti-authoritarian appeal to philosophy with which I began spoke of truth, as well as reason. Perhaps the most shocking of the findings ascribed to postpositivist philosophy of science was the alleged insight that rational inquirers in the theoretical sciences do not make truth-claims. Certainly theoretical scientists often are in no position to claim that all relevant evidence would support their favored theory in every possible rational framework. In these cases, at least, a denial of truth would be the outcome of taking a familiar step, a characteristic move of the positivists in their discussions of moral judgments: the fact that two people could disagree when neither is burdened by ignorance or unreason might be taken to show that they are not disagreeing about how to describe the facts.

This move is a misstep. It would either reflect lingering positivist prejudice or an idealization of access to truth (perhaps a "metaphysics of presence"). A justified truth-claim is a justified claim to have successfully exercised a capacity for detection. Reference, in other words, is what conveys success in detection. The cases of radical disagreement that the new philosophies of science bring to the fore are cases in which people disagree as to what constitutes detection. Maxwell was in a position to take himself to have ways of revealing ether stress (sometimes in charming popular lecture-demonstrations). But Neumann was in a position to assert that action-at-a-distance had been detected. The evenhanded concern and respect that are our way of telling better from worse political systems would be a sentimental distortion for Aristotle. Because of their different positions concerning what constitutes detection, each antagonist is in a position to claim that the other has a false belief. But neither has a neutral argument, begging no question which the rival framework answers differently. And neither is in a position to charge the other with irrationality or neglect of relevant data.

Admitting that the hypothesis one accepts might be rejected by someone who is not burdened by unreason or ignorance of relevant data does not make it irrational to go on to express one's acceptance as a truth-claim. However, such is the diversity of scientific practice that one's acceptance need not be expressible in that way. Sometimes scientists employ theories without believing them. Such nonbelievers may employ different theories—i.e., theories which could not all describe the underlying causes of the phenomenon—without disagreeing as to their truth, or the truth of any proposition. Thus, the physicists who thought it premature to decide between ether-stress and action-at-a-distance still relied on theories to summarize shared and uncontroversial expectations concerning charge, movement, and magnetism. And in this agnostic reliance, some preferred one theory to another. After all, Maxwell's and Neumann's principles concerning the causes of motion were two different ways of integrating electromagnetic theory with the rest of physics A noncommittal user of the electromagnetic equations could prefer one or the other fit, without taking such fit to be a sign of truth. Or the rational preference for one theory or the other might reflect the needs of the moment, as when an ether stress model supplies a physical feel for Maxwell's mathematical complexities.

One tells whether a good scientist is concerned with the truth of a theory by examining his practice, to see what attitude would make that practice rational. Thus, Maxwell, unlike the agnostics, did not merely employ the ether hypothesis as part of a convenient model for electromagnetic phenomena. In other fields the hypothesis guided him in forming expectations that he could not otherwise have justified. At the end of his presentation of the molecular-kinetic theory, in his *Theory of Heat,* he notes that hot bodies can radiate heat through a space devoid of molecules. Because he believes that the ether is a universal medium of energy propagation, he concludes that radiant heating is due to ether perturbations caused by the motion of molecules (which can constitute the hotness of the body). Mere convenient modeling of electromagnetic regularities would not sustain this guess about radiation. And it is a guess in physics, not a mere metaphysical gloss on physics. Given his principles of motion, Maxwell's ether-based expectation forces the conclusion that the emitted energy of radiant heat must be subject to continuous variations and must give rise to the usual wave-based processes of interference and reinforcement. This leads to further consequences, derived by Rayleigh and others, consequences whose gross conflict with observations were an important stimulus in the quantum revolution.

In the great wars of literary theory, when people promote rival ways of learning, are they making contrary truth-claims? An assumed general analogy with rational uses of scientific theories will not provide an answer. Even if both sides are rational and well-informed, each could be making a truth-claim while conforming to rational scientific uses of theories. On the other hand, each could be using without believing.

A Scandal about Content

The light that the new approaches to science will shed on literary theory may prove to be a by-product of the effort to overcome an anomaly. If the mixed verdicts on the many issues faced under the heading of "scientific realism" are right, a new account of content is needed. The change in the theory of content seems to clarify disputes as to what could count as literary meaning and what such reading reveals.

According to those mixed verdicts, important scientific hypotheses may be subject to rational, empirically informed dissent (as antirealists like to say), even though we participants in the current consensus are in a position to claim that the hypotheses are approximately true (as realists like to say).

This mixed verdict is mixed up, an unintelligible combination, according to current theories of content. I have already described the impossibility for positivism of genuine disagreement as to truth among rational inquirers possessing the same evidence. The verdict is also incoherent in the so-called "conceptual role semantics" that Harman and others developed out of important antipositivist arguments of Quine's.[4] There, a belief-state has its content in virtue of its role in the production of relations between observational input and verbal and other behavioral output. The other field for ascribing content, the task of determining whether one person's utterance has the same content as another's, is taken to be the enterprise of constructing a scheme that correlates their respective total patterns of use, a scheme that is internally simple while matching similar dispositions and preserving similarities in actual usage. When people differ in their responses to the same inputs, this will at once require an ascription of difference in beliefs and a translation scheme departing from the one that simply matches phonologically identical utterances. In such cases, there is supposed to be no distinction between genuine disagreement, reflecting disagreement in belief, and merely verbal disagreement, reflecting differences in meaning. My confinement of Maxwell's disagreement with Neumann, or Aristotle's disagreement with us, to the former category would be a kind of philosophical witch lore, presupposing a distinction that does not exist.

A causal theory of reference, deriving from powerful criticisms of positivism in Kripke, Putnam, and others, is often taken to be the other main rival to positivist accounts of content. According to such a theory, the reference of a term is determined by the causal origins of its use. Of course, all causal influences cannot equally determine reference in such a theory. A baby's whine from the next room may lead me to say a cat is there. Such a misstep may have occurred when I was taught "cat" usage. Yet what is in the next room does not fall under the extension of "cat" as I employed it. Presumably, the defectiveness of my way of responding is what excludes the cause of my utterance from the extension of the term. The extension of a natural-kind term is determined by its application by people responding well to past and present causes. If content is determined by the nature of the causal origin, the standards of good functioning must be extremely general, not tailored to the particular act of reference in question in light of noncausal knowledge of its content. So general, topic-neutral standards of rational inference, imposing limits on dissent as severe as the positivists' canon, would be required by a full-fledged causal theory. (This is one of the reasons why Putnam, Kripke, and others who uncovered causal aspects of content neglected by positivism were wise in not advancing a full-fledged causal theory.)[5]

In all of these very different theories of meaning, the ascription of content is part of the description of how we would operate as well-functioning individual computers, connecting inputs from the great keyboard of observation with outputs on the great monitor of behavior. We *are*, very broadly speaking, computers, and such a perspective can certainly contribute important descriptions of how we manage to refer. Still, the question of whether different processings are similar enough to engage with the same subject matter is not well resolved in this perspective. (Think of the physiological way of describing how Pollini plays piano during a certain period of time, which does not provide a description of what makes his playing a performance of the last Beethoven sonata.) Help in resolving the question about shared content comes from another perspective, which emphasizes communicative intentions relying on social phenomena.

In seeking help from the alternative approach, Grice's account of meaning is a good place to begin. Adapting some of his proposals to our purposes (and ignoring the virtually infinite complications that his proposals acquired over the years), we can connect content with communicative intentions in the following way. In uttering the sentence S, a person means that p just in case she intends her saying S to be a reason for any relevant hearers to believe that p, a reason in virtue of the hearers' grasp of certain linguistic conventions and their recognition, relying on these conventions, of her intention so to induce belief that p. It is important, here, that the intended recognition rely on linguistic conventions. When I tell my little girl, "This is absolutely the messiest room I have ever seen," I intend that my words be a reason to believe that I am angry and intend that they provide this reason through the listener's recognition of this intention. But I do not use those words to assert that I am angry. This is not part of the very content of those words, when I use them, even though I am using the saying of those words to convey that message as well. (Grice would identify the content in question as "the timeless meaning in a language of a sentence-type, applied to a particular token utterance." Elsewhere—though not in this particular case—he tended to avoid appeals to conventions in his theory of meaning, but his reasons need not detain us now.)[6]

What is the source of our prolific access to conventions when we communicate? Such authoritative performances as a scientific conference's fixing the reference of "meter" are rare. And, in any case, the source of their linguistic authority remains to be explained.

Granted, one is often aware of a certain consensus among all those with whom one expects to communicate. There are features, say, that every such person takes typical bearers of a term to have and expects others to ascribe. Such a consensus may provide the raw materials for linguistic conventions.

But much of it is discarded or modified along the way. I believe and expect others to believe that all elephant populations derive from either Africa or Asia. But in saying that Jumbo is an elephant, I do not assert African-or-Asian-ancestry, even if I intend to convey such belief about Jumbo in virtue of recognition of my intention to do so by my utterance.

With very few exceptions, the conventions that fix content do not depend on explicit public declarations of common loyalty to rules. So we had better take advantage of the rich philosophical discussion of tacit commitments and uncodified conventions, starting in seventeenth- and eighteenth-century political philosophy, and most recently advanced by Lewis and Gauthier.[7] As Locke and Hume emphasize, people engaged in common projects can have a tacit commitment to follow a certain rule because of the evident instrumental rationality of the practice dictated by the rule. Suppose that people are engaged in a common project, committed to its goals, and aware that others are similarly committed. Moreover, each can see that conformity to some practice would advance the goals of the project if (nearly) everyone conforms, each can expect (nearly) everyone to be aware of that advantage, and each can expect conformity to that practice to be more advantageous under the circumstances than any alternative. Then, without any explicit declarations of loyalty to the practice, each is tacitly committed to conform to it provided that too many others do not indicate unwillingness to do the same. If, in addition, conformity would be advantageous if most others also conform, disadvantageous if they don't, then actual conformity to the rule motivates those committed to the common project in the same way as declared loyalty to a codified convention would. One may speak, in such cases, of regulation by a tacit convention. In short, a tacit convention is a practice, burdensome if not generally observed, which each participant in a common project can justify as the best means of advancing the project should others be willing to do the same.

Someone uses a term to refer to something only if she intentionally uses the term to convey information about it in a project of advancing learning through cooperation. (I will use "term" very broadly, to include sentences, with the state of affairs described as the referent. Reference can occur in private projects of advancing learning through laying down communicative ties with oneself at a later time. But all the disagreements of interest in this essay concern common meanings, shared projects, and social learning.) Evidently, conventions that determine the content of a referential use of words are fixed by generally accessible pragmatic rationales concerning tactics that would contribute to advancing learning through communication. These rationales will also fix the scope of understanding, of common engagement with a single content, including the engagement required for genuine disagreement. Genuine disagreement requires the rejection of some of the beliefs intended to be recognized by means of the tacit conventions.

The beliefs that one expects cooperators to have, especially the ones that one expects one's words to bring to mind, are the raw material for tacit communicative conventions. But learning would rarely be advanced by a practice of taking on this whole baggage of belief whenever someone uttering words in the language is so trusted that his saying is a basis for believing. In part, this is a matter of convenience, avoiding pointless complexities in the accumulation and revision of beliefs and needless complexities in testing for competence. (Someone who doesn't know about elephant ancestry may still be a useful contributor to the basic projects of animal classification.) Above all, it is a matter of rational openness to surprises. As time goes on or as the number of cooperators increases, someone who meets all conditions for trust that are readily applicable may have good reason to believe that the current consensus is wrong. If too much of the current consensus is taken to be conveyed by current means of utterance, he will be unable to contribute to the advance of learning by means of the old words, without clumsy hedges or confusing new coinages. Perhaps, if each of us could instantaneously and effortlessly signal the totality of our observations and observational expectations, there would be no need to avoid such clumsiness and confusion by using conventions to distinguish content from underlying belief. That is why the distinction between difference in content and difference in underlying belief looks like witch lore in computational theories that ignore our actual limitations and their impact on our need to rely on one another.

The right limit on the scope of a term is the one that narrows the scope in ways that make it an effective discriminator in the tasks of learning in which it is employed, but no narrower. Of course, such rationales are affected in subtle ways by the presence of alternatives employed at the same level of discrimination, and by beliefs concerning expertise among communicators or concerning deviousness in the environment. What is most important, though, is the need to rely on two kinds of mere social contingencies in the rationales determining content: features that every cooperator in the common project can be expected to associate with the term, and goals of the common project in which the cooperators are engaged, goals in light of which cooperators can regard restrictions as useful or pointless.

Here are three examples, in fragmentary sketch, of how given associations and projects fix the limits of content.

1. Ancient Greeks thought, and expected one another to think, that objects to which the term "*naus*" applied were objects made of wood,

reeds, or leather constructed to transport people or cargo across stretches of water on which those objects were meant to float. But a statement that something was made of iron, but a *naus* nonetheless, would have been a disagreement with their *naus* lore, not a departure from their meanings. Our boat talk does not differ in subject matter from their *naus* talk. This is because of the purposes of the talk. The ancient Greeks used the term to communicate in ways that advanced projects of finding, improving on, and preparing for transportation. It advances such projects if plain and common classifications are relevantly discriminating yet otherwise broad. A term referring indifferently to boats and to wagons would not be a useful basic term for classifying means of transportation. But a conventional requirement of woodenness might inhibit the project. The object answering to one's need for water transport might have an unforeseen composition. The object approaching the harbor might have a surprising composition, but call for the usual preparations. Suppose, on the other hand, that the Greeks had been extremely concerned to tear up old boats and use them for firewood. If this wreck and burn project were so important, then the limited understanding of "*naus*" would serve their concerns. In speaking of steel ships, we would be addressing ourselves to a different content.

2. A plain natural-kind term such as "gold" will evoke certain features on the part of virtually all basically competent language users, for example, glittery yellow, heavy, and malleable. The reference of a common natural kind term should be controlled by these common associations, but not too directly. These terms are used in the project of making nature useful. If actual possession of the properties were required, the term would be an ineffective means of finding items that lack the commonly associated features but can be worked up so that they possess them. But the mere capacity to acquire those features is not of interest, either, if acquisition adds to nature rather than developing what is naturally there. Gold in low grade ore is gold, but lead is not gold even though it can be gilded. The limit on content that advances our common projects must take into account both the reason for breadth and the reason for narrowness.

Suppose that the samples found in nature which display the commonly associated features typically have those features because of certain properties which are also found in other stuff. Because of these underlying properties, the other stuff would manifest those commonly associated features if we could put it in the same situation or arrangement. The grouping together of all such stuff is the classification that will best serve the purpose of making nature useful through communicating facts as to what is there. Of course, a specific, accurate description of the underlying properties provides ideal help. Yet someone ignorant of the best-established detailed description, or disbelieving it for good reasons, may also contribute to the common project. Best to have a convention that "gold" is taken to refer to whatever has the underlying nature (if any) typically producing glittery yellow and so forth in typical local samples. That is, the beliefs asserted using the term ascribe whatever it is that typically underlies the features among our samples. We can then use a technical vocabulary to record the best-established current belief as to what gold is. Note that mere contingencies about our samples will, then, conspire with contingent purposes to fix limits to content. If Attic "*khrusos*" were typically a malleable form of iron pyrites, our "gold" talk would have a different content from their "*khrusos*" talk.

Maxwell and Neumann's disagreement about substances and causes is a bit more complex, requiring a deeper discussion than I can give here of the basis for accepting hypotheses as genuine hypotheses about causes. But I hope these remarks on natural kinds suggest the communicative good sense of a liberal understanding of what each theorist asserted, i.e., an understanding that does not deprive them of a common subject matter. Both theorists had an adequate rationale for extending the received repertoire of causes of motion. Our common projects of gaining control over nature are advanced if we take hypotheses which are grounded in such rationales to be hypotheses about the causes of motion.[8]

3. The main tasks of moral discourse are to reconcile conflicts by means of rational appeals to conscience and to encourage personal growth in the face of temptations. As we have seen, conscience and integrity make different demands of different people, rational and informed. Still, the basic catalogs of goods and bads seem to be the same. (Aristotle, too, thought drudgery a cost and imposition.) Different judgments are due to different rankings, in the face of painful tradeoffs. It would only interfere with the task of ending conflict through persuasion if others were required to rank the basic criteria of moral value in the right way as a condition of employing terms with the same content as one does oneself. The acceptance of the same verbal judgment is a signal of successful mutual persuasion. In a great many particular cases, someone accepting the general catalog of goods and bads may be accessible to such persuasion, even though she has a different general ranking. At the same time, she may be capable of making trouble if persuasion fails. Given the goals of moral discourse, the relevantly, discriminating, otherwise broad convention is that moral assessments be understood as attempts to weigh the general considerations in the right way whatever it may be. So Aristotle did assert what we deny (that certain considerations rightly weighed make certain arrangements desirable) in his judgment of hierarchies.

Reading and Its Limits

A certain kind of indignation seems as much a part of the scene in literary theory as the anti-authoritarian attitude. Often the former is a response to versions of the latter. I have in mind a charge that someone who claims to offer a reading of a text is doing no such thing. He is broadly and intimately acquainted with the text, related texts and, literary history. He is responding in accordance with his own intentional and self-conscious practice. But more's the pity, for that practice of response is not a way of reading a text. It could not be. A response dependent on it could not be an interpretation. The deviant responder has departed so far from a traditional framework for inquiring about texts that he does not really provide readings that compete with more traditional ones. He is simply engaged in a different practice, which is other than reading a literary text.

The previous discussions of science and morality suggest no judgment of this charge. In science and morality, inferences radically departing from standard frameworks sometimes do and sometimes do not make it impossible to offer a rival hypothesis about the same subject matter. Still, the discussion of how given projects and habits of thought set limits to content should be useful here, as well. And the typology of rational disagreements in science and morality may help to characterize disputes about literary reading, if only by way of contrast.

It might seem wishful thinking to speak of a common project of present-day expert readers of literature. (I must admit to coming away from the documents of their struggles with the unfamiliar thought that Anglo-American philosophers are relatively sweet-tempered.) Still, those who criticize others for taking missteps must think they are all on a common journey. And there is reason to think they are right.

For all their differences, people who claim to offer readings of literary texts are engaged in ways of responding that are (they hope) highly dependent on what words are in the text and what not. Moreover, they are all interested in some process of decoding what is there. By decoding I mean an ongoing process of seeking explanations of why some words appear where others might, explanations judged on the assumption of some or all of the conventions, standard maxims, and circumstances by which the intentions of an actual author might be constructed. Such conventions include linguistic conventions, standard conversational maxims enjoining coherence, economy, and relevance, and conventions of genre. (For convenience sake, I will put the maxims under the heading of conventions in the rest of this section, although they don't quite fit the category, being useful even when they are not widely observed.) When features of the text are explained as due to observance of such conventions, this explanatory activity may be a matter of belief or it may be a pretense of the moment sustaining a particular game of explanation hunting. Even if what is assumed is believed, much or very little of the available bundle of conventions and circumstances may be assumed.

Before, I proposed that rational inquiry is the pursuit of the best explanation of the data, a search in which one sifts through data using framework principles, hoping to deploy all available principles and data that would make a difference to the end result. In effect, I have just stipulated that decoding could be but need not be such earnest explanatory pursuit of the intentions which actually gave rise to the words in the text. When principles, data, or beliefs relevant to the earnest pursuit are left out, decoding is a game of learning, or a game based on the process of learning. However, there are limits to such freedom from constraint. If nothing, not even the barest linguistic convention, is imposed as a constraint on explaining, the response does not depend on the text and we are outside of the practice I am describing.

Literary reading is different from other ways of reading, a fact to which people appeal when, for example, they disentangle different ways of reading the Bible, or a young child's and a grownup's way of taking in *Alice in Wonderland*. Literary reading is a process of response that depends on decoding in which the dominant interest is in the process itself, rather than the propositions decoded. To take a not too vulgar example, on the rare occasions when I can read Bryan Miller's restaurant reviews with a dominant interest in finding a place to eat, I am not subjecting his output to a literary reading. But often I sit in Ithaca, enjoying the process of understanding his nuanced allusions and of taking in the economy and rhythm those allusions create. This is a literary reading of the text. Here, as on occasions of greater literary importance, the process of decoding may be interesting because the decoder has a definite view of the real world (needed to appreciate Bryan Miller's suave economy in describing it) or an abiding engagement in certain loves, hatreds, and values. I'm not dispassionate, just in no position to put the number of stars to use.[9]

This broad connection with certain activities and interests, or something like it, is surely in the common fund of beliefs about the processes of reading that fit the term "literary." Any category much broader would not make basic discriminations of which we have a need—as in specifying that one's intense interest in the King James version is neither purely historical nor a matter of religious belief. So if there is a common project to which reports and arguments about literary reading contribute, it is directed toward the advancement of some interest in one's process of decoding, together with other processes strongly and immediately dependent on it.

Further restrictions of the scope of "literary reading" will now concern some restriction on the interests that might dominate or on the processes of decoding that might be of interest. To begin with the first, there are many different interests that do dominate people's decodings of literary texts, even decodings whose relevance to literary reading is not at all in controversy. They differ from person to person, and people sometimes dispute their appropriateness to literary reading. An interest in participating in a certain tradition of response to canonical texts is one example of such a contentious interest. Still, it is striking that a certain goal is part of the practices of response that everyone regards as literary reading. Everyone thinks that genuine literary reading, yielding accurate interpretations, can sometimes be dominated by an interest in enjoying the appropriate process involving decoding. Of course, by "enjoyment" I mean both plain enjoyment and stress that one is glad to have undergone. Since decoding is learning or a game based on learning, Aristotle was right in what he said at the start of literary theory: our general interest in literature is part of our enjoyment of learning, a mere pleasure in the exercise of a capacity, which is shared by children and the mightiest inquirers.

If enjoyment could be a sufficient interest in literary reading, what would be the generally available rationale for restricting the phrase to certain specific processes of decoding? As we have seen, if there is no such rationale, there is no such restriction on what could be spoken of as literary reading. One restrictive proposal would be this: all processes of reading worthy of the name involve the same process of decoding. The basic terms for distinguishing different ways of reading simply mark off different dominant interests. So literary reading cannot involve different procedures from those of the earnest pursuit of underlying explanations of the text involved in nonliterary reading. This proposal eventually leads to intentionalist misreading.

Any sane homogenizing proposal ("Reading is always the same process") will depend on an abstract and flexible description of the strategies of nonliterary reading. Otherwise, appropriate interpretations of the trial scene in *The Merchant of Venice* will have to be appropriate interpretations of an actual court report. The way out of such foolishness is the reminder that nonliterary reading requires identification of the genre conventions meant to govern the text or utterance. It just happens that special genres are most apt to serve literary interests in reading. But this sensible reminder is inadequate for the reading of much literature, including much of the best (as everyone would acknowledge, on reflection). The reading of such literature requires the acknowledgment that it departs from genre conventions. Rimbaud's prose poems are one example. Shakespeare's plays were once another. Thus, the kind of nonliterary decoding which is literary decoding as well would have to be the attempt to reconstruct what the writer intended to convey, what she meant by writing as she did, a process in which knowledge of the writer's individual intentions is decisive.

This is one of the initial targets of the anti-authoritarian attitude. Appeals to new philosophies of science failed to destroy the target. Rather, it should be destroyed by appeals to the practice of everyone, or nearly everyone, engaged in the exchange of purported literary readings. The individual writer's intentions are not absolutely decisive. Granted, there is a standard way of reading in which the writer's intentions are relatively important. In the standard way of reading, one prefers explanations of textual facts that are constrained by the writer's actual loyalties to conventions, her actual intentions, and her actual circumstances, so far as one knows them. The preference is strong, but it is not absolute, since a constraint might be rejected if it interfered with a relevant interest in decoding, which might be mere enjoyment. In one of the documents at the start of Richards' *Practical Criticism*, a student offers a truly bad reading of "Margaret are you grieving / Over Goldengrove unleaving?": the poem expresses an old man's sour condemnation of a little girl's grief at the end of summer as mere self-centered petulance on her part. Evidently, the bad student thinks that "It is the blight man was born for, / It is Margaret you mourn for" refers to the blight of self-centeredness and Margaret's exaggerated attachment to herself. Suppose that a trove of diaries and letters were discovered tomorrow, which included decisive biographical evidence that Hopkins meant to convey just that condemnation. Surely, the bad reading would not be transformed into the right one. No one, or virtually no one, engaged in literary reading is committed to such bloody-minded denial of enjoyment of literary reading. And it is the goal of the common project that determines the meaning of the terms employed to advance it. Someone proposing absolute submission to historical intentions as a way of responding to texts is not describing a standard that we do impose or rationally should in the practice we denote by "literary reading." Of course, someone might still recommend absolute submission as better than reading a work of literature in a literary way. But clearly, this is not the intention of actual absolutists, E. D. Hirsch, for example.

Literary reading involves options of downplaying information that are not available to the same extent in nonliterary reading. So one restrictive rationale, the homogenizing proposal, is invalid. The other plausible rationale would be that certain kinds of decodings should be excluded from the practice since otherwise the practice will serve the appropriate interests less well. One outcome of such a rationale would be the understanding that reading literature depends on whatever form of decoding would serve the most appropriate interests best.

Such restrictive rationales may have very different premises, often corresponding to different interests taken to be appropriate. But all appeal to the fear that unworthy responses would drive worthy ones out of circulation. After all, the most diverse kinds of decodings are now associated with "literary reading." Each can support enjoyment, the interest whose relevance is universally acknowledged. Why exclude communications from the project of talking about readings when those communications could enhance enjoyment? The answer must be that in the rational practice of literary reading, an interpretation or other understanding once accepted is put in a kind of archive. Thereafter, other ways of responding are to be excluded as misreading, if they yield contrary understandings. More precisely, they are to be excluded in the absence of reasons to abandon the archival reading in favor of the rival.

As we have seen, scientific practice sometimes is this archival, sometimes not. (Moral practice always is, on important matters, but this is a specific demand of moral responsibility.) As before, the right anti-authoritarian arguments specifically consider literary practice. Two ways of understanding a text are incompatible if a single process of reading it, serving relevant interests, could not be guided by both or result in both. It would beg the question to suppose at the outset that readings are ever incompatible in any stronger sense. But even the standard way of reading, applied in light of actually available knowledge, produces such incompatible understandings.

For example, one might interpret *Lear* as expressing the conflict between an older way of life and politics, based on personal ties and kinship, and a new way, based on self-aggrandizing individualism. The Soviet film of *Lear* is a powerful embodiment of this interpretation. One might interpret the same text as an expression of the torment of letting go, the problems of retirement. As in the first interpretation, Lear tries to have it both ways and so inevitably fails, but he is destroyed by different ambitions in the two readings. Or one could interpret Lear's grandly self-destructive urge as a pursuit of the timeless incestuous attachments that dare not be acted out, as in Olivier's version.

A reading governed by all these interpretations would be a mess, serving no interest. This is especially clear in a play, where we know how messy the corresponding performance would be. But different readings, each governed by a different interpretation, could sustain a terrible enjoyment that makes *Lear* of interest. Even if one reading were to be most worthwhile, that would be no reason for never having recourse to another. Imagine a world in which every deviation from the best way of performing *Lear* up until now were strenuously avoided until it was shown to be at least as good.

The goals of those who engage in the practice of offering purported literary readings do not make such single-minded self-denial rational. When interpretations are incompatible and corresponding ways of reading are of different worth, it would often be irrational not to indulge in both (on different occasions).

There is no rationale, based on shared goals in our actual practice of communication, for any restriction on the scope of "literary reading" that is narrower than this: a way of decoding the text that is of some relevant interest (which might be a mere interest in enjoyment) to the person as she engages in the process of decoding. So any such process does count as literary reading.

In scientific and moral inquiry, we encountered a variety of cases in which such liberality concerning the subject matter of a field was a prelude to poignant confrontations over that subject matter. That Maxwell and Neumann both made statements about the causes of motion, that Aristotle and we moderns all engage in the moral assessment of social arrangements was a precondition for saying that each side was in a position to make a claim entailing the falsehood of claims made by the other. Influenced in part by the enduring fierceness of literary struggles, one might take this situation as the right analogy for literary inquiry: different frameworks for rational literary inquiry, which put informed practitioners in a position to make interpretative claims, at the same time require the rejection of claims based on other frameworks as false, though rational and informed. But this would be a bad analogy. The specific arguments against the archival view, which helped to establish the relevance of different responses to a common subject matter, are also arguments against supposing that differences in informed and relevantly interesting response include the assertion by each side that the other's response is false.

Even among those who employ the standard way of reading, the acceptance of one interpretation as guiding the reading in which one chooses to engage, does not entail the rejection as false of an incompatible interpretation which could guide an informed reading serving a relevant interest. The standard practice of reading, the common and uncontroversial one, is not employed as a means of detecting underlying facts that exist independent of the value of the practice to a practitioner. What is true for common and uncontroversial practices will certainly be true for any nonstandard ways of reading that count as literary reading, nonetheless. Suppose a nonstandard way of reading serves a relevant interest as it unfolds. Suppose, for example, it serves the interest in enjoying decoding (as some surely do). Just by that token, the interpretations that it yields should not be rejected by any informed and rational practitioner. Literary inquirers are not like Maxwell and Neumann, pursuing facts that would exist regardless of what serves the interests of rational inquirers.

A way of decoding a text is a valid source of literary understanding (valid interpretations, for example) just in case such a process of decoding, and other processes immediately and directly depending on it, are themselves of relevant interest to those engaged in them; and interest in enjoyment is enough. Among current approaches to literary understanding, this proposal is especially close to Iser's and to Booth's. For Iser, valid interpretation is determined by a process of decoding that satisfies a relevant interest in the process, and he unashamedly asserts the relevance of pleasure.[10] However, he seems to regard just one way of reading as appropriate to literature, the pursuit of an underlying intention that would explain all of the choices of words encountered in the text, surprising choices that make this pursuit difficult if the text is any good (282–85). Though this is probably characteristic of most of the most interesting decoding, I do not see why the pursuit of maximal consistency should be made a dominant aspect of any process of literary reading worthy of the name.

Booth also bases interpretation on appropriate experiences of reading. And he emphasizes the existence of different processes of reading, which he takes to yield diverse interpretations, some incompatible yet equally valid. Still, he shows due concern to limit this pluralism. Here, his means of setting limits seem to be different from those implied by my proposal, stricter all told yet sometimes lax in describing an aspect of critical judgment. In Booth's account, critics are to be judged by the vitality, justice, and understanding that they display in their critical communications. Vitality is supposed to be the tendency to enliven the responses of readers. But surely there is a further question of what enhancements are relevant to valid interpretation. A way of reading may serve no relevant interest even if it enlivens reading by swelling smug pride in Anglo-Saxon virtue. As for "justice," it is said to require the avoidance of double standards. But a critic who insists that only the standard way of reading is right and employs this demand fairly would still seem to be plain wrong. Since the first two virtues are described in such permissive ways, much depends on the third virtue, "understanding." Its characteristic goal is said to be entering the mind of another.[11] According to Booth's further explications, this other need not be the actual author. At the outer limit of nonsubmission to actual authorial intentions, understanding may view the text as created to achieve a valuable goal, which the actual writer may or may not have been pursuing. At times this seems to be an injunction to make the reading as worthwhile as possible. Usually the assumed standard of worth seems to be the unity in diversity that Iser's reader pursues (Booth, *Critical Understanding* chap. 7). In any case, the limit placed on literary reading seems stricter than my own approach could support.

Of the many questions my account might provoke, I have time to address myself to only two that I find especially troubling. First, if literary readers should be so receptive to diversity and incompatibility, why is literary discussion especially combative when different ways of reading are the topic? Mistakes and bad analogies to one side, there are good reasons for combat here. Important interests are not served equally well by different ways of reading. A process of decoding in which one prefers explanations of what is in the text that fit actual loyalties and intentions of the writer is more apt to serve an interest in taking part in a great chain of production and interpretation, in which writers and certain critics maintain and elaborate an abiding tradition. A process of decoding in which one suspends normal maxims of coherence, relevance, or economy is more apt to serve an interest in subversion or in eruptions of Barthesian pleasure. (In any case, these interests are best served if one avails oneself of the nonstandard process when the interests require this move. A standard reading of Jane Austen would be bad if it were placid or utterly unsubversive.) Critics are right to persuade people to indulge in some ways of reading more, some less—because of the importance of certain interests. Here their justifications are, in part, ethical and, broadly, political, which helps to explain the heat of the argument.

The other question concerns the dirty little secret of anti-authoritarianism, the continuing centrality of the standard way of reading. Before a student overindulges in more playful or subversive ways of reading, he or she had better start by becoming good at the practice of decoding in which one submits one's explanations of what is there to the constraints of the standard maxims, and to such knowledge of conventional loyalties and intentions as a writer could reasonably expect reasonably hardworking readers to acquire. Similarly, there are possibilities of interpretation that one would hate to miss, without which one would not care deeply about a text that does matter. These possibilities nearly all result from the standard way of reading that I have just evoked. (Or so I find, despite my anti-authoritarian sympathies.) Indeed, most of the subversion and fun of the nonstandard ways depends on acknowledgment of the force of the standard way of reading.

I think that the source of this centrality is embarrassingly simple: it is very hard to create a text the decoding of which is of much intrinsic interest. Extracting the message or discovering the origin of a text is usually trouble endured for the sake of the end result. Even most good writers do no more than minimize the trouble. So a text whose literary reading is worthwhile is not apt to be an accident. Moreover, the interest of decoding as such is largely some interest (including some enjoyment) in the posing and overcoming of problems. Such problems are created by the constraints of genre and of whatever writer's projects are assumed to guide the writing, i.e., so assumed in the reader's game of explanation. A writer committed to the hard work of engaging such interest will respect constraints of coherence, relevance, and economy, since they are the most prolific source of verbal problems while any reasonably competent language user is prodigiously good at recognizing the corresponding solutions. Short of happy accidents, the most worthwhile achievements will then be recovered by readers seeking to locate the intended achievements of writers who cope with the standard constraints.

One can imagine another world of writing, easier if not happier. Even in the real world, there are happy accidents. "Lightness falls from the air" is a much better line for a notable lyric than "Lightness falls from the hair"—but I gather it began as a misprint for the latter. If fitness in literary creation were typically advanced through such random mutations, like fitness in biological evolution, then the standard way of reading might be of marginal interest. Indignant responses to the anti-authoritarian impulse sometimes take the form of protests that reading is not easy. Perhaps the grain of truth in literary authoritarianism is that writing is not easy.

NOTES

1. James Clark Maxwell, *A Treatise on Electricity and Magnetism*, 3d ed. (1891; New York: Dover, 1954), 2: 492.

2. Karl Gottfried Neumann, *Das Newton'sche Princip der Fernwirkungen* (Leipzig: B. G. Treubner, 1896), v, 22, 27.

3. In *Fact and Method* (Princeton: Princeton University Press, 1987), I argue at length for the rejection of the positivist demand for a canon of general rules of method, the rejection that I have simply assumed for present purposes. There, I also develop in detail the account of rational scientific inquiry that I employ here in its broadest outlines. I try to fill in the present sketch of truth and justification in moral inquiry in "Ways of Moral Learning," *Philosophical Review* (1985), and *Moral Differences: Truth, Justice and Conscience in a World of Conflict* (Princeton: Princeton University Press, 1992). *Moral Differences* also includes a more detailed description and defense of the account of content that I will employ in this essay.

4. See, for example, Gilbert Harman, *Thought* (Princeton: Princeton University Press, 1973).

5. See, for example, Saul Kripke, "Naming and Necessity," in G. Harman and D. Davidson, eds., *The Semantics of Natural Language* (Dordrecht: Reidel, 1972), and Hilary Putnam, "The Meaning of 'Meaning' " in K. Gunderson, *Language, Mind and Knowledge* (Minneapolis: University of Minnesota Press, 1975).

6. For Grice's basic account of meaning see H. Paul Grice, "Meaning," *Philosophical Review* (1957). For the later elaborations see his *Studies in the Way of Words* (Cambridge: Harvard University Press, 1989.)

7. See David Lewis, *Convention* (Cambridge: Harvard University Press, 1969); David Gauthier, "David Hume: Contractarian," *Philosophical Review* (1979).

8. See *Fact and Method,* chap. 2, especially 72–86, 104f., for some further details.

9. As a further mark of the relevance that reality can have to literary reading, appraisals of truth can be part of assessments of literary adequacy, for example, of the aptness, depth, or superficiality with which ideas are expressed. I explore this bearing of truth, which helps to separate my account of literary reading from formalism, in "Truth in Beauty," *American Philosophical Quarterly* (1979).

10. See, for example, Wolfgang Iser, *The Implied Reader* (Baltimore: Johns Hopkins Press, 1974), 275.

11. See Wayne Booth, *Critical Understanding* (Chicago: University of Chicago Press, 1979), 262.

CHAPTER 6

An Antirepresentationalist View: Comments on Richard Miller, van Fraassen/Sigman, and Churchland

RICHARD RORTY

Philosophy of science has often tried to use realistic painting as a model for its account of scientific truth. One can pair off parts of a realistic painting, or a photograph, with objects which were before the eye of the painter, or the camera, and note that the parts are related as the objects are related. The realistic philosopher of science would like to do something of the same sort with the sentences that make up true scientific theories. She thinks that unless such pairing is possible, she will not be able to give sense to her claim that science tells us how the world is in itself, apart from human needs and desires.

Pragmatists like myself do not wish to make this latter claim, since we see all uses of language—including scientific theory construction—as ways of gratifying such needs and desires. We do not think there *is* a "way the world is in itself." Part of our strategy against the realist is to draw attention to the difficulty of finding objects in the world to pair off with the signs which make up "Force equals mass times acceleration," or "The speed of light is finite," or mathematical equations using imaginary numbers. We pragmatists suggest that the whole idea of truth as accurate representation needs to be abandoned. We agree with Donald Davidson when he says:

> Beliefs are true or false, but they represent nothing. It is good to be rid of representations, and with them the correspondence theory of truth, for it is thinking there are representations that engenders thoughts of relativism.[1]

Davidson's point about the source of thoughts of relativism gets spelled out when he goes on to say, "Representations *are* relative to a scheme; a map represents Mexico, say—but only relative to a mercator, or some other projection." I take his point to be that we should restrict the term "representation" to things like maps and codes—things for which we can spell out rules of projection which pair objects with other objects, and thus embody criteria of accurate representation. If we extend the notion of representation beyond such things, we shall burden ourselves with a lot of philosophical worries we need not have.

In particular, if we worry about what rules of projection connect sentences like "$F = MA$" or "There are lots of transfinite cardinals" or "Love is better than hate" with bits of reality, we get nowhere. So Davidson suggests we drop the metaphor of "scheme and content," and that of "relativity to a scheme," for all cases in which we are not prepared to specify such rules. This means dropping the notion of "representation" and "correspondence" for these cases, while retaining the notion of "truth." We Davidsonians think that such disquotational banalities as "The sentence '$F = MA$' is true if and only if $F = MA$" capture all that remains of Aristotle's claim that true beliefs say of what is that it is, while making no use of metaphors of projection, correspondence, or representation.

What Richard Miller has identified as "the hot topics" of contemporary analytic philosophy—scientific realism and moral realism—leave us Davidsonians cold. For debates between realists and antirealists take for granted that *some* beliefs *do* stand in a relation of correspondence to reality, and then go on to discuss which others do. These debaters take seriously the question of whether there is "a fact of the matter" to be true to in morals or in literary criticism, while assuming that there is such a fact in the case of at least some nontheoretical portions of natural science. We Davidsonians have no use for this notion of "a fact of the matter." We take the truths uttered by physicists, moralists, and literary critics to be true in exactly the same familiar sense, a sense which requires no philosophical gloss.

What difference does it make whether we take these hot topics seriously or, with Davidson, chill them out? One difference will be in our attitude toward Miller's phrase "using without believing." Miller explicates this phrase by saying that Maxwell "did not merely employ the ether hypothesis as part of a convenient model for electromagnetic phenomena." Rather, because he *believed* it, because he thought it *true,* Maxwell went on to form expectations capable of being overthrown. We pragmatists who follow Bain and Peirce in thinking of a belief as a habit of action rather than a representation will describe Maxwell's behavior differently. We shall not distinguish between "a convenient model" and a "belief," but only between assenting to a sentence in some limited range of situations and assenting to it in a larger range of situations. We think of the behavior of Maxwell's instrumentalist opponents as analogous to our habit of saying, "The sun is dropping behind the mountains" in nonastrophysical contexts but not in astrophysical ones. So we shall not say that Maxwell both used and believed certain sentences about the ether, whereas his opponents used them without believing them. Rather, we shall say that Maxwell used these sentences in contexts in which his opponents did not use them.

Another way of putting this alternative, antirepresentationalist, view of the matter is to say that one person may infer from the sentence "The sun is dropping behind the mountains" to the sentence "The sun moves and the earth is at rest" and another may not. Analogously, a physicist who found the ether merely a convenient model would not have made certain inferences which Maxwell made from certain sentences containing the term "luminiferous ether." But this difference in inference patterns does not show that Maxwell was making a "truth-claim" when he asserted those sentences and that the other physicist was not. It will merely show that they used the same sentence in different ranges of situations.

It is tempting to think that an adequate theory of meaning, or of reference, will explain differing uses of the same string of marks or noises. Perhaps it will, but perhaps the temptation to look for such an explanatory theory is a result of a picture which holds representationalist philosophers captive—the picture of language use as a matter of obedience to rules of projection, and of semantical theories as descriptions of those rules. We antirepresentationalists are inclined to agree with Davidson that "what interpreter and speaker share, to the extent that communication succeeds, is not learned and so is not a language governed by rules or conventions known to speaker and interpreter in advance."[2] All they share are what Davidson calls "passing theories" about what linguistic behavior each can be expected to exhibit under various conditions. As Davidson says, "there are no rules for arriving at passing theories, no rules in any strict sense, as opposed to rough maxims and methodological generalities" ("Nice Derangement" 446).

This means that, as Davidson continues, "there is no such thing as a language, not if a language is anything like what many philosophers and linguists have supposed. . . . We must give up the idea of a clearly defined shared structure which language-users acquire and then apply to cases."

So much for the antirepresentationalist view. What difference does adopting this view make for our sense of the differences between literature, literary criticism, and science? In the first place, it makes us pragmatists suspicious of the following question, posed by Miller:

> In the great wars of literary theory, when people promote rival ways of learning, are they making contrary truth-claims?

We are suspicious because, as I have already said, we reject Miller's implied alternative possibility, that the opposing camps may be "using without believing." We are inclined to replace Miller's question with the following substitute: "Do the opposing camps share any common purpose by reference to which they can argue about which of them is right?" That is, we try to change the subject from accuracy of representation to utility. We do not ask, with Miller, whether Maxwell and Neumann, or Aristotle and Rawls, or Freudian and deconstructionist readers of Shelley, "share a common subject matter"—something they all hope to represent accurately. Instead, we ask only whether they share common concerns, and whether these concerns are such as to provide criteria for settling the disputes between them.

We pragmatists think of physics, in the spirit of William James and Ian Hacking, as "the science of the ways of taking hold of bodies and pushing them."[3] So we think that it is a common concern for efficient pushing, rather than a common desire for what realists call "a literally true account of the physical world," that makes the physicists a community of rational inquirers. The question whether the interpreters of "The Triumph of Life" form such a community will be settled by seeing whether there is something every interpreter wants to do with that text *other* than place it within a context which relates it as closely as possible to something he or she cares a lot about.

My own hunch is that there is no such common concern. That is, it seems to me that offering readings of literary texts is *just* a way of putting them in contexts which strike readers as important. C. S. Lewis thought Christianity important, Paul de Man thought the presence of a nothingness important, E. D. Hirsch thinks authorial intention important, Eve Kosofsky Sedgwick thinks homophobia important, and so on. Most battles between alternative readings of literary texts seem like battles about what is important. The question of "accurate representation" will arise only if one takes seriously claims to the effect that a given text is *really* about, e.g., incest rather than class struggle, or *really* about the Incarnation rather than the impossibility of reading. For the use of "really" suggests that one reader has been successful in a task at which other readers have failed—the task of representing the text more accurately than other readers have represented it, according to some agreed-upon scheme of projection. In particular it suggests that that reader has succeeded in representing what the text itself *really* represents.

The phrase "a literally true account of the physical world" (quoted from Leplin by van Fraassen) can be given a relaxed, pragmatic sense by erasing "literally" (as either redundant or pointless), and by making reference to a shared concern with efficient pushing. But the phrase "discovering what the text is *really* about" could be given such a sense only if we take the task of the reader to be something like what Miller calls "decoding." He defines "decoding" as

> an ongoing process of seeking explanations of why some words appear where others might, explanations judged on the assumption of some or all of the conventions, standard maxims, and circumstances by which the intentions of an actual author might be constructed. (129)

If that Hirsch-like task is what all those who deserve the name of "reader" are doing, then it would, indeed, be the case that, in Miller's words,

> in the rational practice of literary reading, an interpretation or other understanding once accepted is put in a kind of archive. Thereafter, other ways of responding are to be excluded as misreading, if they yield contrary understandings. (119)

But, as Miller rightly says, any such Hirsch-like view would exclude most so-called "literary readers." So it seems better to adopt Miller's tolerant, pluralistic, anti-authoritarian view that

> way of decoding a text is a valid source of literary understanding . . . just in case such a process of decoding, and other processes immediately and directly depending on it, are themselves of relevant interest to those engaged in them; and interest in enjoyment is enough. (121)

Still, I should prefer to drop Miller's term "decoding," and to substitute something like "close reading." Such a substitution preserves Miller's point that one doesn't count as an "expert literary reader" unless one presents one's view as, at least in part, an explanation of why this word rather than that occurs at a given place in the text. But it abandons the idea that there is a common concern which binds all close readers together—a concern which supplies an analogy between their activity and that of the physicists. As far as I can see, the only such common concern is the project Schiller called "the aesthetic education of mankind." This project seems to me far more important than the physicists' project, but equally insusceptible to being described in representationalist terms.

Bas van Fraassen and Jill Sigman are not realists, but they still find a use for the notion of "representation" when discussing the evaluation and use of scientific theories. (Although I am informed by van Fraassen that his and Sigman's views on this matter are, in fact, different, it is difficult to disentangle them on the basis of their text. For convenience, therefore, I will discuss their positions as a single one, which I infer from their joint paper.) They grant that the attempt to see scientific truth as accuracy of representation, and to see representation in terms of pairwise matchings, does not get us very far. But, they suggest, we can retain the analogy between representational art and natural science by noting the way in which "interpretation-as" supplements "representation-of" in discussions of art, and adapting the former notion for the purposes of philosophy of science.

I agree with most of what they say in their paper, but I find myself wanting to change "interpret as" to "use for" throughout. I agree that "when attention is directed to how art (and also science) represents *as*, interpretation takes on a crucial role, at various levels, and the pristine simplicity of the idea of mere representation, in the paradigmatic sense of a geometric projection, is altogether lost." But I would want to direct attention to how the products of the artist and of the scientist are *used*—yoked to the service of whatever purpose a fellow scientist, a successor artist, a critic, or a philosopher of science may happen to have—rather than to "how they are interpreted to represent as. . . ." When van Fraassen and Sigman say that "work is open if . . . it does not dictate its own interpretation," I should substitute "does not dictate its own use—does not dictate what context in which to put it." I should then, of course, round up the usual arguments (drawn from Derrida, Stanley Fish, et al.) to show that *all* works are open in *that* sense.[4]

I confess that I am not sure whether there is a nonverbal issue between me and van Fraassen and Sigman here. I suspect there is, but I cannot put my finger on it. I can only say that my suspicions are aroused in the final section of their paper, where they talk about criteria. There they say things like "We have some idea of what is a faithful representation—as well as of the difficulties inherent in that idea," but doubt that we have one of "what makes for a good or better interpretation." I would deny, in the case of most of the sentences which make up scientific theories, that we have *any* idea of what a faithful representation would be, and so I think "inherent difficulties in the idea" is too mild.

My suspicions are heightened when van Fraassen and Sigman say that a good interpretation "gives us real, new insight," gives us "a sense of discovery," and "suggests a relation between the work and its interpretation which is objectively there." The phrase "objectively there," used in a situation in which we can (as van Fraassen and Sigman admit) produce no criteria to determine whether this relation is there or not, makes us pragmatists nervous. We are willing to use "objectively" only in situations where it can be interpreted as "agreed upon by the relevant community—though not necessarily in accordance with antecedently stated criteria." I doubt that van Fraassen and Sigman would accept this gloss. More generally, I doubt that they would be willing to interpret "agreed to be a good thing to represent the universe as" simply as "agreed to be what is referred to by the subject-terms of a useful system of beliefs, a system helpful in letting us push bodies around."

To sum up: I entirely agree with van Fraassen and Sigman when they say about interpretation of works of art that

> the communal judgment that the interpretation is strained, forced, malapropos, or egregious will typically seem to be made in terms of fidelity to the original text, but will largely get its bite from expectations of the role this reading or staging could play in the evolving tradition of interpretative responses focused on this work. (97)

But I am not sure they would agree with me when I say that the communal judgment that a physical theory is false, or that an interpretation of a physical theory is a bad one, will seem to be made in terms of its fidelity to the way things are—but will get *all* of its bite from disappointed expectations about the role this theory might play in our communal project of pushing bodies around.

I turn now to Paul Churchland's paper, which raises rather different issues. Churchland says that connectionism is naturalistic and reductionistic. I have trouble seeing in what sense it is reductionistic, for I have trouble seeing any thesis about hardware as reductionistic in its attitude toward software. I should have thought that Charles Taylor (the antireductionist whom Churchland has chiefly in mind) would not object to the claim that brains are physical systems which work by physical laws. For Taylor is saying merely that we are not going to get much light on any of the issues to which the topic of "human nature" has been supposed relevant by understanding those laws.

Taylor seems to me right about this. A physicalistic understanding of how the brain works will not tell us much about human nature, in any sense in which "human nature" has been used by philosophers. The only philosophical view endangered by such an account would be Cartesian dualism, or perhaps Thomas Nagel's notion of prelinguistic phenomenological givenness, a notion which Nagel takes to entail some form of panpsychism.

Churchland grants that "the features of the world that are maximally important for explaining the behavior of humans are not the simple ones that can be defined in the vocabulary of a naturalistic physics, but rather the much more subtle and complex features that constitute our social culture." This strikes me as granting Taylor all that he needs. Taylor ought to be able to grant that, as Churchland says, this point is "wholly consistent with a reductionist program for understanding human cognition," if connectionism is an example of such a program. For connectionism tells you how brains come to detect subtle and complex features of objects without telling you anything about those subtle and complex features. Understanding how the network comes to distinguish mines from rocks tells you nothing about mines and rocks, just as understanding how the same hardware can both process words and solve differential equations tells you nothing about either prose or mathematics. I should have thought that this latter point was all the antireductionism Taylor wanted.

Perhaps the sting of Churchland's view lies in the suggestion, frequent in his writings, that connectionism may reveal mistakes and misconceptions in our commonsense categories. I do not see commonsense "folk" psychology as endangered by connectionism, any more than carpentry is endangered by particle physics. Like Taylor, I have trouble seeing how a better understanding of how to push our brains around could change our views on desirable directions or methods for social change. Churchland's suggestion seems to me as dubious as B. F. Skinner's claim that psychology has shown, or might show, that the notions of freedom and dignity were obsolete.

Let me conclude with a comment on Churchland's suggestion that the high-dimensional activation vector is a "more fundamental, general, and vastly more powerful means of representation than is the sentence."[5] I have just as much trouble seeing why it is useful to think of such a vector as a "means of representation" as I do seeing why we should think of a sentence as such a means. These vectors, and sentential attitudes, are both likely to enter into our best explanations of how we manage to do the various things we do. For example, certain vectors may be part of the best explanation of how we learn languages, and certain sentential attitudes the best explanation of how we put our linguistic abilities to use in worshiping the gods, fomenting revolutions against injustice, and so on. But I cannot see the use of raising the question of how "powerfully" either vectors or sentential attitudes *represent*. Any node in any causal transaction—for example, a hardware state of a computer, a wetware state of a brain, or an intentional state of a human being—can, if one likes, be described as a "representation" of some earlier node. But—to return to the Davidsonian point with which I began—if there is to be a point to so describing it, we shall have to sketch something like "rules of projection" which provide criteria for the accuracy of the purported representation. I do not see how this could be done, either for most English sentences or for the connectionists' high-level vectors.

NOTES

1. Donald Davidson, "The Myth of the Subjective," *Relativism: Interpretation and Confrontation,* ed. Michael Krausz (Notre Dame: Notre Dame University Press, 1989), 165–66.

2. Donald Davidson, "A Nice Derangement of Epitaphs," in *Truth and Interpretation: Perspectives on the Philosophy of Donald Davidson,* ed. E. LePore (Oxford: Blackwell, 1986), 445.

3. The quotation is from a Professor W. S. Franklin, who is cited by James as exemplifying Ostwald's view that "all realities influence our practice, and that influence is their meaning for us." See William James, *Pragmatism* (New York: Longmans, 1947), 48–49.

4. See my "Inquiry as Recontextualization: A Non-Dualistic View of Interpretation," in my *Objectivity, Relativism and Truth: Philosophical Papers, vol. 1* (Cambridge: Cambridge University Press, 1991).

5. I am quoting here from a letter from Churchland, outlining what he intended to say at the conference.

CHAPTER 7

Why Realism Matters: Literary Knowledge and the Philosophy of Science

PAISLEY LIVINGSTON

It has been said that when the members of a field start to pay attention to philosophers of science, this is a sure sign that the field is in deep trouble. I am inclined to disagree, however, because I doubt that there are any fields that have no use for epistemological reflection and because I think that the philosophy of science is an invaluable resource. Literary research, which is my primary concern, is surely no exception. In this paper I shall take up the question of what some different philosophies of science have to offer theorists who want to reflect on the nature and status of *research* in the literary disciplines. I shall begin with the extremes of contemporary poststructuralism and traditional positivism, and then I shall move on to discuss some alternatives to those extremes.[1]

A positivist or, more precisely, a logical empiricist philosophy of science offers an idealized model of the type of explanation that it is supposed to be the business of scientists to produce; it also proposes various standards of confirmation that are meant to make it possible to know when there is enough evidence to support belief in a given explanation or theory. All of this is couched as a logical reconstruction of the rationality of scientific judgment. It should be clear that the products of literary research do not correspond to such models and are unlikely ever to do so, so theorists who believe in such a philosophy of science are most likely to decide that criticism is necessarily nonexplanatory and nonscientific. Thus critics must either bite the bullet and try to imagine how they can conform to the covering law model and other positivist strictures, or swerve away from science altogether. In its neo-Kantian versions, the latter option generates dichotomies between two different families of disciplines, i.e., those that explain and those that understand; those that discover laws and those that invent particularities and values. Worst of all, science is supposed to be purely objective and value-free, while the humanities only express values and various subjective experiences.

A number of different poststructuralist philosophies of science have precisely the opposite implications for the literary scholar's self-understanding. These philosophies characterize the work and findings of physics and biology in terms that were once reserved for the discourses of the humanities: the findings of natural science are inventions, not discoveries, and the success of science's particular, historically determined discourses owes nothing to the kind of autonomous epistemic value that science was sometimes thought to have. According to this story, literary scholars are freed from the myth of science's epistemic superiority; theorists need no longer try to solve the "crisis" in criticism by looking for ways to remedy the noncumulative and contradictory nature of literary criticism's results. There is no special epistemic reason to believe in any of science's claims: as far as knowledge is concerned, "anything goes." Thus, the supposed "truth" of epistemic relativism, for the sciences and for the humanities, is thought to justify a total shift of focus: instead of talking about the logic of explanation and confirmation, we should focus uniquely on the nonepistemic values and practical aims of discourse. In recent literary criticism, this often amounts to the idea that scholars should first get clear about their political and/or gender allegiances, and then produce a discourse that will advance those interests.

We should be reluctant to embrace either of the two extreme positions that I have just evoked. For a start, there are many good reasons for doubting that any of the positivist philosophies of science are adequate characterizations of the rationality of the natural sciences, for this rationality has various dimensions and limitations that go unmentioned in the logical reconstructions. We should not apply these norms to work that is done in the anthropological disciplines. On the other hand, there are problems with the idea that epistemic values should be entirely replaced by practical ones. For example, it seems unlikely that we can best advance our political goal of creating a more just and ecologically sound world order by ceasing to evaluate the reasons and evidence that may be given for different descriptions and explanations of states of affairs in the world, and of schemes for bringing about desired changes.

Fortunately, there are many other positions and arguments in the philosophy of science, and their implications for literary research largely remain to be explored. In discussing these alternatives, I shall focus here on three positions: a very general form of realism, scientific realism, and a moderate form of antirealism.

To begin with the last, moderate antirealism grants science's ability to achieve an intersubjectively reliable plotting of empirical regularities. Yet the moderate antirealist deems it reasonable to withhold belief in the theoretical entities postulated by science. According to this particular form of antirealism, science has no "foundations," in the sense that its empirical adequacy may not be a sign of truthful reference to unobservable entities. As Richard Miller puts it in *Fact and Method,* a field may be said to have a foundation "if investigators should require the true description of underlying causes" that generate the observed empirical facts (503). If a field is to have foundations, it is not enough, then, that explanations successfully cope with the phenomena; they must, on the contrary, get at the underlying causes. If we believe that some branch of science has successfully done this, then we are scientific realists. The moderate antirealist thinks this is a leap of faith, and withholds belief; yet this does not mean that the moderate antirealist pretends to know that the postulated entities and causes do not exist. That is the leap of the extreme antirealist, who purports to know that science never has provided us with any properly epistemic warrant for belief in a theory—and never will.

It seems quite clear that at the present time literary research does not constitute a field with any systematic foundations in the specified sense. This fact is hardly surprising given that literary criticism constitutes a field or discipline only in the very loosest sense of the word. The object domain is extremely open-ended, being basically composed of whatever items various national traditions happen to have preserved under the vaguely defined rubrics of "literature" and "criticism," words that evoke any number of multifaceted items, as well as a broad range of phenomena that are in one way or another thought to be significantly related to them. The "entities" dealt with by this field are an ontological *auberge espagnole,* for they include past and present agents, actions, and events, mental states and attitudes, physical artifacts, institutions and conventions, symbolic inscriptions and utterances—and their aesthetic qualities. It is not uncommon for literary critics to debate over angels, demons, and vampires. Moreover, critics' attitudes toward this vast and variegated object domain are not on the whole particularly disciplinary, for the open-ended collection of literary phenomena may be approached in terms of any number of perspectives, notions, and interests. There is no general agreement about a privileged level of description at which the central and determinant entities and processes are located. To illustrate this point, I propose the following sample of statements that critics can make and defend in reference to "a single" literary item—the play *Mascarade,* by Ludvig Holberg:

1. *Mascarade* is a typical comedy of intrigue influenced by the Italian *teatro delle maschere.*[2]

2. In writing *Mascarade,* Holberg used half of a play by Joachim Richard Paulli as his basis.

3. While writing *Mascarade,* Holberg intended to create a play that would express his idea that society should allow a "reasonable freedom" (*en fornuftig Frihed*) to its members; this intention was linked to his desire to oppose the state's repressive policy of prohibiting masquerades and gambling.

4. *Mascarade* is Holberg's unintended expression of his unconscious oedipal ambivalence toward his father, represented in the figure of Heronimus; other figures represent facets of Holberg's psyche, including contrasting rebellious and obsequious sons.

5. *Mascarade's* representation of the carnivalesque dimensions of masquerades exemplifies Bakhtin's emphasis on the critical and revolutionary dimensions of popular festivities.

6. *Mascarade* conveys Holberg's philosophical belief, also expressed in his Epistle 347, that masquerades and carnival rightfully express the natural equality of master and slave.

7. *Mascarade* has had an important political and social function in the constitution of the national literary culture of Denmark.

8. *Mascarade* manifests the essential instability of language, for in its incessant displacements, tropisms, and figural processes it paradoxically subverts the Subject's claim to coherence and grounding.

9. *Mascarade* is not particularly original: its style is clumsy and uninspired, and the plot clearly reflects Holberg's slavish imitation of Molière. Perhaps its greatest merit was to have served as the inspiration for Carl Nielsen's lovely opera of the same name.

10. Early in 1724, Ludvig Holberg composed the script for *Mascarade* at his home on the Købmagergade in Copenhagen. The play was first performed in late February 1774, at the Lille Grønnegade Theatre, and was first published in 1731 in *Den danske Skue-Plads.*

Confronted with the diversity of such claims, it would hardly seem wise to adopt the realist stance that the critics really are referring to a single determinate entity (or domain of entities and processes) with their talk of *Mascarade* and its "meanings." Imagine the folly of asserting earnestly that the eighteenth-century play did mean what statement number (8) puts in its mouth, and that statement (6) is also true, and that the two statements really are about the same entity. If we recoil at that prospect, what framework of compelling reasons and principles will allow us to delete items from the list until we are left with a set of assertions about a world where they could all be true? Answering that question is what would be involved in seeking to establish realist foundations for literary criticism. In the absence of such a framework, it seems we must conclude that critics display remarkably different ways of "coping" with the rather different phenomena their assumptions and approaches select for them.

Many literary scholars have sought to give their field a more sharply circumscribed disciplinary basis, and although such tendencies are an important vein of literary pedagogy and research, their status remains a matter of much debate.[3] Essentially, the attempt to orient research toward a "literary specificity" of texts and utterances has typically amounted to trying to discover and emphasize what may be loosely identified as the texts' aesthetic qualities; by focusing on the latter, it is sometimes thought, we study literature as literature. Yet this approach is highly problematic, and there are good reasons why it is unlikely to provide literary research with realist foundations. Briefly, many of the aesthetic notions depend on various assumptions (at once philosophical and ideological) that critics today have good reasons to reject. For example, critics challenge the assumption that the doctrine of aesthetic autonomy refers correctly to the processes that have actually been at work in the writing and reading of texts. What is more, the attempt to erect an aesthetic framework of literary analysis has a way, not of erecting disciplinary boundaries and realist foundations, but of leading, on the contrary, to additional interdisciplinary borrowings, which has the effect of making the question of the foundations of literary research depend on that of the foundations (and nonfoundations) of other fields. For example, there is good reason to think that the aesthetic properties of literary works of art bear an essential relation to meaning; consequently, the critic or scholar who tries to analyze literature's aesthetic properties ends up taking at least an implicit stance on a number of topics—such as the nature of "reference"—that the students of language tend to group beneath the rubrics "semantics" and "pragmatics." It is unsurprising, then, that the attempt to probe the specifically aesthetic qualities of literary works of art has typically led critics to have recourse to various linguistic and/or rhetorical terminologies. Yet which doctrine of language is to provide the foundation for a realist aesthetics?

It may be instructive in this context to evoke the work of Siegfried Schmidt. Working in collaboration with colleagues from a range of fields, Schmidt has sought to lay the "foundations" for an empirical science of literature, and argues that an autonomous system of literary communication emerged toward the end of the eighteenth century as part of thegeneralized trend of specialization and functional differentiation in

Western societies. The specificity and autonomy of literary actions are constituted by agents' adherence to a set of aesthetic conventions. Briefly, these conventions require a bracketing of evaluative criteria based on truth and/or utility. When readers read a text as literature, they set the latter criteria aside in order to engage in free and playful explorations of linguistic features, multiple meanings, and fictional worlds. To read literature as literature is not to seek to discover a text's or author's true meanings and values; even less is it to enquire into the causal conditions behind literary phenomena. Instead, reading literature as literature is like an exercise in applied constructivism, for the reader "constitutes"—in some suitably strong sense of the word—the reality of the text, while understanding that a plurality of such constructive actions is at once possible and desirable.

In Schmidt's view, criticism has a proper object domain (those actions and artifacts generated within the autonomous literary system), as well as its own specific approach to that domain, an approach that consists of a pluralistic interpretation and evaluation of literary works of art. Yet given that these critical activities must be governed by the aesthetic conventions, criticism cannot be a form of research. Schmidt allows that reading literature and writing about it may be beneficial for any number of reasons, but the aim of such practices is not to make any contribution to knowledge. Rather, literary criticism is simply one part of the system in which literary works are produced, distributed, and consumed. It is not the business of literary criticism to produce a genuine knowledge of that system: criticism is governed by the aesthetic conventions, and should a critic begin to make genuine knowledge claims about literature or about the aesthetic conventions that make it possible, in the same instant these conventions would be violated, and the utterance would no longer be an act of criticism.

In Schmidt's view, to make assertions about the reality of the literary system is to adopt the role of the *Literaturwissenschaftler,* whose science of literature investigates the literary system from the outside. Unlike criticism, literary science can explain and describe the aesthetic conventions constitutive of literature. And in Schmidt's conception and practice (which are admirable for their breadth, clarity, and detail), this empirical science of literary systems is an essentially interdisciplinary enterprise. A branch of systems-theoretical sociology and historiography, it draws on philosophical semantics, aspects of cognitive psychology, and the theory of autopoiesis.[4] Thus, an author who has formulated one of the most extreme statements of the autonomy and specificity of the literary system concludes that genuine research concerning literary matters must be interdisciplinary. Oddly enough, the orientations of the field turn out to be extraliterary, and criticism, as Schmidt defines it, is totally lacking in realist foundations. As long as criticism is an aesthetic enterprise it can have no foundations, for it does not have the task of referring truthfully to the determinate features of some class of entities.

Although it is easy to show that the field of literary studies does not presently have foundations in the specified sense, what follows from this fact is less obvious, and a number of difficult questions arise. Does the explanatory value—or other cognitive status—of literary research suffer as a result? Does a lack of foundations in literary research mean that "anything goes"? And if the literary field has no foundations, does that mean that none should be sought, or that it could never have any?

In regard to the first question, Miller states in *Fact and Method* that although he thinks a realist stance is warranted in regard to aspects of science (for example, belief in genes, molecules, electrons, and continental drift is rationally compelling), the absence of foundations in some field does not in itself warrant anyone to yield a negative judgment of that field's explanatory efforts. Successfully coping with phenomena in a variety of ways is already an important cognitive achievement. Yet on the other hand, Miller contends that the absence of foundations in literary studies does not mean that "anything goes." But how, one wants to know, are we to decide what does not "go"? It is not a matter of holding up a canonical model of explanation so as to pass "scientific" judgment on some theory's interpretive rewards, for it is granted that literary critics can usefully ask and answer a lot of different questions without having to work with one theory that truthfully describes the invisible causes of literary phenomena. In a nonfoundational assessment of literary research, the epistemic standards to be brought into play are basic norms of reasonable enquiry as well as what Miller refers to as Level III truisms, that is, beliefs that all reasonable people are committed to in response to experiences that almost all humans have. Certain banal beliefs, such as our belief in the existence of automobiles, "command more than tentative assent because reason and evidence cannot dictate the switch to their negation" (222). Arguments over what does and does not constitute genuine literary research should be settled reasonably and fairly by drawing upon such shared background assumptions, belief in which amounts to a basic realist stance.

The key point here is that the literary field does not have to have foundations for it to be possible for critics to make some reasonable epistemic judgments, or for it to be possible to conceive of ways in which literary research may be improved. Skeptical and relativistic critical theorists often construct elaborate metaphysical and linguistic arguments why criticism must be a noncumulative and circular exercise, yet much more ordinary explanations for actual cases of such failings may be given. For example, it is hardly surprising that critics' various responses to the question of "the meaning" of a particular work are discontinuous and framework-relative, for any number of assertions can be plausibly understood as responding to that question, which is essentially vague and ill posed. Critical inquiry gets off to a false start when it begins with the general question of the meaning of some literary item. Given that this question is ill posed, it is not a mystery that the "central debate" of recent critical theory, which reflects on what is called "validity in interpretation," seems to lead to the conclusion that anything goes because all facts are "overdetermined" by theoretical prejudices. Critics necessarily work with some prejudices or theories in disambiguating the vague question of meaning, and these background beliefs vary quite wildly today. It is important to note that writing and publishing elaborate elucidations of the meanings of literary works is best understood as an aesthetic activity, the underlying assumption of which is that an important way to experience the value of a literary work is to develop, write up, and publish a detailed interpretation of it. Many theorists today are expressing doubts about this particular aesthetic assumption and are looking for alternatives to it.

Forms of literary research that diverge from this sort of aesthetic hermeneutics do not begin with the vague question of "meaning," but take up more specific queries that may be raised in regard to various literary phenomena. For example, instead of seeking to elaborate a particular systematic interpretation of a particular work, historically oriented research can attempt to describe the different background attitudes and situations that made possible a wide range of responses to a work in a particular historical context. More generally, the point is that a historical and cultural orientation that seeks to explain the causes and consequences of literary practices and artifacts is a major alternative to romantic aesthetics and to its academic vestiges in literary criticism.

Another kind of cognitive goal for literary research amounts to trying to complexify and develop theoretical models within the human sciences. A literary scholar who adopts this strategy is not simply looking for ways to lend meaning to a text; nor is such a critic interested only in ways in which a particular set of background assumptions can be shown to match some of the features of a text. Instead, the critic's goal is to explore the text's heuristic value in the context of a particular theoretical problematic. An example of such a contribution is René Girard's elaboration of ideas about the role of imitation in human motivational processes, the so-called theory of mimetic desire that Girard first elaborated in his readings of a number of major European novels. It should be noted that

Girard's various statements about the patterns of intersubjective mediation in these novels should not be taken to provide any compelling confirmation of the theory of mimetic desire: not only could these novels' depictions of human desire be skewed, but Girard's choice of documents, and his manner of reading them, could manifest a confirmation bias. Yet Girard's hypothesis nonetheless retains its heuristic value in spite of these possibilities, and researchers in a number of disciplines, including economics and political philosophy, have found these intuitions useful.[5]

My advocacy of the general line of enquiry that I have just mentioned is linked to a stance on the literary field's interdisciplinary relations. As the notion of literature is extremely open-ended and multifaceted, literary researchers are led to draw on the discourses of a range of disciplines, such as linguistics, history, psychology, and sociology. That literary research is typically interdisciplinary raises the issue of the reasonableness of the different strategies of cross-disciplinary mediation practiced by critics and theorists. An important discussion of this issue is Thomas Pavel's recent book *Le mirage linguistique* (translated in English as *The Feud of Language*), which incisively describes the distorted and selective appropriations of linguistics that have characterized structuralist and poststructuralist theories in France and elsewhere. Pavel does not claim that the shortcomings of these theories are only a matter of a purely epistemic error, for he sketches a hypothesis about some of the sociocultural conditions that could have given rise to the linguistic mirage. Nonetheless, his study also underscores some epistemic norms that literary scholars should take more seriously.

So far I have discussed some ways in which epistemic norms are relevant to literary studies understood as a nonfoundational and diverse field having a range of cognitive and practical aims. Is it also possible to develop an argument in support of the possibility and desirability of discovering foundations for literary research—in the sense of a theory of the causal processes behind literary phenomena? Recently a lot of literary theorists have spent a lot of time making arguments to the effect that no such foundations could ever be discovered; the very least one can say, then, is that some members of the field are invested in the topic and seem to think it makes a difference. Indeed, if it were truly known that it was impossible ever to describe the causal conditions of any literary or cultural phenomenon, then there would be no use engaging in that sort of explanatory effort. Yet does anyone in fact know any such thing? I have my doubts, and suspect instead that what has been established is that it is impossible to provide an empirically founded scientific description of an absolutely unconditioned condition, an "Origin" with a capital O. Yet it does not follow from this that there is not a more humble kind of causal process waiting to be explored by humanistic researchers. Thus it seems reasonable to me to ask in which direction literary theorists should look in search for a set of field-specific substantive principles that could guide some of their explanatory efforts. This means that literary theorists should not dogmatically assume that an antirealist self-definition is necessarily appropriate to their field.

It could very well be that literary scholars cannot consistently hold to a moderate antirealist stance, the reason being that they are already committed to belief in a number of unobservable, theoretic processes and entities. That would mean that critics must be either realists or extreme antirealists. Arguments for the latter position are common enough in the field, and typically run as follows. It is assumed that once we begin to make statements about the meanings of texts, we leave the domain of reasonable argumentation and cross over into a patchwork world of irreconcilable frameworks. This would be the case because readers must rely on any number of uncontrolled and untestable theoretical background assumptions. Theory, then, in the form of the reader's various background beliefs, interests, and prejudices, is thought to overdetermine the "facts" or textual evidence in the production of meanings. Moreover, the meanings arrived at in different theory-driven processes of reading can be understood and evaluated only within a compatible framework, which implies that between the different theories and frameworks there is "radical meaning variation." How could there be a rational evaluation, then, of the relative epistemic merits of a Lacanian reading of a Shakespeare sonnet and an interpretation of it by John Crowe Ransom? The "textual input" may be "the same," but the "poems" rendered by the theory-laden interpretations of this input are not.[6] Thus we may conclude that interpretations of a text are not about any real entity, for the only plausible way of construing the status of "the text's meanings" is that statements about them are reports on aspects of readers' individual experiences of a textual input.

My criticism of this argument is essentially that reasonable attitudes about which statements about meaning can reasonably be believed or doubted do not correspond to a sharp division between a "textual input" (an observable sequence of "signifiers") and theory-driven readings or interpretations (a contradictory array of projected "signifieds"). The division in question is not a good indication concerning reasonable judgments about what exists, nor can we use it to decide which statements have a purely instrumental status and which we hold true or at least approximately true. Another way to put this point is to say that it is reductive to claim that all readings have the same status as different ways of "coping." To support this contention, I would point to cases of banal, truistic readings that we may expect anyone but the wild skeptic to accept. These examples will not be cases of exciting literary criticism, but they do stand as crucial counterexamples to extreme antirealist pronouncements, and they are also the kinds of claims that can sometimes provide reliable evidence for more interesting enquiries. For example, anyone who has read some of the most famous plays by Molière and who reads Holberg's *Mascarade* in Danish or in a moderately faithful translation may be expected to agree that the latter play is a comedy and that its plot structure and characterizations bear certain broad similarities to those in Molière's works.[7] With a little background evidence about Holberg's vast erudition, about his travels through Europe (including Paris), and about the early history of theater in Denmark, plus a few assumptions about human cognition and motivation, we can reach the conclusion that the similarities between the works of the French master and those of Holberg were not coincidental. In short, we have here a well-established case of "influence"—indeed, a literary truism.

What kinds of evidence would allow this truism to be made the object of reasonable doubt? It is surely the case that we have no direct access to Holberg's brain states and mental attitudes, so we cannot point to them as direct evidence that (*a*) he read, saw performed, and thought about some representative sample of Molière's plays; (*b*) he had certain ideas about the salient features of Molière's comedies; and (*c*) he applied these attitudes about Molière in writing *Mascarade*, intending to endow the play with those traits that would later provide evidence of a case of literary influence; (*d*) it was actually the latter intention that made *Mascarade* have the features in question. So even if it be granted that *Mascarade* does bear important similarities to Molière's comedies, doubts about the causal role of the "influence" could be based on doubts about any or all of (*a*)–(*d*). What direct observations can be made to support such claims as (*a*)–(*d*)? None. Yet in the example at hand, there seems to be enough surrounding evidence for inferences (*a*)–(*d*) and no particularly significant evidence contradicting them. The explanatory link here is partly theoretical, but only a very far-reaching form of skepticism can threaten our realism in regard to it. It must be acknowledged, however, that finer-grained claims about the specific nature of the influence could be subject to reasonable doubt. For example, when a critic proclaims that the influence was 50 percent Molière, 50 percent Regnard, we need much better evidence than we presently have. The point to be retained here is that some readings are guided by theoretical principles that it would be extremely unreasonable to distrust. The consequence is that there are cases where interpretations can provide reliable explanations in response to certain kinds of questions. That means that many critics often already take the "leap" to realism about theoretical entities and processes, and that they are well warranted to do so.

Another argument suggests that the sharp dichotomy between literal observation and theory-driven reading, where reasonable grounds are denied the latter, is self-defeating. Why? The idea here is that identifying a symbolic token as such (that is, as a token of a particular type of character or symbol) is already a kind of observation that is not reducible to perception alone. The background beliefs that similarly must "always already" be in place to make possible the recognition of a text as text are quite extensive. Although we may recognize a curve in a river or a highway as an *S,* we do not literally judge them to be texts: it is metaphorical—or theological—to speak of the "prose of the world." We should call something a text only if we believe that some sentient agent produced it, and we usually assume that this agent was acting on a certain sort of intention (except, perhaps, in cases of genuinely compulsive and unintentional scribbling). Consider the case of a textual artifact that results from a surrealist exercise in "automatic writing." We are right to think that such texts are not fully determined by the author's conscious intentions, but we none the less must assume that there was an agent acting on the intention to write (that the intention was to write in an uncontrolled and spontaneous manner does not alter this more basic fact). Moreover, we know that this first decision is followed by a second one: when the surrealist writing experiment is over, the writer must decide whether to publish the results (and in most cases, the surrealists decided to destroy their automatic writings). The case of the *cadavre exquis,* a text produced when different agents add lines to it without having seen those already written, merely shows that a particular kind of "we-intention" can motivate the production of a textual artifact.[8]

The foregoing remarks raise the crucial issue of the relation between literary explanations and assumptions about agency. I shall conclude this paper by arguing that such assumptions are crucial to literary research. Whatever foundations—and short of that, explanatory progress—are to be had in literary research will be achieved by improving the principles of agency upon which criticism depends. Please note from the outset that my emphasis on concepts of agency does not entail the view that author criticism is the only genuine form of literary enquiry; even less does it mean that I think the key to a text's meanings resides in the writer's conscious intentions.

Why are notions of agency central to literary explanations? The answer involves what I take to be some fairly uncontroversial, yet highly significant, facts about symbolic artifacts and the causal powers that they may be expected to exert under normal conditions. An artifact is something produced by the work of an agent or agents. In other words, no artifacts are literally "self-organizing," which implies that realistic causal explanations of the production of artifacts require true (or approximately true) descriptions of the pertinent doings of the agent or agents involved in making them. Now, although not all artifacts are texts, all texts are artifacts. That is, texts come into existence only as a result of some agent's behavior. Agency, then, is a necessary ingredient in any explanation that describes the conditions of the production of literary texts.

Does a similar claim hold in relation to explanations dealing with the conditions of the reception of literary works? I believe so, but the point is subtle. Some artifacts, once they have been created by an agent, have causal powers of their own. Thus they can figure as proximate causes in the explanation of some subsequent event. To grasp this, one need only think of an engine which, once it has been constructed and set in operation, is able to continue producing various effects for some time, including effects that were never intended by the machine's creator. An explanation of the proximate causes of the latter effects need not refer to the agent who fabricated the machine; i.e., that agent's conscious intentions would not be the sole proximate cause figuring in an adequate explanation. But what kinds of causal powers of this sort can symbolic artifacts (texts, discourses, etc.) have? It is important to note that the semantic and aesthetic properties of a symbolic artifact (e.g., a text or discourse) have no significant autonomous causal powers. Under certain conditions, a book (i.e., the physical object) could have some causal effect on the family pet, but *Hamlet* could never do so. Whatever effectiveness the work's semantic and aesthetic properties may have requires the contribution of rather complicated human cognitive and affective processes. One way of putting this is to say that the "intentionality" of a work of art is always on loan from someone. It follows that genuine explanations of a work's semantic and aesthetic effects require descriptions of the pertinent doings of the readers and writers in question.

My argument, then, is that explanations of the creation and use of symbolic artifacts require reference to agents and to their intentional attitudes—and hence to such items as desires, actions, and beliefs. In short, explanations of literary phenomena—such as the truism about influence evoked above—require assumptions about agency. Whatever foundations literary criticism could eventually be given would lie in this direction. In this regard, the underlying orientations and assumptions of criticism's current approaches fall into two categories, namely, those that recognize that successful enquiries concerning artifacts and meanings require psychological assumptions, and those that do not. As I have already suggested, there are good reasons to think that the latter are not likely to lead to any truly explanatory forms of criticism. In apsychological criticism, idealist assumptions about such entities as form and meaning (which cannot plausibly be thought to have the necessary causal powers of their own) typically vitiate any reference to effective causal agents. Aesthetic properties are totally detached from the agents whose thoughts and perceptions are the necessary conditions of such phenomenal qualities. Works of art, genres, traditions, tropes, and so on are said to act, mean, and interact on their own, and the critic freely invents his or her map of their various imaginary relations, tracing the evolution of themes and figures, plotting similarities and differences. In this manner, literary critics have perpetuated the method of historiography in which the figures of a disembodied *Geist* remain the sole object. The result is the crazy quilt of framework relativism.

Various sociological approaches to literary study have not succeeded in breaking with the idealist tradition. A central problem has been the failure of critical theorists to grasp the most basic lessons of methodological individualism. Critics ask how a particular work "reflects" or "contests" some social totality or dominant discourse, but they fail to reflect sufficiently on the ontological status of the latter, endowing it with dubious causal powers. Moreover, such critics typically fail to confront the difficult epistemological problems that are raised by this kind of sociological holism, which typically begins and ends with some set of untested speculative theses about the nature of global structures, moments, systems, and sets of institutions. The heroic critic takes on the monumental task of mediating back and forth between claims about the social totality and the particular work, but the results of these dialectical efforts are easily challenged by historians who are closer to the facts.[9] Another typical shortcoming of holist sociologies, and of the literary criticisms inscribed within them, is that they typically fail to attend sufficiently to the processes at work in the individual agent's assimilation of, and resistance to, the influences, discourses, etc., of the putative social totality. Holist critics fail to ask in what concrete ways the many faces of the totality make themselves known to the individual agent. We are simply supposed to take it for granted that social orders are "habitus forming." The shortcoming just evoked is only aggravated when the apparent emphasis on pragmatics and human interaction is vitiated by a tendency to focus uniquely on discursive and symbolic levels of description: the sociology of texts and artifacts is replaced by the artifact of a textual society. Ultimately we are back in the imaginary museums, libraries, and theme parks where the critics weave and unweave their *correspondances générales*.

I suggest, then, that the kinds of causal processes that we are most likely to discover in a sociocultural field such as literature involve the capacities of agents and of the systems of their interaction, which means that any quest for substantive principles should focus on the models of agency at the heart of literary enquiry. At the present time, however, we are hardly in a position to speak of foundations in this regard, for the various fields that could potentially contribute some of the needed substantive principles are themselves "self-questioning." Yet it is none the less possible to speak of research strategies and lines of enquiry that can and cannot presently be identified as deserving a high degree of priority in literary theory. For example, we are warranted to say that the burden of proof today belongs on the shoulders of the literary critic who believes that some strain of psychoanalysis can be taken as the sole source of the psychological principles and methods guiding literary enquiry. What is the epistemic justification for the choice of Freudian assumptions about development, sexuality, language learning, creativity, meaning, and so on? In the absence of good answers to such questions, criticism's failure to explore the alternatives is a flagrant weakness.[10] And as I have suggested above, references to pragmatic and political agendas is not a sufficient excuse for failing to shoulder the burden of proof in question.

The next step in my argument involves the contention that intentional explanations of behavior (or more properly speaking, of "action") rely on some very basic assumptions about the rationality of the agent: if we did not assume that there were any regularities or systematic connections between a creature's behavior and the semantic content of some of the intentional attitudes that we might attribute to that creature, then there would be no point in trying to explain or predict this being's behavior in terms of such attitudes. The very notion of agency and of an intentional action entails, then, some very general (yet moderate) form of rationality.[11] The privileged status of the rationality heuristic flows from here, as it is this heuristic that enables us to identify particular cases of both rational and irrational behavior. Yet the nature of this general rationality condition is a factual question, as is the question of which agents and behaviors satisfy it. All particular definitions of general rationality conditions, and any specific attribution of rationality to a particular entity or class of them, should be deemed hypotheses requiring evidential support. A number of different hypotheses and models of bounded, minimal, and moderate rationality are today available.[12]

It is important to point out that my emphasis on the topic of agency in literary enquiry does not involve the assumption that authors consciously formulate an intention in regard to every feature of the texts they write. A distinction between the intended results and unintended consequences of an action is basic to the framework of action theory, and focusing on the ways in which intentions generate actions does not entail an inability to analyze and explain the many unintended consequences that actions have.[13] In recent work in action theory, emphasis has been placed precisely on the ways in which agents intentionally produce certain consequences without having acted with the specific intention of doing so; for example, some unintended consequences are the expected by-product of an action aimed at a rather different goal.[14] It should also be noted that the framework of intentional action explanations does not preclude attention to the emergence of unintended consequences of social interaction. Of special interest are cases where two or more agents' actions are guided by reciprocal expectations of the others' actions. For example, while writing, authors make decisions in function of certain expectations about readers' future beliefs and preferences. Moreover, some of these authorial expectations may concern the readers' future expectations about what the author is most likely to have believed and intended.[15]

It is also important to stress the fact that my emphasis on the topic of agency does not amount to a proposal that literary criticism should focus exclusively on authors and on the conditions of their creation of literary utterances and artifacts. I am not saying that "speaker's meaning" is the key to the meaning and qualities of a literary work, for I believe that there are genuine literary enquiries that do not take the speaker's intended meanings as their object. Literary explanations concern both the writing and reading of texts, and the conditions of the former do not magically govern the conditions of the latter. Analyses of the processes by means of which readers make sense (and nonsense) of texts today emphasize the reader's pragmatic and purposeful orientation toward the textual input, as well as the reader's application of extensive background beliefs and knowledge to this textual input.[16] Critics should explore the possibility that the various actions that readers may perform in relation to a text are explicable in terms of beliefs, desires, and intentions, only some of which have the author's putative intentions as their object.

Concepts of agency have an additional importance in literary inquiry because of the role that beliefs and attitudes about agents play in readers' comprehension of texts. In relation to discourses in which there is any form of psychological verisimilitude (which means all or almost all literary works, and certainly all narrative discourse), a crucial part of the background knowledge applied by readers concerns the practical reasoning and purposeful action of the depicted agents.[17] Readers' judgments of the coherence and incoherence of discourses are probably correlated to their identification of textual elements' consistent co-reference to an agent or agents. The point here is not that readers of literature read "only for the plot." A model of the role of background beliefs about agency cannot alone explain all aspects of reading. Yet beliefs and attitudes about agents are likely to be a necessary and important element in any adequate descriptive model of literary comprehension. The hypothesis that needs to be explored, then, is that an important part of readers' comprehension of narrated stories is their filling in of the text's reports on characters' actions, a completion task that requires the activation of an extensive network of background beliefs about agency.

In short, to suggest that the framework of intentional explanation should be taken as being basic to literary inquiry is not to argue that criticism should return to its former crippling reliance on a great man theory of history, with its idealization of the powers of singular individuals. Instead, the goal in applying the rationality heuristic should be to examine the psychological processes at work in the formation and transformation of literary artifacts and institutions. My point is not that authors and readers should be thought of in relation to some substantive and highly normative standard of Rationality; rather, the point is that if we are to produce genuine explanations of literary phenomena, we must attend to the multiple forms that the practical reason and unreason of agents may take.

To conclude, I return to my title. Why does realism matter? The question amounts to asking for a practical justification of an epistemic stance, and that justification should refer to the epistemic values that this stance alone can promote. In a very broad sense, realism is the notion that there is a reality that exists independently of our minds, and that we can know aspects of this reality. The epistemic value of this notion resides in the cognitive achievements it makes possible, and some endeavors indeed require the belief that inquiry can sometimes result in our discovering something about what is actually the case. In the context of the literary disciplines, such a realist attitude matters because a lot of literary theorists have already leaped to extreme, antirealist conclusions. These conclusions have the effect of diverting attention away from various avenues of research, and in some cases, of prompting a rejection of the notion that there have ever been or could be any genuine discoveries in critical theory or practice. Such extreme, antirealist conclusions foreclose on a range of epistemic values and have a tendency to lead to a rather truncated research agenda. Literary research is badly served by the idea that we know for certain that discoveries and explanations are forever impossible; it is better served by confidence that there is a world of texts and actions to be explored.

Yet this is only an argument for a rather general sense of realism. What about scientific realism, which concerns, more specifically, our reasons for believing in some of science's theoretical inferences about the existence of certain kinds of entities and processes? Why does scientific realism matter to literary knowledge? It matters, first of all, because literary scholars have often thought that the way to defend the status of the humanities was to diminish the epistemic achievements of science; similarly they criticize the abuses of science in contemporary society by denying the possibility of epistemic demarcation. These are dubious strategies; I do not think that theoretical agnosticism is the best response to the political, ethical, ecological, and cultural problems that surround the role of science in the modern world.

Scientific realism also has important implications for literary scholars' self-understandings. Theoretical agnosticism has the consequence of reinforcing a business-as-usual attitude in literary scholarship at a time when epistemic reflection has begun to reveal the problematic nature of many of the assumptions behind traditional literary criticism. Scientific realism says that theories can and should be rationally compared; critical agnosticism gives up on such debate in advance. Scientific realism can motivate literary researchers to engage in theoretical reflection and debate, and to strive for new kinds of explanatory achievements; it motivates them to remain open to new lines of enquiry and to developments in other fields. Such an orientation may have many beneficial, unforeseeable results, even in a field as diverse and self-questioning as literature.

NOTES

1. For background, see Boyd; Boyd, Gasper, and Trout; Van Fraassen; Leplin; Livingston, *Literary Knowledge;* Miller; Siegel.

2. The play is a "tipica commedia d'intreccio influenzata da teatro delle 'maschere' italiano" (D'Amico 6: 360). For background, and sources of the other sample statements, see Argentsinger; Brix; Holberg; Jansen. Some of these sample claims actually have been made by critics, and some are probably correct, yet that is not my present concern.

3. For intelligent surveys of this issue, see Aron; Todorov, "Notion of Literature," *Théories*.

4. In his most recent statements, Schmidt has tended to fold the entirety of the "empirical literary science" back into an extreme version of the constructivist epistemology. Thus he begins a recent essay by citing Musil's "Das Sein ist das Delirium vieler" and ends with Maturana's "Wenn ein Traum geteilt wird, ensteht ein Universum" (*Kunst* 6, 49).

5. For a reconstruction of the theory of mimetic desire, see my *Models of Desire*. For work in economics inspired by some of Girard's insights, see Orléan, "Mimétisme," "Théorie," "Money."

6. For a recent example of this idea, see Smith 4.

7. Jansen puts the basic intuition as follows: "Molière was the first to create comedies of great value around the character of a single person. Holberg, then, first exercised himself in comedies of character, presenting a cavalcade of fools" (62). With a little effort a more precise formulation of the similarities could be provided, but the present argument does not require one.

8. For the concept of "we-intention," see Tuomela, *Theory.* For a detailed account of the nature and functions of intentions, see Mele, *Springs.*

9. At which point the extremists resort to what Pavel has identified as the "esquive empirico-transcendentale" (136). This is the tactic of dodging back and forth between wild empirical theses and claims that the goal is not to make empirical claims but to undertake a radical philosophical reflection on transcendental conditions, grounds, and differences. The obscurity and profundity of the latter are supposed to conceal the absurdity of the former.

10. An approach that critics might explore is that of Cummins, who provides a rigorous example of how psychodynamics may be inscribed within a functionalist research program. It is a pity that literary psychoanalysts have not referred to this text.

11. This point is contested by Levin, but her argument refers to the kinds of strong standards of rationality (i.e., the canons of decision theory) that theories of bounded and minimal rationality reject.

12. For an extensive discussion of the topic, see my *Literature and Rationality.* The notion of bounded rationality was introduced by Simon, *Models.* For background on theories of rationality,see Agassi and Jarvie; Benn and Mortimore; Bicchieri; Brand; Bratman; Cherniak; Elster, *Ulysses, Explaining, Sour Grapes;* Føllesdal; Mele; Simon, *Reason.*

13. For background, see Brand; Dretske; Tuomela, *Human Action, Theory.*

14. See Bratman; Elster, *Ulysses, Sour Grapes.*

15. In some cases, literary inquiry can seek to explain systematic interactions between writers and readers mediated by symbolic artifacts. For details, see my *Literary Knowledge.*

16. For background, see Johnson-Laird.

17. On this point, see Wilensky.

WORKS CITED

Agassi, Joseph, and Jarvie, Ian Charles, eds. *Rationality: The Critical View.* Dordrecht: Martinus Nijhoff, 1987.

Argentsinger, Gerald S. *Ludvig Holberg's Comedies.* Carbondale and Edwardsville: Southern Illinois University Press, 1983.

Aron, Thomas. *Littérature et littérarité: un essai de mise au point.* Paris: Belles Lettres, 1984.

Benn, Stanley I., and Mortimore, Geoffrey W., eds. *Rationality and the Social Sciences: Contributions to the Philosophy and Methodology of the Social Sciences.* London: Routledge & Kegan Paul, 1976.

Bicchieri, Cristina. "Rationality and Predictability in Economics." *British Journal for the Philosophy of Science* 38 (1987): 501–13.

Boyd, Richard N. "On the Current Status of the Issue of Scientific Realism." *Erkenntnis* 19 (1983): 45–90.

Boyd, Richard N.; Gasper, Philip; and Trout, J.D., eds. *The Philosophy of Science*. Cambridge: MIT Press, 1991.

Brand, Myles. *Intending and Acting: Toward a Naturalized Action Theory*. Cambridge: MIT Press, 1984.

Bratman, Michael E. *Intention, Plans, and Practical Reason*. Cambridge: Harvard University Press, 1987.

Brix, Hans. *Ludvig Holbergs Komedier: den danske skueplads*. Copenhagen: Gyldendalske, 1942.

Cherniak, Christopher. *Minimal Rationality*. Cambridge: MIT Press, 1986.

Cummins, Richard. *The Nature of Psychological Explanation*. Cambridge: MIT Press, 1982.

D'Amico, Sivio, ed. *Enciclopedia dell Spettacolo*. Rome: Le Maschere, 1959.

Dretske, Fred. *Explaining Behavior: Reasons in a World of Causes*. Cambridge: MIT Press, 1988.

Elster, Jon. *Explaining Technical Change: A Case Study in the Philosophy of Science*. Cambridge: Cambridge University Press, 1983.

Elster, Jon. *Sour Grapes: Studies in the Subversion of Rationality*. Cambridge: Cambridge University Press, 1983.

Elster, Jon. *Ulysses and the Sirens: Studies in Rationality and Irrationality*. Cambridge: Cambridge University Press, 1979.

Føllesdal, Dagfinn. "Hva er rasjonalitet?" *Norsk Filosofisk Tidsskrift* 4 (1988): 203–12.

Fraassen, Bas van. *The Scientific Image*. Oxford: Oxford University Press, 1980.

Girard, René. *Des choses cachées depuis la fondation du monde*. Paris: Grasset, 1978. Translated by Stephen Bann and Michael Metteer, under the title *Things Hidden Since the Foundation of the World*. London: Athlone Press; Stanford: Stanford University Press, 1987.

Girard, René. *Mensonge romantique et vérit romanesque*. Paris: Grasset, 1961. Translated by Yvonne Freccero, under the title *Deceit, Desire, and the Novel*. Baltimore: Johns Hopkins University Press, 1966.

Holberg, Ludvig. *Værker i tolv bind*. Ed. F. J. Billeskov Jansen. Copenhagen: Rosenkilde & Bagger, 1969.

Jansen, F. J. Billeskov. *Ludvig Holberg*. New York: Twayne, 1974.

Johnson-Laird, P. N. *Mental Models: Towards a Cognitive Science of Language, Inference, and Consciousness*. Cambridge: Cambridge University Press, 1983.

Leplin, Jarrett, ed. *Scientific Realism*. Berkeley: University of California Press, 1984.

Levin, Janet. "Must Reasons be Rational?" *Philosophy of Science* 55 (1988): 199–217.

Livingston, Paisley. *Literary Knowledge: Humanistic Inquiry and the Philosophy of Science*. Ithaca and London: Cornell University Press, 1988.

Livingston, Paisley. *Literature and Rationality: Ideas of Agency in Theory and Fiction*. Cambridge: Cambridge University Press, 1991.

Livingston, Paisley. *Models of Desire: René Girard and the Psychology of Mimesis*. Baltimore: Johns Hopkins University Press, 1992.

Mele, Alfred R. *Irrationality: An Essay on Akrasia. Self-Deception, and Self-Control*. New York: Oxford University Press, 1987.

Mele, Alfred R., *Springs of Action: Understanding Intentional Behavior*. New York: Oxford University Press, 1992.

Miller, Richard W. *Fact and Method: Explanation, Confirmation and Reality in the Natural and the Social Sciences*. Princeton: Princeton University Press, 1987.

Orlén, André. "Mimétisme et anticipations rationelles: une perspective keynésienne," *Recherches Economiques de Louvain* 52 (1986): 45–66.

Orléan, André. "Money and Mimetic Speculation." In *Violence and Truth: On the Work of René Girard*, Ed. Paul Dumouchel. London: Athlone Press; Stanford: Stanford University Press, 1988. 101–12.

Orléan, André. "La théorie mimétique face aux phénomènes économiques." In *To Honor René Girard, ed. Alphonse Juilland. Stanford French Review* 10 (1986): 121–34.

Pavel, Thomas. *Le mirage linguistique*. Paris: Minuit, 1988.

Schmidt, Siegfried J. *Foundation for the Empirical Study of Literature: The Components of a Basic Theory*. Trans. and rev. by Robert de Beaugrande. Hamburg: Helmut Buske, 1982.

Schmidt, Siegfried J. *Kunst: Pluralismen, Revolten*. Bern: Benteli, 1987.

Schmidt, Siegfried J. *Die Selbstorganisation des Sozialsystems Literatur im 18. Jahrhundert*. Frankfurt: Suhrkamp, 1989.

Siegel, Harvey. *Relativism Refuted: A Critique of Contemporary Epistemological Relativism*. Dordrecht: Reidel, 1987.

Simon, Herbert A. *Models of Man*. New York: John Wiley, 1957.

Simon, Herbert A. *Reason in Human Affairs*. Stanford: Stanford University Press, 1983.

Smith, Barbara Herrnstein. *Contingencies of Value: Alternative Perspectives for Critical Theory*. Cambridge: Harvard University Press, 1988.

Todorov, Tzvetan. "The Notion of Literature." *New Literary History* 5 (1973): 5–16.

Todorov, Tzvetan. *Théories du symbole*. Paris: Seuil, 1977.

Tuomela, Raimo. *Human Action and Its Explanation: A Study on the Philosophical Foundations of Psychology*. Dordrecht: Reidel, 1977.

Tuomela, Raimo. *A Theory of Social Action*. Dordrecht: Reidel, 1984.

Wilensky, Robert. *Planning and Understanding: A Computational Approach to Human Reasoning*. Reading, Mass.: Addison-Wesley, 1983.

CHAPTER 8

Is Literary Theory a Science?

J. HILLIS MILLER

By outraged recapitulation evoked . . .

William Faulkner, *Absalom, Absalom!*

In the labyrinth of contemporary narrative theory, the path marked "Realism" or "Mimesis" is frequently trod. It looks like it ought to be easy to attain clarity about mimesis, then take a stand, but this is not the case. Part of the difficulty arises from the way criticism in this area tends to express itself in either/or dichotomies: either realism or vacuous, free-floating fiction; either solid ground in social and historical reference, the reproduction of something really there, or narcissistic self-reference, the novel turned back on itself in sterile contemplation of its own narrative processes; either the representation of some verifiable and objective truth, or the merely relative, some partial, subjective truth, therefore no truth at all. The use of speech act theory has done much to break these binary deadlocks. If novels are seen as a way of doing things with words as well as a way of reflecting (or not reflecting) a preexisting reality, some clarity is obtained in narrative theory. The relation between fiction's performative and constative functions is not a binary opposition but the contradictory inherence of two incompatible linguistic usages.

A major form of criticism, however, assumes that the question of "realism" is the most important theoretical issue. Such criticism tends to presuppose that a good novel is validated by its correspondence to some extralinguistic reality: social, historical, biographical, psychological, or even "spiritual." This form of criticism has its roots in the condemnation of literature by Plato and its justification by Aristotle along moral or psychological lines. Criticism in this tradition is still prone to moralistic pontification: "Good heavens, of what possible use is literature if it is not solidly grounded in reality?" Part of the difficulty may arise from the attempt to develop an "atheoretical" accounting for fiction, an accounting pragmatically empirical, rooted in historical, sociological, economic, and material facts, whereas the terms of the debate—"realism," "imitation," "reference," "fact," "ground," and the rest—are metaphysical through and through. They cannot be detached from their metaphysical implications without begging all the questions that the accounting is meant to ask and answer. It will not do to say, "Everyone knows what is meant by 'realism.' It is a representation in words of real life." The words used to say this recreate the problem they are meant to solve. They retie the Gordian knot they try to cut with pragmatic common sense. My attempt here will be to follow through the lines of this knot rather than to untie it or to cut it. Such a following through is like a schematic drawing of a complex sailors' knot.

The questions asked by so-called "scientific realism" in philosophy may seem at first glance to be rather different from those asked in investigations by literary critics of "realism" in fiction. The former is concerned with classic epistemological questions: the relations among sensation, perception, and theory; the other minds problem; the mind/body problem. The latter ask what it means to make "realism" a criterion of value in fiction. Considerable translation and bridge building are necessary to negotiate from one of these discourses to the other. Nevertheless, my argument here has several common starting points with "scientific realism" as it is represented by Paul Churchland. I agree with Churchland that "all knowledge (even perceptual knowledge) is theoretical" and that "there is no such thing as *non*theoretical understanding." For me too "our self-conception, our commonsense 'theory of persons' is false." More broadly, I agree with Churchland that "our current modes of conceptual exploitation are rooted, in substantial measure, not in the nature of our perceptual environment, but rather in the structure and content of our common language, and in the process by which each child acquires the use of that language. By this process each of us grows into a conformity with the current conceptual template. In large measure we *learn,* from others, to perceive the world as everyone else perceives it. But if this is so, then we might have learned, and may yet learn, to conceive/perceive the world in ways other than those supplied by our present culture."[1] I would agree with this except in holding that since the changes Churchland has in mind would need to be not changes in perception but fundamental changes in language, they would be exceedingly difficult to bring off, more difficult than Churchland's formulations may make it sound. If the mind is plastic, language is not so easily reshaped.

A more familiar expression of this these days in literary study asserts that perceptions of the world and representations of the world in literature are "ideological" through and through. Language is the primary creator and enforcer of ideological presuppositions, defining ideology, with Althusser, as "the expression of the relation between men and their 'world,' that is, the (overdetermined) unity of the real relation and the imaginary relation between them and their real conditions of existence."[2]

Ludwig Wittgenstein's way of putting this is to say that "a picture held us" and then patiently, in example after example, to show that the picture is drawn with words. One example he gives is the presupposition that a picture or a face refers to a person other than itself of which it is the representation. "We are, as it were," says Wittgenstein, "under an optical delusion which by some sort of reflection makes us think that there are two objects where there is only one. The delusion is assisted by our using the verb 'to have,' saying 'The face *has* a particular expression.' Things look different when, instead of this, we say: 'This *is* a peculiar face.' What a thing *is,* we mean, is bound up with it; what it has can be separated from it."[3]

What is at stake in the translation from Churchland's way of putting it to the Marxist or Foucauldian language of "critique of ideology" to Wittgenstein's exploration of "language games" to my rhetorical or "deconstructive" procedures can be told only by careful examination of examples of such translation. The translation is never neutral or innocent. Each is situated and has its own institutional and political agenda.

Is literary theory, then, a science? I answer a wary "yes, of course" to that question. The project of literary study in the various forms of its institutionalization in our culture, primarily, these days, within the university, is to account for literature, to produce knowledge of literature and of its contexts, for example of the various ways throughout history that literature has been accounted for. Literary theory is part of that vast attempt to account for everything that is the reason for being of the modern research university. But literary theory, like scientific realism as Churchland describes it, and like other forms of "accounting for" in the immense multidisciplinary enterprise of university research, has another function, one asymmetrical to the purely cognitive one. Just as Churchland's scientific realism has as one of its goals a transformation of those linguistic structures we take in with mother's milk, so that we may come to see the world differently, so literary theory is, among other things, a critique of ideology, for example of the millennial ideology of mimetic realism. "Critique of ideology" is performative as well as constative, though the two functions work at cross-purposes, since the performative effect of teaching or writing about literature is always to some degree blind to what it does, however clear that teaching or writing may be about what it knows. Nevertheless, literary theory, like other forms of science, would change things as they are, not just describe them. Literary theory is productive. It makes something happen. It is oriented toward the future of those new forms of literature, new forms of democracy, new forms of the study of literature, whose contours we can as yet hardly foresee, since it is our own affirmative activity, in part, that will bring these about. For our part in that, we must take responsibility, just as scientific realism must take responsibility if it succeeds in teaching us to "conceive/perceive the world in ways other than those supplied by our present culture."

A specific problematic is associated with the region of narrative theory focusing on "realism." It seems relatively easy to define exactly what one means by "realism," and yet it turns out to be impossible to do so unequivocally. Clarity is possible here, but noncontradiction is not possible, no neat division into an either/or choice, for reasons I shall try to identify. Key terms in this area are mimesis, imitation, representation, reproduction, report, realism, referential, self-referential, relation, relative, relativity. No one of these words means exactly the same things as any of the others. They overlap or intertwine in a chain, a concatenation of related terms. "Imitation" is not quite the same thing as "mimesis," either as a Greek word or in any strict English usage, even though the words are etymologically related. "Imitation" in English suggests something factitious, even factitiously factitious, as in "imitation plastic." An imitation is a copy that in one way or another advertises the fact that it is a copy. "Mimesis" as used, for example, by Aristotle, on the other hand, still carries some of the force of its origin in dance or mime. Mimesis is an inward act of reproduction whereby the thing imitated is internalized by the imitator and so learned. In mimesis the thing imitated is then turned into an action and thereby externalized, brought out into the open for the imitator or for those who watch the imitation. In mimesis the imitated becomes exposed to knowledge. It is natural to man, says Aristotle, to take pleasure in imitating and in beholding acts of imitation. Man takes pleasure in these because he learns by them, as children learn by imitating the adult world. What is learned is the nature of things as they are, including human things.

The same sorts of distinctions could be made among all the other words in the tangle of terms that in one way or another must be used in discussing "realism" in the novel. "Reproduction," to give another example, is not the same as "imitation," since it calls attention to the way the presence of things present in "reality" is already the result of their "production," their being drawn out into the open where they stand there, out in the sunlight. "Reproduction" copies this act in producing a simulacrum of the original production. Reproduction draws out into visibility another object modeled on the first act of drawing out. A somewhat similar concept or figure, a concept in a figure or figurative concept, is present in the word "represent." Something has to be present or to have been present in the first place in order to be presented again in a representation of it. Both "reproduction" and "represent" show how impossible it is to detach a theory of storytelling as truth of correspondence from the seemingly contradictory notion that art is revelation, "unveiling," the uncovering of a hidden truth. Rather than untangling these words and laying each thread side by side with the others, I shall limit myself here to several key points about them and about the concept of realism they must be used to express.

Many of these words carry the mark of repetition in their prefixes: reproduction; re-presentation; re-ference; re-lativity; re-port; or re-lation. The telling is always a retelling, the presenting or producing again of something that has already been presented, produced, or carried over. No telling, presenting, or producing in narrative is ever the first but is always the repetition of an earlier such act. A narrative, for example a realistic novel, is the pursuing over again of a track already laid down, a "following across" or *diegesis* rather than a drawing out, *exegesis,* or a reading into, *eisegesis.*

What is distinctive about theories of the novel focusing on its need to be "realistic" is the insistence on the necessity of correspondence to solid nonlinguistic fact. Though a realistic novel may be recognized to be a detour away from reality into fiction, a line of words leading into a region of nonexistence, nevertheless, if it is to have value, if it is to be valid, if it is to pass current as genuine for the individual or for the community who "consume" it, it must rise from the real and return to the real. Moreover, at every point along the line of narration, and in its contours as a storyline, it must correspond, in however indirect a fashion, or by however many complicated relays, to the real. It must be grounded in psychological, historical, biographical, or economic fact.

Any theory of "mimesis" must focus on this relation between the story and what it represents. The "re-" in so many of the words used to express such a theory is the sign of the dependence of the representation on what is represented, its mimicry of it. A realistic novel does over again in words what has already in one way or another been done, outside language. On the other hand, the "re-" in "reference," "representation," "reproduction," "report," or "relation" indicates a disturbing kinship between the two acts, disturbing, that is, if one wants to think of the real as unequivocally there, solid and perdurable fact. What the narration does in words—that is, present the real—repeats an act of presentation, making present, or production in reality itself. If a telling is always a retelling, then that reality must in some way already be a telling.

A basic problem in theories of fiction holding that a good novel must be a realistic copy of things as they are has to do not so much with the nature of such copies as with their function. Only if a mimesis is an exact copy of reality as we know it will it be valid, but if it shows us only what we know already, of what possible use is it? The reading of a novel is a detour away from reality that returns the reader back to the real, that is, back to where he was already. What practical value is there in learning again what we already know? On the other hand, if the novel brings something into existence that did not exist before, if it adds to reality, for example by expressing its author's relative point of view on human reality, then it is factitious, not adequately governed at every point by its correspondence to the real, by its absolute truth telling, its verisimilitude, and so it is of no use. In fact, it is probably a positive evil. To read such a novel is to make a permanent detour away from the real and to be in danger of being lost forever among cloudy fictions. Our Victorian great-grandfathers and great-grandmothers may have been right to fear novel reading as a dangerous pastime. Have not novels themselves, from *Don Quixote* to *Madame Bovary* to *Lord Jim,* contained their own warning labels, "May be hazardous to your moral health," in the form of characters who are in one way or another led astray by reading novels? This double bind is intrinsic to the modern theory of realism and underlies all its permutations, for example the specific version that was the reigning theory of the novel in Victorian England. If the novel is fully adequate, it is useless. If it is fictitious it is factitious, and so useless or worse. As I have elsewhere argued,[4] only the notion that a novel has in one way or another a performative rather than a constative function in the society for which it is written will provide an escape from the sterile oscillations of the traditional paradigm of realism. Recognition that novels are performative, however, provides an escape only by generating new problems in its turn.

The traditional paradigm of realism nevertheless still has great force. As Jacques Derrida has argued, it has governed Occidental thinking in this region of philosophy and literary theory from Plato's *Republic, Cratylus,* and *Sophist* down to present-day Marxist or sociological theories of realism. Derrida's formulation, in a footnote for "La double séance," is elegantly succinct. This is the conclusion of the footnote, but the whole note, as well as the discussion of Plato and then of Mallarmé's *Mimique* in the main body of Derrida's essay, is relevant to my argument here:

Schema of this "logic": 1. *Mimesis.* Mimesis produces the double of the thing. If the double is faithful and perfectly like its model, no qualitative difference separates it from the model. Three consequences: a) the double—the imitation—is nothing, is worth nothing in itself. b) The imitation has a value only in relation to its model; it is good when the model is good, bad when the model is bad. It is neutral and transparent in itself. c) If *mimesis* is worth nothing and is nothing in itself, it is nothing of value or being, it is in itself negative; it is therefore an evil. To imitate is an evil in itself and not only when this takes the form of imitating something evil. 2. Like its model or not, the imitation is something since there is such a thing as mimesis and products of mimesis (*mimèmes*). This non-being "exists" in some way (*Sophist*). Therefore a) adding itself to the model, the imitation functions as a supplement and ceases to be a nothing and a non-value. b) Adding itself to the "existent" model, the imitation is not the same, and were it absolutely like the model, it is never absolutely like the model (*Cratylus*). Therefore never absolutely true. c) Supplement of the model, but not able to equal it, it is inferior to it in its essence at the very moment in which it can replace it and be thereby "first." This schema (two propositions and six possible consequences) forms a kind of logical machine; it programs the prototypes of all the propositions inscribed in Plato's discourse and in those of the tradition. According to a complex but implacable law, this machine distributes all the clichés of the criticism to come.[5]

By another "complex but implacable law" and as a strange consequence of the working of this machine, those who attempt to talk, however reasonably or even "scientifically," about the relations of fiction to truth tend to become, in spite of themselves, subdued to what they work in. They extend the work of fiction rather than escaping from it, encompassing it, or seeing all around it from the outside. The commentator on a novel gets caught up in the fiction. He or she begins to speak of the characters as if they were real people and so becomes another fictional character, the imitator of an imitation. The critic imitates the voice of the narrator, a fictional "personage" in the novel like the rest. To put this another way, the commentator becomes another narrator added in supplement to the narrator or narrators already inscribed in the text.

It is exceedingly difficult to avoid doing this. Nor can I hope to avoid it when I discuss, for example, such a novel as Faulkner's *Absalom, Absalom!*. Our culture has always feared this tendency of fictions to turn those who read them into fictions, with possibly dangerous consequences in the "real world." The fictional fabric of *Absalom, Absalom!* is made up of the telling and retelling of the "same" story over and over by a series of narrators, the "omniscient" narrator, Miss Rosa, Mr. Compson, Sutpen, Quentin, and Shreve. Each storyteller tries to put the ingredients of the tale together and make it come out right, so he or she can understand it and have done with it. Any conceivable critical essay on *Absalom, Absalom!* is a repetition of those acts of narration, a repetition in which the critic attempts once more to put the ingredients of the tale together and make it come out right, so he can understand it and have done with it. In this effort the critic becomes one narrator the more added in supplement to all those narrators inside the text. But the novel itself, and its sister novel, *The Sound and the Fury,* show the possibly mortal danger of narration.

Of this inability of commentators on fiction to extricate themselves from the problems they describe, Plato's *Sophist* is a spectacular grandfatherly example. It is an example especially relevant to my search for a solid grounding somewhere for the interpretation of novels. Along with Aristotle's *Poetics* and Plato's condemnation of Homer in the *Republic* for practicing "double" rather than "simple" diegesis, the *Sophist* is a locus classicus for the Western theory of mimesis. The dialogue has been abundantly discussed in the context of current criticism, for example by Gilles Deleuze in *Logique du sens* and in the collection of essays by Jacques Derrida and others entitled *Mimesis: des articulations.* Philippe Lacoue-Labarthe, in *La fiction du politique: Heidegger, l'art et la politique,* has analyzed the political implications of the aporia of the traditional concept of mimesis.[6] The *Sophist* is especially relevant as an example here not only because of its status as an "origin" but because it shows the philosopher who searches for a true theory of fiction becoming tangled in his own lines of inquiry and remaining astray within the corridors of fiction.

The model of the hunt for the Sophist is the search for a definition of angling or fishing with a line. The Eleatic Stranger easily proceeds by the Platonic logic of division and subdivision to catch the angler. Each region of reality as soon as it is identified is further subdivided until the art of angling is located: "One half of all art was acquisitive," says the Stranger, "half of the acquisitive art was conquest or taking by force, half of this was hunting, and half of hunting was hunting animals; half of this was hunting water animals; of this again, the under half was fishing; half of fishing was striking; a part of striking was fishing with a barb, and one half of this again, being the kind which strikes with a hook or draws the fish from below upward, is the art which we have been seeking, and which from the nature of the operation is denoted angling or drawing up."[7]

Plato's (or the Stranger's) choice of examples is not fortuitous. It is another example of Plato's art or wit. The art of the angler doubles the Stranger's activity of angling for the true and genuine Sophist. The angler seeks to catch fish on a hooked line. The Stranger too is an acquisitive hunter. He is even a hunter whose instrument of acquisition is a line. He is the double or mime of the angler, or the angler is the Stranger's double. The Stranger follows a line of discourse in an attempt to track down and catch the angler, then the Sophist. In both cases, moreover, the hunter is hunted, the fisher becomes fish, since the angler is angled for. The Eleatic Stranger is himself obliquely the mysterious prey the dialogue seeks to identify.

The attempt to track down the Sophist, however, even though it takes the successful search for the angler as its model, differs essentially. Though the Sophist too is, like the Stranger and like the angler, man engaged in an acquisitive art, something goes wrong when the Stranger tries to track him by division and subdivision. Since the Sophist is a false simulacrum of the true philosopher, he involves an element of the fictive, the false, in short, of *mimesis*. This makes him a protean figure, a shape changer. He is therefore exceedingly difficult to track down. Whatever line of investigation the Stranger follows leads eventually to a fork in the road where it is impossible to decide on which track to proceed. The Sophist seems either to have disappeared or, absurdly, to have left his footprints down both lines at once. The Sophist, for example, is both a case of the art of acquisition and a case of the art of production. He therefore cannot be tracked down by making a choice between the two possibilities when that particular fork is reached. He has left his spoor down both roads. One or the other, or both, must be false leads. What the Sophist produces are phantasms, illusions, "mimèmes" of true knowledge. The Sophist uses those to make money and to catch the souls of the young men who come to him. Any track he lays down will be a false track. The Sophist and therefore mimesis itself cannot be reached and captured because they always double, bifurcate. The "real and genuine mimesis" is always on the other track from the one the tracker chooses. Space is lacking here to make the detour necessary to recapitulate the indefatigable skill with which the Stranger follows the elusive Sophist down corridor after corridor, dividing and subdividing with admirable athletic energy, until the Sophist vanishes at last into a kind of ultimate insubstantiality. Here is the climactic definition of the Sophist:

Theatetus: We cannot surely call him wise, because we set him down as ignorant, but as a mimic of the wise man he will clearly assume a title derived from this, and I now see that here is the man who must be truly described as the real and genuine sophist.
Stranger: Shall we, then, as before collect all the elements of his description, from the end to the beginning, and draw our threads together in a knot?
Theatetus: By all means.
Stranger: The art of contradiction making, descended from an insincere kind of conceited mimicry of resemblance-making breed, derived from image-making, distinguished as a portion, not divine but human, of production, that presents a shadow play of words—such are the blood and lineage which can, with perfect truth, be assigned to the authentic sophist. (1016–1017, 268b–d)

"Authentic sophist"; "real and genuine sophist": the phrases are oxymorons, as is the notion that the Sophist is engendered and has "blood," a bloodline or lineage, since, as a case of ungrounded mimicry, the Sophist's reality is his unreality. He is a ghost, not a body. The Sophist is not what he is, or is what he is not, or he is what is not. The focus of the dialogue is on the question of the existence of such nonexistences. To try to retrace the thread leading to such a contradiction, to tie it in a neat knot, is to try to weave the wind. The "lineage" of the Sophist is itself a series of contradictions, a long line of unfounded shadows, and shadows further divided and subdivided within shadows, phantasms behind phantasms.

As other commentators have observed, the ultimate irony of this dialogue is that the final definition of the art of the "real and genuine sophist" can with difficulty be distinguished from the art of Socrates, the true sage. One of the last forks in the path before the final subdivision that allows the Stranger to corner the Sophist and claim to catch him at last turns on the distinction between those whose mimicry of justice and virtue is based on true knowledge and those whose mimicry is based on ignorance. The Sophist is of course an example of the latter, but Socrates too made ignorance the basis of his ironic argumentation. Socrates might seem to differ only in claiming to have knowledge of his ignorance, but the Sophist too is said to be "insincere" (1016) in that he knows that he does not have true knowledge. What is the difference between the the Sophist's insincerity and Socrates' irony? The difference is minimal, perhaps nonexistent. Socrates was given the hemlock for doing just what the Stranger says the Sophist does. Socrates too was a seducer and corrupter of the youth of Athens, leading them astray by ironical reasoning producing a beguiling semblance of truth. He too "uses short arguments in private and forces others to contradict themselves in conversation" (1016).

The Sophist is the mimic, simulacrum, or phantasm of the sage, though to which of the two subdivisions of mimesis he belongs in his mimicry cannot certainly be told. Is he an example of the making of likenesses (*eikastiké*), defined as "creating a copy that conforms to the proportions of the original" (978), or is he an example of mere semblance making (*phantastiké*), "the kind which only appears to be a likeness of a well-made figure" (979)? It cannot be known for certain, since the model, Socrates, the true sage, is himself an ironist and mimic of the arguments of others. He is not solidly enough what he is, self-identical, to be imitated either truly or falsely. Socrates too is not what he is. To copy him accurately, in a true likeness, might paradoxically require mimesis in the sense of *phantastiké*.

The Stranger's entire line of argument, with its parricidal refutation of Parmenides, turns on the need to demonstrate that "what is not" can exist, whatever Parmenides said. Fictions, semblances, or acts of mimicry that are not controlled by semblance to real things nevertheless *are* something. They have being. Once that is admitted, the possibility of a permanent detour into a realm of ungrounded fiction exists or even becomes inevitable. All the permutations of the logical machine of mimesis begin their to and fro motion.

What of Plato himself, or what of his dialogue, the *Sophist*? Plato is without doubt an adept in the art of mimicry that is the topic of this dialogue. The *Sophist,* like Plato's other dialogues, is a great work of mimesis employing "double diegesis." Plato plays the role of the Eleatic Stranger, Theatetus, and the rest, speaking for them and miming their modes of thought and their personalities. As Nietzsche centuries later in *The Birth of Tragedy* was to observe, Plato in his dialogues brought a new art form into existence: the novel.

Is the *Sophist* a work of *eikastiké* or of *phantastiké*? The evidence suggests it is the latter, the "kind which only appears to be a likeness of a well-made figure." Socrates and probably Theatetus were historical personages, even though the dialogues in which Socrates or Theatetus speaks undoubtedly never occurred in just the way Plato says they did, if they occurred at all. The performance of the Eleatic Stranger is even less plausible as an "eikon" of an actual personage who spoke just these words in just this way. Socrates himself appears just at the beginning of the *Sophist* to set the stage and then disappears into silence, never to speak again in this dialogue. He becomes one of the listeners to what the Stranger says. He and the reader of the dialogue are in the same place. Socrates becomes the reader or the reader becomes him. Both become silent auditors or readers, witnesses, of the Stranger's zealous tracking to and fro in search of the true and genuine Sophist. Socrates sets the stage for this by saying that perhaps the Eleatic Stranger is not a man at all but the god of Strangers "who intends to observe and expose our weakness in philosophical discourse, like a very spirit of refutation" (958, 216b). In saying this Socrates identifies at the start the main topic of the essay, the extreme difficulty of telling the true from the sham philosopher: "Such men—the genuine, not the sham philosophers, as they go from city to city surveying from a height the life beneath them, appear, owing to the world's blindness, to wear all sorts of shapes. To some they seem of no account, to others above all worth; now they wear the guise of statesmen, now of sophists, and sometimes they may give the impression of simply being mad" (959, 216c). In saying this, Socrates puts doubts in the reader's mind about the identity and nature of the Stranger and calls attention to the way the dialogue is an example of the problems it raises. In the end the reader must decide whether the Stranger is a Sophist or a true sage. It is urgently necessary, but impossible, to decide, since the dialogue itself takes away the cognitive measures by which a decision might be made.

The same thing is accomplished by the odd presence of another speechless auditor of the Stranger's discourse with Theatetus. This is that young friend of the latter whose name is also Socrates and who is also interested in philosophy. In fact, both Theatetus and the Young Socrates are in different ways the replica of Socrates, as the latter observes to Theodorus near the beginning of Plato's next dialogue, the *Statesman:* "They might be said to have some sort of kinship with me. Theatetus, according to you, is like me in looks and Socrates bears the same name. Sharing a name entails kinship in some sense."[8] If Socrates is kin to Theatetus, represented by him in another version of his famous ugliness, he becomes through this doubling not the sage but the novice philosopher who says, "yes, indeed," to the arguments of another. The Young Socrates, on the other hand, plays no role at all in the *Sophist* except as a silent double of the "real" Socrates, at least in name. This discreetly and ironically calls attention to the fact that the Socrates Plato invents in his dialogue is the phantasm of the real historical Socrates. Just as in the *Republic* double diegesis—Homer's pretending to be Ulysses and making him the narrator who tells part of the *Odyssey*—is condemned in an act of double diegesis whereby Plato pretends to be Socrates and the rest, so in the *Sophist, phantastiké,* the Sophist's skill in making ungrounded likenesses, is condemned in a brilliant act of *phantastiké.* Both texts are striking confirmations of my proposed law that the one who interprets fictions becomes a fiction and a maker of fictions.

Nor have I been exempt from this law. In order to enter the movement within the theory and practice of mimesis, it has been necessary to read an example. This has meant evoking the ghosts of the Eleatic Stranger, Theatetus, and the two Socrateses in a recapitulation, a miniature narrative. All theories and practices of realism in the novel remain within the alternations I have described and mimed, that is, within the contradictory inherence of the good imitation within the bad, the bad within the good. It is impossible to get outside this contradiction, since it reinscribes itself in any conceivable theory or practice by which we might attempt to put ourselves outside it. That of course would remain to be proved by an exhaustive analysis of historical modes and the invention of new ones.

The diverse forms of modern fiction and modern theories of fiction might be defined as an approach to fulfilling that agenda. Two signal forms of modern mimetic theory and practice conspicuously displace the traditional notion of mimetic realism. One shifts from the imitation of an objective reality to the imitation of some subjective perspective on reality. The other thinks of fiction as imitation of the illusory collective ideology of a nationality or class at a certain historical moment.

The development of the modern Western genre we call "the novel" from the Renaissance to the present is the history of various forms of the first displacement. George Eliot, for example, in chapter 17 of *Adam Bede* (1859), locus classicus of the Victorian theory of realism in England, defines her project as the "effort" "to give a faithful account of men and things as they have mirrored themselves in my mind." She goes on to say, "The mirror is doubtless defective; the outlines will sometimes be disturbed, the reflection faint or confused." George Eliot's aim is not the direct mimesis of external reality, but a representation in words of that reality as it is mirrored in her mind. As I have elsewhere shown,[9] Eliot's theory and practice reinscribes the traditional contradictions of mimetic realism, as I have defined them here, within the post-Renaissance concept of realism as the faithful representation of individual subjectivities as they reflect reality.

Something similar can be said of more recent and often extremely sophisticated attempts—inspired by Foucault, by such Marxists as Althusser, and by the "new historicists"—to define realism in fiction as the necessary reflection, in the fine grain and texture of the work, of a given ideology. An example much studied is the reflection by anamorphosis of the bourgeois ideology of nascent capitalism in eighteenth-century English fiction. The hegemonic ideology "hales" or "interpellates" the author, willy-nilly, whether he or she knows it or not. This makes the work, if it is read at the proper angle, an accurate, "realistic" mimesis of the ideology in question. That ideology, though it was the mistaking of a linguistic reality for a material one, wielded an all too effective power over the everyday lives of people of the time and place where that ideology "reigned." But ideology is precisely the force of the unreal within the real.

Novels, however, do not merely reflect the ideologies of their times. They also contribute, performatively, to the creation of those ideologies. In the same way, those new histories presenting the novel as the reflection of ideology rather than as the reflection of individual subjectivity or of external reality create in their turn a new ideological presupposition about the relation of literature to reality. They remake history. To put this another way, if these new theories are a critique of ideology, they are themselves manifestly ideological.

But the novels these theorists discuss do not passively reflect the ideologies of their day. They also functioned for readers of their own time, and may function in a different way again for us, as critiques of the ideologies they reflect. George Meredith's *The Egoist*, for example, is a powerful indictment of the ideologies of selfhood and of the role of women in Victorian middle-class society, even though those ideologies are at the end of the novel reaffirmed in a new form. Though the demonstration of this is perhaps only now beginning to be made, seeing mimetic realism as reflection and critique of ideology is yet another displaced reinscription of the Platonic paradigm whereby constative representation and constitutive performative language are irreconcilably mixed, recapitulation and evocation. In realistic fiction of any time or place in our tradition, the projected, groundless phantasm and the genuine reproduction of the real occur in a single indistinguishable operation of narrating language.

I began this essay by saying that the questions asked by so-called "scientific realism" in philosophy sound somewhat different from those asked in investigations by literary critics of "realism" in fiction. Nevertheless I claim that "scientific realism" inherits from a tradition that goes back to Plato the same terminology, the same figures, and the same conceptual formulations. The philosophers of "scientific realism," like literary critics dealing with "realism" in the novel, can with difficulty, if at all, extricate themselves from the aporias generated by these terms, figures, and concepts.

NOTES

1. Paul M. Churchland, *Scientific Realism and the Plasticity of Mind* (Cambridge: Cambridge University Press, 1979), 2, 5, 7.
2. Louis Althusser, *For Marx,* trans. Ben Brewster (New York: Vintage Books, 1970), 233–34.
3. Ludwig Wittgenstein, "The Brown Book," *The Blue and Brown Books* (New York: Harper and Row, 1965), 162.
4. In a chapter entitled "Character" in *Ariadne's Thread* (New Haven: Yale University Press, 1992).
5. Jacques Derrida, "The Double Session," *Dissemination,* trans. Barbara Johnson (Chicago: University of Chicago Press, 1981), 187 n. 14.
6. Philippe Lacoue-Labarthe, *La fiction du politique: Heidegger, l'part et la politique* (Paris: Christian Bourgeois, 1987), 114–33.
7. Plato, *The Sophist,* trans. B. Jowett, *Collected Dialoques,* ed. Edith Hamilton and Huntington Cairns, Bollingen Series 71 (New York: Pantheon Books, 1964), 963. Further citations will be identified by page numbers from this edition.
8. Plato, *The Statesman,* trans. J. P. Skamp, *Collected Dialogues,* 1020, 257d–2592.
9. In J. Hillis Miller, "Reading Writing: Eliot," *The Ethics of Reading* (New York: Columbia University Press, 1987), 61–80.

CHAPTER 9

Tlön and Truth: Reflections on Literary Theory and Philosophy

ROBERT SCHOLES

Introduction

The text that follows here is the one which was distributed and from which I read (with some omissions for the sake of brevity) at the conference on Realism and Representation. I have left those words unchanged. It is now clear to me, however, for a variety of reasons that I shall discuss in my Afterword, that my paper contained some mistakes or confusions that require some attempt at rectification. I have chosen to do things this way, rather than to simply improve the initial text and thus hide my mistakes, because I think the process involved is crucial to our whole topic at the conference. If we can get things wrong, we can also get them right, but we can do so, I should think, only in the light of some ideal of rightness which we might as well think of as truth—our truth, local truth, discursive truth.

At this point I also want to say what I said before reading the paper and reiterated in my remarks during our concluding discussion. That is, I want to insist that, as far as I could tell, all the participants at the conference believed that what they said was an adequate account of the topics discussed. Every one of us spoke as if our texts were the best possible verbal presentation of some matter, and we stood prepared to defend or emend those presentations in response to criticism. For myself, I can say that I proceeded by reducing schools of thought to representative figures and then reducing the figures to a few typical words or phrases that I hoped would represent them adequately. Obviously, this is a process that is fraught with opportunities for error.

My Afterword is in fact an acknowledgment that I got something wrong that I must now attempt to set right. This concern about getting things "right" is an essential aspect of our academic discourse, without which we could not operate as we do. I see no reason why we should avoid thinking of it as a concern for "truth," nor do I see how our study and teaching could continue without the fundamental assumption that some descriptions of things are better or worse than others, more or less accurate, more or less fair, more or less comprehensive, more or less clear. How could we do without judgments of this kind? If we do not wish to call these protocols of our discourse a concern for truth, then we had better find some other name for them rather than pretend that we have no such concerns at all. For to deny such concerns would eliminate our very reasons for being and doing what we do and the rationale for the institutions that sustain us in these endeavors.

> Ten years ago any symmetry with a semblance of order—dialectical materialism, anti-Semitism, Nazism—was sufficient to entrance the minds of men. How could one do other than submit to Tlön, to the minute and vast evidence of an orderly planet? It is useless to answer that reality is also orderly. Perhaps it is, but in accordance with divine laws—I translate: inhuman laws—which we never quite grasp. Tlön is surely a labyrinth, but it is a labyrinth devised by men, a labyrinth destined to be deciphered by men.
>
> J. L. Borges, *Labyrinths*

Let us pause for a moment over this epigraph from *Labyrinths*. It occurs in one of Borges' most dazzling texts, "Tlön, Uqbar, Orbis Tertius." In these pages Borges leads us from a conversation with his real friend Bioy Casares, through a supposed copy of a pirated encyclopedia, in which there is a reference to a nonexistent country, Uqbar, where the literature consists mainly of fantasies about an imaginary region named Tlön, to the discovery of a fragment of an "actual" encyclopedia of that place, from which Borges gravely recounts the operations of a language, a literature, a philosophy, and a geometry distinctly different from those we know in this world. As if this were not enough, he then informs us in a "*Postscript (1947)*" that his own foregoing text has previously (1941) been published in an *Anthology of Fantastic Literature,* after which "many things have happened." Among the things that have happened is the discovery of a complete version of the forty volumes of the First Encyclopedia of Tlön, along with Borges' own discovery of how it came into being. It is the work of a secret society, existing over centuries, that ultimately came to be financed by an eccentric American millionaire. The project of this society was first to create an imaginary country but finally to create an imaginary world that could compete with the real world for human attention and belief. In Borges' text the competition is grossly unfair, because humans prefer to believe in a world constructed by the "rigor of chess masters, not of angels." The science and languages of Tlön have already begun to overwhelm those of this world. After another century, "The world will be Tlön" (18).

As a contribution to this conference, Borges' text would be squarely on the mark. It is about realism and representation in the most elaborate and engaging way. It is also, clearly, in its own procedures, anything but what we call "realistic." Still, it resembles in many respects the writing of philosophers, who often concern themselves with counterfactuals in the interest of clarity and problem solving, if not of truth. Borges poses problems and makes assertions, as in the quotation from Tlön used as an epigraph to my text, in which Borges points to dialectical materialism, anti-Semitism, and Nazism as sorts of Tlöns that inspired belief because they offered the kind of rigor or system intelligible to humans, as opposed to the "rigor of angels," the actual world, which is inhuman and therefore unintelligible. The actual world, it is suggested also, is—however unintelligible—better than any fictional world, because it is the work of better beings, angels. The loss of the real or angelic world to the excessively intelligible world of human thinkers is something about which Borges encourages us to think. Are we to celebrate this victory of the human imagination as a triumph of aesthetic thinking—or to lament the loss of a better world, the "natural" or "real" world created by inhuman, angelic imaginations?

The problem as Borges poses it in this text—and to which he returns in others—has affinities with certain positions adopted or presupposed in much of recent literary theory. Certainly, one of the most important implications of "Tlön" is that there is a radical incompatibility between human language and the world, in that human language is intelligible to humans at the cost of being incapable of true or adequate reference to reality. Borges is useful to us not only in that he presents this view of representation very engagingly but also in that he makes clear a presupposition of this view which is often suppressed: that the radical otherness of the world is due to the radical otherness of its making, described by Borges as a "rigor of angels." One of the claims I shall be making is that behind most literary views of the radical inadequacy of language lurk those angels of Borges. In developing my case I shall attempt to explore what I take to be some important differences between the view of reference and representation taken in recent literary theory and the views taken by many scientists and Anglo-American philosophers. Recognizing that there are also significant differences between the pragmatic and the analytic perspectives, for instance, not to mention the nuances attributable to individual thinkers, I shall maintain, nevertheless, that these groups are broadly opposed to much that is taken for granted by recent literary theory in the United States, and in particular by what is called deconstruction. My concern will not be to adjudicate between these positions so much as to present clearly the nature of their differences and what is at stake in them. As a member of the "literary" party—though not, perhaps, in good standing—I shall also maintain that literary theoreticians ought to be more worried about these differences than they appear to be. Whether philosophers and scientists ought to be worried, I leave to them. The topic can be approached by comparing recent deconstructive theory to American pragmatist thought.

Pragmatism is useful here because there is obviously some sympathy between pragmatism and deconstruction, a sympathy embodied in the texts of Richard Rorty and Stanley Fish, for instance, as they relate to those of Jacques Derrida. Pragmatism is also useful because one of the founders of American pragmatism, Charles S. Peirce, is also frequently cited as a father (or uncle) of structuralist and semiotic thought, which in turn is believed to have been *aufgehoben* by deconstruction. Peirce is interesting because, though his notion of "unlimited semiosis" has been incorporated in poststructuralist thought, he would never have accepted some of the crucial premises of deconstruction. In many matters he ranged himself with the scientists, saying of himself on one occasion, "I am saturated, through and through, with the spirit of the physical sciences" (Peirce 1). Nevertheless, he took the problem of signs as seriously as it has ever been taken, and he had some very interesting things to say about truth and belief. In discussing the concept of *reality* Peirce proposed that it would be helpful to distinguish it from its "opposite," *fiction*. He put the matter this way, using a dream as his example of the fictional:

> a dream has a real existence as a mental phenomenon, if somebody has really dreamt it; that he dreamt so and so, does not depend on what anybody thinks was dreamt, but is completely independent of all opinion on the subject. On the other hand, considering, not the fact of dreaming but the thing dreamt, it retains its pecularities by virtue of no other fact than that it was dreamt to possess them. Thus we may define the real as that whose characters are independent of what anybody may think them to be. (36)

That Peirce should choose dreaming to represent fiction is itself interesting, and we shall return to this choice, but, for the moment, we must attend to the point he is trying to make. As I read him, he is saying that no one can deny the fact that a dreamer has had a dream. Dreaming is real. But what is dreamt depends exclusively upon the dreamer and has no existence apart from the dreamer. Dreams, therefore, are real insofar as they exist but fictional insofar as they represent or refer. "Thus," he says (and how can one not love the human frailty of a philosopher's thuses?), "we may define the real as that whose characters are independent of what anybody may think them to be." Because a dream may exist with no one—including the dreamer—knowing exactly what was dreamt, it exists beyond all opinion and is therefore real. To the extent that some particular things were dreamt, however, those things are simply the work of the dreamer and have no larger claims to truth. But suppose the dreamer dreamt he was dreaming? Or dreamt some other very believable thing? Consider, for instance, the following case:

A philosopher is dreaming. In his dream he is in a court of law, being sworn in as a witness. He is asked to swear that he will "tell the truth, the whole truth, and nothing but the truth." On reflection he finds it impossible to swear to any such thing. It is not that he has scruples, that he wants to lie or evade his responsibilities. Far from it. But when he considers what this oath means, he wonders how anyone has ever sworn it. After all, however much truth one tells, there will inevitably be some left over, including the truth that one has indeed just completed one's testimony. And, however much one wishes to avoid including in one's testimony things that are grossly and obviously false, how can one promise to avoid entirely things that are only somewhat true or relatively true, or true only at certain times, not to mention all the things that are indifferent with respect to truth such as questions, phatic expressions, and matters of common opinion presented as no more than that, without regard to their absolute veracity. The more one thinks about it, the more the common legal oath assumes the proportions of a monstrous impossibility. How, then, can one swear to accomplish something that a little reflection demonstrates to be simply impossible? Would not swearing to an impossibility already be a violation of the oath itself? The judge demands a "yes or no" answer. "Do you so swear or not?" In his dream, the philosopher begins to sweat. When he wakes, the sheets of his bed are wet with perspiration.

Regarding this dream, we may ask many questions. One such question might concern the source of this dream. In classical terms, did it come to the dreamer through the gate of horn or the gate of ivory? Is it a true dream or a false one? Or is it possible that it is partly true and partly false? Does the perspiration on the sheets, for instance, confirm the sweat of the dream, making that part of the dream, at least, true? What theory of truth would enable us to adjudicate even such a tiny truth claim? Does the waking in bed disconfirm the truth of the courtroom itself? If a man is in bed he cannot be in a courtroom. But perhaps he has just returned from being in that courtroom. Most of us, I suppose, would not wish to argue that the courtroom and the bedroom exist on the same plane of reality—except here in my text, where both are made of words and have exactly the same level of textual existence, as if I had dreamt them both. But even if we regarded the courtroom as clearly an imaginary rather than a real place and the bedroom as a real one (within the fiction of my text), we would still be faced with a major problem: the truth or falsehood of what the dream said about truth itself. In the dream the dreamer came to believe that it is impossible to tell the whole truth and nothing but the truth. Is this the truth about truth? And if it were, would it make the dream true, in one sense, even though plainly imaginary in another?

As Peirce well knew, the problem is not one of truth but of belief. He said very plainly that we can never hope to reason our way to "absolute certainty, absolute exactitude, and absolute universality" (56), but he knew that we cannot live without belief. With respect to our dream, then, the question becomes—What might make such a dream believable? For Peirce the scientific or inductive method was the best there was for approaching the truth, and he was quite willing to accept what he knew to be the necessary condition of such a method: a belief that Real things exist which "affect our senses according to regular laws," so that "we can ascertain by reasoning how things really and truly are" (18). According to Peirce, however, such knowledge can never be absolutely certain, because it is achieved by "judging the proportion of something in a whole collection by the proportion found in a sample" (56). Peirce called these assumptions about truth and reality "fallibilism," a name which underscores their undogmatic quality. I have brought Peirce into this discussion because he represents with some adequacy views that still prevail in our scientific community (by and large) and, indeed, in our shared, public culture—to the extent that we have one. I am also hoping that his intellectual presence will help me sharpen the contrast between these fallibilistic or pragmatic assumptions and certain views that are current among literary theoreticians.

I do not mean to make of Peirce a mere foil, however, since I personally find his pragmatism very congenial, even if I cannot fully share his assumptions, and even though I believe that his treatment of the dream example, for instance, solves no problems but simply moves them over into the area of interpretation: the question thus becoming how one would interpret this or that dream as truthful or realistic as opposed to merely fanciful or "fictional." Personally I doubt if there was ever a dream that would not yield some truth if rightly interpreted. But I have introduced Peirce also to remind those interested that the best thinkers in this country have, for a century, denied the possibility of absolute certainty, absolute exactitude, and absolute universality. They have, in short, been skeptical of Truth with a capital *T*, while insisting that we could attain reasonable beliefs without it. Peirce, for instance, took the following line on Kant's proof of a geometrical axiom:

> Had Kant merely said, I shall adopt for the present the belief that the three angles of a triangle are equal to two right angles because nobody but brother Lambert and some Italian has ever called it into question, his attitude would be well enough. But on the contrary, he and those who today represent his school distinctly maintain the proposition is *proved* and the Lambertists *refuted,* by what comes merely to general disinclination to think with them. (17)

This seems to me a quintessentially pragmatist view, in which a thorough skepticism about absolute proof is sustained by a faith in the results of continuing investigation. Until more investigators than "some Italian" join brother Lambert there is simply no need to bother with him, and especially there is no need to try to "prove" what is verified practically, day after day, by surveyors and builders. Contemporary deconstructive writers share Peirce's skepticism about absolute proof. They do not, however, share his faith in progressive knowledge building toward consensus. The best discussion I have seen of the relationship between pragmatism and deconstruction is that in Jonathan Culler's clear and clever book *On Deconstruction.* Culler devotes only a few pages to this question, and these are based mainly on his reading of Richard Rorty's *Philosophy and the Mirror of Nature,* but he brings the issues into focus with his typical perspicacity.

> There are two major obstacles to identifying deconstruction with pragmatism. First, deconstruction cannot be content with the pragmatist conception of truth. The appeal to consensus and convention—truth as what is validated by our accepted methods of validation—works to treat the norm as a foundation, and, as Derrida's discussions of Austin and Searle suggest, norms are produced by acts of exclusion. . . . If, as Rorty observes, to analyze propositions to determine their objectivity means "finding out whether there is general agreement among sane and rational men on what would count as confirming their truth," objectivity is constituted by excluding the views of those who do not count as sane and rational men: women, children, poets, prophets, madmen. One frequently finds general agreement, but consensuses adduced to serve as foundations are not given but produced—produced by exclusions of this sort.
>
> (153, quoting Rorty, *Philosophy and the Mirror of Nature* 337)

Culler argues that the pragmatist's truth by consensus is based on acts of exclusion (a phrase that cannot escape political overtones in this culture). In so doing he elides the difference between Derrida's claim (that Austin and Searle have no right to exclude certain cases from their discussions of speech acts) and Culler's own claim: that certain classes of people should not be excluded from determining what is "true." There are several problems with this elision, but the major problem is that it blurs the distinction between what counts as evidence and who gets to judge what counts. What counts as evidence is the specific quarrel that Derrida has with Austin. Who gets to judge is another matter. Who gets to judge the issue between Derrida and Austin? Madmen? Prophets? Poets? Children? Perhaps, but this is not an ethical issue, though Culler tries to make it one. The issue is not who *should* settle disputes of this kind. The issue is how they *will* be settled, which is to say that it is a strictly pragmatic issue. Madmen, prophets, and even literary critics may take part in such a decision, but their effectiveness will depend upon their ability to persuade others to a consensus on the disputed points. Those excluded from consensus are very likely to have interesting things to say, but they cannot prevail except by persuading a significant body of others that their views are valuable. Decision by consensus is part of a cultural package that includes empirical science, government by consent and participation, freedom of thought and expression, and trial by a jury of one's peers. Are the masters of deconstruction really opposed to all this?

Culler's list of the excluded is also, of course, tendentious. He catches Rorty out in his masculinist pronoun use (for which Rorty has atoned—or attempted to atone—in the pronouns of *Contingency, Irony, and Solidarity*) and includes women in the list of those excluded from the pragmatist's "general agreement among sane and rational men." In all this, however, I think he is merely taking advantage of local problems in an uncautious formulation. Because of this, I don't believe that Culler's views ought to be convincing to the audience of sane and rational readers that he is so clearly addressing with his own text—an audience which can scarcely be imagined to include children and madmen. As for the other items in this tendentious list, I doubt if most poets would want to be excluded from the ranks of the sane and rational. Certainly, there is no reason to assume that Rorty meant to exclude them. Prophets are a problem on several grounds, one of which is that the category seems to include everyone from religious fanatics to scientists a bit ahead of their time—but, again, there is no reason to assume that a prophet has to be insane, or that any sane person must always agree with the majority about any matter whatsoever.

The major problem, however, with the way that Culler uses Rorty's words is that he has taken them out of context in a damaging manner. In the quoted passage Rorty is talking specifically about what "positivists" mean by "analysis." He is not presenting his own position, or any specifically pragmatist position. Therefore, it is a little worse than tendentious to quote Rorty's words as representing either his own or a typically pragmatist position. In particular, the words "sane and rational men," of which Culler makes so much, are more typical of the discourse of positivism than that of pragmatism. It is true, however, that Rorty is arguing for a consensus theory of truth rather than a correspondence theory. But what does Culler, or any deconstructive critic, mean when he uses the word *truth*? Culler argues that "since deconstruction attempts to view systems from the outside as well as the inside, it tries to keep alive the possibility that the eccentricity of women, poets, prophets, and madmen might yield truths about the system to which they are marginal—truths contradicting the consensus and not demonstrable within a framework yet developed" (153–54). There are some problems with this formulation that need to be explored. First of all, it depends to some extent upon a reflex of sympathy for the oppressed and the outlaw. The strongest challenges to scientific paradigms, for instance, come not from children and madmen but from scientists who bring one paradigm or conceptual scheme or system to bear upon another. Such individuals both are and are not marginal.

Another problem in Culler's formulation lies in his own use of the word *truth*. Since the proper use of that word is what is being disputed, his use of it in this context effectively begs the disputed question or displaces it, since we must now ask how the new "truth" would be determined to be true. Culler's view—and perhaps I should make clear that I have considerable sympathy with it—also raises the question of whether or not it is possible to view a system from the "outside." On this topic we can fruitfully contrast Culler's view with Donald Davidson's, since Davidson is convinced that "there is no chance that someone can take up a vantage point for comparing conceptual schemes by temporarily shedding his own" (185). On this matter as on certain others the pragmatist view, which I see as mediating between the analytic and the literary, is especially attractive. By conceptual labor or by play—or, most likely, by some combination of the two—a person might produce a text that challenged or violated the intellectual system or conceptual scheme under which the text was conceived. But the effectiveness of such a challenge would be decided in the long run by its ability to gain acceptance from others, its ability to move toward consensus. In this matter Davidson seems to have an "all-or-nothing" view of conceptual schemes—which is useful to him since he wants to argue that they do not exist. This is a move not unlike some of Derrida's. Culler's position, which could fairly be called "semiotic," makes more sense if one considers "systems" or "conceptual schemes" as never being fully systematic or fully closed. The semiotic notion of codes and the pragmatist notion of consensus come together here, I should say, in opposition to the deconstructive and the analytic notion of all-or-nothing conceptual schemes. This very opposition, however, should probably be seen as the opposition of a middle to two very different extremes: extremes which are precisely "all" and "nothing."

Returning to the question of how "truth" is to be determined, however, most people would accept the possibility of a "marginal" person saying something that is later regarded as true. This happens all the time. And, still later, this same something may again be regarded as untrue. The issue is always and only how this "regarding as true" is to be achieved. Some analytic philosophers would say that the ultimate system is simply the world itself, which will have a hand in determining what is regarded as true. Donald Davidson claims that "successful communication proves the existence of a shared, and largely true, view of the world" (201). Charles Peirce himself believed something similar: "The opinion which is fated to be ultimately agreed to by all who investigate, is what we mean by the truth, and the object represented in this opinion is the real. That is the way I would explain reality" (38). It is the world that plays the role of fate in this view. It is the world that makes consensus possible. For Peirce, however, such a consensus could be achieved only by those "who investigate"—a group that obviously excludes those who cannot or will not "investigate"—but this is not an exclusion by fiat. Like other exclusions in a pluralist society, it is based on opportunity and capacity, which is to say that it is only relatively fair and just. But even Culler suggests that the truths of the marginalized are truths because they will be "demonstrable within a framework" that must someday be developed. Davidson's view—that ordinary language is already full of truth—is the radical one on this topic. But let us pursue a bit further Culler's way of discussing truth.

Culler's position raises two questions. First, what will guide humanity to the new framework in which the truths of the marginalized will be "demonstrable"? And, second, to whom will the "demonstrable" be demonstrated? If the new framework is reached purely by chance—as I think Richard Rorty would say—then the word *truth* does not apply until that framework is achieved. If, on the other hand, the new framework is reached through interaction with the system that is "reality" or "the world," then it may be reasonable to speak of truths as yet unrecognized. My point is that the deconstructive position, as Culler explains it, depends upon contradictory assumptions about the nature of truth itself. "Truths" not yet demonstrable are "truths" only if their demonstration is inevitable because the world itself will support it. That is, they must be truths of some correspondence perceived only by those with special gifts. The child and the madman, in this formulation, must be supposed to be in touch with a deeper, more primordial truth than the sane and rational sluggards against whom they are ranged. Behind this formulation we can see Plato and Nietzsche, holding hands.

Many believing deconstructivists, however, accept as an article of faith that it is impossible to utter the truth because there is an unbridgeable gap between human language and the world. According to this view, everything we speak or write is fictional because there is no such thing as the literal meaning of words. This view runs almost perfectly counter to the position of Donald Davidson in "The Method of Truth in Metaphysics," where we find him saying things like, "Successful communication proves the existence of a shared, and largely true, view of the world" (*Truth and Interpretation* 201). Davidson also argues, in "What Metaphors Mean," to the effect that there is always and only the literal meaning of words, which refer quite adequately to actual states of affairs. The meaning of metaphors, in Davidson's view, is not in language but in the world, in which we find the "objects" that a metaphor invites us to compare (255–56). All that metaphors do, in this view, is to name the objects that are to be brought together. They do not specify the meaning of the conjunction. If we may take Davidson, for the moment, at least, to represent the "analytical" view of language, it will be useful to explore further the differences between his view of metaphor and that of most literary theoreticians.

Culler has taken up this position of Davidson's in his chapter on metaphor in *The Pursuit of Signs,* and made what I take to be some very serious objections to it, despite admitting that Davidson's argument "has definite attractions" (207). In responding to Davidson's position, however, he does not directly take up the question of "objects." Still, Culler's position on this question may be inferred from his text. He argues that responses to metaphor are not "purely random or idiosyncratic," because they are governed by "norms, conventions, codes, structures." If I have read him rightly, he largely agrees with Umberto Eco that in interpreting (or in constructing) metaphors, we are guided not by some direct perception of "objects" but by "a network of conventional associations" (209) that is attached to the words brought together in a metaphor. Davidson asserts that metaphors belong strictly to speech acts themselves, rather than to language. In this view the literal incompatibility of meanings forces the interpreter out of language and into the world of objects. Culler counters this position with the view that language or cultural coding continues to operate in the individual speech act. Davidson's position is essentially Aristotelian: the best metaphors are made by those who have an eye for resemblances. Culler, on the other hand, is close to Eco's view that makers of especially interesting metaphors are not those who see "objects" more fully but those who can work the system of verbal associations more elaborately. This is one of those places where the literary and philosophical perspectives seem most clearly opposed, and I find myself drawn toward the literary position, doubtless because of my own predispositions and conditioning. That is, I think Culler is righter than Davidson on this point. More important, perhaps, this emerges as a place where further discussion is definitely needed.

Davidson opens his discussion of metaphor with a metaphor of his own:

> Metaphor is the dreamwork of language and, like all dreamwork, its interpretation reflects as much on the interpreter as on the originator. The interpretation of dreams requires collaboration between a dreamer and a waker, even if they be the same person; and the act of interpretation is itself a work of the imagination. So too understanding a metaphor is as much a creative endeavour as making a metaphor, and as little guided by rules. (245)

This is an attractive formulation in some respects, but the use of Freud's crucial term "dreamwork" should remind us that the Freudian interpretation of dreams, though it is certainly creative, is just as certainly guided by a system of beliefs about the unconscious. Freudian dream interpretation is a highly allegorical process, in which the story of the dream is interpreted in relation to a developed set of concepts such as "Oedipus" and "castration," and a set of devices such as "condensation" and "displacement." Granted, another system of interpretation will yield another interpretive result, but is there such a thing as a "free" interpretation, an interpretation without presuppositions, without allegory? I am inclined to doubt it. I rather think that in Davidson's "analytic" formulation words like "imagination" and "creative" function in a way that seems from the literary perspective to be both impoverished and deficient in rigor.

There is something more at stake, however, in the differences between the "analytic" and the "literary" views of language and metaphor. Davidson, for instance, appears to accept without question the distinction between literal and figurative meaning, assigning the literal to language and the figurative to utterances or speech acts. For many literary theoreticians, however, it is an article of faith that metaphors go all the way down, that there is no "literal" level to language at all. This position gets considerable comfort and support from a much quoted passage of Nietzsche's:

> What is truth? A moving army of metaphors, metonymies and anthropomorphisms, in short a summa of human relationships that are being poetically and rhetorically sublimated, transposed, and beautified until, after long and repeated use, a people considers them as solid, canonical, and unavoidable. Truths are

illusions whose illusionary nature has been forgotten, metaphors that have been used up and have lost their imprint and that now operate as mere metal, no longer as coins.

(Culler, *Signs* 203–4)

This passage is often quoted as if it proved something—that is, as if it told the truth about truth, or the truth about the relationship between language and reality. Taken in this light, it then becomes part of a larger "deconstructive" argument which goes something like this. Human perception is always already structured by language. That is, we "make sense" of the world around us only because we are linguistic or semiotic creatures, already shaped by our capacity for language. This formulation can be presented as a logical argument. Because perception is always coded by language, and because language is never "literal" but always figurative, perception is never accurate, is always distorted. Derridean deconstruction is founded upon this belief. Derrida himself has called it "l'intention première—et l'horizon lointain" (the immediate intention—and the ultimate horizon) of his major essay on the topic (*La Voix et le phénomène*). In that text he argues "que *la perception n'existe pas* ou que ce qu'on appelle perception n'est pas originaire, et que d'une certaine manière tout 'commence' par la 're-présentation'" (that *perception does not exist,* or that what is called perception is not originary, and that somehow everything 'begins' by 're-presentation'—his emphasis). Derrida's program, as he makes entirely clear, is one of insisting on the existence of "la différence du 'signe' au coeur de l' 'originaire' " (the difference of the 'sign' at the heart of the 'originary' [50]).

Combined with Nietzsche's assertion of the essential figurativeness of all language, Derrida's position yields the deconstructive dogma that perception itself is always figurative, never literal, always distorted, never accurate. Up to a point, this elaborately developed position claims no more than Borges does in the epigraph to this essay: that the world we live in was not made by humans and therefore eludes, to some degree, human understanding. But many deconstructive writers move beyond this position to assume that, since no perception is unmediated, all perceptions have the same zero degree of validity or truth. Or, rather, they all seem reluctant to open the question of how degrees of truth might be discussed or tested. This is precisely the subject I wish to consider (however briefly and inadequately) in the conclusion of this discussion. As Borges put it, in an essay on Zeno's second paradox, "It is hazardous to think that a coordination of words (philosophies are nothing else) can have much resemblance to the universe. It is also hazardous to think that one of these famous coordinations does not resemble it a little more than others, even in an infinitesimal way" (*Other* 114).

The position of Borges and the position of Derrida share a certain modernist angst, a touch of nostalgia for the eternal and essential, for things-in-themselves. Because we cannot capture the truly true in words (says Borges) or even in perception (adds Derrida), we are fundamentally alienated from our world. Not being made by humans, Borges tells us, this world is inhuman. To this I want to reply that humans were made in and by this world, that humans are thoroughly worldly. On this earth, in particular, we are at home, as we would not be on Mercury, for instance, or Saturn, but we have no reason to believe that matter and energy, even on those planets, function differently than they do on ours—though we personally could not survive unaided in those worlds. In any case, this world is ours because we are its creatures, quite literally, and it would be very strange indeed if we were perpetually mistaken about it. It is this view, or something like it, that appears to support the analytic philosopher's faith in the literal truthfulness of most language. It is because language is regarded as already mostly true that the study of ordinary language is so important to analytic philosophers like Davidson. On the other hand, it is because they believe that the very capacity for language distances human beings from the truth that deconstructive writers find a perpetual need to undo or deconstruct verbal formulations. I am suggesting, however, that the deconstructive quest is motivated by the absence of Truth. Deconstruction is driven by nostalgia for a lost angelic world. The extreme differences between the analytic and the deconstructive positions, however, lead to a paradoxically similar result. Both analytic and deconstructive thinkers look to language as the field of their inquiries. Because the truth either is or is not in language, it is language that must be either analyzed or deconstructed.

Coming to the end of these reflections, I find myself facing the somewhat surprising and unwelcome conclusion that extreme positions in both literary theory and philosophy are united not only in their extremity but in the linguistic object of their interest. They are also, of course, extremely opposed in their assumptions about that linguistic object. Given this, we should probably be skeptical about whether analytic philosophy and deconstructive literary theory can say anything useful—or even interesting—to one another. On the other hand, in pragmatic philosophy and semiotic literary theory, we have two discourses with many common interests and assumptions—enough, at least, to negotiate fruitfully over the differences between them. If literary theory and philosophy can offer one another useful dialogue over the matters of truth and representation, it will be most likely to occur at the point where these two disciplines already seem near enough to converse easily and negotiate differences.

I do not want deconstructive and analytic thinkers to stop doing what they do. More power to them, I should say. On the other hand, I can see more possibilities for fruitful interaction between pragmatic and semiotic thinkers. If a bridge between philosophy and literary theory can be built—and I believe it might be very productive to build it—the point where semiotics and pragmatism face one another is probably the right place to begin construction. In this connection I should note that Richard Rorty has claimed that both analytical philosophy and Continental post-structuralism lead inevitably to pragmatism. As he puts it, "On my view James and Dewey were not only waiting at the end of the dialectical road which analytical philosophy travelled, but are waiting at the end of the road which, for example, Foucault and Deleuze are currently travelling" (*Consequences* xviii). The inevitability of this process is perhaps only a claim made for polemical purposes, but I think there is something to what Rorty says. My major reservation, of course, has to do with the pragmatic view that speech acts can be discussed without consideration of signs and codes. Here, I should say, is where Peirce needs to be put back alongside James and Dewey as one of those waiting at the end of the road. Certainly, there are some things to be negotiated between semiotics and pragmatism. All I am claiming here is that, for a variety of reasons, it is both possible and important to negotiate them.

Afterword

One of the functions of a conference such as the one recorded in these pages is to provide the occasion for interactions that may lead us to clearer and more accurate views of the matter of the conference or some other things of importance. Without some notion of progress toward the truth about truth (which might, of course, be that there is no truth about truth), the conference itself would have been a mere junket, a purely social function. In my own case, I can say that sufficient interaction resulted for me to become aware of certain problems in my presentation. This awareness is largely the result of some conversation and correspondence with Richard Rorty (though I must absolve him of any responsibility for my specific revisions) and my subsequent reading or rereading of certain crucial texts by Rorty and Donald Davidson. I now see two difficulties in my original paper that must be addressed.

The first difficulty involves my discussion of what is at stake in the different views of metaphor proposed by Davidson and Jonathan Culler, which might have been clarified if I had focused on the following remark of Davidson's: "a metaphor doesn't say anything beyond its literal meaning (nor does its maker say anything, in using the metaphor, beyond the literal). This is not, of course, to deny that a metaphor has a point, nor that a point can be brought out by using further words" (246). The issue that needs pursuing, here, is what Davidson might mean by "a point," and whether having a point is not a way of trying to say something. It seems to me that if we get the point of something we have decoded an encoded meaning. At other moments in his essay Davidson seems to take a position that would deny to metaphor anything so simple as a single "point": "there is no limit to what a metaphor calls to our attention" (263). It is hard to see how these statements can be reconciled, but I suspect that if he had to give up one of them, Davidson would give up the notion of a point to metaphor and hold on to the lack of limits. But surely there are many things that any particular metaphor does *not* call to our attention, things that are simply irrelevant? If this is so, then there are indeed limits to metaphorical meaning. In this respect I would describe metaphor as effective to the extent that it offers us not an unlimited process of analogical exploration but a shape or structure that organizes the possibilities of analogy in terms of greater or lesser relevance to the matter at hand.

Davidson wants to deny that a metaphor has any shape or structure, that it is governed by any method or protocols of reading. For him, the only meaning in a metaphor is a literal meaning strictly limited by the preexisting semantic structure of language. The important thing about a metaphor, then, is not that it conveys a meaning but that it encourages the reader to use it in ways that are not limited by language. This move is of a piece with his argument against "the very idea of a conceptual scheme." In the essay of that title Davidson elegantly demonstrates that we can find no languages or other systems of thought that cannot be translated into one another, because only if they are translatable can we recognize them as languages in the first place. And if they are translatable, then they cannot function as schemes that limit their users to a world bounded by any one of them. For Davidson the world gives boundaries to language. It is not the other way around. Thus, if we give up "the dualism of scheme and world, we do not give up the world, but reestablish unmediated touch with the familiar objects whose antics make our sentences and opinions true or false" (198). This position is strongly opposed to the views of most semioticians, for whom codes, schemas, paradigms, and discourses are the main objects of study, precisely because they are held to enable and constrain what we believe and utter.

In itself, and insofar as Davidson represents analytic philosophy, this is not a great problem for the position I developed in my paper; however, to the extent that, as Richard Rorty has argued in a number of papers, Davidson is articulating a pragmatist position, it pretty well undoes my conclusion that semioticians and pragmatists may have useful things to say to one another. The gap may simply be too wide to bridge. Either my conclusion is too optimistic, or, by claiming Davidson as a fellow pragmatist, Rorty is actually demonstrating that he is himself more of an analytical philosopher and less of a pragmatist than he has claimed. This is a matter that will have to be left open.

WORKS CITED

Borges, Jorge Luis. *Labyrinths*. New York: New Directions, 1964.

Borges, Jorge Luis. *Other Inquisitions*. New York: Simon and Schuster, 1968.

Culler, Jonathan. *On Deconstruction*. Ithaca: Cornell University Press, 1983.

Culler, Jonathan. *The Pursuit of Signs*. Ithaca: Cornell University Press, 1981.

Davidson, Donald. *Truth and Interpretation*. Oxford: Clarendon Press, 1986.

Derrida, Jacques. *La voix et le phénomène*. Paris: Presses Universitaires de France, 1967.

Peirce, Charles Sanders. *Philosophical Writings of Peirce*. ed. Justus Buchler. New York: Dover, 1955.

Rorty, Richard. *Consequences of Pragmatism*. Minneapolis: University of Minnesota Press, 1982.

Rorty, Richard. *Contingency, Irony, and Solidarity*. Cambridge: Cambridge University Press, 1989.

Rorty, Richard. *Philosophy and the Mirror of Nature*. Princeton: Princeton University Press, 1979.

CHAPTER 10

A Comment on Robert Scholes's "Tlön and Truth"

RICHARD RORTY

Professor Scholes thinks of deconstructionists as claiming that we are cut off from the world made by Borges' angels—as believing that our statements and perceptions are "always distorted." He suggests that "Deconstruction is driven by nostalgia for a lost angelic world." I agree that much in Derrida's writing suggests such nostalgia, but I think it important to note that Derrida explicitly condemns this kind of nostalgia when it occurs in Heidegger. (See the end of Derrida's "The Ends of Man.") Further, and more important: Derrida's view of thought as always in language, and of language as getting its meaning from differential practices rather than from representational relations to reality, *should* lead Derrida to say that the whole idea of an angelic world is one of which we cannot make any sense (that is, any good use).

Borges' angelic world is the world of things in themselves—the world which has the nature it does apart from the fact that it is described in some particular way. But once you give up the idea that language is an attempt to represent or correspond to something which is what it is independently of how it is described—as Derrida seems to do, at least most of the time—you have no reason to hang on to the notion that there *is* anything of that sort, anything like what Nelson Goodman calls The Way The World Is. So, a fortiori, you have no reason to feel sad that language doesn't get you in touch with it. I see Derrida's importance as consisting in the help he gives us to *stop* being nostalgic, and I am baffled by the popularity of nostalgia among those who claim to be his followers (e.g., among the de Manians). It seems to me that they just didn't get the message.

Davidson is explicitly committed, as I think all those who adopt his holistic account of language and thought should be, to the claim that beliefs do not *represent* anything—that truth has nothing to do with representation. The nice thing about Davidson is that it never occurs to him that his nonrepresentationalist account of language and belief is an occasion for nostalgia. He just waves aside the angelic world as a bit of fantasy which we have now gotten beyond. The angelic world is a useful peg for Borges to hang stories on, just as the Olympian deities and the Incarnation were handy pegs for earlier writers to hang stories on; but none of these fantasies is something for which philosophers are obliged to make room. Davidson can happily agree with the claim (made in Scholes's "Foreword") that "some descriptions of things are better or worse than others, more or less accurate, more or less fair, more or less comprehensive, more or less clear." But he will insist that adjectives like "accurate," "better," "clear," "true," and so on have nothing to do with a relation between descriptions and things-as-they-are-under-no-description. They are, rather, ways of describing the relation between a description and the rest of the human practices within which the use of that description occurred.

On my view, Derrida and Davidson don't exactly have useful things to say to each other. Rather, they both are already saying the same thing—namely, that "the relation between language and reality" is a topic on which there is nothing interesting, nothing bracing or saddening, to be said. The only relations between the marks and noises that make up language and the rest of the universe are plain, ordinary, philosophically uncontroversial causal relations. (Why did he say that? Because he he had just been bitten by a snake. Why did he pick up the cigarette butt? Because the sergeant ordered him to.) So language cannot be "out of touch with reality" in the only sense that matters. That sense is a *causal* sense. As long as there are language-using organisms there will be causes and effects which are uses of language—marks, noises, brain states, etc.—by those organisms. Once we see the relation of language to reality as causal rather than representational, we do not know how to raise the question whether language gets us beyond fictions, nor how to phrase the traditional exchanges between dogmatic logocentrists and skeptical logocentrists.

For both Derrida and Davidson, the "literal meaning" of a metaphor is just what the words composing the metaphor would be interpreted to mean by unimaginative souls who go by the book (the book that contains the lexicon and the grammar of the language as it was before the metaphor in question got dead). This is quite compatible with saying, as Nietzsche does, that all words started off as metaphors. For the latter point just says that, the *first* time anybody used a word in a certain way, that word didn't yet have a fixed use, and hence wasn't part of a practice which lexica and grammars might have captured.

As I understand Scholes, he thinks that if truth is a moving army of metaphors, it follows that language is never literal and perception is always distorted. But all it takes for moving armies of metaphors to produce literal truth is for the soldiers to be killed off—for the metaphors to be used predictably enough so that their use is codifiable by the lexicographers. Scholes seems to me to run together the pre-Derridean and pre-Davidsonian sense of "literal" as "use which represents reality-as-it-is-apart-from-description" with the post-Derridean and post-Davidsonian sense of "literal" as meaning "standard, unsurprising use." I admit that Nietzsche himself often ran these two together (thus producing his paradoxical and pointless claim that truth is just a useful fiction), but there is no reason why we should continue to do so. (On Nietzsche's struggles to overcome this paradox, see Maudmarie Clark's recent book.)[1] Once you view literal truth as the sort of thing you get with the help of sufficiently dead metaphors, then there *can* be metaphors all the way down. For now you don't need to halt the regress of metaphors with "an accurate representation of reality as it is apart from any description" (the old, pre-Derridean and pre-Davidsonian sense of "literal truth").

Is perception always distorted? As compared with what? Once you go over to the Derrida-Davidson nonrepresentationalist view, you will no longer use the distorted-nondistorted distinction except within the context of some linguistic practice. "His account was distorted" means something like "It wasn't the sort of account we can rely on." But "All accounts are always distorted, so we can never rely on any of them" is as silly as "All books are always forgeries, so you can never trust any of them." You cannot say that what was thought the exception is really the rule without losing the pejorative force of the term originally used to describe the exception, and thereby trivializing your claim.

I can sum up by adverting to the penultimate paragraph of Scholes's "Afterword." Contrary to what he there suggests, one can say *both* that (as Davidson puts it) we are in "unmediated touch" with snakes and sergeants and that "codes, schemas, paradigms, and discourses" (construed as the regularities characteristic of linguistic practices) do indeed (as "the semioticians" say) "enable and constrain what we believe and utter." No regular, predictable tossing about of marks and noises, no beliefs and utterances—so the semioticians are quite right. No causal relations to snakes and sergeants, no regular, predictable tossing about of marks and noises—so Davidson is quite right.

But don't those "codes, schemas, paradigms, and discourses" *mediate? No.* You would think they mediated only if you thought of them as coming *between* us and the snakes and sergeants, the snakes and sergeants *in themselves,* as they were before any linguistic practice came along which made it possible to so describe them. But do you have any idea what it means for something to be a snake (or anything else, even a Thing-in-Itself) *in itself,* as opposed to being correctly described as a snake (or a Thing-in-Itself) by users of English? If you do, then you are nostalgic for an angelic world—one in which the snakiness of the snake (or the in-itselfness of the in-itself) shows up as such without your having the word "snake" (or "in-itself") in your vocabulary.

There is a story that, when asked by Eve why he named a certain animal "elephant," Adam replied, "Well, it just *looked* like an elephant." Only if you can make sense of such a situation will you be able to talk about "always distorted perception," for only then will you be able to make sense of "*un*distorted perception" (undistorted by codes, schemas, etc.). But to make sense of that story you are going to have to make sense of the idea that something can look like something to you without looking like anything you can put a name to.

As I see it, what Scholes's semioticians study are not "codes, schemas, paradigms, and discourses" as mediating entities that get between us and reality. What they study under this heading are just our habits of tossing marks and noises around in predictable ways. These are reasonable things to study, but study of them raises no problems about the nature or possibility of truth. Nothing *could* raise such problems, once you give up the representationalist notions which Davidson and Derrida both give up. For giving up on these notions means giving up on the notion that "codes, schemas, paradigms, and discourses" are *media*—and maybe always already distorting media—of representation. (But Davidson, alas, does not speak for most analytic philosophers, any more than Derrida speaks for most semioticians.)

NOTE

1. Maudmarie Clark, *Nietzsche on Truth and Philosophy* (Cambridge: Cambridge University Press, 1990).

Part 4

Modernism and Literary Realism

CHAPTER 11

Wave Theory and the Rise of Literary Modernism

GILLIAN BEER

When I first imagined this essay I set it in the late 1920s and 1930s, the period when the elegant expositions of Eddington and Jeans, and the fame of Einstein, were communicating to nonscientists how modern physics crazed categories and dislimned boundaries. As Eddington wrote: "In the scientific world the conception of substance is wholly lacking. . . . For this reason the scientific world often shakes us by its appearance of unreality. It offers nothing to satisfy our demand for the concrete. How should it, when we cannot formulate that demand?" (274)

By the late 1920s waves in motion are all the universe consists in—and they are probably fictitious, "ondes fictives," as de Broglie called them, or as Jeans suggests in *The Mysterious Universe:* "the ethers and their undulations, the waves which form in the universe, are in all probability fictitious . . . they exist in our minds" (79). He is thus led, long before Baudrillard, to equalize representations and enactments: "The motion of electrons and atoms does not resemble those of the parts of a locomotive so much as those of the dancers in a cotillion. And if the 'true essence of substances' is for ever unknowable, it does not matter whether the cotillion is danced at a ball in real life, or on a cinematograph screen, or in a story of Boccaccio" (136). "The universe," he asserts, "is best pictured . . . as consisting of pure thought."

How does literary realism engage with a scientific system that denies substance, dissolves difference, and in the early thirties insists that the universe is best understood as mind? The problem is that in such a formation all realism's work has, paradoxically, been done for it: the difficult forging of likeness between symbol and substance is prematurely accomplished; indeed, there is an "always already" complete fusion between represented and representable. The loss of the contradictions at the heart of the realist enterprise saps its energy even while it ensures its continuance.

Wave theory seems to make a single process a sufficient explanation of all phenomena. This universalizing impulse is counterset in later-nineteenth-century scientific writing by an insistence on relativizing, the relativizing both of our knowledge and of possible descriptions. The relativizing of description is crucial both for advances in quantum mechanics and in modernism. Wave-particle duality and complementarity and *The Waste Land* alike draw on this resource.

Realism in writing is founded on paradox. The term "real*ism*" declares itself as approximation, or servitor: an attempt to mimic an "other" which it must also match. The twin goals of realism are cohering and observing, at once. The "other" that realism serves is assumed as prior, already *there:* out there, in there. If necessary, to be made there.

Sometimes the impossible nature of that "other" is manifest. Such is the case with "psychological realism," which is predicated on the fiction that we can enter another person's consciousness. Sometimes, as in social realism, the project is predicated on a contradiction: on the reader's supposed ignorance of low-life or of technical vocabularies, which that reader is yet then also to recognize so as to vouch for the authenticity of the text.

Realism is stretched further when its topic is the unseen, the unheard, the unregistered: that which lies beyond the reach of our unaided senses. It is also then released from some of the constraints of mimesis. Many nineteenth-century scientists hypothetically filled the zones of space with a transmissive medium, lumeniferous ether, using an old term, aether, in a new guise. Wave theory, acoustics, radiation, all seemed to indicate that our senses are contracted and that we are battered by continuous events beyond their registration: sound waves, air waves, the irreversible transformations of thermodynamic energy. Such theories produced also a space for the idea of the unconscious.

As I approached the topic of realism and representation, therefore, it seemed to me that it might be more productive to focus on a period when realism is usually described as being in the ascendant and to illustrate through a single example, that of the great physicist James Clerk Maxwell, the restiveness about representation in the later nineteenth century—a restiveness shared, and crossing to and fro, between physicists, philosophers, and poets. Maxwell is most often held up as an example of the modes of thought and the attitudes to physical models before quantum mechanics (see Harman). As I shall demonstrate, he was acutely aware of problems of representation and was averse to materialism. Clerk Maxwell is, moreover, a particularly apt choice for those of us living in the postmodern era in which he has become more broadly famous through the trope of Maxwell's Demon, and its figuring in Pynchon's *The Crying of Lot 49*. Like many others of my literary generation I first heard of him and his work through that book—and, at the time, was not sure whether he was a figment of Pynchon's imagination.

My remarks here, therefore, are primarily concerned with the conditions for modernism rather than with samples of literary works. Among Victorian scientists we uncover anxieties about the relativity of knowledge, about determinism, about imaging a stochastic universe instead of a teleological one, about manifestation, symbol, and discourse (Beer, "Reader's Wager"). These anxieties refined (and shared) the conditions necessary to the rise of modernism and of quantum mechanics alike. They were argued at large in the major generalist journals of the time, such as the *Academy,* the *Westminster Review,* the *Nineteenth Century,* and the *Cornhill Magazine.*

Key terms, I would suggest, are often formulated at the moment that their explanatory power begins to wane. "Realism" and "determinism" would be strong nineteenth-century examples. The *OED*'s first example for "determinism" is 1846, and for "realism" it is the late 1830s in philosophy, the late 1850s in art and literature. Multiple, nondualistic forms of representation were proving to be necessary to the advance of the physical sciences. Probability and statistics were the means of stabilizing laws from the random behavior of molecules. C. S. Peirce, arguing for a "universe of chance" in "The Doctrine of Necessity Examined" (1892), was, as Ian Hacking points out, impressed by the statistical mechanics of Maxwell.

Maxwell derived the classical deterministic laws of gases from the postulation of purely random behavior of molecules. Peirce conjectured that something similar would prove to be the case with all the most firm deterministic laws of physics. Hacking goes on to observe the interplay between sociology and physics in this invocation of statistical explanation: "Maxwell had been led to his model and his analysis after reading an account of Quetelet's research into social phenomena. In a sense he modelled his random distribution of molecular motion on social interactions. Maxwell himself may have held, at least for a time, that his models were more than models" (Olby 70).

In the period that concerns me in this essay the margins between models, thought experiments, social occurrences, and mechanical events were a central topic for dispute. How to represent the relations between the all-inclusive laws of thermodynamics and their incommensurate, diverse, and evanescent manifestations? "She arrived in tears and a sedan chair"—the rhetorical figure of zeugma is, I think, useful here.

The acceptance of multiple, incommensurable outcomes driven by a single verb opened the way alike to modernist literature and thought and to wave-particle theory.

Nineteenth-century scientists from Helmholtz to Thomson, Clausius to Clerk Maxwell, were pursuing a single explanation of cosmic processes that would include light, heat, and sound and that would construe them all as motion, passing irreversibly beyond the reach of the senses and dissipating irregularly through the ether (that crucial explanatory substance that ebbed quietly out of the universe early in the twentieth century, going the way of eighteenth-century *phlogiston,* the material principle of combustibility) (Cantor and Hodge passim, esp. 309–40).

Ideas of flux were of course in no way new: all things fleet away; we never step into the same river twice; *alles geht vorbei.* Such Heraclitean tropes were familiar, and were themselves resources, and assurances, for working scientists of the time. What was unfamiliar was the universalizing of wave theory (as thermodynamics continued to be called) to account for all phenomena. Unfamiliar, too, were the twin emphases in the laws of thermodynamics on the constancy of energy within a system and the tendency to increasing disorganization (entropy always tends to increase to a maximum).

There is no need for agreement between legendary and scientific accounts for the release of new imaginative energies. It helps, though, if the phenomena under description are already familiar both in canonical literature and in daily life. This is the case both in thermodynamics and in chaos theory, where observed but hitherto excluded phenomena move into the center of meaning. Even phenomena like the sun and the waves and tides are, after all, inflected differently at different times in the same place.

Educated people in Victorian Britain read Heraclitus, Lucretius, and Ovid in their youth, and often continued to read them in adulthood. All these writers emphasized the wavelike flow of energies. Moreover, people in nineteenth-century Britain were far more conscious of the manifest waves of the sea than we are. They experienced their action. They, or their kin and acquaintance, were obliged to take sea voyages, often long ones. Emigration, imperialism, and trade depended on protracted sea journeys. Even crossing the Channel to Europe in unstabilized boats gave—and can still give—an unforgettable physical experience of wave activity. Fishing was a major industry with a high death toll, the matter of Victorian ballads such as Kingsley's "Men must work and women must weep." The fashion for sea bathing was, in the mid-nineteenth century, still sufficiently new to add a frisson to being buffeted on chill British shores. (Lying on the beach was *not* then an acceptable alternative.) So there was a manifest social complex of referents which could overlap, incompletely but persuasively, with fresh scientific theory. Waves were not only the visible waves of the sea, now, but any kind of periodic disturbance in a medium or in space. The physicist John Tyndall, traveling to the Alps, describes in a continuous implied argument seasickness, heat as a mode of motion, the intellect as a function of temperature, a thunderstorm, the sound of agitated water, the "sonorous vibrations" of air bubbles, reflected light, and human sleepers in a carriage "each burning the slow fire which we call life" (*Hours of Exercise* 59–65).

In 1858 Herbert Spencer, the economist and philosopher, wrote to Tyndall, shaken by Tyndall's exposition to him of the second law of thermodynamics: "That which was new to me in your position . . . was that equilibration was death. Regarding, as I have done, equilibration as the ultimate and *highest* state of society, I had assumed it to be not only the ultimate but also the highest state of the universe. And your assertion that when equilibrium was reached life must cease, staggered me" (Duncan 104). The assumption that a congruity must exist between ideal representations of society and the universe is not peculiar to the Victorians. Such congruity is sought persistently, even at high cost, as now chaos theory has been eagerly seized upon by nonscientists as reinvesting the erratic with meaning and thus surcharging social description with significance—a significance that need no longer depend upon equilibration.

When familiar ideas and phenomena become the focus of scientific theory and research they acquire, for the moment, a new dignity. Half understood and rapidly received, they move across into other fields of enquiry, and they cluster, unstably transformed, amidst the needs and anxieties of a community. I have argued elsewhere that that process informed the new significations of solar physics in Victorian society: the coming death of the sun was no longer a matter of legendary history only, though those precedent legends (Balder dead, the fall of the Incas, Max Müller's solar interpretations of Aryan myth) inform the scientific enquiry, and its reception (*Sun Is God*). Helmholtz, Thomson, Clerk Maxwell made that heat death of the universe seem imminent not by moving it forward temporally, but by changing the level of assent demanded. No longer an as-if story, nor a foundational one, the new physics counted up the number of years likely to intervene before the death of the sun. Their sums varied (anything from 25 to 20 million years) but their totals did not: the earth will become too cold for life.

Stephen Brush, in his invaluable two-volume study *The Kind of Motion We Call Heat: A History of the Kinetic Theory of Gases in the Nineteenth Century,* observes the inductive problem of thermodynamics:

It is difficult to conceive of a time when people did not know that heat flows from hot bodies to cold bodies. Our problem is to understand how this apparently trivial example of irreversibility was translated into an illustration of a general law of nature, the Principle of Dissipation of Energy, and as such was seen to be in conflict with Newtonian mechanics. (551)

One might turn that argument around and say that for most people, once observed, it was not easy to know where the application of the principle stopped. It could be made into a description of mind; it could become grounds for spiritualism; it could provide a vocabulary for degenerationism; it could dislimn all boundaries and disturb all organizations. Happily, it began to play all these parts in early modernism. As Pater puts it in *Plato and Platonism:*

These opinions too, coming and going, these conjectures as to what under-lay the sensible world, were themselves but fluid elements on the changing surface of existence.

Surface we say; but was there really anything beneath it. . . . Was not the very essence of thought itself also such perpetual motion? . . . The principle of disintegration [is] inherent in the primary elements alike of matter and of the soul . . . the principle of lapse, of waste, was, in fact, in one self. (14–15)

Such lapsing could also produce resistance, a flow to be staunched, as T. E. Hulme later attempted to do.

At the end of his essay on Helmholtz, Clerk Maxwell invites the reader to join him in observing Helmholtz observing the waves of the sea.

Now that we are no longer under the sway of that irresistible power which has been bearing us along through the depths of mathematics, anatomy, and music, we may venture to observe from a safe distance the whole figure of the intellectual giant as he sits on some lofty cliff watching the waves, great and small, as each pursues its independent course on the surface of the sea below.

(*Scientific Papers* 2:598)

The scene is heroic and dizzying: Helmholtz is a "giant," Maxwell and the reader are at "a safe distance" released momentarily from "that irresistible power which has been bearing us along" in an imaginative likeness to the action of thermodynamics; the waves are each "independent."

Maxwell continues by quoting Helmholtz, taking us into the pleasures and difficulties of vision, in the double sense peculiarly apt for Helmholtz, who for so long worked on optics, on acoustics, on energy:

"I must own," he [Helmholtz] says, "that whenever I attentively observe this spectacle, it awakens in me a peculiar kind of intellectual pleasure, because here is laid open before the bodily eye what, in the case of the waves of the invisible atmospheric ocean, can be rendered intelligible only to the eye of the understanding, and by the help of a long series of complicated propositions." (598)

Instead of series and complexity, Helmholtz here delights in instantaneity. The visible waves *vouch for* as well as represent the "invisible atmospheric ocean." They give it the effortless "reality" of the manifest. The intensity of the scene is imbued also with Maxwell's own scientific nostalgia, for manifestation, for models, for sufficient equivalence, for an escape from the impasse of theories which mean that "we are once more on a pathless sea, starless, windless and poleless" (letter to Tait, 11 Nov. 1874, Add 7655/Ib/72).

Many later-nineteenth-century scientists, and in particular Maxwell, were scrupulously aware of the problems of representation, problems not only intrinsic to language but specific to the theoretical work in which they were engaged. In *The Meaning of Truth* (1904) William James argued that "up to about 1850 almost everyone believed that sciences expressed truths that were exact copies of a definite code of non-human realities."

> But the enormously rapid multiplication of theories in these latter days has well-nigh upset the notion of any one of them being a more literally objective kind of thing than another. There are so many geometries, so many logics, so many physical and chemical hypotheses, so many classifications, each one of them good for so much yet not good for everything, that the notion that even the truest formula may be a human device not a literal transcript has dawned upon us. We hear scientific laws now treated as so much "conceptual shorthand," true so far as they are useful but no farther. Our mind has become tolerant of symbol instead of reproduction, of approximation instead of exactness, of plasticity instead of rigor. "Energetics," measuring the bare face of sensible phenomena so as to describe in a single formula all their changes of "level," is the last word of this scientific humanism. (40–41)

We do not need entirely to agree with James's view of science before 1850 to find some reinforcement of what he is arguing in the work of late-nineteenth-century scientists, especially those concerned with "energetics." Not only in the social theorizing-out from evolutionary ideas, but in the fields of physics and mathematics, we find a heightened awareness of the instability of language, certainly, and also—more strikingly—of the insufficiency of symbol and of algebra.

In the number of the *Westminster Review* in which Walter Pater's important early essay "Coleridge's Writings" was first published (29 new series, Jan. 1866) George Grote reviewed John Stuart Mill on *The Philosophy of William Hamilton.* This is *not* the same William Hamilton whose initiating work on quaternion vectors Maxwell was studying at that same time (a useful reminder of the principle that things do not fit neatly but remain recalcitrant). But all these writers, philosophers and mathematicians alike, are concerned with the issue of the relativity of knowledge. Pater in his essay argues that "modern thought is distinguished from ancient by its cultivation of the 'relative' spirit in place of the 'absolute.' " Hamilton, says Grote, advances the doctrine of the Relativity of Knowledge and yet elsewhere (in his dissertation on Reid) argues "that our knowledge is only partly, not wholly, relative; that the secondary qualities of matter, indeed, are known to us only relatively, but that the primary qualities are known to us as they are in themselves, or as they exist objectively, and that they may be even evolved by demonstration *a priori*" (12).

The argument concerning the relativity of knowledge is absolutely necessary to the emergence of modernism. And it is particularly in the cognate confusion between method and findings that connections between late-nineteenth-century physics and mathematics and protomodernist texts can, I believe, be uncovered.

Take, for example, Cayley's mathematics. These caused extreme distress to more conservatively minded astronomers, such as the highly effective scientific writer Richard Proctor. In particular, Proctor attacked Cayley's "Address at the opening of the 1883 meeting of the British Association" (*Universe of Suns,* 303). In his essay "Dream Space" Proctor challenged what he saw as the *unreal* nature of the non-Euclidean geometry that Cayley pursued, in which Cayley considered four-dimensional space, worlds in which two and two make three, and inhabitants of "a perfectly smooth sphere" who would with "a more extended experience and more accurate measurements" be taught "that any two lines, if produced far enough each way, would meet in two points; they would in fact arrive at a spherical geometry, accurately representing the properties of the space in which they lived" (308).

Proctor is appalled by these alternative worlds and by Cayley's disturbance (by his interposing of the word *seems*) of axioms such as that odd and even numbers succeed each other alternately ad infinitum. Cayley pointed out that "because a proposition is observed to hold good for a long series of generations, 1,000 numbers, 2,000 numbers, as the case may be, this is not only no proof, it is absolutely no evidence, that the proposition is a true proposition holding good for all numbers whatever; there are in the Theory of Numbers very remarkable instances of propositions observed to hold good for very long series of numbers which are nevertheless untrue" (quoted in Proctor 306).

The mathematician W. K. Clifford similarly argued in his essay "Aims of Scientific Thought" (1872) that the apparently stable generalizing process of scientific induction is often only simile making, and that prediction is an unsound gridding of past events upon the future. He questioned the view that Nature is reasonable, "inasmuch as every effect has a cause" (1:170). "What," he asks, "do we mean by this?" "The word represented by 'Cause' has sixty-four meanings in Plato and forty-eight in Aristotle" (170–71). We develop habits of mind that take for granted laws "so familiar that you seem to see how the beginning must have followed from the end." When sequences of outcome will not conform to the established simile, the majesty of mystery is invoked: "The cause of that event is a mystery which must remain for ever unknown to me." With some asperity he observes, "On equally just grounds the nervous system of my umbrella is a mystery which must for ever remain unknown to me. My umbrella has no nervous system" (172).

This emphasis among mathematicians on conditionality and relativity is a far cry from the position of a contemporary such as T. H. Huxley, who claims "that there is not a curve of the waves, not a note in the howling chorus, not a rainbow glint on a bubble which is other than a necessary consequence of the ascertained laws of nature; and that with sufficient knowledge of the conditions competent physico-mathematical skill could account for, and indeed, predict, every one of these 'chance' events" (Darwin 1:553–55). Realism was put in question in this debate since it depends not only upon representations of interlocked events laterally, but upon the reader's acquiescence in the logic of sequence.

What most disquieted Proctor intellectually (and what most materially makes for my argument that scientific questioning and protomodernism are closely interconnected) is that, as Proctor observes, Cayley's paper was enthusiastically taken up by the *Times,* the *Globe,* and the *Spectator.* The generalist journals and the newspapers made new ideas rapidly available to people throughout the country. Demonstrations by traveling lecturers such as Proctor and Tyndall, with experiments set up on stage, made a dramatic impact on their audiences. Such lectures were arresting entertainment, expanding the scope of the senses and putting credence to the test. Yet such demonstrations also asserted the real presence of unforeseen phenomena "out there": singing flames, invisible rays made visible, artificial blue skies. Materialism became a form of magic spectacle, and the spectacle implied both the relativity of knowledge and the actuality of phenomena beyond the customary reach of our unaided senses.

In the Conclusion to *The Renaissance* Pater presents physical life as perpetual motion, perpetually unobserved: "the passage of the blood, the waste and repairing of the lenses of the eye, the modification of the tissues of the brain under every ray of light and sound—processes which science reduces to simpler and more elementary forces" (233). At the same time, Helmholtzian optics newly established the eye as an uncertain arbiter, an imperfect organ. Helmholtz, indeed, argued that "the impressions of sense are the mere *signs* of external things" (quoted in Tyndall, *Fragments of Science* 1:193).

Rosalind Krauss has recently emphasized in *The Originality of the Avant-Garde and Other Modernist Myths* that painters from the 1870s and impressionism "had to confront a particular fact: the physiological screen through which light passes to the human brain is not transparent, like a window pane; it is like a filter, involved in a set of specific distortions" (15). In the last edition of *The Origin* Darwin pinpoints Helmholtz's emphasis on the imperfection of the eye as according with the processes of natural selection which do not guarantee absolute perfection. The contradictions between these various recognitions were themselves startling representations of the relativity of knowledge.

Human beings are adept at living in multiple and conflicted epistemologies, or we could not survive. In postmodernism we have even attempted to domesticate that awareness of conflicted multiplicity, as Don de Lillo demonstrates in his novel *White Noise*. In the late nineteenth century, play, vertigo, and denial were all provoked in readers by the disequilibrium and illimitability that the new physics was attempting to grip in symbols. Clerk Maxwell indeed hoped that "the intelligent public" would be weaned from determinism by being "led in pursuit of the arcana of science to the study of the singularities and instabilities, rather than the continuities and stabilities of things" (Campbell and Garnett 444).

Among scientific workers themselves the referentiality of language became a dilemma to be argued through. Nor was mathematics naively seen as an escape from the problems of language. The correspondence between Faraday and others concerning the term "force" makes that clear.

"Relativism" of representation need not at all, of course, infringe upon a belief in the actuality of phenomena under description. Indeed, an awareness of slippages within representation—the scrupling at terms and disavowal of any exact reference—may be a form of hyperrealism: an assertion that there is an "out there" so powerfully sui generis that it cannot be captured by already existing terms. The race in science between neologism and agreed nomenclature shows that tendency in action.

In the late 1850s Tyndall thanks Maxwell for offprints in dynamics, the perception of colors, and for his monograph "The Lines of Force." His tone seems a trifle tart: "I never doubted the possibility of giving Faraday's notions a mathematical form, and you would probably be one of the last to deny the possibility of a totally different imagery by which the phenomena might be represented" (7 Nov. 1857, Add 7655/II/13).

Clerk Maxwell's correspondence with Tait in particular (now in the Cambridge University Library to whom I am grateful for permission to quote the material in this essay) is a fruitful source of these debates concerning representation and phenomena. Maxwell's struggle to establish exact terms is undertaken with a serious merriment that is alert to the multivocality of language and tries to yoke that to his purposes. He is both lighthearted and exacting in his attempts to control what he calls "plurality." In the following passage he seeks the apt and stringent word. He toys with sexual reference and escapes it. He controls the *pace* implied by the chosen term.

The discussion is about the vocabulary of vector quantities. (Vector quantities are measures of motion in which both magnitude and direction must be stated: displacement and velocity are examples of vector quantities.)

> the vector part I would call the twist of the vector function (Here the word twist has nothing to do with a screw or helix.) If the words *turn* or *version* would do they would do better than twist for twist suggests a screw. Twirl is free from the screw notion and is sufficiently racy. Perhaps it is too dynamical for pure mathematicians so for Cayley's sake I might say curl (after the fashion of Scroll). (7 Nov. 1870, Add 7655/Ib/16; Beer, Introduction)

Maxwell is chary of the overabundance of connotation and recognizes the difficulty of honing any word to one limited notion, particularly when a field is new. How to say little enough is the problem. But he is also well aware that mathematical symbols are no simple alternative to the communicative problems of language. Language, after all, is composed of grammar and syntax quite as fundamentally as of semantics, and Maxwell felt the lack of a secure grammar in the current mathematical field of quaternions derived from W. R. Hamilton's work. He complained of the want of a "Grammar of Quaternions" and "the proper position of . . . Contents, Notation, Syntax, Prosody, Nablady" (4 and 9 Oct. 1872 Ib/49, 50).

By the end of that sentence he has moved across the spectrum into his own punning habit of mind, between music and geometry. Tait, in Maxwell's repertory, is the "Chief Musician upon Nabla" because "Nabla was the name of an Assyrian harp of the shape ▼. ▼ is a quaternion operator . . . invented by Sir W. R. Hamilton, whose use and properties were first fully discussed by Professor Tait" (Campbell and Garnett 634 n. 1).

Maxwell was an extraordinarily skillful parodic poet. In his poem addressed "To the Chief Musician Upon Nabla: A Tyndallic Ode" he uses quaternion rhymes in a performance, half celebration, half mockery, of John Tyndall's scientific demonstrations. The opening stanzas of this long ode run:

I come from fields of fractured ice,
  Whose wounds are cured by squeezing,
Melting they cool, but in a trice,
  Get warm again by freezing.
Here, in the frosty air, the sprays
  With fern-like hoar-frost bristle,
There, liquid stars their watery rays
  Shoot through the solid crystal.

I come from empyrean fires—
  From microscopic spaces,
Where molecules with fierce desires,
  Shiver in hot embraces.
The atoms clash, the spectra flash,
  Projected on the screen,
The double D, magnesian b,
  And Thallium's living green.

Precisely equivalent passages to the scenes described in these and the ensuing stanzas of this poem can be found in Tyndall's 1865 Rede lecture on radiation (*Fragments of Science* 1:28–73), in his *Heat as a Mode of Motion,* and in his paper "On the Blue Colour of the Sky, and the Polarisation of Skylight" (*Fragments* 1:109–30).

A week later in his correspondence with Tait, Maxwell returns to the problem of representational orders: "the interaction of many is necessary for the full development of a new notation. . . . Algebra is very far from O.K. after now some centuries. . . . We put down everything, payments, debts, receipts, cash, credit, in a row or column and trust to good sense in totting up" (9 Oct. 1872, Add 7655/Ib/50). In 1873 he proposed a spoof question for the Cambridge Natural Sciences Tripos: "General Exercise: Interpret every 4ion [i.e., Quaternion] expression in literary geometrical terms."

Maxwell is careful to preserve a distinction between our knowledge of the world and the possible nature of the world, as did Schrödinger and Einstein later. Thus, in his *Britannica* article "Diffusion," Maxwell argues that the idea of entropy depends on our knowledge of the system and is not itself an observable property of the system: "Now, confusion, like the correlative term order, is not a property of material things in themselves, but only in relation to the mind which perceives them" (quoted in Brush 592–93).

Maxwell repeatedly uses the tardy and distanced form of denomination that Helmholtz also recommended to the scientist: "the motion *called* heat." This power of distancing himself from terms allows a limber play of attention across even those concepts most necessary to his projects. He jokes about the ether, which yet (as his contemporary R. T. Glazebrook wrote concerning Maxwell) seemed to be for scientists at the time the remaining secret to be unlocked: "In light waves periodic changes in the ether are taking place. . . . The laws of these vibrations, when they are completely known, will give us the secret of the ether" (*DNB* 15:120).

Maxwell combines the extreme of skepticism with the extreme of faith, remaining always devout while teasing out the obduracies of the invisible material world. Indeed, for his theological comfort he needs that distinction between what he calls in another letter "the ignorance and finitude of human science" and the enduring energies and dissipations of the universe. In the space between them his God can remain stable, even while Maxwell himself experiences through his study of Clausius, as he remarks wryly, "that state of disgregation in which one becomes conscious of the increase of the general sum of Entropy" (12 Feb. 1872, Ib/43).

Maxwell struggles, with great self-discipline and skepticism, against a temptation in epistemology, where, for example, evolutionism employs the branching model to represent the procedures by which theory is formed as well as the theory that is formed, thus confirming its own theorization. This tendency, I have already suggested, proved fruitful in modernist writing where it could be reconceived as imitative form. Maxwell avoided merging his mode of explanation with the topic studied, but he was highly conscious of the changing functions of metaphor as they extend across scientific fields, shifting from technical description toward generalization that allows productive switching to take place between two fields.

By means of the finitude of mathematical symbols and theorems Maxwell sought to wrest his own representation away from any likeness to the entropic processes he described. But he was also acute about the instability even of mathematical symbols. To Tait he wrote that he "should make a supplementary book on Quaternions explaining the true principles of dots and brackets and defining the limits of the sway of symbols" (14 June 1871, Ib/30).

He concludes this postcard by writing out a "Sylvestrian sonnet" "Tasso to Eleonora" without remark. The poem is thereby made to bear upon the theoretical problems they are surveying in their study of thermodynamics. The octave runs:

> Calm, pure, and mirroring the blue above
> To whom comminglingly my life's streams flow,
> Making that one which many seemed but now,

Thou art the sum and ocean of my love.
What though my soul rebellious pulses prove:
These are the gusts that o'er the surface play,
The fleeting colours painted on the spray;
They cannot in its depths the oceans move.

The writing-out of the poem in the context of this correspondence produces an implicit analysis that he need not spell out. Here, current topics in science are serenely reimagined in the traditional tropes of love sonnets: the blue of the sky (which Tyndall had recently shown to be the result of the polarization of sunlight by particles in the upper atmosphere), the expanding of a single explanatory system to encompass light, heat, sound; the conserving of energy through the whole system; the fleeting colors of the spectrum in the turning wave; and the recognition that the particles of water do not move forward but simply up and down, the disturbances being at right angles to the direction of propagation. All these subjects are to be found in the work of Helmholtz and Maxwell, and are set forth with ravishing clarity in Tyndall's essays gathered in *Fragments of Science.* The tropes of Renaissance poetry are the current topics of science, Maxwell indicates. Recontextualising the sonnet draws attention to the complexities of limiting "the sway of symbols." Language is fertile with fresh reference.

Maxwell has an unusual spatial capacity in his thought that allows him to hold geometry, poetry, logic, statistics, and joke alongside each other without seeking resolution or hierarchy among them, in a manner that actualizes Bakhtin's idea of the polyphonic. This ranging is achieved without muddle. Even his puns are models of precision.

Maxwell warns against popular expository rhetorics, which he calls "the sensationalist" and "the hierophantic":

> The sensationalist says "I am now going to grapple with the Forces of the Universe and if I succeed in this extremely delicate experiment you will see for yourselves exactly how the world is kept going." The Hierophant says "I do not expect to make you or the like of you understand a word of what I say, but you may see for yourselves in what a mass of absurdity the subject is involved." (23 Dec. 1867)

Up to now in this argument I have concentrated on the writings of Clerk Maxwell, partly because he is so clear and adept a thinker about communicative questions and also because his work has continued to be of profound importance in the development of physical theory. But Clerk Maxwell's influence took time to be felt and acknowledged in cultural circles beyond science.

John Tyndall, in the physical sciences, was the writer who most spoke to his contemporaries, conveying to a general readership information about current scientific work and illuminating its penumbra of meaning. His effect can still be felt in the writing of Virginia Woolf, particularly *The Waves,* as I have argued elsewhere ("Victorians in Virginia Woolf"). He wrote in a style at once easy and incandescent. He was the person whom Pater read, Hopkins read, and in her youth Woolf read—indeed, he was the one writer you could scarcely have avoided scanning on scientific subjects if you read the generalist journals of the later nineteenth century.

Tyndall provoked controversy by his atheism, materialism, and insistence upon the imagination: itself an intriguing mix of preoccupations. He was from Ireland, not part of the social establishment, making his way from the ordnance survey of Ireland to the Preston Mechanics' Institute and thence as a mature student to Marburg University in Germany where he studied chemistry and math. He was an atheist but "redeemable," Hopkins hoped, and a materialist of a lofty, even transcendent, cast of mind (Beer, "Helmholtz, Tyndall, Gerard Manley Hopkins: Leaps of the Prepared Imagination"). Much of the power in his writing came from his making visible to the imagination forces beyond the reach of sense. These paradoxical qualities meant that his work posed questions about cosmic order and extent. His work on radiation emphasized "the incessant dissolution of limits" (*Fragments* 1:2). His picturing of the outmost reaches of space was figured as sensation:

> It is the transported shiver of bodies countless millions of miles distant, which translates itself in human consciousness into the splendour of the firmament at night. (4)

Heat and light are both modes of motion and

> in the spaces of the universe both classes of undulations incessantly commingle. Here the waves issuing from uncounted centres cross, coincide, oppose, and pass through each other, without confusion or ultimate extinction. Every star is seen across the entanglement of wave-motions produced by all other stars. It is the ceaseless thrill caused by those distant orbs collectively in the ether, that constitutes what we call the "temperature of space." (1:34)

Tyndall prefers words that are at once precise, sensational, and evaluative: here, "thrill" technically signifies penetration and oscillation, and also communicates excitement. This talent for rousing sensation in the reader meant that, despite his specifying precise meanings for terms such as force, radiation, absorption, his work offered mental images that could be symbolically reapplied, even though his own position was firmly grounded in materialism. He sets as epigraph to his most famous essay, "The Scientific Use of the Imagination" (1870), a passage from Emerson whose last four lines run:

> The rushing metamorphosis
> Dissolving all that fixture is,

> Melts things that be to things that seem,
> And solid nature to a dream.

The tendency of Tyndall's own rhetoric was not dissolution but making visible. His particular major contribution to research was on the "obscure rays" of the sun and their powers, as well as on ice crystallization, and on the blue of the sky.

Tyndall's making visible, in his theoretical and experimental demonstrations, of the "dark rays" of the sun was—for some beholders—not unlike the appearance of the aura in spiritualism. Azure and wave motion, the stirring topics of then current scientific enquiry, enter early modernism alongside spiritual emanations. If ether, why not aura? If dark rays, why not invisible presences? And if a "medium" of transmission (the ether) is required for energy, why not for voices from beyond? Spiritualist seances and scientific demonstrations did not seem very different in their effects. Signs; science; séances: how were they to be distinguished? Photography, with its apparent authenticity of real presences, could be used to confirm spiritualism. The Victorian camera takes snapshots of emanations, by an optical and chemical process that seemed to parallel spiritualism's insistence on "manifestation."

The "dark rays" of Tyndall's own experimental work manifested otherwise invisible presences and claimed for them a more than symbolic form. In an essay, "Science and the Spirits" (*Fragments* 1:444–52), Tyndall sets himself in competition with the medium at a seance. Both claim to bring hidden "real" phenomena within the scope of the senses. In this unremarked essay Tyndall gives a vivid account of a tussle between himself and the medium for control of interpretation. He and she are, equally, storytellers. Whose narratives more satisfyingly expound wave processes? Whose please the listeners more? Whose describe a "real" world?

> Our host here deprecated discussion, as it "exhausted the medium." The wonderful narratives were resumed; but I had narratives of my own quite as wonderful. These spirits, indeed, seemed clumsy creations, compared with those with which my own work had made me familiar. I therefore began to match the wonders related to me by other wonders. A lady present discoursed on spiritual atmospheres, which she could see as beautiful colours when she closed her eyes. I professed myself able to see similar colours, and, more than that, to be able to see the interior of my own eyes. The medium affirmed that she could see actual waves of light coming from the sun. I retorted that men of science could tell the exact number of waves emitted in a second, and also their exact length. The medium spoke of the performances of the spirits on musical instruments. I said that such a performance was gross, in comparison with a kind of music which had been discovered some time previously by a scientific man. Standing at a distance of twenty feet from a jet of gas, he could command the flame to emit a

melodious note; it would obey and continue its song for hours. . . . These were acknowledged to be as great marvels as any of those of spiritdom. The spirits were then consulted, and I was pronounced to be a first-class medium. (1:447)

(This "siren song" is alluded to in the Maxwell poem I quoted earlier.) Tyndall triumphs, or believes himself so to do, but the exchange also takes us back to his early letter to Maxwell, arguing for variety of representations. Tyndall's materialism makes room for variety of interpretation and representation, but within the pale of scientific debate. Single truth and hyperrealism prevail. That scene of debate between scientist and medium, both conjurors of demonstrations, both claiming a higher validity for their performance, suggests also a context (which I shall not here develop further) for Yeats's early poetry.

The idea of the universe as waves, of the parallels between light, heat, and sound, and the single process expressed through them, enters late-nineteenth-century writing with a fresh urgency. Flux, the vortex, the ocean, the aura, the "sea of forces flowing and rushing together," as Nietzsche called it, so important in modernism, are all elements of a repertoire shifting across fields.

In this paper I have concentrated on issues of representation among British scientific writers of the later nineteenth century concerned with wave theory, rather than on the famous philosophical examples of Nietzsche and of Bergson in the formation of early modernism. One of the oddities of modernist chronology is the frequency of time warps, delays of reception which have sustained the insistence on novelty so important to modernist ideology. Let me conclude by glancing at this oddity since it has its bearing on questions of representation and realism. In French writing of the later nineteenth century science and symbolism are not at odds: witness Mallarmé's "L'azur," and the great and hideous invocation of the ocean in Lautréamont's *Maldoror*. Lautréamont idealizes mathematical signs in his sadomasochistic ecstasies which, in a series of cantos, flow associatively through reformations and deformations of the human body and psyche: "Ainsi, les êtres humains, ces vagues vivantes, meurent l'un après l'autre, d'une manière monotone; mais sans laisser de bruit écumeux (1.9) . . . "Les bras nageant aveuglement dans les eaux ironiques de l'éther" (2.5). Lautréamont, like Gerard Hopkins (and, so far as nonscientific circles go, like Clerk Maxwell too), is a curious example of the time-crumpling nature of modernist reception. (When Woolf came to write *The Waves* she was responding both to Einstein and to Tyndall simultaneously.)

Lautréamont died in the 1870s yet his heyday was in the period of surrealism in the 1920s. Similarly Hopkins appears as the first poet in the *Faber Book of Modern Verse,* reft away from the period in which he himself lived among the surrounding languages of poets like Swinburne, writers like Maxwell and Tyndall.

The force of scientific ideas in literary works is to provoke resistance as often as it is to persuade acquiescence or extension. In his essay "Bergson's Theory of Art" in *Speculations,* T. E. Hulme describes the activity of the mind through a forced extension of the waves metaphor:

> It is as if the surface of our mind was a sea in a continual state of motion, that there were so many waves on it, their existence was so transient, and they interfered so much with each other, that one was unable to perceive them. The artist by making a fixed model of one of these transient waves enables you to isolate it out and to perceive it in yourself. (150–51)

The important modernist principle here is that of *falsification:* to model or to fix a wave is to interfere fundamentally with its representation. The violent seizure of the provoked image is one important strain in modernism: as in the vortex, the interpenetrating cones. Hulme sees science, and indeed all thought, as the art of reduction in the service of power:

> to reduce the complex and inevitably disconnected world of grit and cinders to a few ideal counters, which we can move about and so form an ungritlike picture of reality—one flattering to our sense of power over the world. . . . In the end this is true too of mathematics.
>
> ("Cinders," *Speculations* 224)

That emphasis on arrest and power is one important element in modernism. It is set in energetic opposition to entropy and to the evanishing of substance. Yet the metaphor of cinders also recalls the degradation of energy through the entropic process and calls on that as the "real" against the stylization of art. A different expression of modernist creativity, which does draw on wave theory without quarrel, is that of oceanic communality. It is voiced alike by Woolf in *The Waves* and by Schrödinger. Schrödinger, like Woolf, like Jung indeed, wrote of "conscious awareness as something emerging in individuals like tips of waves from a deep and common ocean" (quoted in MacKinnon 221).

The questioning of substance in twentieth-century physics, and the formulation of wave-particle theory, gave realism a new lease of life (if in a manner somewhat analogous to the move in theology from literalism to the hermeneutics of myth). It is harder to deny an "out-there" that is undifferentiated, or irresolute, or composed of "ondes fictives" than it is to challenge substantive phenomena. Realism spurns paradox: it seeks referential (and reverential) equivalence, the one-to-one locking of word and thing. But it has come to depend on paradox and on the logic of zeugma.

WORKS CITED

The writing of this essay, as of those listed under my name below, was made possible by the award of a British Academy Research Readership. I would like to thank the Academy for its support. I am grateful to the Cambridge University Library for permission to quote from James Clerk Maxwell's correspondence.

Beer, Gillian. "The Death of the Sun: Victorian Solar Physics and Solar Myth." In *The Sun Is God: Painting, Literature, and Mythology in the Nineteenth Century,* ed. B. Bullen. Oxford: Clarendon Press, 1989.

Beer, Gillian. "Helmholtz, Tyndall, Gerard Manley Hopkins: Leaps of the Prepared Imagination." *Comparative Criticism* 13 (1991)

Beer, Gillian. Introduction. Rhetoric and Science special number, edited with Herminio Martins, *History of the Human Sciences* (May 1990).

Beer, Gillian. "The Reader's Wager: Lots, Sorts, and Futures." *Essays in Criticism* 40:2 (April 1990).

Beer, Gillian. "The Victorians in Virginia Woolf." *Arguing with the Past.* London: Routledge, 1989.

Benson, Donald R. " 'Catching Light': Physics and Art in Walter Pater's Cultural Context." In *One Culture,* ed. George Levine. Madison: University of Wisconsin Press, 1989. 143–63

Brush, Stephen G. *The Kind of Motion We Call Heat: A History of the Kinetic Theory of Gases in the Nineteenth Century,* 2 vols. Amsterdam: North-Holland Publishing Company, 1976.

Campbell, Lewis, and Garnett, William. *The Life of James Clerk Maxwell with a Selection from His Correspondence and Occasional Writings and a Sketch of His Contributions to Science.* London: Macmillan, 1882.

Cantor, G. N., and Hodge, M. J. S. *Conceptions of Ether: Studies in the History of Ether Theories, 1740–1900.* Cambridge: Cambridge University Press, 1981.

Churchland, Paul. *Scientific Realism and the Plasticity of Mind.* Cambridge: Cambridge University Press, 1979.

Clifford, W. K. *Lectures and Essays.* 2 vols. 1879; London: Macmillan, 1901.

Darwin, Charles. *Life and Letters of Charles Darwin.* Ed. F. Darwin. 2 vols. New York: Dutton, 1959.

De Lillo, Don. *White Noise.* Harmondsworth: Penguin, 1988.

Dictionary of National Biography. Ed. L. Stephen. Vol. 15. London: Smith Elder, 1888.

Duncan, David. *The Life and Letters of Herbert Spencer.* London: Methuen, 1908.

Eddington, Arthur. *The Nature of the Physical World.* Cambridge: Cambridge University Press, 1928.

Girard, René. *"To double business bound": Essays on Literature, Mimesis, and Anthropology.* Baltimore and London: Johns Hopkins University Press, 1978.

Goethe's Theory of Colours. Trans. Charles Lock Eastlake. London: John Murray, 1840; reissued Cass, 1967.

Harman, P. M. *Energy, Force, and Matter: The Conceptual Development of Nineteenth-Century Physics.* Cambridge: Cambridge University Press, 1982.

Helmholtz, H. von. *Epistemological Writings.* The Paul Hertz/Moritz Schlick Centenary Edition of 1921 with notes and commentary by the editors Robert S. Cohen and Yehuda Elkana. Dordrecht: D. Reidel, 1977.

Helmholtz, H. von. "On the Conservation of Force; a Physical Memoir" (1847). In *Scientific Memoirs Selected from the Transactions of Foreign Academies of Science: Natural Philosophy,* ed. John Tyndall and William Francis. London: Taylor and Francis, 1853.

Helmholtz, Hermann. *Popular Lectures on Scientific Subjects.* Series 1 and 2. London: Longmans, 1870, 1881.

Holton, Gerald. *The Thematic Origins of Scientific Thought: Kepler to Einstein.* Cambridge: Harvard University Press, 1973.

Hopkins, Gerard M. *The Journals and Papers of Gerard Manley Hopkins.* Ed. Humphry House and Graham Storey. Oxford: Oxford University Press, 1958.

Hulme, T. E. *Speculations: Essays on Humanism and the Philosophy of Art.* Ed. Herbert Read with a foreword by Jacob Epstein. London: Kegan Paul, Trench, Trubner, 1924.

Inman, Billie A. *Walter Pater's Reading: A Bibliography of His Library Borrowing and Literary References, 1853–1873.* New York: Garland, 1981.

James, William. *Pragmatism* and *The Meaning of Truth.* Introduction by A. J. Ayer. Cambridge: Harvard University Press, 1978.

Jeans, James. *The Mysterious Universe.* Cambridge: Cambridge University Press, 1930.

Karl, Frederick R. *Modern and Modernism: The Sovereignty of the Artist, 1885–1925.* New York: Atheneum, 1985.

Krauss, Rosalind E. *The Originality of the Avant-Garde and Other Modernist Myths.* Cambridge: MIT Press, 1985.

Lautréamont [Isidore Ducasse]. *Maldoror.* Trans. A. Lykiard. London: Allison and Busby, 1970.

Levenson, Michael H. *A Genealogy of Modernism: A Study of English Literary Doctrine, 1908–1922.* Cambridge: Cambridge University Press, 1984.

Lyotard, J. F. *The Post-Modern Condition: A Report on Knowledge.* Manchester: Manchester University Press, 1984.

McGrath, F. C. *The Sensible Spirit: Walter Pater and the Modernist Paradigm.* Tampa: University Press of Florida, 1986.

MacKinnon, Edward M. *Scientific Explanation and Atomic Physics.* Chicago and London: University of Chicago Press, 1982.

Maxwell, James Clerk. Holograph Correspondence. Cambridge University Library.

Maxwell, James Clerk. *The Scientific Papers of James Clerk Maxwell.* Ed. W. D. Niven. 2 vols. Cambridge: Cambridge University Press, 1890.

The Scientific Letters and Papers of James Clerk Maxwell, ed. P. M. Harman, vol. I 1846–1862, Cambridge: Cambridge University Press, 1990.

Nietzsche, Friedrich. *The Will to Power.* New York: Vintage, 1968.

Olby, Robert, et al., eds. *Companion to the History of Modern Science.* London: Routledge, 1989.

Pater, Walter. *Plato and Platonism: A Series of Lectures.* 1893; London: Basil Blackwell, 1967.

Pater, Walter. *The Renaissance.* London: Macmillan, 1910.

Popper, Karl R. *Quantum Theory and the Schism in Physics.* London: Hutchinson, 1982.

Proctor, Richard. *The Universe of Suns and Other Science Gleanings.* London: Chatto and Windus, 1884.

Pynchon, Thomas. *The Crying of Lot 49.* Harmondsworth: Penguin, 1967.

Schrödinger, Erwin. *Science and the Human Temperament.* London: Allen and Unwin, 1935.

Schwartz, Sanford. *The Matrix of Modernism: Pound, Eliot, and Early Twentieth Century Thought.* Princeton: Princeton University Press, 1985.

Simons, Herbert W., ed. *Rhetoric in the Human Sciences.* London: Sage, 1988.

Tyndall, John. *Fragments of Science: A Series of Detached Essays, Addresses, and Reviews.* 2 vols. 10th impression. London: Longmans, Green, 1899

Tyndall, John. *Hours of Exercise in the Alps.* London: Longmans, Green, 1871.

Wheaton, Bruce R. *The Tiger and the Shark: Empirical Roots of Wave-Particle Dualism.* Cambridge: Cambridge University Press, 1983.

Zaniello, Tom. *Hopkins in the Age of Darwin.* Iowa City: University of Iowa Press, 1988.

CHAPTER 12

The Crisis of Realism in Postmodern Time

ELIZABETH DEEDS ERMARTH

History is a thing of the past in more than one sense. Most obviously, the historical construction of temporality aligns the past in a structure of significance that informs present and future. But also, and as I have argued elsewhere, history is itself a construct, one that belongs to an era of about five hundred years lasting (roughly) from the Renaissance through the late nineteenth century. This representational construction of time, the historical convention, made possible across a wide range of cultural expression certain definitions and practices that we still take for granted. Without the production by modern culture of neutral space and time, those homogeneous media in which mutually informative measurement is possible, modern science would have been unthinkable, and so too, for that matter, would certain forms of political organization. These representational conventions, for example, have everything to do with certain habitual conceptions of identity, simple location, structure, consciousness, the subject, and social "laws." What interests me in postmodernism is the disappearance of precisely these media that have been so crucial to the development of, among other things, modern science.

After a brief, initial discussion of what postmodern time is like, I will concentrate on two weaknesses that postmodernism has located in the representational convention of temporality, which is to say, the convention of historical time. First, what might postmodern time be like? Just as pictorial art since cubism has forsaken the neutral homogenized space of realism, treating that space as itself a phenomenon, so postmodern narratives like *Jealousy,* or *Hopscotch,* or *Ada* have forsaken the neutral, homogenized time of realism, treating that (historical) time as itself a phenomenon. My discussion of history and representation—of history *as* fundamentally a representational convention—is too complex to summarize here but I assume it throughout the present essay, especially the idea that historical time is a highly artificial convention: a temporal corollary of single-point perspective in painting that, in a single stroke, rationalizes consciousness and neutralizes (homogenizes) time.[1] Where the representational conventions of neutral, homogeneous space and time provide common ground in the media of time and space, postmodern narrative looks elsewhere for its common ground. To put it in other terms, the constant in postmodern narrative—the controlling denominator which makes all definitions mutually relative to one another—is no longer the time of history, the time of project, the time of Newton and Kant, the time of clocks and capital. Narrative no longer inscribes the time which makes possible that perception of invariant identities like "subject" or "object"; instead it concentrates phenomenologically on the reader-events which collapse the distances between object and subject, inside and outside. In postmodern narrative we experience temporality as an imaginary ambience containing tensions, fields, tectonics, values. Time, too, can stumble, we learn in *One Hundred Years of Solitude,* "and splinter and leave an eternalized fragment in a room."[2] Time, in other words, is not neutral and absolute, but a function of position, in narrative literally of reader position. In short, postmodern temporality makes time itself part of a system of value and emphasis. The sentence read *is* time, and time is a sentence: a defined part of a defined sequence which comes to an end before another sequence, another *conjugation* begins. The "distance" or perspective necessary to maintaining historical time simply is unavailable where time is defined by such specific formulation. Postmodern time is coextensive with the event, not a medium for recollecting it in tranquility.

This focus on the event collapses the distinction between invention and reality, a distinction that is another form of the habitual inclination toward transcending the moment and the detail that is fostered by historical thinking. Nineteenth-century narrative, even at its most reflexive, for example in the novels of George Eliot or George Meredith, still did not ask readers to make this new move of considering one's own responses as text; rather this earlier narrative asked readers to consider readable parallels that were "like" life, and in the 1990s most "popular" novels still permit readers this detachment; that is their particular charm. The purpose of such reading is still the same: ultimately it is a way of reaffirming the existence and operability of historical time.

Postmodern narrative denies the dissociation of art from life, making the act of reading and interpretation the subject of the book. In these redefinitions, acts of reading and interpretation take on new meaning for readers who must continuously recognize that when they read, as when they do other things, their consciousness is active, not passive; that, in short, reading time is not life neutralized or bracketed, but life in full exercise. In the reading of any text whether or not it is a printed book, every interpreter continues to undergo the warps and deformations that never-neutral life always entails. As we read and decipher, we coinvent; and this active attention to reader awareness belongs to a broad redefinition of what constitutes a "text." We are always deciphering a text: the Republican convention, the intentions of a friend, Hiroshima, the emergence of mass media, *glasnost,* the behavior of a relative, the painting of Paul Klee—all are texts, constructs, readable inventions. We are constantly reading, interpreting the constructions we find ourselves occupying and thus coinventing, including the book we hold in our hands whether it be Tolstoy or Borges. Unlike the older narrative conventions that naturalized themselves and effectively neutralized the active moment, postmodern narrative constantly reminds us that each day we invent, coinvent, reinvent Paris, Detroit, and Gaza, in intensely realized detail. To read postmodern narrative is to participate self-consciously in the invention and deformation of value.

There's no place like a Borges story to discover the priority of invention and the link between that invention and time. In "Tlön, Uqbar, Orbis Tertius," for example, the reader must endure the gradual revelation that a fictional world is taking over the so-called "real" one (this "real" one is wittily defined as the world of Sir Thomas Browne). In this fictional world everything is subjective; heresy is "materialism" or faith in a verifiable objectivity. The foundation of its geometry is "the surface, not the point. This system rejects the principle of parallelism, and states that, as man moves about, he alters the forms which surround him. The arithmetical system is based on the idea of indefinite numbers." This counterintuitive system belongs to a culture with values diametrically opposed to those of representation and science; to the inhabitants of Tlön, who know that any system is arbitrary, the elevation of one system above others by calling it "truth" is merely impoverishing and simple-minded:

> The metaphysicians of Tlön are not looking for truth, or even for an approximation of truth; they are after a kind of amazement. They consider metaphysics a branch of fantastic literature. They know that a system is nothing more than the subordination of all the aspects of the universe to some one of them. . . . One of the schools in Tlön has reached the point of denying time. It reasons that the

present is undefined, that the future has no other reality than as present hope, that the past is no more than present memory.*

. . . .

*Russell (*the analysis of mind,* 1921, page 159) conjectures that our planet was created a few moments ago, and provided with a humanity which "remembers" an illusory past.

This story forces readers gradually into the position where the invented country of Uqbar, and its invented country of Tlön, eclipse the so-called "real" world like a black hole suddenly visible. This invented—literally fantastic—world becomes the primary reality to which the rationalist's researches become strictly marginal. This Spinozist universe is a series of mental processes whose unfolding is what we call time.[3] Looked at one way, novels like *Anna Karenina* or *Middlemarch* are precisely this: a series of mental processes whose unfolding is what we call time; but neither Tolstoy nor George Eliot sought primarily to make readers aware of that fact. The difference in postmodern narrative is that the novelist seeks precisely to make that mental unfolding evident to the point of making it the primary text.

As for history, Borges celebrates it as the mode of fantasy that founds entire cultural formations. The true historical date, as he writes in "The Modesty of History,"[4] is not the day of an action, but the day of its perpetuation. This act of recording is an event unparalleled even by the battle recorded or by the retort between royalties. But Borges' historian is not the social scientist scanning developments from past to future; the Borgesian historian is the one who introduces into language and thus into the reservoir of human awareness a theme that was formerly unformed or mute.

I now want to turn to two of the weaknesses in the representational convention of time that may account in part for its eclipse. First, this convention entails a perpetual flight from the concrete which poses certain problems for those who must deal with material limitation and death; second, and as a kind of underside to the achievement of neutrality and objectivity, this convention produces a kind of rationalist disorientation about questions of value. These will be my focus for the remainder of this paper.

The first of these weaknesses, a fatal tendency to transcend whatever is concrete and particular, has been variously noted among twentieth-century writers. Whether or not this weakness for transcendence is endemic to humanism, or merely to one form of it, is a separate issue, although it is worth noting that Renaissance humanism was preceded by an *a*historical medieval humanism of the kind Etienne Gilson has characterized as "a humanism of the present."[5] The perpetual mediation of historical thinking—between aspect and depth, primary and secondary characteristics, inside and outside, public and private—requires a kind of estrangement from the present that entails dematerialization, abstraction, disembodiment. The rationalization of consciousness that supports historical thinking always seeks to *transcend* the present, concrete, arbitrarily and absolutely limited moment by linking it with past and future, cause and project. The present requires a future to complete or at least improve it, and consequently a dialectical method for getting there from here or, in a word, for achieving transcendence of this inadequate present. By emphasizing what is linear, developmental, and mediate, historical thinking by definition trivializes the concrete, specific detail and trivializes the finite and present moment.

Practically speaking—and this is what concerns postmodern novelists—this means that to live in historical time is to live with one's immediate present effectively neutralized. To the extent that we are all historians culturally we always inhabit a *dematerialized present* where particular, practical, concrete, specific experience is something we can only anticipate or recollect. This convention even commits us to the paradoxical position of habitually striving to transcend our transcendence in order to arrive (ultimately) at reunion with real presence which is always posited There but never Here. The ultimate problem with this liability in historical thinking is one that Heidegger identified: it makes the subject of death inaccessible. Historical time, to use Heidegger's terms, is "public time" or the time of "nobody." But "nobody" never dies. Heidegger's famously difficult language is nevertheless adequate to this famously difficult subject:

> the "they" never dies because it *cannot* die; for death is in each case mine, and only in anticipatory resoluteness does it get authentically understood in an existentiell manner. Nevertheless, the "they," which never dies and which misunderstands Being-towards-the-end, gives a characteristic interpretation to fleeing in the face of death. To the very end "it always has more time." Here a way of "having time" in the sense that one can lose it makes itself known. "Right now, this! then that! And that is barely over, when. . . ." How is "time" in its course to be touched even the least bit when a man who has been present-at-hand "in time" no longer exists? Time goes on, just as indeed it already "was" when a man "came into life." The only time one knows is the public time which has been levelled off and which belongs to everyone—and that means, to nobody.[6]

To exist in historical or "inauthentic" time is to exist as nobody and thence, Heidegger's logic goes, to act like an immortal or at least to act like someone who is able to pretend that finitude is not absolute and that it can be mediated by various means: achieving fame or amassing a fortune, endowing a building or a person with one's name or some other measure to guarantee survival according to the logic of historical time. But the authentic future for every *Dasein*, or being-in-the-world, necessarily involves the absolute end of that being.

Heidegger's most important perception, for my purposes, is that the idea of infinity deflects attention from the ultimate human necessity of facing death. Heidegger claims that this "fleeing *in the face of death*" is the very ground of historical thinking (or what he calls the inauthentic temporality) because it exists in order to cover up the fact that existential time ends and is not mediated. Dying itself is not the issue nor is that a specifically human event. But facing our necessity with recognition, living as if we were mortal, that is the specific challenge of Heideggerian *Dasein*. Heidegger's insistence on restructuring philosophical discourse so as to include the fact of death remains an important reminder of how far the conventions of transcendence belonging to history have enabled us to make the subject of death taboo. To use Marguerite Duras's far more elegant and harrowing words, "People ought to be told such things. Ought to be taught that immortality is mortal, that it can die. . . . It's while it's being lived that life is immortal, while it's still alive. . . . Look at the dead sands of the desert, the dead bodies of children: there's no path for immortality there, it must halt and seek another way."[7]

The second weakness of the historical convention, because of its formal emphasis on neutrality, is its inclination to depreciate questions of value. This weakness is not unrelated to the first because if death becomes part of my picture—that is, if my own inevitable finitude becomes part of the discourse in which I make my choices and commitments—then questions of value cannot be infinitely deferred. I might have to ask, for example, of any use of time and attention, is it worth it? But these are questions of value in the most obvious sense and ones that can never be completely avoided. Questions of value, however, come in more powerful and less obvious forms, and ones that the historical convention has elaborate mechanisms for deflecting. In brief, historical temporality is the ultimate medium for sustaining the value of "neutrality." By linking past and future the historical convention creates a putatively neutral medium in which "events" take place freely, albeit according to certain laws of causality which can be 'discovered' through comparisons of widely separate instances, and in which "free" human projects can be formed and pursued. Preserving this neutrality, it can even be argued, is the chief purpose of thinking historically in the first place, although that purpose may not be mentioned directly.

The very establishment of this medium, however, entails the segregation of the (depreciated) present moment which, to the historical mind, is only an intersection, a neutral crossroads for various different and unrelated tracks of causality. Instead of seeing any cultural moment synchronically, as a homeostatic unit or "cultural formation," the historically minded person treats any cultural moment as merely a neutral locus for the various historical threads that run "through" it. History, we might say, is the great creator of disciplines and the great segregator of culture; it diverts into separate "courses" various functions of a cultural formation, and those functions, thus orphaned, find new context in the sequence from past to future. One thinks of the disciplinary distinctions of academia, where textbooks on such fields as Western civilization are careful to segregate art from politics, and one century from another, and where even a restricted field of study like literature has defined everything from the curriculum to the vocabulary of scholarship in historical terms. We teach and discuss the history of genres; we teach and discuss the cultural causes of literary or textual phenomena or we see those phenomena as manifestations of cultural and historical development; we are inescapably engaged, it seems, in the language of "background" and event, the language of depth, the language of representation. And literary studies are only one instance of the massive cultural commitment to such thinking. The practice of such historicism—it is a key convention in the education of young people—has the unspoken but powerful rationale of reencoding the idea that both the medium of events and the method of the investigator are imbued with a fine neutrality.

It is precisely its insistence on questions of *value* that has made feminist theory so powerful an extension of other theoretical writing based in linguistics, anthropology, and phenomenology. Julia Kristeva, for example, supports the view that history is a discourse of appropriation and grasp that supports the values and the exclusions of patriarchy, and she concerns herself with the "sociosymbolic contract" whereby we agree to think of "time as project, teleology, linear and prospective unfolding; time as departure, progression, and arrival—in other words, the time of history." Kristeva has in view nothing less than the "religious crisis of our civilization" and a revision of "the very principle of sociality." The linear convention of time belongs to what Kristeva calls the symbolic disposition of language, that is, the disposition to state, qualify, and conclude rather than the disposition to play, multiply, and diversify. This is a convention that fosters what Kristeva claims a psychoanalyst would call "obsessional time": a zeal to master time in which can be discerned "the true structure of the slave." Kristeva describes this "time of history" as one that is "totalizing" in its universal sweep and, consequently, "totalitarian" toward what it excludes as "nonessential or even nonexistent" Such a critique of historical time sounds very much like Heidegger's critique of inauthentic temporality; and such agendas are among the several ways in which theoretical feminism has extended and specified the postmodern experimental effort: an effort to redefine Western metaphysics and to reformulate social codes by starting with the most intimate, the most practical, the most apparently "innocent" of daily practices. Heidegger's critique of inauthentic temporality ("nobody's" time) implicitly engages his argument in questions of value and questions of proportion.[8]

The postmodern idea that time and space are themselves defined, limited, discontinuous is so counterintuitive that it may seem almost unthinkable. Yet this is precisely what postmodern narratives establish—an alternative temporality—and precisely what they ask of their readers: to think what seems unthinkable. And in this the postmodern narrative project very much resembles the discourse analysis that has developed across disciplines, eroding their boundaries. Breaking down the convention of historical time reveals the arbitrariness of its "neutrality," and this opening permits us, no, forces us to focus on precisely those questions of value and proportion that history defers. This is also the effect of discourse analysis, and especially feminist versions: precisely that they permit us to shift disciplinary discussion to questions of value. If these questions sometimes seem tautological, that is generally because they are the most important questions and because it is precisely such tautologies, unseen and unexamined, that tend to become the invisible footmen of discourse. The value of neutrality, for instance, is not so much mentioned by historical narratives as it is silently taken for granted by them. While the old historicism masks questions of value with all their implications for commitment and choice, the new disciplinary work based on Foucault and philosophical linguistics brings such questions into focus. For example, when scholars speak in the same breath of Shakespeare and the *conquistadores,* they employ a method that refocuses the cultural moment as a homeostatic entity and consequently dissolves the neutrality of the present which now appears as syntax-bound and value-laden and certainly no longer a neutral site for the displacement of value. Questions of value even leak into matters of methodology itself, wiping out any putative neutrality that may still remain there.[9]

Whatever this new effort is called, and there is considerable terminological difficulty about that at the moment, it is clearly difficult work: difficult largely because it involves ending one's tenure as an implied spectator or neutral historian and accepting a position in the frame of reference. To see the cultural moment as a single frame means to refocus on the difference between cultural moments and between large discursive practices, which means to see every method including my own, every value including my own, every language including my own as historically limited—even the method I use to arrive at this recognition. This is heady stuff. If I accomplished this perilous work I would in effect de-"naturalize" my own deepest preoccupations; I would dematerialize the very ladder under my feet. I would (to use Stephen Greenblatt's phrase for one form of modernism) *improvise* my own beliefs in the act of discussing and situating them. Postmodern improvisation, that is, requires a truly "self"-reflexive activity. Unlike the historian, who improvises on the beliefs of others, for example of past generations, the postmodern interpreter is forced to improvise on his or her *own* beliefs. And once new practices unsettle habits, I face the choice among practices which means that I squarely face questions of value. It is this necessity at the heart of postmodern narrative (and discourse analysis) that really unsettles the complacent reader-writer-citizen and that partly accounts for the reaction against it.

The costs as well as the benefits of historical thinking have by now been widely perceived, especially its entail of dissociation between discrete, textured, phenomenal experience on the one hand and generalized, metaphysical consciousness on the other. In fact this dissociation, of which Conrad's Kurtz is a particularly famous representative, had already proved by the end of the nineteenth century to be a definitive, determining liability. What postmodern writers inherited was the necessity to deal with the liabilities of a cultural discourse which had made possible world war and other world disasters, and it is only with an eye on social and political conditions of the twentieth century that we can hope to understand the phenomenon of postmodern narrative and its critique of representation in anything like adequate ways.

The best definition of postmodern narrative might be precisely that it resolutely *does not operate* according to any form of historical time, that is, representational time, and in many cases directly parodies or disputes that time and the generalizations it allows to form. Such subversion necessarily precedes those experiments with new forms of temporality that postmodern narrative makes possible. In such narrative, the infinite future does not exist, nor does the finite subject, or at least they are so massively attenuated that they no longer function as controlling conventions. For postmodernism, historical time is a thing of the past in more than one sense. History now is not just the convention where the present belongs to a controlled pattern of meaning governed by the past and opened to a future. History now is also in the interesting position of confronting its own historicity.

NOTES

This essay appeared in a slightly different form in my book *Sequel to History: Postmodernism and the Crisis of Representational Time* (Princeton, 1992).

1. A more complete discussion can be found in the first one hundred pages of my *Realism and Consensus in the English Novel* (Princeton: Princeton University Press, 1983), a history of consciousness between (roughly) 1500 and 1900: an exploration of the conventions of time and space as they developed in painting, mathematics, and particularly narrative in the modern era, which is to say the period between the early Renaissance and the late nineteenth century.

2. Gabriel Garcia Marquez, *One Hundred Years of Solitude* (*Cien Años de Soledad,* 1967), trans. Gregory Rabassa (New York: Harper and Row, 1970), 322.

3. Jorge Luis Borges, *Ficciones* (New York: Grove Press, 1962), 24–28.

4. Jorge Luis Borges, *A Personal Anthology* (*Antólogia Personal,* 1961) (New York: Grove Press, 1967), 179–83.

5. "It is often said, and it is in a sense fair to say, that the Middle Ages remained almost completely a stranger to history, at least in the way the Renaissance understood it and as we still understand it today [Gilson writes in 1932]. Its humanism is very different from the historical humanism which characterizes the Renaissance, it is a humanism of the present, or, if you prefer, of the timeless." Compared with medieval humanism, says Gilson, the Renaissance and particularly Erasmian humanism displays "a passion for historical difference." "Le Moyen Age et le naturalisme antique," *Archives d'histoire doctrinale et littéraire du Moyen Age* 7 (1932): 35–36 (translation mine).

6. *Being and Time,* translated from Martin Heidegger's *Sein und Zeit* (1927) by John Macquarrie and Edward Robinson (New York: Harper and Row, 1962), 477 (2.6.81).

7. *Dasein* (literally, Being-there-ness) is Heidegger's term for that phenomenological event of being-in-the-world. "Dasein traverses the span of time granted to it between the two boundaries (birth and death), and it does so in such a way that, in each case, it is 'actual' only in the 'now', and hopes, as it were, through the sequence of 'nows' of its own 'time.' . . . Dasein does not fill up a track or stretch 'of life.' . . . It stretches *itself* along in such a way that its own Being is not anything more cosmically structured. The principal thesis of the ordinary way of interpreting time—namely that time is 'infinite'—makes manifest most impressively the way in which world-time and accordingly temporality in general have been levelled off and covered up by such an interpretation." (476 [2.6.81]). By "world-time" he means the time that is "sighted" by the use of clocks (see 474 [2.6.81]).

Marguerite Duras, *The Lover,* trans. Barbara Bray (New York: Random House, 1985), 105–6, from *L'Amant* (Paris: Minuit, 1984), 128–29): "Il faudrait prévenir les gens de ces choses-là. Leur apprendre que l'immortalité est mortelle, qu'elle peut mourir. . . . Que c'est tandis qu'elle se vit que la vie est immortelle, tandis qu'elle est en vie. . . . Regardez les sables morts des déserts, le corps mort des enfants: l'immortalité ne passe pas par là, elle s'arrête et contourne."

8. Kristeva notes that women's experience has demonstrated that the cultural formation supporting the idea of history—and with it what Heidegger calls inauthentic temporality—has not been accessible to change from within; "the assumption by women of executive, industrial, and cultural power has not, up to the present time, radically changed the nature of this power" which has "inhaled" women and turned them into "the pillars of the existing governments, guardians of the status quo, the most zealous protectors of the established order." Nor has the effort to outline or speak or write a "countersociety" escaped the danger of merely reiterating "in reverse ways the logic of what is supposedly being rejected." She does find, however, that a "new generation of women" is potentially moving beyond these cul de sacs and "is showing that its major social concern has become the sociosymbolic contract as a sacrificial contract." "Women's Time," trans. Alice Jardine and Harry Blake, *Signs: Journal of Women in Culture and Society* 7, no. 1 (1981): 32–33, 17, 21–27.

9. I allude here specifically to Stephen Greenblatt's seminal essay, "Improvisation and Power," in *Literature and Society* (English Institute Essays for 1978), ed. Edward Said (Baltimore: Johns Hopkins University Press, 1980), 57–99.

CHAPTER 13

Modernism and Literary Realism: Response

BRUCE ROBBINS

Both in the papers by Gillian Beer and Elizabeth Ermarth on modernism and in the papers on cultural studies to follow, there is a tendency to translate the realism debate out of the epistemological language in which it is usually formulated and into social terms, terms like "consensus," "solidarity," "community," and "the public." Most explicit in the pragmatism of Richard Rorty and Robert Scholes, this translation is implicit in Harriet Ritvo's argument that eighteenth-century taxonomy, while "establishing a natural order," served at the same time to "help define and dignify the place of both the discipline [of zoology] and its adherents in the human intellectual order." It is what Ludmilla Jordanova accomplishes in describing the museum as a site of legitimating address to "the public as a whole, [where] expertise is exhibited to the nonexpert." And it is what Simon Schaffer proposes, still more pointedly, when he suggests that "debates about the contents of nature are simultaneously debates about the standing of rival representatives." Questions about the accuracy of scientific representations are joined and, for the moment at least, displaced by questions about the social place and interests of science's representatives.

I have two responses to this displacement from the epistemological to the social. First, I think it deserves applause and encouragement. Reformulating the argument over realism as an argument over the size and shape of community seems to me an excellent way around what might otherwise appear to be a theoretical and argumentative impasse. Further, it may allow us to reconceive realism, not as a form or period that we rightly if also repeatedly put behind us, but as a continuing social project that (in some form) one might still want to sign onto. My second point, however, will be that this social reformulation also brings with it its own problems, which must be attended to.

In her admirable conciliation of scientists like Maxwell and Tyndall with aesthetic modernism, Gillian Beer several times describes their object as "phenomena beyond the customary reach of our unaided senses," and describes their project as "making visible to the imagination forces beyond the reach of sense." As a way of disturbing the strange near-consensus in literary studies today to the effect that realism is naive and self-contradictory, it should be pointed out that Gillian Beer's description reproduces almost word for word the classic (in fact, Aristotelian) case *for* realism enunciated by Georg Lukács. To depend on the senses, Lukács says, is to forfeit any chance of comprehending the dynamics of society. "The perceptual image cannot entirely comprehend motion." It is to produce that naive error Lukacs called "naturalism." The task of realism is not "the photographic imitation of reality" but to get "beyond immediate reality."[1]

Raymond Williams, in his critique of the Marxist base/superstructure model, remarks that the problem is not too little significance attributed to the superstructure, but too little attention paid to the complexity of the base.[2] Here, analogously, it is only an impoverished notion of "reality" (as the evidence of the senses) that is to blame for the caricatural notion of realism which can so easily be dismissed. Fredric Jameson, a more recent champion, keeps the project of realism alive in just this way by reinscribing it within an enriched reality—a reality that is inaccessible to the unaided senses, he says, for sociopolitical reasons. In the nineteenth century, Jameson writes, the era both of realism and of imperialism, the truth of experience "no longer coincides with the place in which it takes place. The truth of that limited daily experience of London lies, rather, in India or Jamaica or Hong Kong; it is bound up with the whole colonial system of the British Empire that determines the very quality of the individual's subjective life. Yet those structural coordinates are no longer accessible to immediate lived experience." It is this sense of realism as formed around an "absent global colonial system" that enables Jameson to see it as continuous rather than discontinuous with modernism—indeed, as something that can include the postmodern reflexivity described by Elizabeth Ermarth—and to see both as falling within a project that is not merely aesthetic but also cognitive. This project, which he calls "cognitive mapping," offers to provide verbal maps—the metaphor insists on their provisional, nonauthoritative plurality—enabling people to feel their way around a social reality assumed to be dispersed, an "(unrepresentable, imaginary) global social totality."[3]

The real gain here is not the assumption of an ultimately intelligible totality—nothing could be less self-evident—but rather the methodological principle: if cognitive difficulty inheres in the fatality of language, it also emerges from the social predicament of living in an asymmetrical and complexly interrelated political space. (As Robert Scholes puts it, "the radical otherness of the world is due to the radical otherness of its making.") Realism can then be seen as the task of mapping and remapping this space, very likely in "postmodern" literary forms rather than in the nineteenth-century narrative norm fetishized by Lukács. There is no need to assume (as Jameson's argument might suggest) that the end of social action is an ideal social transparency beyond any need for interpretative effort. On the contrary, one could justifiably feel that this mapping would *be* an action in society: the sort of "performative" that J. Hillis Miller proposes in this volume.

At the conference where Jameson presented this argument, he was asked why it seemed to be the specific task of *aesthetics* to account for totality—and not the task of, say, political economy.[4] Like Gillian Beer's bringing together of scientists and artists *as artistic modernists,* in other words on the territory of aesthetics, Jameson's argument makes a disciplinary case for literary criticism. Disciplines, which define the particular actors who perform the act of representation, are clearly a key term in the social displacement of the realism debate. For as attention turns from the representations to the representatives, disputes about meaning shift accordingly, and the inadequacy of our habitual notion of (simple, unified) disciplinary identity suddenly becomes visible.

Those of you who belong to literature departments may have asked yourselves, as I have asked myself, why it is that the construction of an argument in our discipline so often relies on using "naive realism" as a negative or scapegoat term that a given author, text, period, or genre can be shown to rise sophisticatedly and self-consciously above. The repetitiveness of this rhetorical structure ought to suggest what in any case the organizer of this conference has long argued: that "naive realism" in this sense is not realistically accurate but rather a fiction enlisted for its usefulness in generating arguments. There must be other, less simplistic ways of generating arguments than this blatant strawmanism. Why then do we persist in it? The answer, I think, is that such arguments are ritualistic reiterations of what the discipline of literary criticism takes to be its founding postulates, reenactments of its creation myth. Realism is not any old subject for criticism; it's what we have told ourselves we exist by not being. The tradition that runs from the romantics through Matthew Arnold and into the era of modern professionalization insists on defining the distinctness and autonomy of literature against a (largely unexamined) backdrop of scientific or positivistic realism. Every time a text is triumphantly shown to transcend realism, therefore, the demonstration is only partly about the text; it is also a pious exercise in disciplinary self-corroboration, a demonstration that the discipline of literary criticism is justified in its distinctness and autonomy.

My own impatience with this form of argument comes only secondarily from the fact that arguments of this form are exceedingly tedious. It comes first and foremost from my sense that the disciplinary self-understanding thus corroborated is a major if longstanding mistake. James Clifford has described how anthropology, in trying to found a new professional authority on the "scientific" ethnography, was forced to relegate "amateur" travel writing to the triviality of mere literariness. If literariness can so easily be equated with triviality—Richard Miller's example of reading *New York Times* restaurant reviews while living in Ithaca comes to mind as well—then literary criticism has only itself to blame. In trying to establish its own professional authority, it has in effect embraced the triviality end of the same opposition. Literature may be trivial, but at least it's all ours.

One would have thought that the point, for us as for anthropology, was to reject the science/literature opposition as such. To say, as we are fond of saying, that after all ethnography too is a literary form is also to say, as we are less fond of saying, that the literary is among other things a vehicle of information—mediated, imperfectly reliable, open to multiple interpretations, and so on, but a vehicle of information nonetheless. This is, after all, part of the public service that the teaching of literature actually performs in the classroom: the transmission of cultural history to students who very possibly will get *all* their history, social and political history as well as cultural history, from us, or from nobody. In its own mind, the discipline has generally stressed its professional claims, via research, to a unique identity that differentiated it from science. Neither its pedagogy nor the other ways in which, like science, it too plays a cognitive role have figured prominently in its disciplinary legitimation. But at a time when, as George Levine's report indicates, public pressure makes it urgent to "[Speak] for the Humanities," it seems stupid not to claim public credit for full services rendered.[5]

Public credit is certainly one thing the debate over realism has been about. To judge from the frequency with which one hears the term "consensus," whether joined to or substituted for realism, what we *want* out of realism may no longer be an unavailable certainty on which to ground our knowledge, or a straw man to define ourselves against, but rather common values, common purposes, community: all of them often associated with (epistemological) realism, but also separable from it. The suggestion is not just that we have to settle for a "consensus" rather than a "correspondence" theory of truth, but that maybe in this way we can actually have what we really want most out of realism.

This refocusing of desire onto the territory of society is most explicit in the talk given by Robert Scholes. "A thorough skepticism about absolute proof," Scholes says, "is sustained by a faith in the results of continuing investigation"—a faith, in other words, in "progressive knowledge building toward consensus." Among other things, this is a tiny allegory of professionalization, a story about the building of professions. And it's worth noting how very faithful a translation of realism it offers. Progressive temporality, which according to Lukács and Jameson is at the very heart of realist narrative, is now displaced to the temporality of *scholarship,* of "continuing investigation." And the notorious, much-decried "closure" of realist narrative becomes the boundedness or enclosure of the community of investigators. As the issue of knowledge becomes an issue of community, the supposed object of the realist novel—progressive temporality in a bounded social context—becomes the subject of professionalism: the ongoing professional community.

The antithetical word "professionalism," which is probably used as often to condemn as to praise, is one sign that the displacement of the realism debate from epistemology to community in no way *resolves* the debate. Community isn't necessarily any easier to delimit or achieve than certainty is. Knowledge about communities that produce knowledge is itself the product of knowledge-producing communities, and their (or our) knowledge and interests also invite continual investigation. The debate goes on, within the terms of community, over any given discipline's territory and borders, domestic and foreign adversaries. If professional "progress" is not an ever closer proximity to reality, then what is it? Ever tighter professional solidarity? Or perhaps, as Richard Rorty has suggested, the *expansion* of the professional community? After all, how "public" *is* a profession? If we are no longer to ask what realism excludes, we now have to ask whom the community of interpreters may exclude.

Here we switch, in other words, from representation in its literary sense to reprepresentation in its political sense. Within a discussion of the shift from the epistemological to the social, it needs to be said I think that these two senses of representation are historically very much entangled with one another. One specifically social reason for the theoretical suspicion of representation, at least since the 1960s, has been the sensitivity of actual, vocal constituencies (racial, ethnic, sexual, and so on), especially since the sixties, about their misrepresentation and underrepresentation in the dominant cultural discourses. But the simple refusal of representation certainly does not represent these constituencies, who are also of course demanding representation at the same time.

All of this is the context for Robert Scholes's answer to Jonathan Culler's list of those excluded from the pragmatist "consensus":

"women, children, poets, prophets, madmen." In effect, what Scholes does is point to an incoherence in deconstructive rhetorical practice: behind deconstruction's supposed refusal of representation, or at any rate its purist extremity of representative suspicion, he correctly exposes a rhetoric of representation, an appeal to the oppressed, the suffering, the marginalized that marshals their collective moral weight on behalf of interests it claims to share with them.

I agree entirely. Appeals like this one have I think helped deconstruction make a public case for its legitimacy, if only a covert one. Where I don't agree is with the implication that this is a *criticism* of deconstruction—that there is something unseemly or frankly unethical about such appeals, even when they drag the oppressed and marginalized into the argument for moral support, or by the same token that pragmatism itself can afford to spurn the rhetoric of political representation.

In any case, the need for disciplines to legitimate themselves would make nonrepresentation an impossibility. No professional community, however self-enclosed, can do without public representation to its "outside," and representation of this sort is precisely what I take Scholes himself to be doing, rather successfully, when he insists on a model of shared reasonableness as opposed to deconstructive esotericism. As a displacement of the debate (that keeps the debate alive), this argues in effect that the interests of our profession are better served if we buy into a discursive mode that will bring us into communication with more folks rather than a mode that will make us appear to the public more distinctive but also more isolated. The issue is not between representation and nonrepresentation, in other words, but between differing representations.

By way of conclusion, I would like to dissociate myself, briefly and schematically, from the purist horror of representation that Scholes and Culler, and indeed our discipline itself, seem to share. It's not just that the reductio ad absurdum offers us a world in which no one would be empowered to represent anyone but him- or herself; it's not just that insistence on the absolute singularity, uniqueness, incommensurability of given groups or cultures reinscribes the privileges of the literary, *the* place of the particular which is not to be sullied by the common touch of public concepts. The crucial point is the restriction of community, the political isolationism, that is the other side of its piety. In lieu of fuller argument, I offer a few words in defense of representation from S. P. Mohanty:

> To believe that you have your space and I mine; to believe, further, that there can be no responsible way in which I can adjudicate between your space . . . and mine by developing a set of general criteria which would have interpretive validity in both contexts . . .—to believe both these things is also to assert something quite large. Quite simply, it is to assert that *all spaces are equivalent:* that they have

equal value, that since the lowest common principle of evaluation is all that I can invoke, I cannot—and consequently need not—think about how your space impinges on mine, or how my history is defined together with yours. If that is the case, I may have started by declaring a pious political wish, but I end by denying that I have to take you seriously. Plurality instead of a single homogeneous space, yes. But also, unfortunately, debilitatingly insular spaces. . . . To the extent that our initial interest in relativism was motivated by a political respect for other selves, other spaces, other contexts, relativism seems now to be an unacceptable theoretical position. For it might encourage a greater sensitivity to the context of production of cultural ideas, but it will not, given the terms of its formulation, enable what Talal Asad calls for—a "genuine dialogue" between anthropologist and native, the ex-colonizer and the ex-colonized.[6]

Talk of "consensus" can make us feel very much at home in our world. But it is a very big world; we remember how big if we translate Borges' "Orbis Tertius," quoted by Scholes and Ermarth, back into the phrase "Third World"—a sort of return of consensus' repressed. If the project of realism can be conceived as the project of community building in this shared but very unequally shared space, then there's still plenty for it to do.

NOTES

1. Georg Lukács, "Art and Objective Truth," *Writer and Critic,* ed. and trans. Arthur D. Kahn (New York: Grosset and Dunlap, 1971).
2. Raymond Williams, *Marxism and Literature* (Oxford: Oxford University Press, 1977), 75–82.
3. Fredric Jameson, "Cognitive Mapping," in Cary Nelson and Lawrence Grossberg, eds., *Marxism and the Interpretation of Culture* (Urbana: University of Illinois Press, 1987), 356.
4. The questioner is Nancy Fraser. In Nelson and Grossberg, *Marxism,* 358.
5. George Levine et al., *Speaking for the Humanities* (New York: American Council of Learned Societies, 1989). Occasional Paper, no. 7.
6. S. P. Mohanty, "Us and Them: On the Philosophical Bases of Political Criticism," *Yale Journal of Criticism* 2, no. 2 (Spring 1989): 1–31.

Part 5

Science in Culture: Representations

CHAPTER 14

Zoological Taxonomy and Real Life

HARRIET RITVO

It was a truth almost universally acknowledged by British naturalists of the eighteenth and early nineteenth centuries that taxonomy had provided the foundation of their discipline and continued to shape its development. "Without a systematic classification," according to William Turton, the editor of one of the many versions of Linnaeus published in England during that period, the student of zoology "wanders in obscurity and uncertainty, and must collect the whole of its habits and peculiarities, before he can ascertain the individual he is examining."[1] Writing a generation earlier and for a somewhat broader audience, Richard Brookes made a more sweeping claim. "Although the multitude of Nature's productions . . . seems at first to bewilder," he reassured his audience that armed with a properly systematic understanding, "the mind by degrees . . . finds nature in almost every instance acting with her usual simplicity."[2] And this utility extended beyond the animal kingdom. Besides establishing a natural order, a well-conceived zoological system could help define and dignify the place of both the discipline and its adherents in the human intellectual order. Benjamin Stillingfleet, another interpreter of Linnaeus, made the ability to give a plant or animal "its true name according to some system" a kind of sine qua non, observing sternly that "he who cannot go thus far . . . does not deserve the name of a naturalist."[3] Many of his fellow naturalists viewed the disciplinary stakes as higher than merely the exclusion of the unprepared. Without system, they feared, natural history would be "but a confused, undisciplined crowd of subjects" and naturalists "mere collectors of curiosities and superficial trifles . . ., objects of ridicule rather than respect."[4]

That is to say, Enlightenment naturalists identified classification as the boundary between their own scholarly pursuits and what they viewed as the benighted and muddled efforts of their predecessors. And they made this boundary quite difficult to cross, both temporally and methodologically; taxonomy itself became a characteristic of the highest taxonomical significance. Thus, for example, most English systematizers considered themselves the intellectual descendants of John Ray, who published systematic catalogues of both plants and animals in the late seventeenth century, but they viewed Ray as a prodigy without immediate intellectual ancestors. The standard praise of Ray emphasized the discontinuity that separated his work from well-known Renaissance and classical compilations on related topics, placing equal emphasis on Ray's virtues and the defects of the competition. As Thomas Pennant put it, "so correct was his genius, that we view a systematic arrangement arise even from the Chaos of *Aldrovandus* and *Gesner*."[5] Brookes, who considered "no systematical writer has been more happy than he [Ray]," dismissed the writings of Aldrovandus as "insupportably tedious and disgusting" and those of Gesner as "so incomplete as scarce to deserve mentioning" (1:x–xi).

The initial enthusiasm for classification moderated during the first decades of the nineteenth century, and by 1834 William Jardine, the editor of *The Naturalist's Library,* an extensive and successful series that launched an era of sophisticated zoological popularization, could proclaim that "the age of superstitious reverence for categories . . . has long passed away."[6] Nevertheless, the pioneer taxonomists continued to occupy prominent positions in the zoological pantheon enshrined by Jardine and his collaborators, and the sudden emergence of systematic taxonomy continued to symbolize the reincarnation of natural history as a scientific study. The sketches of distinguished zoologists (many distinguished primarily for their contributions to classification) that began each volume of *The Naturalist's Library* echoed the judgments and preoccupations of the eighteenth century. Thus, again, Gesner's subdivisions were "altogether arbitrary and useless"; Pliny's "most obvious defect is the want of any thing like system"; in general, "with the exception of Aristotle, neither the philosophers of antiquity, nor those . . . succeeding the revival of learning" studied nature with "that accuracy of observation and reference to organic structure, so necessary for . . . determining . . . the classes, orders, genera, and species."[7] Although Aristotle's well-developed interest in animal classification (as well as his extrazoological reputation) exempted him from this wide-ranging and contemptuous dismissal, eighteenth- and nineteenth-century naturalists took care to stress the uniqueness of his position. Most acknowledgments of Aristotle's anachronistic insight were constrained by the observations that he had been largely ignored and that little scientific progress had occurred between his time and the beginning of the modern taxonomical era.[8]

Figure 14.1. An imposing portrait of John Ray, the frontispiece of James Duncan's volume on beetles in *The Naturalist's Library*. Although nineteenth-century taxonomists had largely discarded the practices of their Enlightenment predecessors, they continued to invoke their heroic presence. By permission of the Houghton Library, Harvard University.

Embodied in this simultaneous celebration of Enlightenment achievements and disparagement of the past was a radical redefinition of the enterprise of natural history. This redefinition was based on two related claims. The first, that systematic taxonomy was entirely new, relocated an ancient and highly traditional study within the emerging network of rational science. The second, that the simple existence of a formal system was more important than the relative merits of particular modes of classifying (although there was also plenty of argument between patrons of rival systems), subordinated the empirical to the abstract, the content to the form. Both the claims and the redefinition have generally been accepted by subsequent commentators, whatever their assessment of the systems themselves or of their social or intellectual consequences; this story of heroic innovation has come to constitute one of the founding myths of modern biology. For example, in the succeeding period, increasing attention to comparative anatomy inspired many taxonomists (and other biologists) to disparage the particular systems constructed by their predecessors as artificial or based on inappropriately chosen characteristics. Thus, George Shaw, a Linnaean of such enthusiastic orthodoxy that he threatened to destroy specimens of species not listed in the twelfth edition of the *Systema Naturae,* controlled the classification of the British Museum's natural history collections until his death in 1813; but as soon afterward as decently possible his assistants switched to a new system based on Cuvierian anatomical principles.[9] Nevertheless, even as they jettisoned eighteenth-century categories, such revisionists continued to respect the trailblazing of their predecessors. Thus, in the midst of a distinctively mid-nineteenth-century taxonomical debate[10] a combatant could stop to acknowledge that "it is but in times comparatively modern that this branch of knowledge can be said to have risen to sufficient rank to be looked upon as a science at all."[11]

Modern interpreters with widely differing scholarly preoccupations have echoed the traditional zoological consensus. The eighteenth century was "the great age of classification," a time when "Natural History was . . . above all . . . a set of rules for arranging statements in series, an obligatory set of schemata of dependence, or order, and of succession."[12] The systems so constituted embodied "a novel way of looking at things, . . . which was more detached, more objective, less man-centered than that of the past"; they were distinctive, path-breaking, and significant.[13] Nor did the fact that they were ultimately superseded or modified by taxonomies that could be characterized, depending on the inclinations of the analyst, as more historical, more anatomical, or more natural compromise their privileged historical position.[14] Instead, in some Whiggish versions of the history of biology, the introduction of systematic taxonomy has been viewed as the opening battle in a protracted triumph of human intelligence over nature, and, within the human realm, of science over superstition.[15]

The enduring appeal of this Promethean version of the origin of taxonomy has rested on more concrete foundations than the desire of naturalists to enhance their own intellectual stature and that of their discipline. Its strongest corroboration has been provided by the voluminous literature of natural history. The contrast between the orderly catalogues of the Enlightenment and the chaotic miscellanies of the preceding ages was both striking and ubiquitous; it was obvious even if unsophisticated zoological primers written for eighteenth-century children were compared with the most elaborate Renaissance productions. For example, Edward Topsell's massive *History of Four-Footed Beastes,* which was published in 1607, purported to offer information that was complete, accurate, and up-to-date. But despite the fact that its entries included a good deal of relatively fresh material—Conrad Gesner, the sixteenth-century Swiss scholar whose yet more massive work Topsell condensed, had even commissioned correspondents to provide him with new observations on so familiar a creature as the dog—it clearly belonged to the bestiary tradition that stretched back through the middle ages to antiquity.[16] That is, it was distinguished by both plenitude of detail and paucity of organization; no readily apparent principle determined the order of the entries for different animals or, within the entries, what material should be included—or even what constituted fact. The long entry on the domestic cat began with the role of cats in ancient Egyptian society, then went on to discuss, among other things, which kinds of cats were best, their eyesight, their hunting methods and favorite prey, their capacity to love and hate, the diseases they suffered, the diseases they caused, and the diseases they could cure or alleviate (for example, the fat of a cat might be efficacious against gout), all with reference to such classical authorities as Pliny and Galen.[17] The entry on unicorns was longer, just as detailed, and derived from equally authoritative sources (711–21). Altogether, this massive work seemed like a jumble, a promiscuous mix of ancient wisdom and modern observation, which implicitly defined people as passive receivers of random information about the natural world.[18]

Even the superficial appearance of eighteenth-century natural histories was calculated to produce a very different impression. Most authors prefaced their work with both verbal and visual proclamations of their concern with order. The minimum was an alphabetical table of contents, such as Thomas Bewick used in his very popular but not particularly learned *A General History of Quadrupeds.* Bewick rather apologetically characterized the table as "our disregard of system," even though it did not represent the organization of his entries, which, like those of many naturalists influenced by Buffon, reflected a loose notion of kinds.[19] More serious audiences were offered more elaborate representations. In his *British Zoology,* Thomas Pennant followed his prefatory (and anti-Linnaean) announcement that "we shall, to avoid the perplexity, arising from forming a new system, adopt . . . that of the inestimable *Ray*" with a genus-by-genus schema of quadrupeds,

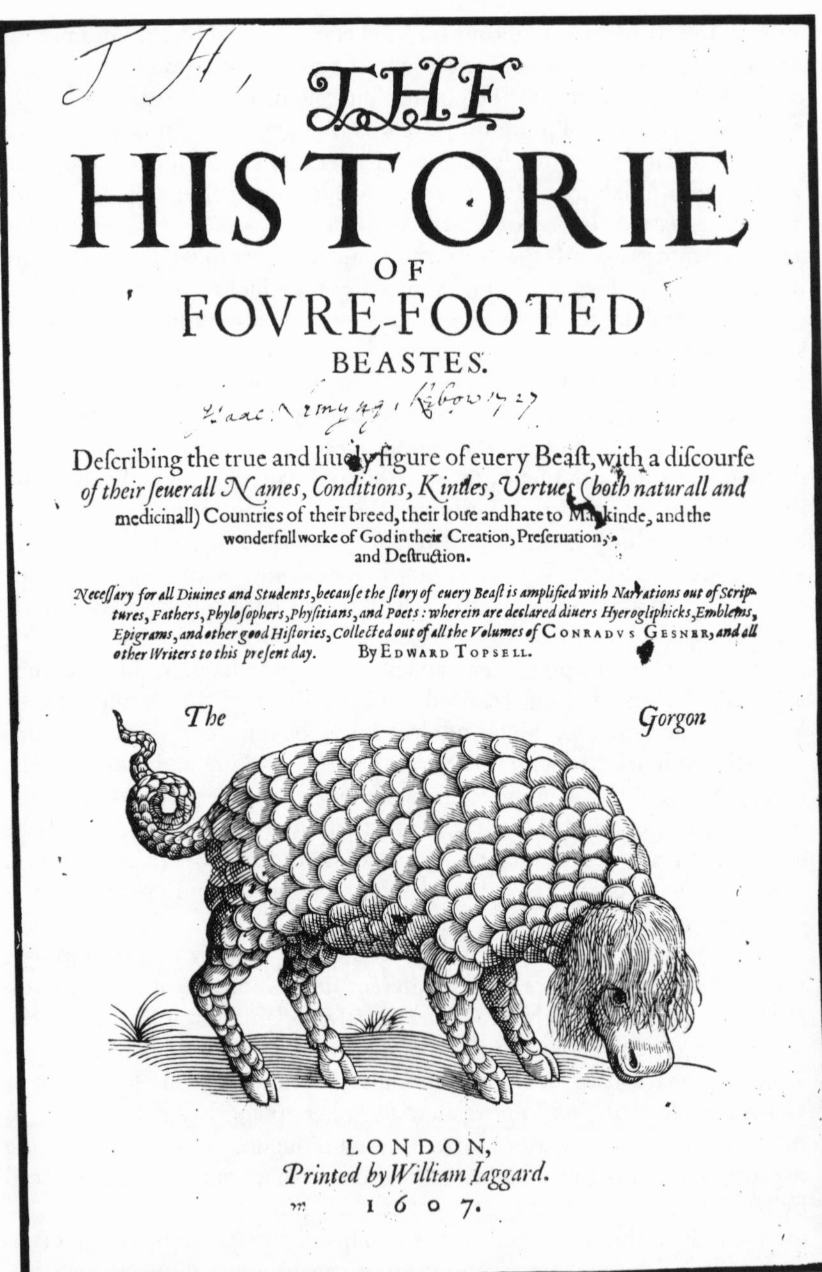

THE

HISTORIE

OF

FOVRE-FOOTED

BEASTES.

Deſcribing the true and liuely figure of euery Beaſt, with a diſcourſe *of their ſeuerall Names, Conditions, Kindes, Vertues (both naturall and* medicinall) Countries of their breed, their loue and hate to Mankinde, and the wonderfull worke of God in their Creation, Preſeruation, and Deſtruction.

Neceſſary for all Diuines and Students, becauſe the ſtory of euery Beaſt is amplified with Narrations out of Scriptures, Fathers, Phyloſophers, Phyſitians, and Poets: wherein are declared diuers Hyeroglyphicks, Emblems, Epigrams, and other good Hiſtories, Collected out of all the Volumes of CONRADVS GESNER, *and all other Writers to this preſent day.* By EDWARD TOPSELL.

LONDON,

Printed by William Iaggard.

1607.

Figure 14.2. The title page of Topsell's *Historie of Foure-Footed Beastes,* which shows its debt to the bestiary tradition. By permission of the Houghton Library, Harvard University.

based primarily on the conformation of their feet.[20] John Church straddled the fence in *A Cabinet of Quadrupeds,* confessing that the "systematic arrangement . . . of Mr. Pennant . . . takes the lead; but for the use of those who may prefer the Linnaean arrangement, it has been added"; following the preface, both systems were displayed in tabular form.[21] The rage for order could even influence adherents of Buffon, who had resisted the introduction of scientific taxonomy both by precept and by example; one of his late-eighteenth-century translators noted with embarrassment that Buffon's "strictures upon the writings of Sir Charles Linnaeus . . . could not be inserted with any degree of propriety," and then, "as the Count de Buffon has observed no systematic order in his History of Quadrupeds," sneaked in a table in which Buffon's genera were laid out against those of Pennant.[22]

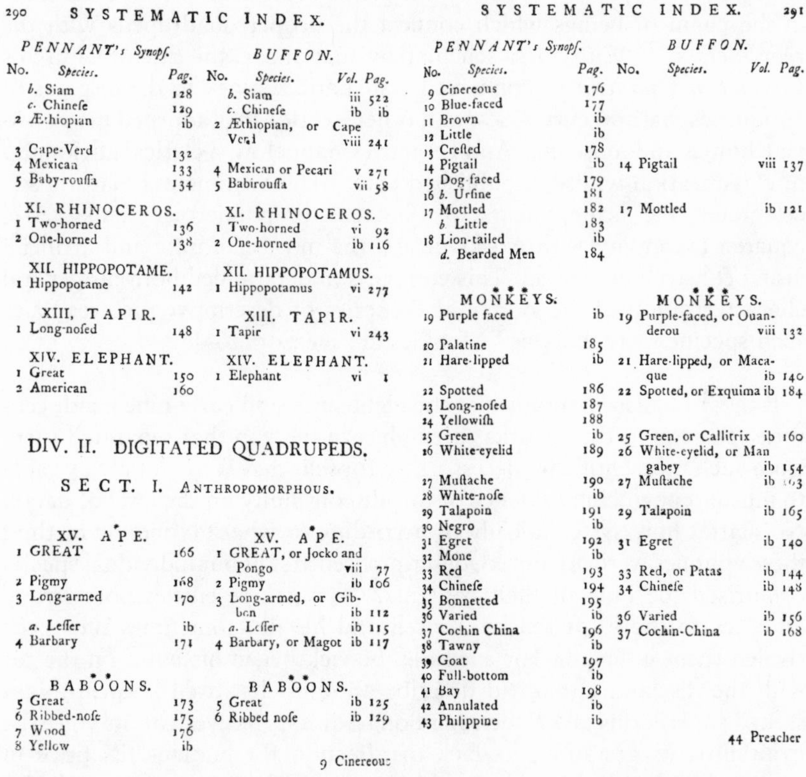

290 SYSTEMATIC INDEX.

PENNANT's Synopſ.			*BUFFON.*			
No.	*Species.*	*Pag.*	No.	*Species.*	*Vol.*	*Pag.*
	b. Siam	128		*b.* Siam	iii	522
	c. Chineſe	129		*c.* Chineſe	ib	ib
2	Æthiopian	ib	2	Æthiopian, or Cape Verd	viii	241
3	Cape-Verd	132				
4	Mexican	133	4	Mexican or Pecari	v	271
5	Baby-rouſſa	134	5	Babirouſſa	vii	58
	XI. RHINOCEROS.			XI. RHINOCEROS.		
1	Two-horned	136	1	Two-horned	vi	92
2	One-horned	138	2	One-horned	ib	116
	XII. HIPPOPOTAME.			XII. HIPPOPOTAMUS.		
1	Hippopotame	142	1	Hippopotamus	vi	277
	XIII, TAPIR.			XIII. TAPIR.		
1	Long-noſed	148	1	Tapir	vi	243
	XIV. ELEPHANT.			XIV. ELEPHANT.		
1	Great	150	1	Elephant	vi	1
2	American	160				

DIV. II. DIGITATED QUADRUPEDS.

SECT. I. ANTHROPOMORPHOUS.

No.	*Species.*	*Pag.*	No.	*Species.*	*Vol.*	*Pag.*
	XV. APE.			XV. APE.		
1	GREAT	166	1	GREAT, or Jocko and Pongo	viii	77
2	Pigmy	168	2	Pigmy	ib	106
3	Long-armed	170	3	Long-armed, or Gibbon	ib	112
	a. Leſſer	ib		*a.* Leſſer	ib	115
4	Barbary	171	4	Barbary, or Magot	ib	117
	BABOONS.			BABOONS.		
5	Great	173	5	Great	ib	125
6	Ribbed-noſe	175	6	Ribbed noſe	ib	129
7	Wood	176				
8	Yellow	ib				

9 Cinereous

SYSTEMATIC INDEX. 291

PENNANT's Synopſ.			*BUFFON.*			
No.	*Species.*	*Pag.*	No.	*Species.*	*Vol.*	*Pag.*
9	Cinereous	176				
10	Blue-faced	177				
11	Brown	ib				
12	Little	ib				
13	Creſted	178				
14	Pigtail	ib	14	Pigtail	viii	137
15	Dog-faced	179				
16	*b.* Urſine	181				
17	Mottled	182	17	Mottled	ib	121
	b Little	183				
18	Lion-tailed	ib				
	d. Bearded Men	184				
	MONKEYS.			MONKEYS.		
19	Purple faced	ib	19	Purple-faced, or Ouanderou	viii	132
20	Palatine	185				
21	Hare-lipped	ib	21	Hare-lipped, or Macaque	ib	140
22	Spotted	186	22	Spotted, or Exquima	ib	184
23	Long-noſed	187				
24	Yellowiſh	188				
25	Green	ib	25	Green, or Callitrix	ib	160
26	White-eyelid	189	26	White-eyelid, or Mangabey	ib	154
27	Muſtache	190	27	Muſtache	ib	163
28	White-noſe	ib				
29	Talapoin	191	29	Talapoin	ib	165
30	Negro	ib				
31	Egret	192	31	Egret	ib	140
32	Mone	ib				
33	Red	193	33	Red, or Patas	ib	144
34	Chineſe	194	34	Chineſe	ib	148
35	Bonnetted	195				
36	Varied	ib	36	Varied	ib	156
37	Cochin China	196	37	Cochin-China	ib	168
38	Tawny	ib				
39	Goat	197				
40	Full-bottom	ib				
41	Bay	198				
42	Annulated	ib				
43	Philippine	ib				

44 Preacher

Figure 14.3. An anonymous translator of Buffon apologetically introduced this systematic index in his version of the *Natural History.* By permission of the Houghton Library, Harvard University.

The metaphors with which taxonomists characterized the relationships between the elements that constituted their systems also stressed orderly visual display. John Ray's eighteenth-century biographer characterized his system of classification as a series of framed "tables."[23] English versions of Buffon included references to quadrupeds as a polygonous group, as well as to "the circle of natural beings" and the "scale" of nature.[24] The image of nature as a chain recurred frequently, determining many references to individual species as links between other kinds of animals. Thus the "Mouflon . . . may be considered as . . . forming the link" between sheep and goats (Bewick, *General History* 74), as, on increasingly abstract taxonomic levels, "the Hunting Leopard [cheetah] forms a sort of connecting link" between cats and dogs,[25] the swine genus "may . . . form . . . a link between the cloven-footed, the whole-footed, and the digitated quadrupeds,"[26] and the scaly manises (pangolins) "approach so nearly the genus of Lizards, as to be the links in the chain of beings which connect the proper quadrupeds with the reptile class."[27] With a less schematic visual image, the title of Church's *Cabinet of Quadrupeds* connected systematic zoology to the displays of antiquities, natural curiosities, and other exotica that adorned many private homes and museums. And Leonard Chappelow, a clerical aficionado of classification whose unpublished epic, "The Sentimental Naturalist," celebrated the achievements of Linnaeus in ponderous blank verse, equated taxonomy with works of art, the most elaborate and artificial visual constructions of all. This comparison determined both his general characterization of the system as "a series of descriptive pictures" and such specific metaphors as "Monkies are mezzotintos."[28]

If most English naturalists of the eighteenth and early nineteenth centuries structured their works to emphasize the gap that separated them from such unscientific predecessors as Topsell, they were not always able to muster convincing evidence of this discontinuity on the level of detail. No matter how systematically or according to what taxonomic method these volumes were organized, descriptive entries about individual species comprised the bulk of their contents. Often, these entries bore strong affinities to those offered by Topsell and his ilk; sometimes they even rivaled them in length. For example, Bewick began his entry on the cat with the disclaimer that "to describe an animal so well known, might seem a superfluous task," then went on to discuss its eyesight, its voice, its irritability, its gestation, its lack of affection for humans, its price in medieval Wales, and its relationship to Dick Whittington (*General History* 231–34). Addressing a less popular audience, Pennant noted, among other things, that wild and domestic cats came from the same stock, that Angora cats degenerated in England but were adorned with silver collars in China, that tortoiseshells were black, white, and orange, that cats purred when pleased and washed their faces at the approach of a storm, and that although many people hated them they were much loved by the "Mahometans" (Pennant, *History* 1:295–97).

Nor, when they were worked out in detail, did the systems themselves unambiguously support the assertion that they represented a new departure in the study of animals. Often, on the contrary, they reflected competing, if unacknowledged, principles of organization that seemed to undermine both their schematic novelty and their implicit claim to be based on objective scientific analysis of the natural world. (This claim was readily apparent in systems derived from the work of Ray or Linnaeus, which used categories based on such physical structures as feet and teeth. And even the kinds into which followers of the unsystematic Buffon tended to divide their creatures—the horse kind, the deer kind, the hog kind, the cat kind, the weasel kind, the otter kind, the ape kind, and so forth—embodied it in attenuated form.[29]) These competing principles usually divided animals into groups based not on their physical characteristics but on subjective perceptions of them. An ancient category like "vermin," long used by hunters and farmers to describe noxious animals—animals "necessary to be hunted," as one seventeenth-century manual of venery put it—survived in the taxonomy of Ray and Pennant only superficially transfigured by the claim that it alluded to the wormlike forms of the weasels, martens, and polecats most frequently so castigated.[30] Thus, rather than analyzing nature exclusively on its own terms—the claim embodied in their formal systems—naturalists often implicitly presented it in terms of its relationship to people, echoing the kind of anthropocentric and sentimental projection characteristic of the bestiary tradition they had so emphatically discarded and (then as now) of much nonscientific discourse about animals.

Richard Brookes introduced one of the most powerful and highly constructed sets of subjective categories in *The Natural History of Quadrupeds*. He proclaimed himself a follower of Ray, and therefore, like most naturalists in this camp, he used a range of physical characteristics to group mammals, with foot conformation preeminent (*Natural History* 1:xi). This method yielded the following order: horses (undivided hoofs); ruminants (cloven hoofs); the hippopotamus, elephant, and others (anomalous hoofs); camels; monkeys (the first of the animals without hoofs); humans; cats; dogs; weasels; hares; the hedgehog, armadillo, and mole (divided feet and long snouts); bats; and, finally, sloths. Yet he also asserted, and in the synoptic introduction where his methodological consciousness might be presumed to be highest, that "the most obvious and simple division . . . of Quadrupedes, is into the Domestic and Savage" (1:xxvi). Obvious though it might be, however, this division implied a taxonomic structure that cut across the formal organization established in Brookes's synoptic summary (unless, perhaps, that summary was taken to represent a progression from familiar to exotic animals, rather than an analysis of mammals based on feet).

Brookes was not the only naturalist to address this dichotomy, nor was such an address inevitably subversive of manifest systems. The differences, for example, between wild animals and the domesticated creatures that most closely resembled them fit easily into routine subgeneric analysis. Thus the uncompromisingly Linnaean George Shaw defined the "common ox" as "the Bison reduced to a domestic state, in which . . . it runs into . . . many varieties . . . differing widely in size, form, and colour."[31] Observed over the range of domestic species, however, such characteristics invited generalization, and these generalizations might lead to the formation of categories more difficult to assimilate into a taxonomy based on the principles of Linnaeus, Ray, or even Buffon. Thus it was commonplace to notice that, as one retailer of Buffon put it, "domestic animals in very few respects resemble wild ones; their nature, their size, and their form are less constant . . . especially in the exterior parts of the body (*Barr's Buffon* 7:24). Related, if less firmly anchored in objective observation, was the assertion that "all Animals, except ourselves . . . are strangers to pain and sickness. . . . We speak of wild animals only. Those that are tame . . . partake of our miseries."[32]

And often, like Brookes, zoological writers treated the distinction between wild and domestic animals as primary rather than contingent, the basis for taxonomic discrimination rather than the occasion for description and explanation. Thus William Swainson defined domestication not as a human accomplishment, but as an innate, divinely inculcated propensity "to submit . . . cheerfully and willingly." In consequence, it had systematic significance, cropping up in "every instance among the more perfect animals [of] the rasorial type."[33] Many naturalists used domestic animals as taxonomic models, typically claiming that "each class of quadrupeds may be ranged under some one of the domestic kinds"; thus domestic animals both exemplified and limited the range of mammalian possibilities (Goldsmith, *History* 2:302). (That Oliver Goldsmith, among others, made this assertion even though the resulting system left many animals—elephants, hippopotamuses, giraffes, camels, bears, tapirs, badgers, and sloths, to name a few—uncategorized illustrated the appeal of a classification based on domestication.) The categories of wild and domestic might be perceived as so disparate that they required a connecting link; thus, "as the cat may be said to be only half domestic; he forms the shade between the real wild and real domestic animals" (*Barr's Buffon* 6:13).

The dichotomy between wild and domestic animals was equally influential at lower taxonomic levels. William Jardine offered separate entries on the reindeer of North America and those of Eurasia, not because he doubted that they belonged to a single species (although, as an afterthought, he suggested that "they present different varieties in the different countries . . . which may ultimately lead to a distinction of the species"), but because "in the one he is hunted in a state of nature, while in the other the greater proportion of the race is under the guidance and protection of man."[34] Similarly privileging relationship to humanity over physical characteristics, he revised a colleague's placement of the "subgenus *Taurus* [that containing domestic cattle] last in the series of Bovine Animals. We have treated it first, as containing animals of the most importance."[35] Another indication of the taxonomic significance of domestication was that animals perceived to differ only in this attribute—that is, animals that were anatomically similar and that were believed to interbreed—were frequently placed in separate species. Thus, although Pennant, along with many others, identified the European

Figure 14.4. In Thomas Bewick's engraving of a Chillingham wild bull, pose and background combine to emphasize the animal's distinction from ordinary cattle.

wild cat as the "stock and origin" of the domestic cat, one was *Felis sylvestris* and the other was *Felis catus* (*History* 1:295). Analogously, he referred to what were known as the wild cattle of Chillingham, an unruly strain of white animals preserved in the parks of several great houses, mostly for decoration or hunting rather than for the dairy or the slaughterhouse, as *Bisontes scotici,* putting them into a separate genus or subgenus from the *Bos taurus* that grazed on ordinary British pastures (1:16–17). Indeed the fact of domestication appeared so important to some naturalists that they tended to accord breeds of domestic animals the same taxonomical status as species of wild animals, despite the fact that variability within species was widely recognized as one of the most frequent results of domestication. Bewick presented "The Arabian Horse," "The Race-Horse," "The Hunter," "The Black Horse," and "The Common Cart Horse" in separate entries analogous to those devoted to "The Ass" and "The Zebra" (*General History* 1–23). Following Linnaeus, Shaw tagged many dog breeds with Latinate binomials that at least sounded like the names of species—for example, the hound was *Canis sagax,* the shepherd's dog was *Canis domesticus,* and the Pomeranian was *Canis pomeranus* (*General Zoology* I (1):277–80). And if divisions based on the dichotomy between wild and domestic animals came into explicit conflict with divisions based on the principles of systematic taxonomy, sometimes it was the latter that gave way. Thus, when Edward Bennett admitted that "it would . . . appear . . . impossible to offer" a physical description of the domestic dog that would distinguish it from the wolf and other wild canines, he did not conclude that they should all be considered a single species. Instead, to reify the division based on domestication, he introduced a new and circular criterion: "it is to the moral and intellectual qualities of the dog that we must look for those remarkable peculiarities which distinguish him" (*Tower Menagerie* 85–86).

Thus, if the fact or form of systematic taxonomy helped to place natural history in the mainstream of Enlightenment science, its detailed elaboration could compromise that position. As they resurrected traditional modes of analysis and undermined systematic categories, alternative principles of classification also challenged more fundamental taxonomic claims to intellectual comprehensiveness. Any scientific system, whether natural or artificial, was necessarily universal: flexible enough in its structure to provide an appropriate location for any animal, but sufficiently rigid in its organizing principles to exclude anything that did not belong. Nature, abetted by the efforts of Enlightenment explorers, made it difficult for systematizers to live up to these standards. Part of the problem was simply quantitative. In the half century between Ray and Linnaeus, the number of known kinds of mammals doubled from one hundred fifty to approximately three hundred, and naturalists could feel oppressed by the pace as well as the volume of discovery.[36] For example, in terms echoed by many of his colleagues, Brookes apologized to his readers for the fact that "as this is a science that continually improves, new matter arises even during the short period between printing and publication" (*Natural History* 1:xvi).

In principle, the difficulties produced by the profusion of nature could be overcome by assiduous application. Its variety however, might raise more intransigent problems, as William Frederic Martyn, a naturalist who disparaged system, suggested by contrasting "the ineffectual attempts of the profoundest scholars . . . on the scale of systematic arrangement" and "the sublime disorder of Nature . . . too prolific to enumerate or arrange."[37] He underscored his radical dissatisfaction with taxonomy by arranging his own zoological survey as a dictionary, structured only by the arbitrary order of the alphabet; perhaps as a culminating gesture of resistance, his volumes lacked pagination as well as taxonomic organization. But Martyn's rejection of system was less radical than his opening declaration and his alphabetical arrangement suggested. The entry for "Animal" included appreciative summaries of the work of Ray, Klein, Brisson, and Linnaeus; that for "Quadrupeds" referred approvingly to Pennant's division of them into "digitated, hoofed, pinnated, and winged." He defined many terms drawn from systematic nomenclature, such as "Agriae" ("an order of quadrupeds destitute of teeth, but furnished with long cylindrical tongues") and "Glis" ("in a limited sense . . . only . . . the dormouse; but according to Linnaeus, the Glires constitute the fourth order of the mammalia").

Thus Martyn was protesting not at the attempts of naturalists to group species, whether to discern their natural affinities or simply for efficient reference, but at the necessity, imposed by systematic theory, to unite all these groups in a single pattern. (A fellow dictionarist, the anonymous compiler of *A Dictionary of Natural History,* was more intransigent, claiming that "concerning the futility of systems in this part of literature, every person conversant herewith must be satisfied."[38]) Perhaps the character of the dominant structure, or structural metaphor, exacerbated Martyn's sense that such a pattern impoverished and misrepresented the phenomena it claimed to describe. The chain of being, embodied in the ubiquitous rhetoric of links and connections, was an insistently linear image, implying a single series that extended from one end of the animal kingdom to the other. And although he was among the most vigorous protesters, Martyn was not the only naturalist to acknowledge its constricting tyranny; even in the usage of admirers of system, its metaphoric overtones could easily slip from connection to confinement. Pennant noted with regret that "Buffon seems to think it beneath him to shackle his lively spirit with systematic arrangement" (*History* 1:vi); in arranging his *Natural History of Cornwall,* William Borlase warned that although "order, connexion, rank, and relation must be strictly observed," nevertheless "there must be no shackles" (*Natural History* viii).

To some extent the tension between the systematic metaphor of the chain and the disorderly variety of nature indicated an ongoing change in paradigm, as a result of which the linear image was supplanted by the more complex bush or tree. But it also demonstrated the continuing influence of pre-Enlightenment and nonscientific categories, which encouraged even the most disciplined systematizers to identify connections that undermined the notion of a linear order of life. That is, when taxonomists described the connections between specific animals and groups of animals, they did not always apply the same criteria they had announced in their prefatory systematic synopses, nor did these lower-level linkages necessarily reflect the prescribed structural design. For example, the metaphor of the chain implied that mammals or quadrupeds, universally acknowledged to head the zoological chain, would be connected to lower animals by a single intermediary group. But systematists frequently offered inconsistent testimony as to the identity, and even the unity, of that group. They were apt to suggest multiple links between mammals and other vertebrates, and to locate those links in mammalian groups that were liminal or problematic not in scientific terms, but in terms of ordinary language and folk classification.[39]

Thus Church began his description of the bat by noting that it "seems to form a connecting link in the great chain of nature, between the Quadrupeds and the winged inhabitants of the air," even though, as was widely recognized by naturalists, "it is evidently related to the four-footed tribe, both by its internal and external formation" (*Cabinet* 2:n.p.); in his more poetic vein, Chappelow characterized bats as "an uncouth, plumeless race of beastly birds" ("Sentimental Naturalist" 100). And one such connection did not necessarily preempt others. While Bewick agreed that the bat "seems to possess a middle nature between four-footed animals and birds," he also asserted that the walrus, which seemed "to partake greatly of the nature of fishes . . . may be considered as the last step in the scale of Nature, by which we are conducted from one great division of the animal world to the other" (*General History* 506, 513). He probably gave this mediating role to the walrus because he considered whales and dolphins, which did not appear in his *General History of Quadrupeds,* to be incontestably fish, even though, as with bats, the consensus of naturalists was that "their whole internal structure resembles that of other Mammalia" (Shaw, *General Zoology* II (2):471). (Bewick's treatment of cetaceans was not confined to popular writers; Pennant made the same omission in his *History of Quadrupeds,* and another serious naturalist, John Reinhold Forster, explicitly classified the cetaceans as fish in his *Catalogue of the Animals of North America.*)[40]

Although systematizers thus accommodated distinctions based on such traditional environmental attributes—"the fish of the sea" and "the fowl of the air" in the taxonomy of Genesis—with apparent ease, they had more trouble dealing with genuinely liminal creatures, that is, creatures whose anomalies were not part of conventional beast lore. In the 1790s naturalists became aware of the echidna and the platypus, egg-laying mammals that might have seemed created to confirm the theory embedded in the chain metaphor.[41] Bewick responded to the platypus, the more spectacular of the two, with confusion, characterizing it as "an animal *sui generis;* it appears to possess a three fold nature, that of a fish, a bird, and a quadruped, and is related to nothing we have hitherto seen." He declined not only to classify it, but even to name it, referring to it only as "an amphibious animal" (*General History* 523, 526). Shaw responded to it with suspicion, wondering whether "some arts of deception" might have been practiced on the first specimen he saw; after he was reassured, he nevertheless described it as having "the beak of a Duck engrafted on the head of a quadruped."[42] Once the initial shock had dissipated, zoologists accepted the platypus on more or less its own anatomical terms, even though, as Swainson noted, one of their most striking features, the cloaca, was "highly curious, but not well adapted for popular details" (*Natural History* 219). They placed it "at the termination of the set of links, which led from man downwards" (Smith, *Mammalia* 80), where it could be either analogous "to the Class of Birds"[43] or evincing "a considerable approach towards the class Reptilia."[44]

Creatures of myth sometimes fared better than such startling new discoveries—the plausible impossible, as often in nonscientific discourse, preferred to the possible implausible. For example, the zoological literature of the eighteenth and early nineteenth centuries contained many references to mermaids, unicorns, and sea serpents, even though the credulity of classical and Renaissance bestiarists with regard to such improbabilities was part of the standard Enlightenment brief against them. Rather than simply dismissing these creatures as imaginary, naturalists often tried to account for the persistent reports of their

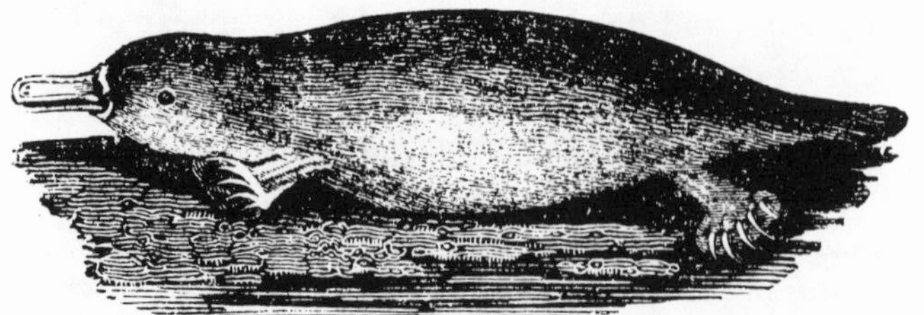

Figure 14.5. So puzzling did the platypus at first appear to European naturalists that Thomas Bewick declined even to give it a name in his *General History of Quadrupeds*. By permission of the Houghton Library, Harvard University.

existence. Thus Jardine remarked of the oryx that "this group is remarkable, as it is supposed that from some of its members the far-famed Unicorn would be made out" (*Ruminating Animals, Part I* 201); Robert Hamilton identified whales, walrus, and seals as "the original types of nearly all these wondrous tales" about mermaids.[45] Others were still more respectful, even accepting. Martyn discriminated between the unicorn, which he dismissed as a creature, "which, if it ever did exist, is now to be found no more," and the mermaid, "partly a fish, and partly of the human species," for which "there seems to be sufficient evidence to establish its reality" (*New Dictionary*).

Martyn, as already noted, was unsympathetic to systematizing, at least in its most comprehensive form. But not even the most carefully elaborated taxonomy would necessarily exclude such prodigies; it could dictate the form of subsidiary categories, but not their content. Indeed, sometimes systems could seem to mandate violations of the natural order, to blur rather than demarcate the boundary between myth and science. The quinary system was formulated by William MacLeay in 1819 and popularized by William Swainson a decade and a half later, at least in part as a response to the narrow restrictiveness of the chain of nature. It arranged animals within a set of complexly embedded circles, which took account of both anatomical affinities and less concrete (and often more traditional) similarities.[46] The system was designed to be predictive as well as descriptive. Each circle was supposed to contain five subcategories, and if the current state of zoological knowledge left one unfilled, it remained as a niche for some creature or group of creatures yet to be discovered. Thus Swainson took the absence of an aquatic group (one of the five was supposed to be "natatorial") in the circle of Quadrumana, which otherwise included apes, monkeys, lemurs, and bats, to indicate that although "we do not . . . believe in the existence of mermaids as

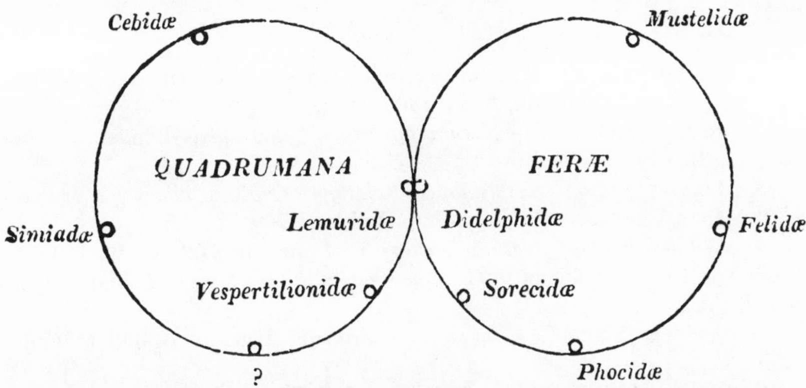

Figure 14.6. These taxonomical circles, from William Swainson's *On the Natural History and Classification of Quadrupeds,* show the connection of Quadrumana (roughly, Primates) and Ferae (roughly, Carnivora) through the lemurs and opossums. Swainson thought that the gap represented by the question mark at the bottom of the circle of Quadrumana might be filled by the mermaid.

depicted . . . by the old writers . . . some such animal has really been created." Similarly, with regard to the circle of Ungulata, he reasoned that the "obvious hiatus . . . between the horse and the camel" would ultimately be filled "by some animal agreeing more or less with the unicorn" (*Natural History* 96–97, 189).

Swainson's reasoning epitomized the ambiguous relationship of scientific systematizing to the zoological universe it ostensibly catalogued. The trappings of Enlightenment classification—whether elaborately hierarchical categories or binomial nomenclature—could legitimize any mode of discrimination and arrangement. Systematic form, whether in the version proposed by Linnaeus, or by Ray, or by any of their followers or competitors, was linked to its content only by assertion. It could accommodate categories like "domesticated animal" or "vermin" as easily as "carnivore," "ungulate," or "rodent." Indeed, the powerful symbolism of their structures may have made these systems particularly vulnerable to subversion, by camouflaging aberrant categories. That is, there was no clear way of distinguishing between the appearance of order and order itself.[47] And the more that taxonomic categories seem to reflect alternative (and inevitably inconsistent, and therefore undermining) ways of classifying, the harder it becomes to claim that the systems they constituted had either the rationality or the novelty or the power that have generally been attributed to them. Rather than consolidating human intellectual dominion over the variety of nature and the vagaries of mind, they demonstrated the difficulty of those attempts.

NOTES

1. Carl von Linné, *A General System of Nature . . .*, ed. and trans. William Turton (London: Lackington, Allen, 1806), 1:vi.

2. Richard Brookes, *The Natural History of Quadrupeds* (London: J. Newbery, 1763), 1:ix.

3. Linnaeus, *Miscellaneous Tracts Relating to Natural History,* trans. and ed. Benjamin Stillingfleet (London: R. J. Dodsley, 1759), xx–xxi.

4. William Borlase, *Natural History of Cornwall* (Oxford: W. Jackson, 1768), viii; Richard Pulteney, *A General View of the Writings of Linnaeus* (London: J. Mawman, 1805), 11.

5. Thomas Pennant, *History of Quadrupeds* (London: B. and J. White, 1793), 1:i.

6. William Jardine, "Memoir of Aristotle," *The Natural History of Gallinaceous Birds, Part I* (Edinburgh: W. H. Lizars, 1834), 19.

7. Charles Hamilton Smith, "Memoir of Gesner," *The Natural History of Horses* (Edinburgh: W. H. Lizars, 1841), 42; Andrew Crichton, "Memoir of Pliny," Prideaux John Selby, *The Natural History of Gallinaceous Birds, Part III. Pigeons* (Edinburgh: W. H. Lizars, 1834), 74; Charles Hamilton Smith, *Introduction to Mammalia* (Edinburgh: W. H. Lizars, 1846), 75.

8. English naturalists were not the only ones to make this kind of observation. For example, Lamarck claimed that nothing of note regarding animal classification appeared between Aristotle and Linnaeus (J. B. Lamarck, *Zoological Philosophy,* trans. H. Elliot [Chicago: University of Chicago Press, 1984], 62). In a similar vein G. E. R. Lloyd has recently described Aristotle's taxonomical method as "in a manner comparable to that of much later taxonomists such as Linnaeus" (*Science, Folklore and Ideology: Studies in the Life Sciences in Ancient Greece* [Cambridge: Cambridge University Press, 1983], 17). Patriotic Englishmen were, however, uniquely inclined to terminate the hiatus with John Ray, frequently referred to as "our countryman" or even "our illustrious countryman" (Cymmrodorion Society, *The British Zoology* [London: J. and J. March, 1766], 48). This theme has occasionally been sounded by later historians; for example, David Elliston Allen recently lamented that "in the absence of continuing interpreters much of the New Learning was forgotten. The great classificatory advances embodied in the work of Ray and his contemporaries, the foundation for the system based on natural structural affinities that was ultimately to triumph, fell into such disuse that the inferior 'artificial' system of Linnaeus was later able to brush it aside with little difficulty—and in the process considerably retarded the development of biological systematics." *The Naturalist in Britain* (Harmondsworth, Middlesex: Penguin, 1978), 19–20.

9. A. E. Gunther, *The Founders of Science at the British Museum, 1753–1900* (Halesworth, Suffolk: Halesworth Press, 1980), 36–50.

10. The debate was about the quinary system, discussed further below.

11. H. T. Turner, "An Essay on Classification," *Zoologist* 5 (1847): 1943–55.

12. Barbara Maria Stafford, *Voyage into Substance: Art, Science, Nature, and the Illustrated Travel Account, 1760–1840* (Cambridge: MIT Press, 1984),

54; Michel Foucault, *The Archeology of Knowledge,* trans. A. M. Smith (New York: Harper and Row, 1976), 57. On the general enterprise of scientific classification, see David Knight, *Ordering the World: A History of Classifying Man* (London: Burnett Books, 1981).

13. Keith Thomas, *Man and the Natural World: A History of the Modern Sensibility* (New York: Pantheon, 1983), 52.

14. Michel Foucault, *The Order of Things* (New York: Vintage, 1973), xxii–xxiii; Michael J. Novacek, "Characters and Cladograms: Examples from Zoological Systematics," in H. M. Hoenigswald and L. F. Wiener, eds., *Biological Metaphor and Cladistic Classification* (Philadelphia: University of Pennsylvania Press, 1987), 181–92; Mary P. Winsor, *Starfish, Jellyfish, and the Order of Life: Issues in Nineteenth-Century Science* (New Haven: Yale University Press, 1976), 1.

15. Of the scholars cited in this paragraph, Winsor and Novacek have the strongest affinities with this viewpoint.

16. Johannes Caius, *Of Englishe Dogges,* trans. Abraham Fleming (London: Rychard Johnes, 1576), translator's preface, n.p.

17. Edward Topsell, *The Historie of Foure-Footed Beastes* (London: William Iaggard, 1607), 102–7.

18. Harriet Ritvo, *The Animal Estate: The English and Other Creatures in the Victorian Age* (Cambridge: Harvard University Press, 1987), 12–13.

19. Thomas Bewick, *A General History of Quadrupeds* (Newcastle upon Tyne: T. Bewick, 1824), iii, v–x.

20. Thomas Pennant, *British Zoology* (London: Benjamin White, 1768), 1:xiii, xxii–xxiv.

21. John Church, *A Cabinet of Quadrupeds* (London: Darton and Harvey, 1805), 1:n.p.

22. G. L. Leclerc, Comte de Buffon, *Natural History . . . with Occasional Notes . . . by the Translator* (London: W. Strahan and T. Cadell, 1781–85), 3:5, 8:287–301.

23. John Ray, *Select Remains . . . with his Life, By the Late William Derham, D.D.* (London: George Scott, 1740), 21.

24. Oliver Goldsmith, *An History of the Earth and Animated Nature* (London: J. Nourse, 1774), 4:187; G. L. Leclerc, Comte de Buffon, *Barr's Buffon* (London: H. D. Symonds, 1797), 3:326, 5:81.

25. Edward Bennett, *The Tower Menagerie* (London: Robert Jennings, 1829), 61.

26. John Lawrence, *A General Treatise on Cattle* (London: Sherwood, Gilbert, and Piper, 1808), 425–26.

27. Thomas Pennant, *History of Quadrupeds* (London: B. and J. White, 1793), 2:252.

28. Leonard Chappelow, "The Sentimental Naturalist," MS in the Cambridge University Library, ca. 1809, 9, 94.

29. See, for example, Goldsmith, *History* 2:303–5.

30. Nicholas Cox, *The Gentleman's Recreation* (London: Thomas Fabian, 1677), 1:121; Pennant, *History* 1:269.

31. George Shaw, *General Zoology* (London: G. Kearsley, 1800), I (1), 397.

32. [J. Gregory], *A Comparative View of the State and Faculties of Man with those of the Animal World* (London: J. Dodsley, 1772), 13.

33. William Swainson, *On the Natural History and Classification of Quadrupeds* (London: Longman, Rees, Orme, Brown, Green, and Longman, 1835), 137.

34. William Jardine, *The Natural History of the Ruminating Animals, Part I* (Edinburgh: W. H. Lizars, 1835), 133.

35. William Jardine, *The Natural History of the Ruminating Animals, Part II* (Edinburgh: W. H. Lizars, 1836), 236.

36. Janet Browne, *The Secular Ark: Studies in the History of Biogeography* (New Haven: Yale University Press, 1983), 1.

37. William Frederic Martyn, *A New Dictionary of Natural History* (London: Harrison, 1785), Vol. 1, preface, n.p. It has been suggested that W. F. Martyn was the pseudonym of W. F. Mavor, who was the author of several natural history books for children under his own name (R. B. Freeman, *British Natural History Books, 1495–1900* [Folkestone: William Dawson, 1980], 237).

38. *A Dictionary of Natural History; or Complete Summary of Zoology* (London: C. Whittingham, 1802), iii.

39. See John Dupré, "Natural Kinds and Biological Taxa," *Philosophical Review* 90 (1981): 66–90, and Scott Atran, "Origin of the Species and Genus Concepts: An Anthropological Perspective," *Journal of the History of Biology* 20 (1987): 195–279.

40. John Reinhold Forster, *A Catalogue of the Animals of North America* (London: B. White, 1771), 19.

41. Jacob W. Gruber, "What Is It? The Echidna Comes to England," *Archives of Natural History* 11 (1982): 1–15.

42. Shaw, *General Zoology*, I (1), 228–29. Shaw's suspicion that the platypus had been surgically produced was understandable in an era in which stuffed mermaids, composed of the cobbled remains of three or four creatures, were familiar exhibits in London's fairs and taverns (Richard D. Altick, *The Shows of London* [Cambridge: Harvard University Press, 1978], 302–3).

43. *Catalogue of the Animals Preserved in the Museum of the Zoological Society* (London: Richard Taylor, 1829), 15.

44. George R. Waterhouse, *The Natural History of the Marsupialia or Pouched Animals* (Edinburgh: W. H. Lizars, 1841), 322.

45. Robert Hamilton, *Amphibious Carnivora* (Edinburgh: W. H. Lizars, 1829), 293.

46. On the quinary system, see Mario A. DiGregorio, "In Search of the Natural System: Problems of Zoological Classification in Victorian Britain," *History and Philosophy of the Life Sciences* 4 (1982): 232–36, and Adrian Desmond, "The Making of Institutional Zoology in London, 1822–1836: Part I," *History of Science* 23 (1985): 160–164.

47. The past tense may be misleading here. For (among other things) a comparison of the relative objectivity of several late-twentieth-century taxonomical philosophies, see Mark Ridley, *Evolution and Classification: The Reformation of Cladism* (London: Longman, 1986).

CHAPTER 15

Museums: Representing the Real?

LUDMILLA JORDANOVA

I

Museums associated with science and medicine occupy a special place in the history of Western societies because they purport to bring the "real" world to the population as a whole. In order to convince people that they give them privileged access to nature and to the means by which it is understood, scientific and medical museums deploy a number of strategies. These are best understood in terms of realism and representation. Forms of realism are historically constituted. What is regarded as truthful, authentic, or legitimate natural knowledge is a product of a wide range of social and cultural factors. These include the institutions and social groups that promote science and medicine, the ways in which they derive legitimacy and authority, from whom or what, and the techniques deployed for cementing their position. Indeed, the culture as a whole provides support for the distinctive claims of scientific and medical knowledge, as it has done for some time. A full understanding of the special qualities of this kind of museum involves an examination of the historical issues around science and medicine as display.[1]

When objects are presented to visitors for their enlightenment, highly complex relationships are set up. At one level, the objects reveal something to the viewers; a part of what they reveal is known by those who designed the display and selected items with a purpose in mind. At another level, however, quite different relationships emerge between onlookers and objects, relationships that pertain rather to the realm of fantasy than to knowledge. These can be neither controlled nor predicted. Yet this is not the domain of anarchy. Those who set up displays, whether they admit it or not, seek to mobilize the unconscious, semiconscious, emotional, and moral responses of visitors. These diverse responses do not derive directly or solely from the objects on display;

rather they arise from a range of factors including physical layout, modes of representation, labeling practices, and so on. The reactions of visitors and the aims of curators are part of socially embedded cultural patterns, although the links between these phenomena have to be inferred as much by indirect means as by direct evidence. Thus, although we need to be aware that museums relate to the world of fantasy, this recognition does not mean that it is impossible to speak coherently about them.

I became interested in museums because of a general concern with the ways in which the biomedical sciences made themselves visible. It is now well known that many practitioners of these fields were also interested in the visual arts. If it is the case that seeing is the most powerful way of acquiring valid knowledge, allowing the public to view for themselves the prized objects of knowledge has enormous significance. Scientific and medical museums are a way of letting people into science, with its privileged access to nature, into mechanisms of discovery, and into the story of the acquisition of truth. This raises questions about the nature of a public for science, questions that are especially important for historians working on the period since the mid-seventeenth century. "The public" is a problematic concept, often used in careless and slippery ways; for the moment I know no better one, provided that it is carefully defined.[2] There are many publics for science and medicine, including peer groups. They have in common their shared status as an audience—yet the image of "audience" is not quite right; its core metaphor is hearing, while my argument is that looking is the key issue.

Museums are the organizational embodiment of the drive to disseminate specific forms of scientific/medical realism, and by the same token they present—in visual form—the authority of natural knowledge and the order that it has been possible to impose on the natural world. When museums invite visitors to reexperience the knowing-through-looking that others have already experienced, they imply that the privilege accorded to the sense of sight is not confined to the dissemination of knowledge, but extends to its acquisition. Hence, in examining science-as-visual display, we are engaged not merely in a study of what is often called "the popularization of science," but in exploring the special role that vision has been accorded in the scientific and medical enterprises. This is at the heart of "realism" as a historical phenomenon, and a concept of representation is a necessary part of the historian's armory. I use the term "representation" not to mean a valid or exact copy of something original, but to draw attention to transformative processes. The implied contrast with "representation" is "reflection," commonly used by historians to suggest that there are screens onto which past scenes are simply and unproblematically projected. Hogarth's art, for example, has been likened to a mirror of the society he inhabited, enabling us to look at his pictures and see eighteenth-century England before our eyes.[3] This approach denies the existence of the mediating processes between "art" and "life"—*re*-presentation, by contrast, affirms their importance.

At this juncture, I want to reflect briefly on the idea of display. Roget's *Thesaurus* indicates three principal ranges of meaning for the term: (1) appearance, phenomenon, and sight, that is, how things look or appear; (2) manifestation, exhibition, demonstration, unfolding, and unveiling; and (3) ostentation, parade, pomp, showing off.[4] It may be helpful to bear these in mind when talking about museums, in which these three modes are often brought together—natural objects may be displayed primarily to demonstrate their appearance; displays may be constructed both to reveal specific theories and to celebrate the discovery, mastery, beauty, awesomeness and power of nature, science, medicine. Accordingly, complex relationships are set up between nature as it is represented, those who actively represent it, and those who participate in the final representations. These relationships are triggered by a visual display, and inevitably include psychic, social, and political dimensions.

There are certainly problems with interpreting "old" museums. Their design and arrangement reflect a particular historical moment, and if these remain relatively unchanged, the museum comes to be viewed differently, reinvested with fresh meanings. It can be treated as a relic, a frozen moment, or it can acquire new lives. For example, the Hunterian Museum at the Royal College of Surgeons in London is "new," in the sense that it has been rebuilt in the twentieth century following bomb damage.[5] But it is in essence "old" because it is a reconstruction of an earlier museum; it attempts to "freeze" John Hunter's vision of a comparative anatomy museum—an attempt that is inevitably imperfect. The surgeons who continue to use it presumably give it their own significance, possibly as a resource and/or cultural ornament. Although the impossibility of genuinely "freezing" a museum is a problem, the difficulty of grasping the interplay between "old" and "new" is a far greater one. This is not an empirical issue. It is not as if documentary evidence could tell us how to see the museum through earlier eyes, although the accounts of those who made, saw, and used it are revealing. The fact that we may be viewing the same objects fosters the illusion that it is possible to talk about museums as if they were somehow timeless; it gives them a spurious continuity.

The most straightforward way of approaching museums is to treat them as institutions, the history of which can be written in the same way as that of hospitals, schools, banks, or companies. Valuable though this approach may be, it privileges administrative arrangements and fails to come to terms with the central experience of going to a museum: looking at objects. Museums that have survived take on new life; when we visit them now they are, simultaneously, of historical and of contemporary interest. Reactions to them are so various that it seems foolhardy to make generalizations on the subject of museums. Nonetheless, they raise some major issues—realism and representation among them—that cannot be ignored.

There can be no single satisfactory definition of "realism."[6] The common ground would seem to be a commitment to the existence of tight links between something "real" and other versions of it. Realism is a set of representational practices, theories, and assumptions, whether philosophical or aesthetic. It refers viewers/readers on to other supposedly more genuine, authentic, or real states of affairs. In literature and the visual arts a range of strategies is deployed to give that sense of firmness, security, and credibility that is the hallmark of "realism." But no one reading or looking at such work is unaware of its status as art. Scientists and medical practitioners are in a different situation. For the most part, they strive to efface the artfulness of their productions. They want to facilitate a relationship with nature, mediated by themselves: "this is how the world works because my theory/discovery says so." In fact, there is a double representation here, since the theory or discovery is itself a representation, and this representation is in turn re-presented to a public. For this reason representation is a central concept for analyzing science and medicine.[7]

The themes of realism and representation are closely tied to the idea of authenticity. If we see a room, or a photograph of a room, furnished with tables, chairs, books, and so on, we do not doubt that these items are "real," but we still have questions about their provenance. In the Dorset County Museum in Dorchester, we can see Thomas Hardy's study. Visual inspection alone could not reveal whether the items on display were the very ones owned by Hardy or replicas. But the labels and the good faith we have in the museum itself convince us that this is the very chair where Hardy sat and wrote. To describe this phenomenon we need another term in addition to realism; the cult of authenticity is appropriate. (The Dorset County Museum relates to "realism" in another sense, since it contains a number of Hardy items suggesting the factual origins of fictional places/characters that appear in the novels. Here it is not just a question of Hardy writing convincingly about Dorset, but an insistence that he was actually writing about real places/people, and hence, by implication, describing them rather than inventing them. This example suggests how powerfully the appeal to authenticity exerts itself.)

The notion of authenticity has other resonances. It is just about acceptable to speak of an authentic copy, meaning something that is an exact, totally accurate version of another object. Used more metaphorically, authenticity is about something feeling right, and being legitimized by those who deem it authentic. Legitimacy concerns power. Furthermore, if an object is authentic, it is generally believed that it embodies and conveys a kind of reality and by that token permits our unmediated vision of it. Scientific and medical museums sustain just this sense of unmediated vision. Since institutions of science and medicine are loci of power, they guarantee the validity of what is seen and display (show off) their own contributions to the project of making nature and human nature clear and comprehensible. A study of museums should attend to the techniques deployed to achieve these ends.

Science-as-it-is-practiced, like science-as-display, uses a wide range of representational techniques. There is considerable overlap between these two areas; for example, the wax and glass models discussed below both assist in teaching and are suitable for display. Their role in "research" is less clear, but it is now more fully appreciated how central drawings, models, and metaphors are to the research practices of science and medicine.[8] At the same time, there are important differences between the doing of science and the public presentation of it. Museums are places where meanings are stabilized. In doing science or medicine there is less stability; representational techniques may be used more flexibly and idiosyncratically than is possible in a museum. Even when the displays are for students, the process of socialization in which they are engaged makes it likely that ambiguity will be limited.

Drawing out the common ground in terms of representational techniques for "research," teaching, and "display" is nonetheless important. It reminds us of the need to consider mediating processes. In all these cases, nature and knowledge of nature only and necessarily exist in a mediated form—as the products of processes that constantly and subtly transform them. These processes involve representational metamorphoses. It is for this reason that "popularization" is such an unhelpful term, because it slides over, rather than drawing attention to, the mediations involved. It is not productive to say that museums are about "popular" science, although most of them are about the role of "the public" in science.

For most historical periods it is appropriate to talk about science and medicine in terms of the communities that produce them. There is no way of avoiding the fact that these communities interact with other occupations, classes, and social groups. Representations of science and medicine are necessary for such interactions to take place, and these representations are integral to the internal functioning of communities, to pedagogic practices, and to the "dissemination" of ideas and values.

It would be artificial to separate out representational practices into rigid categories, since this encourages the dualistic mentality that underpins "popularization" by putting "real" science on one side, popular science on the other. A common assumption is that what is "popular" is frivolous, trivial, of little historical moment. The constant interplay between different facets of the scientific/medical enterprises, like that between these areas and their social and cultural settings, must always be firmly acknowledged. Examining museums is not peripheral to the study of science and medicine. Museums are not trivial and entertaining epiphenomena. They strike at the heart of the fields they display and of the diverse communities they serve.

II

In pursuing the themes of realism and representation, I shall mention museums of different kinds: biographical, teaching, and public museums, and one that does not clearly fall into any such category. They contain different combinations of the realism associated with authentic objects, the special kind of realism generated by modern science and medicine, and the representational realism of the creative arts. Biographical museums, built around the life of an outstanding individual, are of particular significance because they demonstrate most vividly the ways in which displayed objects are both identified with and reified. I shall consider the Nightingale Museum in St. Thomas' Hospital, London, and the Freud Museum in Hampstead, London. Teaching museums are institutions where scientific or medical instruction still plays a significant role in the life of the museum, where displays are arranged to accord with contemporary practices. The Science Museum in London is the preeminent example of a public museum which appeals to a broad section of the population and provides a combination of entertainment and education. Science and medicine are presented to the public as a whole, expertise is exhibited to the nonexpert. Other museums cannot be so neatly classified. One example is the nineteenth-century operating theater of old St. Thomas' Hospital, built in the roof of a church in the 1820s and used for their female patients until the 1860s. The hospital's herb garret is in the same location. Here the interest is in visiting the actual place where operations were performed. It is completely obsolete, it is not built around a hero or heroine, but neither is it medical knowledge put on display for the public. It is simply an authentic old place where we know medical activities occurred.

The recently-opened and lavish Nightingale Museum occupies a large area in the hospital. It was designed by a professional exhibition designer

Figure 15.1. Old St. Thomas' Operating Theatre. General view of the theater (in use 1822–61). By permission of St. Thomas' Hospital.

and is elegantly modern in presentation. Large amounts of money were raised to start and run the museum, which charges an admission fee and attracts visitors from all over the world. Apparently, the majority of these visitors are nurses for whom the image of Nightingale as a pioneer of their chosen profession has special significance. The displays are chronologically arranged, and include many authentic objects; manuscripts, clothes, pictures, "memorabilia," and so on. There are also lifesize models, of the ward at Scutari, of soldiers of the period. A specially prepared video is shown throughout the day. This concentrates on the places with which Florence Nightingale was associated, such as the various houses she lived in while in England. The overall intention of the museum is to tell the story of her life. At one level, then, it aims at biographical completeness. It achieves this partly by stressing Nightingale's diverse activities, interests, and writings, and partly by putting on display a wide range of objects associated with her. But there are areas that it touches on only rather lightly. It mentions, but does not dwell on, Nightingale's emotional life, her conflicts in the Crimea, and her intense spiritual life. Paradoxically, it creates a heroine out of her, while, at the same time, pointing out to visitors how she has been mythologized.

Perhaps it would be more apt to say that the museum draws attention to the old myth while creating a new one. It has, for example, a slogan: "Florence Nightingale—a woman of fame, power, influence. . . ." Here certainly is a new, supposedly more accurate, representation of "the lady with the lamp."[9] It would not be sufficiently precise to call it a feminist reading of her, but it is a form of presentation consonant with present-day concerns, both with the public role of women and with the professionalization of nurses. The displays give authority to their interpretation of Nightingale as a woman of "fame, power, and influence" by, for example, including a range of historical documents in support of it, and drawing attention to her close links with figures who enjoyed political and military power.

The museum is openly didactic; it instructs viewers in a biography. Its authority to do so derives in part from the presence of authentic objects, and in part from a variety of strategies that imply the historical accuracy of the information provided. A number of representational techniques are deployed to convey a true life story and especially to portray the importance of her "vocation." The setting of the museum is new, the installations are purpose built, hence the sense of authenticity derives from the presence of genuine articles, models, and facsimiles of one kind or another, together with the text provided by the museum. In these respects there is an instructive contrast to be drawn with the Freud Museum.

The Freud Museum is located in Maresfield Gardens, Hampstead, in the house where he lived after coming to England following the rise of fascism, and where he died. Only a part of the original house is open to the public, but the rooms that are include the famous study containing the even more famous couch. The room, it is claimed, is very like Freud's Viennese study; Anna Freud in turn preserved it intact after her father's death. It was her wish that the house be turned into a museum. Other rooms contain special displays, a video of Freud family life with voice-over by Anna, and the room in which she worked. The emphasis is both on preserving authentic objects and on suspending time, so that a room—the place where he died—is maintained precisely how it was. This project is assisted by the existence of photographs taken of Freud's Vienna home shortly before he moved to England. They underwrite the accuracy of the preserved room. There is no attempt here to tell a whole life story; instead an invitation is issued to imagine a great man in situ. Various problems emerge at the museum. Should it explain psychoanalysis to the public? There appears to be no attempt to do this; hence the museum probably serves the already initiated. But why do those already more or less knowledgeable about psychoanalysis want to visit Freud's home? There are two possibilities. They may want to offer homage, in which case the museum is a shrine, or they may be inquisitive about the way the man lived, in which case the museum is a display to satisfy their curiosity. How can it do this? What can we learn from seeing Freud's rugs or his books ranged along shelves? Is it more a matter of physical proximity to his possessions satisfying curiosity?

One possible response to such questions, which respects the emotional dimensions of museums, would develop the "religious" theme just hinted at, by considering the need to be close to sacred objects, for which the relic can stand as a model. It is not just that relics are supposed to be authentic, and that they appeal to some kind of faith in higher powers, but that they must be touched, kissed, approached with the body. Another possibility is to examine the aspect of Freud's life that responds most readily to visual hunger—his impressive collection of statuettes and antiquities.[10] Although it is not possible to see most of them at close hand in the study, a small selection is usually on display upstairs, with explanatory labels. The uncertainties and emotional complexities of the museum project have been resolved by resorting to traditional display techniques; a tiny bit of the British Museum is, as it were, recreated in Hampstead, and the science of psychoanalysis thereby linked with archeology. But the dominant effect of the museum, in its emphasis on Freud's "real" study, is to inculcate a shrine mentality; the objects Freud himself used indeed become relics. Freud was, after all, a healer. This is not at all to denigrate the museum. Rather the contrary; it is to illustrate, in an unusually stark form, that museums serve to nourish fantasies as well as to define "realities." These fantasies are of different kinds, as the two biographical museums illustrate. Freud's house encourages stasis; visitors admire the fully mature man in his own space. The Nightingale Museum, with its strong narrative element, encourages visitors to experience the dynamic development of her vocation.

Museum fantasies are highly complex, and it is appropriate to note their gender and class dimensions. This is evident in the forms of commercial activity museums undertake. The Nightingale Museum tends to play down her elite background, stresses her hard work, and sells items like pens, badges, and bookmarks with her picture and/or the museum slogan on. Its populist style gathers in visitors, especially female nurses, and encourages them to contribute by providing information about the geographical spread of her methods. The Freud Museum is pitched at quite a different, and more upper- and middle-class, level, with its facsimiles of objects in the collection, its mug based on Freud's Beardsley bookplate, and its expensive photographs. Each style encourages different sorts of visitors and generates distinct reactions in them once inside the museum: these styles are one aspect of the fantasies that museums give risė to.

Some of the foregoing remarks could probably have been applied to biographical museums built around those completely unconnected with science or medicine, although the personal qualities emphasized, like those played down, are likely to be somewhat different. In the case of writers and artists, for example, more emphasis is usually placed on their creative genius, and their colorful private lives can be made to appear quite compatible with this. When it comes to those in traditional forms of public life, statesmen and warriors for example, it is possible to concentrate on the visible manifestations of their success; trophies, medals, and other material rewards. On the whole scientists and medical practitioners have less to show for themselves, and this is especially true if their work is rather abstract. Nor do we want to display too much of any private chaos they may have experienced because there is still a strong need for the pioneers, the makers of authoritative knowledge, to be above reproach morally, to embody in their lives the order they impose upon nature.

Using "we" in this way is a bit slippery. I generally mean it to refer to commonplace assumptions that may or may not be shared by scholars. Although those who study science and medicine as historical phenomena may believe themselves to be "above" popular assumptions, there is ample evidence that they are not. We need to remind ourselves of the significance attached to the representation of science, by scholars, by governments, by funding agencies, by practitioners themselves, and of the pervasiveness of a value system that communicates the importance of scientific knowledge, even to small children. It is both necessary and inherently difficult to represent science and medicine. Representations take material forms; books, magazines, TV and radio shows, and so on. Museums are another example. However, some phenomena take on material form more readily than others. There is a dual issue here. The first is how abstractions are rendered palpable, especially in cultural settings where personifications are unacceptable or unfashionable. The second is the need for identification. Even if it is possible to give material form to science and medicine, a certain need easily remains unsatisfied, a need that I would characterize as a drive to identify with objects and people, to have something to mingle with. Perhaps the attraction of museums that include steam engines can be explained in this way, since they are a class of objects that inspires fascination and love—in this case the processes of identification are clear.

In thinking about the past of science, it is easy to turn to its personalities. The cult of personality is driven by many forces—the importance attached to discovery, the conviction that most significant discoveries are made by individuals, the association of novelty, progress, and genius—and it offers everyone, scholars included, something deeply satisfying. It provides a name, an identity, a story, a set of boundaries so familiar that they seem natural (Isaac Newton was born in 1642, he was a posthumous child, he was forty-four when he published the *Principia* . . .). At the same time, there are tacit limits to the depth historians should go in researching these lives—it is reached when the phrase "psychological reductionism" is invoked. It is instructive to recall the almost universal scorn that greeted Frank Manuel's psychohistorical study *A Portrait of Isaac Newton,* the fury when it was first pointed out how indebted Charles Lyell was to his wife's scientific skills, the powerful reactions to the BBC drama series on Freud's life, the ongoing vicious controversies around his treatment of women patients and his relationship with his sister-in-law, and current conflicts over the biography of Melanie Klein.[11] In fact, the whole history of the psychoanalytic movement is saturated with minefields triggered by allegations about the morals of its members. Personalities satisfy the need for identification, but prove dangerous if this is not kept within bounds. Unconventional sexual relationships especially imperil received views of male scientific and medical achievement. Although displaying the life of a famous person, whatever the field of their preeminence, generates problems, particular ones are raised by biographies of practitioners of science and medicine. There are special expectations attached to the links between their professional and their private lives, above all where gender issues are concerned. It may be hard to represent their work visually. The overall display is necessarily affected by the assumptions that inhere in the culture about the general significance of science and medicine. In preparing such museums, curators suffer from invisible controls, which guide them in certain directions and inhibit them from following others. These controls are highly elaborate, and rarely explicit; many agencies have a vested interest in them; they result from centuries of social negotiations over the way science is viewed.

III

The constraints are very different if we turn briefly to museums with a continuing educational function. Much has been written about the origins of such museums, the majority of which were in the field of the life sciences. Usually commentators stress the need to provide organic specimens for those who would not otherwise have a chance to see them at first hand.[12] By presenting museums in purely practical terms, a more searching examination of them is discouraged. There is indeed a material background to zoological and medical collections; the scarcity of corpses for anatomy, the expense of glass and alcohol for preparations, the small number of exotic animals in captivity, and so on. These factors are undeniably relevant. What lies behind them should also be considered—a drive to teach through looking, to display the variety of organic life, to capture the lifelike qualities of organisms, to touch, probe, and dissect.

"Life" is the key issue here. The term has multiple meanings in this context. First, in displaying the full range of living beings, it is possible to convey something about the organic world as a whole. By the late eighteenth century, the interest in taxonomy was coupled for many naturalists with a more abstract interest in "life" and in the newly emerging science of biology. This is true of the founder of one of the most famous of such museums, John Hunter, while his French counterparts, natural philosophers like Lamarck and Cuvier, actually lived and worked in a museum.[13] These savants were interested both in the external appearance of organic beings and in their physiology. There is a second kind of interest in "life"—to display objects in such a way that they *look* alive. This is a challenging demand, unless biological museums become a combination of zoos and butchers' shops, with fresh dissections always on display. Preserving dead animals in bottles does not solve the problem, because they lose color and texture, and hence cease to be "lifelike." It was thus necessary to resort to simulations—mainly in glass and wax—to create a lifelike effect. The bodies of real animals failed to satisfy criteria of "realism"; in death they did not look sufficiently like themselves in life. It would still be possible to say that there were purely practical explanations for this; students would have difficulty recognizing different species if they had never seen their color and shape. This can be conceded, while pointing out that it fails to do justice to the intensity of the drive toward exact replication, to verisimilitude. The glass and wax models are beautiful, even magnificent; they are works of art. Perhaps it would be most productive to see them as both betokening and inviting the worship of the forms they represent and of nature as a whole. They can also be seen as demonstrating human powers, since their craftsmanship is so fine it rivals that of nature itself.

There is a third sense in which "life" is involved. We have discussed displays where organic materials look lifelike. It is also possible for whole animals to be displayed as if in their original context; for example, stuffed animals in dioramas with painted backgrounds. The animals look alive and are located in a plausible setting. Natural history museums are particularly fond of this format, which mixes "real" objects with simulated ones. It is quite straightforward telling the difference, if a viewer so chooses, so there is no question of simple deception. Rather the issue is why we seek such an "illusion" at all. In fact, museums for specialized educative purposes use such techniques relatively little; those designed to educate the masses, like the New York Museum of Natural History, deploy them much more.[14]

The museum founded in 1828 by Robert Grant when he came to University College, London, as their first professor of zoology and comparative anatomy, illustrates some of the issues raised by displaying "life" for teaching purposes. The material is arranged taxonomically and is still heavily used in instructing undergraduates. Models—in wax and glass—are most in evidence on the invertebrate side. There are also skeletons, preparations in bottles, and some stuffed animals. These are not on the whole placed in any kind of setting, but remain as isolated figures. Clearly a large number of the objects are very old. Although not in its original location, it remains in many ways as it was in Grant's day. To a degree, then, it reflects a particular historical moment, a specific stage in the history of zoology. We, inevitably, see it differently. Now it has a dual significance: It continues to be a museum of zoology; it is contemporary, even if in practice some of its specimens were prepared more than a hundred years ago. But it is also a museum of the history of zoology, that reveals, although not by design, a changing scientific discipline, and contains remnants of the past. Grant's own microscopic slides, wrapped in their original paper with his annotations on, survive. These are now "historical" objects and possibly relics. Yet preparations by him that are preserved in alcohol can still be used in teaching and hence are "contemporary." The end result is that there are several "museums" here—a single collection can be seen in quite different ways.

Similar arguments apply to medical museums that continue to play a role in teaching. Collections like the ones at St. Bartholomew's Hospital and the Royal College of Surgeons in Edinburgh have the same dual aspect in being simultaneously historical and contemporary.[15] And in both cases, valuable items in the collections have been "removed" (i.e., stolen). This is, I think, interesting. Since St. Bartholomew's is a teaching collection, the museum and the cases are mostly left unlocked. The museum is not, however, open to the general public except by special permission. Missing objects are most likely to have been taken by staff or students. Specimens in jars were not removed, but old medical instruments, which increasingly have market value, were. The apparent ease with which items can be appropriated perhaps signals an ambiguity in the museum; in part it has a purely practical function, yet it contains valuable objects, just as other museums do. Having both these aspects, the practical and the valuable, such museums are neither one thing nor another.

Ambiguities pose problems for institutions and those who use them. Moreover, they signal deep uncertainties about the value of objects. In the case of fine art, by contrast, value is made totally explicit. "Great" works of art are painted by artists of outstanding ability and cost large amounts of money. There is little ambiguity when two major scales of value usually coincide so conveniently. Values generate behavior; when visiting a fine art museum we know, more or less, how to act, how to adopt a reverent posture, how to determine the place of any particular work on the scale of things. And, because aesthetic objects are involved, an ambiguity that dogs science and medicine museums is ironed out—a lot of human effort/skill/imagination went into making them, which we can admire in a direct way.

Reactions to fine art can be contrasted with reactions to man-made scientific and medical objects, such as instruments, on the one hand, and to bits of nature likely to be displayed in museums, such as anatomical preparations, on the other. Since instruments are meant to be used, we go into aesthetic gear when seeing them only if they are conspicuously beautiful. The creative energy that went into them remains invisible. We mostly lack an adequate knowledge of what they did, and where this is self-evident (for example, saws for amputation), pondering on it can be unpleasant, even painful. A residual reaction remains—did they really do it that way in the past, was this really the great man's own instrument, and so on? These responses affirm the reality of the scientific or medical past. This is just how it was. Take it or leave it. The present is thereby affirmed, without our being aware of it. Of course, sometimes the relief surfaces—"Thank God it's not like that now." And invariably the present becomes associated with comfort, with progress, with mastery over human frailty. To the extent that museums reveal the scientific and medical past, they also speak about the present and the future.

If we cannot respond in any simple way to the beauty of most scientific artifacts, then we certainly cannot to anatomical preparations; colorless pieces of flesh, in yellowish liquid, often displaying bizarre abnormalities. Even if it is assumed that "beauty" is a historical construct, and hence varies with time and place, it is hard to imagine a situation in which the remnants of living tissue are generally given high aesthetic value.[16] The problem can be solved if such objects are useful for teaching, but if they are not, it is difficult to know how to react. The value system that has been established for the arts simply does not apply, and no appropriately appreciative aesthetic language exists in which they can be discussed. The difficulty can be overcome only by establishing the historical interest of such specimens, along the lines of "this model was made by a famous man" or "this preparation enabled a part to be seen for the first time," but even then it requires a great deal of work to really demonstrate the point.

IV

There is less ambiguity in fully public museums, which have a single ostensible function: to present science and medicine to the world. So much conscious effort, and money, goes into techniques of display, and the public face of science is so important, that strenuous attempts are made to eliminate all that is unclear, unstable, and potentially subversive. Take, for example, the Science Museum in London, which sells science to an enormous, eager public. Although it appears to have a coherent overall character, the museum is once again doing two somewhat different things. It is informing the public about (preferably glamorous) contemporary science, and especially those aspects of it that attract most attention, such as the exploration of space. It is also providing insights into the history of science, medicine, and technology. This second task is less openly proclaimed, in that many of the galleries make no direct reference to historical issues at all, and few are organized primarily around a chronological sequence, despite the fact that implicit narratives of "progress" abound.

The notable exception is the two galleries on the history of medicine, which derive from the vast collections amassed by Sir Henry Wellcome, now in the hands of the Science Museum.[17] These two very different galleries both convey a strong sense of the history of medicine as narrative. The first gallery is composed of a set of dioramas and reconstructions, some life-size, others smaller. Although not in strict chronological order, the sense of an unfolding story is nonetheless powerfully conveyed. The life-size displays use realist representational techniques with simulations, such as models of people and replicas of rooms, mixed with authentic objects. While visiting there recently I heard a group discussing the reactions of a mutual friend to the reconstructed surgical theater (an open heart operation in 1980). "He claims it's identical to the one at his hospital," one of them said approvingly, "you really can't tell the difference." The reconstructed scenes are set in believable rooms (in terms of spatial arrangement and overall size); visitors look into them through large windows cut into the walls. What this gallery communicates is a literal sense of looking into the past. The reality of that past is affirmed by the forms of representation, by the subject matter, and by the status of the museum.

Two other features of this first, more popular gallery should be noted. The older scenes tend to be presented on a smaller scale, while life-size ones are used only for nineteenth- and twentieth-century subjects. The dioramas imply that the more recent past is more "real," a subtle way of affirming the value of the present and hope for the future. The second feature of this gallery is the presence of an anomaly—a representation of an African medicine man in the 1930s, a display that relates less to past time than to distant cultures. Most of the other scenes relate to Europe, including the classical world. Again it is possible to see this as an affirmation of our present; the anomaly of "primitive" medicine reinforces the rightness of Western scientific medicine.

This impression is strengthened by the second gallery, which is pitched at a much more sophisticated level, but which, nonetheless, is organized around contrasts between Europe and elsewhere, and between our era and the past. Most of the space is devoted to nineteenth- and twentieth-century *scientific* medicine. There are no specimens in glass bottles here, but an impressively wide range of artifacts related to medicine—books, instruments, experimental apparatus, drugs, advertisements, anatomical models . . . The public face of medicine is conveyed here in two ways. First, the labels and explanatory panels sketch in a view of the history of medicine suitable for mass presentation. Second, the artifacts themselves, as permanent traces of medical activity, are there for all to see. However, this provides little sense of the "doing" bits of medicine or science. We have already noted in relation to biographical exhibits how extraordinarily difficult it is to convey science or medicine as practice. Yet it is not impossible. Without deliberate attempts to represent the processes that constitute these fields, museum audiences can only focus on disembodied objects. The reification of science and medicine as they are publicly presented in museums is striking.

The representation of science and medicine is always tricky. Its representation to "the general public" is an especially fraught area. The uncertainties attached to the status of science and to the esteem in which it is held by "the public" probably mean that progress, achievement, and settled values have to be displayed. It is still worth noting the absence of a sense of process. Perhaps this is a widespread lack in museums, but it is possible in art museums to learn about the variety of media and techniques, preparatory sketches, copying, the models used, even studio practices, while the corresponding features of science and medicine are rarely on display. This makes museums like the Old St. Thomas' Operating Theatre in London especially interesting. Operating theaters are places of action. This side of medicine cannot be adequately conveyed by the walls and furniture alone. Yet the actual operating theater is "real" in a much more literal sense than are the contents of any of the other museums mentioned. At the same time it is not exactly a representation. It is quite simply a place where medical things happened, although this fact alone may not be enough to trigger fantasies of medicine in the past, and thereby to provide a satisfying museum experience. The dominant role film and television have played over the last few decades in recreating the past has led to the expectation that additional representations are required to supplement the effect of the physical location. Without these, visitors would have to do excessive work to fill the gap between what is seen and what is imaginatively "understood."

V

Museums of science and medicine are diverse and complex. They deploy a range and mixture of representational techniques that are designed to convey authority, knowledge, and values. By drawing attention to the ways in which people both identify with and reify displayed objects, I have touched on the realisms that these museums embody. They represent science and medicine both as whole institutions and in their constituent displays; they deploy a variety of means to render some scientific/medical phenomena, but not others, visible; as "cathedrals of science" they serve to inspire awe and affirm a true picture of the world; they are, and have been for at least two hundred years, important engines of realism.[18]

If I had to sum up my arguments in a single visual image it would be Charles Willson Peale's portrait of himself in his own museum, painted in 1822. He is lifting up a heavy curtain in order to reveal his collections to the spectator, and, as a reminder that he is also an artist, his palette is on a table at his side. We can discern at least three Peales here. As an enthusiastic Linnaean, he has organized his zoological specimens so as to demonstrate nature's order to the public. As a painter *exceptionally* preoccupied with techniques for achieving verisimilitude, he has provided portraits of the leading lights of the American Revolution at the top of the cabinets. As a museum keeper, he is unveiling both the truth of nature and the truth of human life to the world at large.[19] Here is a canvas that neatly demonstrates some of the ways in which realist forms of representation have functioned in science-as-display.

Before Peale, the urge to demonstrate the variety of nature in a self-consciously modern way was felt by the Scottish medical practitioners William and John Hunter. The latter's museum, given to the Royal College of Surgeons in 1799, still survives, as we have already noted, in a form fairly similar to its original one. Again, the collections are rigidly classified, not only taxonomically, but into normal and pathological

Figure 15.2. Charles Willson Peale, *The Artist in His Museum* (1822). Courtesy of the Pennsylvania Academy of the Fine Arts, Philadelphia. Gift of Mrs. Sarah Harrison (The Joseph Harrison, Jr., Collection).

specimens. Given John Hunter's interest in comparative anatomy—itself an extraordinarily powerful and historically specific way of visualizing putatively natural difference—the taxonomic concerns are not surprising. But the Hunterian also contains paintings commissioned especially to demonstrate the appearance of other races; large wooden panels with the human nervous and circulatory systems mounted on them; items we might call curiosities, like skeletons of dwarves and giants; displays of his experiments; and demonstrations of operations. Such demonstrations generally used wax, either injected into vessels to maintain their shape, texture, and color, or to form exact likenesses of human tissues. Many of those who founded and ran museums were themselves skilled in the preservation and preparation of specimens and in sketching and painting.

I have stressed the significance of techniques, such as modeling in wax and glass, used to achieve the goal of lifelikeness. We need to know much more about the history of such techniques in order to understand the tacit assumptions about realism and representation that they contain. John Hunter saw his museum as primarily benefiting other medical practitioners and students, and not any undifferentiated public at large.

Figure 15.3. The Hunterian Museum in the Royal College of Surgeons, London. Reproduced by kind permission of the President and Council of the Royal College of Surgeons of England.

His older brother William had similar concerns, manifest not only in his own collections, which included, along with important art and coin collections, innumerable wax models, but also in his lavish book of 1774 on the gravid uterus, with its massive plates.[20] This publication is also science-as-display—doubly so, since the process of dissection is made apparent. Layers of flesh are gradually stripped away; the plates depict ever deeper abdominal spaces. William Hunter unveiled nature, just as Peale did. For both William and John Hunter it was the medical community, diverse as it was, that was the principal audience for their exhibitions. Peale sought to create a commercially successful museum. In effect, a boundary was delineated between different kinds of public, a boundary that was and *is* fraught and unstable. The dynamics around such boundaries are formidably complex. The limitation of vaunting displays of scientific/medical prowess, such as John Hunter's, to a peer group (including students), appears strange at first sight. But restricted access also drives a curiosity among excluded groups. This curiosity has a particular quality in relation to science and medicine, since these domains make claims about their special access to nature's secrets. By extension, their practitioners become the exclusive possessors of such secrets; indeed, they use their possession of them in their general power strategies. This means that getting inside *places* where science/medicine are done, however vicariously or indirectly, has a special attraction. Places like operating theaters are assumed to hold some key to secrets, to allow a peep, as if through the keyhole, of special, exclusive, possibly sacred activities.

Because it touches us so directly, getting inside medicine is a very strong urge. To illustrate this point I referred to a contemporary museum—Old St. Thomas' Operating Theatre. This nineteenth-century operating theater was discovered only relatively recently in the roof of a London church. It is not fantastically revealing, yet enormous public interest has been shown in it. What can it reveal? Is it made more revealing, if, as has been done, a surgical operation is reenacted in that very room? The implication is that such reconstructions serve to trigger our historical imagination because they take place in an authentic location. By historical imagination, people in museums would intend us to understand a realistic, vivid, accurate view of the past. While there are visitors who can fill up this imaginative void for themselves, current museum thinking assumes that the majority cannot, and hence the whole array of new realist techniques currently in vogue is justified.

It is vital to distinguish between museums created by medical/scientific practitioners like the Hunters, who mounted exhibitions for their peers, and the modern creation of historical displays, which ostensively reveal a scientific/medical past, but which are molded by present day concerns. The nature of the publics, whether professional or general, to which displays are addressed has changed radically, largely because of the changing nature of science and medicine themselves. To put it extremely crudely, the current political and economic role of science and medicine both gives them enormous glamour and requires them to mobilize popular support and appreciation. In this context, literalism abounds, and reconstructions and reenactments of past science are everywhere. I used the example of the Wellcome displays at the Science Museum in London. Here the realist drive is taken to extremes in a series of life-size scenes. What kind of an experience for visitors do these dioramas give rise to? Silently, certain kinds of knowledge and insight are withheld, and a comforting present is affirmed.

VI

These questions are not restricted to science and medicine. If we concede that museums engage their visitors at a psychic level as well as at many others, then biographical exhibits—no matter what field their subject was in—will most readily assist in processes of identification. I suggested that the Nightingale and Freud museums related quite differently to the issues of realism and representation, since in the first case the displays served primarily to reconstruct the life of a powerful figure in various fields of health care, and in the second to preserve a site as a kind of guarantee of the authenticity and cultural significance of psychoanalysis. Clearly biographical museums raise distinctive questions—about how the shape of a life, including its troubling, inconsistent, unwelcome, even embarrassing aspects, is conveyed. Yet, since they generally have a narrative dimension, viewers can easily be enticed to identify with a life quest. In Nightingale's case, nurses empathize with her life strategies and feel a sense of referred achievement from her acquisition of "fame, power, and influence." Visitors can emerge strengthened from the museum.

The Nightingale Museum, I argued, criticizes an old myth of her, but produces a new one, a process the Freud Museum takes one stage further; Sigmund Freud becomes a legend, an awesome figure of genius, almost a God. This sacralization has two aspects—the museum is a shrine where we worship the intellectual and personal qualities of the founder of psychoanalysis, but at the same time, since its authenticity is everywhere insisted upon, it is also a document, a faithful testimony to Freud's real life and achievements. Visitors are encouraged to adopt a stance of subservient adoration. This museum is a home and a scientific workplace, a place where death occurred, and a place of public display. A skeptical reaction is called for by this conflation of science-as-practiced and science-as-display, which are, despite their close relationships, two distinct historical phenomena. There is a sleight of hand in the Freud Museum, as in many other museums, which encourages visitors to see them as the same, united through a single powerful personality.

The simple fact is that many aspects of human experience and action, especially those that are abstract, cannot be rendered suitable for exhibition in a museum. The new realism in science and medicine museums, driven as it is by powerful market and political forces, denies this. It seeks to create a set of visual experiences for a mass public that forces itself and its meanings upon viewers. It is to be resisted through an understanding of the history of this potent admixture of realism and representation, in which techniques of representation; the social, political, economic, and cultural history of groups and institutions; the nature of visual culture; relationships between objects, displays, and beholders, all played a part. Science and medicine are not unified, homogeneous domains that somehow press themselves directly, unproblematically upon the public, however that is defined. The historical transformations of realism in the fields of science and medicine are about fantasies and identifications, about awe and homage, about trophies and the fetish.

Museums of science and medicine raise central questions relating to "realism and representation." For much of their history, practitioners in these fields have displayed their achievements, have sought to derive status, power, and recognition through doing so, and have fostered the idea that they, uniquely, offer unmediated access to the "real" world of nature. We can pursue this theme by examining the precise techniques deployed in exhibiting nature, science, and medicine, and by reading museums and their constituent displays as complex texts. Much is thereby revealed about classificatory systems, their history, and their contemporary forms. This approach can be applied to the biographies of those prominent in science and medicine, as well as to organisms, the human body, instruments, and so on. The explicit level of scientific and medical museums is only one small part of them. Just as important are the relationships between objects and beholders. To grasp these another language is required. For this reason it is useful to draw upon religious concepts, like shrine, relic, icon, homage, and the sacred, and upon notions like trophy and fetish with their more heterogeneous resonances. If the ways museums generate fantasies and set up apt settings for visitors' identifications with people, places, and objects are ignored, there is a genuine danger of seeing them as simply instruments of scientific and medical power. However tempting it is to interpret them merely as the tools of an authoritative elite, this must be resisted. To succumb would be, in effect, to take terms like "realism" for granted, to treat them uncritically, and to miss the chance that an emphasis on representation offers for the study of the multiple mediations of science and medicine.

NOTES

I am pleased to offer my heartfelt thanks to the Royal Society of London for their financial assistance and to all the museums mentioned for their warm welcome and courteous help.

1. This paper is a sequel to an earlier essay: "Objects of Knowledge: A Historical Perspective on Museums," in P. Vergo, ed., *The New Museology* (London, 1989), 22–40. On science-as-display see S. Schaffer, "Natural Philosophy and Public Spectacle in the Eighteenth Century," *History of Science* 21 (1983): 1–43.

2. Two exemplary works in this area are: T. Crow, *Painters and Public Life in Eighteenth-Century Paris* (New Haven, 1985), and J. B. Elshtain, *Public Man, Private Woman* (Oxford, 1981). For a recent sociological work that addresses these issues see E. Gamarnikow et al., eds., *The Public and the Private* (London, 1983). It is essential to remember that all notions of a public stand in implicit contrast with a private domain.

3. D. Jarrett, *England in the Age of Hogarth* (St. Albans, 1976).

4. P. M. Roget, *Thesaurus of English Words and Phrases* (Harmondsworth, 1953), 137, 169, 321.

5. On the museum see the useful pamphlet by the current Qvist Curator: E. Allen, *Hunterian Museum* (London, 1974), and V. Negus, *History of the Trustees of the Hunterian Collection* (Edinburgh and London, 1966); the museum also publishes a series of catalogues of its collections.

6. I have attempted to address the question of realism in *Sexual Visions: Images of Gender in Science and Medicine between the Eighteenth and Twentieth Centuries* (Hemel Hempstead, 1989), especially 45ff. Michael Fried's ideas about realism are especially stimulating: *Realism, Writing, Disfiguration: On Thomas Eakins and Stephen Crane* (Chicago, 1987), and *Courbet's Realism* (Chicago, 1990).

7. Although he does not frame it in quite this way, Easlea's analysis of the language used by the scientists involved in producing the first bomb demonstrates the value of attending to processes of representation in modern science: B. Easlea, *Fathering the Unthinkable: Masculinity, Scientists and the Nuclear Arms Race* (London, 1983).

8. Classic work, like that of M. B. Hesse, *Models and Analogies in Science* (Notre Dame, Ind., 1966), is now being developed further by those interested in laboratory and experimental practices and in the complex and creative mental processes involved, for example, F. James, ed., *The Development of the Laboratory: Essays on the Place of Experiment in Industrial Civilization* (Basingstoke, 1989).

9. On representations of Nightingale see A. Hudson Jones, "*The White Angel* (1936): Hollywood's Images of Florence Nightingale," in A. Hudson

Jones, ed., *Images of Nurses: Perspectives from History, Art and Literature* (Philadelphia, 1988), 221–42. For a broader perspective on her legacy, see M. E. Baly, *Florence Nightingale and the Nursing Legacy* (London, 1986), and F. B. Smith, *Florence Nightingale—Reputation and Power* (London, 1982).

10. L. Gamwell and R. Wells, *Sigmund Freud and Art: His Personal Collection of Antiquities* (New York and London, 1989).

11. F. Manuel, *A Portrait of Isaac Newton* (Cambridge, Mass., 1968); P. Gay, *Freud for Historians* (New York, 1985), exposes the fallacious thinking that surrounds the fear of psychological reductionism; J. Masson, *Freud: The Assault: Freud's Suppression of the Seduction Theory* (London, 1984); P. Grosskurth, *Melanie Klein: Her Life and Work* (London, 1987).

12. F. J. Cole, "History of Anatomical Museums," in *A Miscellany Presented to J. M. Mackay* (Liverpool and London, 1914), 302–17.

13. S. J. Cross, "John Hunter, the Animal Oeconomy, and Late Eighteenth-Century Physiological Discourse," *Studies in the History of Biology* 5 (1981): 1–110; P. Corsi, *The Age of Lamarck: Evolutionary Theories in France 1790–1830* (Berkeley, 1988); D. Outram, *Georges Cuvier: Vocation, Science and Authority in Post-Revolutionary France* (Manchester, 1984).

14. D. Haraway, "Teddy Bear Patriarchy: Taxidermy in the Garden of Eden, New York City, 1908–1936," *Social Text* 4 (1984): 20–64.

15. V. C. Medvei and J. L. Thornthon, eds., *The Royal Hospital of Saint Bartholomew, 1123–1973* (London, 1974), esp. chap. 17; V. Tansey and D. E. C. Mekie, *The Museum of the Royal College of Surgeons of Edinburgh* (Edinburgh, 1982).

16. The obvious comparison is with relics. These were valued not for their *beauty* but for their efficacy, which derived from their (supposed) authenticity. It is significant that they were usually touched rather than gazed upon.

17. B. Bracegirdle, *The Wellcome Museum of the History of Medicine* (Norwich, 1981).

18. S. Sheets-Pyenson, "Cathedrals of Science: the Development of Colonial Natural History Museums during the Late Nineteenth Century," *History of Science* 25 (1987): 279–300.

19. C. C. Sellars, *Mr. Peale's Museum: Charles Willson Peale and the First Popular Museum of Natural Science and Art* (New York, 1980); E. P. Richardson, B. Hindle, and L. B. Miller, *Charles Willson Peale and His World* (New York, 1983), esp. part 2.

20. On Hunter's atlas see my "Gender, Generation and Science: William Hunter's Obstetric Atlas," in W. F. Bynum and R. S. Porter, eds., *William Hunter and the Eighteenth-Century Medical World* (Cambridge, 1985), 385–412.

CHAPTER 16

Augustan Realities: Nature's Representatives and Their Cultural Resources in the Early Eighteenth Century

SIMON SCHAFFER

This chapter offers a historical account of the resources that were used in Augustan Britain by natural philosophers who were aiming to make themselves nature's legitimate spokesmen. These resources were fragile and controversial. Representations of nature were stabilized not because their promoters escaped from culture's grip, but because these natural philosophers made their representations grip key interests within culture. Scientific realism is a philosophical position that distracts attention from this cultural work of representatives of nature, and points it toward the adequacy of nature's representations. There is a relationship between the "amnesia" of realism, in which the work that establishes representations is forgotten, and the apparent power of realism as a scientific and literary genre. Scientific realism holds that represented objects exist, constrain, and act independently of their representations. Scientific propositions, however, have a prescriptive role. Cosmologies are also job descriptions. An account of nature recommends specific practices and asserts their legitimacy. This gives such propositions a normative role that historians of science can document. Realist epistemologies, by contrast, treat such propositions as purely descriptive, and thus neglect the work that establishes practices' legitimacy. Furthermore, the work of legitimation also disqualifies other practices. An account of the real contents of nature rules out enterprises that tell different stories about the world. So the polemical work that establishes that a group of representatives are reliable delegates of some natural order can also settle the contents of that order [Collins 100; Woolgar 65].

The shift from interrogating trustworthy pictures to questioning trustworthy depictors makes the agency and the power of representatives more obvious. There are precedents for this move in recent epistemologies of science. In his "anthropological fantasy" about the origins of depiction, Ian Hacking urges that the world was "found by conceptualizing the real as an attribute of representations." He exploits the semantic ambiguities of the term "representative": "lawyers represent clients and represent that their clients are innocent" [*Representing and Intervening* xii, 134–36]. The move is also made by Bruno Latour in his investigation of the sociology of representation: "hundreds of scientific disciplines and instruments constantly bring far away places, objects and times to us which are thus represented. . . . To take full account of this retinue of delegates, sociologists have to look carefully at their [i.e., the delegates'] conflicts over who is the most representative" ["Opening One Eye" 16]. I endorse this suggestion. It is a good way of tracing the construction of rival representational regimes. Such an approach does justice to the force of Gillian Beer's observation that "the enclosing within a community is a necessary condition for assuring stable signification": historians of science need to see how enclosure is achieved, and what happens when it breaks down [45].

Scriblerian Representatives

> Though it shall be demonstrated that modern blood circulates, yet I will still believe, with Hippocrates, that the blood of the Ancients had a flux and reflux from the heart, like a Tide. Consider how Luxury hath introduced new diseases, and with them not improbably alter'd the whole Course of the Fluids. . . . I question not but plausible conjectures may be made even as to the Time when the blood first began to circulate.
>
> *Memoirs of Martinus Scriblerus,* ca. 1714–1720.

In 1714 a group of Augustan wits, including Alexander Pope, Jonathan Swift, and John Gay, began to compose their remarkable *Memoirs of the Extraordinary Life, Works and Discoveries of Martinus Scriblerus*. Their satire was directed against the troubled republic of letters, riven by sects who each claimed to be the legitimate representatives of the moral and the natural order. The *Memoirs* recorded the tribulations of a novice trapped amidst conflicting natural philosophical authorities, in the disputes of Ancients and Moderns, of Newtonians and Cartesians, of Deists and High Churchmen. For example, while his anatomy professor taught him that the blood had always circulated round the body, young Martin's father denied it. Martin faces a characteristic dilemma: which representative can be trusted? On the answer to this question hinges the decision on the plausible contents of the worlds moral and natural. Is it plausible that mere observation of humans now could allow us to judge what humans once were? Is the combination of paternal authority, Hippocratic doctrine, and contemporary accounts of pathological luxury to outweigh modern anatomical pedagogy and the views of the royal physician William Harvey? In such contests, the Scriblerians' audience was persistently reminded that the debates about the contents of nature are simultaneously debates about the standing of rival representatives. Decisions about the natural world hinge on judgments of moral and social worth. In a culture of universal distrust, no knowledge could be securely established. The treatment of virtuosi by the learned Scriblerus, of the courts by the highwayman Macheath, and of Yahoos by the surgeon Gulliver all indicated that to determine what counts as real is to brand one's enemies' views as illusory, fantastical, and diseased. "Besides real Diseases," Gulliver tells the Houyhnhnms, "we are subject to many that are only imaginary, for which the Physicians have invented imaginary Cures" [*Gulliver's Travels* 248].

The chapter that follows describes a historical moment, the early eighteenth century, when rival accounts of nature coexisted in public culture. It analyzes these alternatives, the resources which they could use, and the political and moral implications of the lessons they taught. Traditionally, moments such as these have been used to tell stories about the progress of reason or stories about clashes of incommensurable worldviews. The chapter tells neither story. Contests for legitimacy take place within the cultural field, where political, practical, and moral resources count. Natural philosophy in the period of Scriblerians, and Newtonians, was certainly troubled by these problems of power and knowledge. Consider the claim that white light is a composite of different color-making rays, a claim that played a key role in the establishment and propagation of Newtonian philosophy. The apparent behavior of light depended on which prisms experimenters used. Those who failed to replicate Newton's trials of light rays—as many French and Italian natural philosophers did between 1672 and 1740—were charged by the English with a failure to use reliable glassware. In 1715, Newton's lieutenant in London, J. T. Desaguliers, showed visiting French and Italian natural philosophers how to use English prisms; he instructed them where to buy the right instruments; he tried to undermine the reputation of Venetian glass, hitherto the optical benchmark. The Hanoverian court was packed with Newton's delegates. Desaguliers and Samuel Clarke were both chaplains to the new authorities. Court patronage helped secure Newtonian dealers. Those who accepted this new culture also credited Newton's doctrine: "our Prisms in Italy are of no other use than to amuse Children or hang up as a fine shew in some window in the country," an Italian convert wrote in his popular *Newtonianism for Ladies* (1742). Those who rejected these values also rejected Desaguliers' claim that English prisms vouchsafed Newton's credibility. Against them, London instrument makers reckoned they could dominate the international trade, while courtly writers reproduced the Newtonian view of color by constructing Newtonian natural philosophers as proper spokesmen of nature [Schaffer, "Glass Works" 99]. Newton was notoriously identified with the light he described. In verses of 1727 dedicated to "that most illustrious Patriot" Robert Walpole, James Thomson eulogized Newton, "Britain's boast," in these terms: "Even Light itself, which every thing displays, / Shone undiscovered, till his brighter mind / Untwisted all the shining robe of day" [Nicolson; Ketcham; M. L. Greenberg].

The same link between cultural and natural order is apparent in French efforts to determine the Earth's shape, another vital moment in Newtonianism's fate. The representation of the French kingdom by the work of its servants, the king's engineer, his intendant of fortifications, and the director of his Observatory, provided the context for these efforts. Ancien régime surveyors argued for the close link between their own repute and that of their representation of the Earth's surface. The legend of a 1652 Paris map linked royal power, representational techniques, geometrical adequacy, and the vexed question of the metropolis' size: "This map, having been made according to the rules of geometry, will be esteemed not only because of the great advantages that can be derived for the very service of Your Majesty but also that in the most distant countries those who have believed the reputation of Paris to be above the truth may admire its greatness and beauty" [Marin 169–79]. From 1693 the Observatory was charged with the task of representing the whole of France. Jacques Cassini, its director, presented a preliminary report on the measure of a meridian in 1718 and began the determination of a line of latitude in summer 1733. At this moment, however, the astronomers Maupertuis and Delisle, already convinced Newtonians and amongst those who had made the pilgrimage to London, mounted a scathing attack on the Observatory's techniques. Their assault on Cassini's competence, on the representative adequacy of his maps, was part of their effort to make a crucial test of the adequacy of the new philosophy. The claim that Newton had predicted a flattening at the Earth's poles, and that Cassini had found otherwise, was a careful practical construction the Newtonians placed retrospectively upon Cassini's representation. These were not self-evident predictions simply to be matched with the real planet. Cruciality, here as in the optical case, was an achievement in natural philosophical and in court culture. Maupertuis cleverly made interest with the government. State-sponsored expeditions to Lapland and Peru during the 1730s, equipped, via Desaguliers and George Graham, with the best London-made instruments, were designed to settle this set of issues. Allies of the Observatory remained unmoved by Maupertuis' journey and its results. Maupertuis' northern achievement was accurately described by the amiable critic Voltaire as "simultaneously flattening the poles and the Cassini": it was a tactic which undermined the place of the Observatory as a representative of the French state, of the Earth, and of geodesy [Brunet 1: 58–61; J. Greenberg; Brown].

Neither Newton's doctrine of color, nor Maupertuis' argument that the Earth's poles are flattened, commanded assent through ostensive reference to a preordained natural order. This raises the following questions: are representations credible because the practices employed by representatives already command assent? or do these practices command assent because the items they purport to represent have already become credible? Hacking writes that robust practices realize the items they represent (*Representing and Intervening* 24); Andrew Pickering argues that these items "sustain and legitimate the particular experimental practices inherent in their own production" (14). Here trust is (provisionally) withdrawn from the tools and tactics of the working scientists. This is what "abstention from realism" means. A good way of damaging realism is to withdraw legitimacy from representatives who purport to speak for an autonomous realm of facts. The debate on the formal realism of the novel is also marked by this concern. In the context of the novel's readership Ian Watt appeals to the behavior of "another group of specialists in epistemology, the jury in the court of law" [34]. Here, too, it is held that trust in the narrator carries the realism of the narrative. In reply, McKeon notes the tortured maneuvers in which tale-tellers such as Defoe were compelled to engage to win trust and credit for their tales. It is not that Defoe's honesty and credibility vouchsafed the moral message of his stories—on the contrary, *Robinson Crusoe* was to be distinguished from some "other Jesting with Truth," because "it is design'd and effectually turn'd for instructive and upright Ends, and has its Moral justly apply'd" [McKeon 121; Schaffer, "Defoe's Natural Philosophy"]. Just as epistemologists debate the question whether matters of fact are stabilized by, or stabilize, reliable practices, so literary critics seek to gloss realist texts either as the guarantors of moral values or as guaranteed by them. The problem of credit and trust, a problem of moral order, is fundamental for both sets of protagonists.

Received history has it that the eighteenth century was a crucial period for the establishment of these regimes. The novel and the experimental

Figure 16.1. Natural philosophy at court: an imaginary visit by Louis XIV and Colbert to the Académie Royale des Sciences. In the background, Cassini's Observatory. Reprinted from Claude Perrault, *Mémoires pour servir à l'histoire naturelle des animaux* (1671), frontispiece by Sebastien Le Clerc.

report appeared as legitimate means of representing the moral and the natural order. Both required new cultural practices in the realms of instrumentation, dissemination of information, publication, and social organization. Somehow or other, older, courtly forms of making knowledge failed or were thrust aside. Watt stressed this point and sought to connect formal realism with natural philosophical epistemology (*Rise of the Novel* chap. 1). Gaston Bachelard stressed similar features of natural philosophical life. He argued that new sciences appeared via the development of routine, standard, laboratory practices, which generated phenomena upon which natural philosophers could reason mathematically. This substitution of reasoned discourse upon instrumentally generated phenomena for naive realism he called "phenomeno-technics" (*Rationalisme appliqué* chap. 8). However, although they both made a welcome case for attention to the practices through which these new representations were developed, neither Bachelard nor Watt provided an adequate account of the way representatives won the right to speak. Instead, culture functioned negatively, as an obstacle to be overcome in order to allow representation to become adequate. No doubt prompted by the Stoic view that separation from cultural pollution aids representation of truth, both saw court life, in particular, as a source of danger which these new representatives successfully escaped.

For Watt, classicism and romance were "adverse to the requirements of formal realism"; Defoe and Richardson were "freer to present 'the natural object' in whatever way they wished" because, unlike the French, they did not have to orient themselves toward the court; finally, they were "wholly representative of the new centre of gravity" of the urban bourgeois readership. The move from Whitehall and St. James's to Grub Street and the Exchange was a move from fantasy to reality [Watt 65]. Bachelard drew a similar picture: Desaguliers' or Maupertuis' links with power were simply the marks of their insufficient freedom from the fantasies of polite culture. In his investigations of eighteenth-century electricity and chemistry, he insisted that the supersession of the courtly cabinet of curiosities by the regimented milieu of the scientific academy was the precondition of the appearance of legitimate scientific representatives. Bachelard described the move from the wondrous "Leyden Jar" to the reliable techniques of Voltaic analytic electricity as a path "out of the cultural impasse where words and things lead us" [*Formation de l'esprit* 33; *Rationalisme appliqué* 148–9]. The "gulf which separates the charlatan and the savant" was a gap essential for the appearance of reliable representation through scientific practices [*Formation de l'esprit* 33].

This "gulf," however, was a fraught and complex cultural artifact. Natural philosophy had to enlist other powers to win the right to speak

Figure 16.2. Jonathan Swift's "three eminences": the pulpit, the gallows, and the stage. Reprinted from Jonathan Swift, *A Tale of a Tub,* 3d ed. (1740).

on nature's behalf. The emergence of a group of recognizable delegates of nature was both enabled by and also helped make an accompanying rupture, the schism between patrician and plebeian culture. Such a break might be seen as the withdrawal of the natural philosophers from the pressures of public life: hence the Scriblerian joke that Martin had composed "An Essay on the *Origin* of *Sciences,* written from the Deserts of *Nubia,*" a text on the simian source of ancient learning [Pope, *Memoirs of Scriblerus* 171; *Essay* 286–94]. But instead of seeing this rupture as the *removal* of an obstacle to intimate contact with natural order, it is better seen as the construction of a social order which established a place for those who claimed the office of delegate. In *A Tale of a Tub* (1710) Swift analyzed representatives' search for audience and place: "whoever hath an Ambition to be heard in a Crowd, must press, and squeeze, and thrust, and climb with indefatigable Pains, till he has exalted himself to a certain Degree of Altitude above them." After noting the failure of Philosophy, hitherto, to secure such a stable height, Swift listed the means now used to win an audience: "three wooden Machines . . . the *Pulpit,* the *Ladder* (i.e., the Gallows), and the *Stage-Itinerant.*" Eighteenth-century natural philosophers needed to find their own site amongst the worlds of church, law, and theater [*Tale of a Tub* 34]. This search dominated the realities they purported to represent.

Natural Philosophers Ply Their Trade

> For a miracle to be well established, one would wish it to be performed in the presence of the Académie des Sciences of Paris, or the Royal Society of London, and the faculty of medicine, supported by a detachment of the regiment of guards to control the crowd of people whose indiscretion might prevent the operation of the miracle.
>
> Voltaire, *Philosophical Dictionary,* 1764

Early eighteenth-century natural philosophy provides good cases of the search for authoritative platforms. Baroque savants cobbled together a set of technologies to warrant this authority [Shapin, "Pump and Circumstance"]. These included a material technology of highly tooled instrumentation and publicity networks. It was supposed that instruments like microscopes, prisms, telescopes, air pumps, and electrical machines could be made transparent to nature's messages. These machines became emblematic of the new philosophy. It was also supposed that the press and the theater, the coffeehouse and the academy, could be turned into means for propagating such messages. A literary technology sustained proper conventions of reportage, involving detailed autobiographical circumstantiation and the deliberate naming of eminent witnesses, whose eminence, in a society of orders, was a self-evident badge of credit. A social technology was used to organize human beings in spaces set aside for the purposes of the manufacture of experience. Architecture and morality were supposed to combine here, so that specific individuals proper to testify and supervise this process would be marked out as the key members of the republic of letters. Many were distrusted, either in principle or in fact: the vulgar, the hired hand, womenfolk, "enthusiasts." Every single one of these conventions raised trouble for eighteenth-century culture.

Natural philosophical conduct hinged on conventions of trust. The conduct of eighteenth-century courts and exchanges threatened the basis of credit in traditional culture. Courtiers' status relied entirely on customary means of representation before their lord. In the public sphere of "good society," "a market of opinions," real social power was "exalted, abased, or lost" [Elias 96]. Roger Chartier observes that "the construction of each individual's identity was always at the intersection of that person's own self-representation and the credit accorded or refused by others to that representation" [87]. What seemed most real hinged most on others' judgments—hence an obsession with the fragility of credit and trust with Defoe, Fielding, and their contemporaries, and the Scriblerian project of an "art of political lying." The power of movable credit had immense significance for the possibility of establishing credible testimony. The literary and social technologies of experimental natural philosophy would work only if it were possible to secure a witness's standing *independently* of the event reported. But neither courtiers nor dealers could easily show the real basis of their trustworthiness. Experimenters reckoned they could deal with this trouble by trusting to "inanimate bodies, which are not capable of prepossessions, or giving us partial informations" [Boyle 3: 614–15, 624–28]. The recalcitrance of experimenters' critics, however, demonstrated that inanimate bodies could not "speak for themselves." They still needed spokesmen, whose credit remained in question.

Augustan culture experienced an overwhelming credit crisis during the 1720s. The crisis made courtiers and merchants equally vulnerable. Alongside the South Sea scandal, insurance schemes and other "visionary projects" flourished, rose, and fell. These projects directly challenged received views of the boundaries of reality: satirists imagined "an insurance of ships to the spacious world of the moon . . . noses insured from fire . . . to show bears, monkeys and monsters—I think this is an ample list of projects" [Carswell 141]. Leading entrepreneurs, such as Onslow and Chandos, were notorious backers of schemes such as the Royal Exchange Assurance and habitués of the City's worst financial scandals.

Figure 16.3. The credit crisis of the 1720s: Hogarth's satire against the South Sea Bubble. On the left the devil throws fortune's golden haunches to the crowd, while on the right honor is whipped by villainy and honesty broken on the wheel by self-interest. All this takes place in front of a reworked Monument to the Great Fire. Reprinted from Hogarth, *The South Sea Bubble* (1721), courtesy of the Trustees of the British Museum.

They were also sponsors of the foremost Newtonian natural philosophers, including Desaguliers and William Whiston [Stewart, "Public Lectures"]. Insurance schemes like these may have claimed mathematical warrant for their calculation of real worth; these claims were illusory, and in fact ran counter to the culture of risk and uncertainty which the schemes sustained [Daston, "Domestication of Risk" 244–46]. The new Whig oligarchy seemed mired in the world of fantasy, which had done down more solid creditors in its wake. Defoe launched his series of fictions and his series of works on superstition during the 1720s precisely to analyze this disaster. "It is true that by these delusions the priests got infinite summs of money and this makes it still probable that they would labour hard and use the utmost of their skill to uphold the credit of their oracles," he wrote in his *Political History of the Devil* [248]. Defoe made it crystal clear that this remark was directed at more recent illusionists, whose work was "but an Artificial Trick and Cheat upon the Nation of a Trade in the Air." Furthermore, the manipulation of credit affected all secure beliefs: "Great is the Power of Imagination!" [Pocock 452–54; Schaffer, "Defoe's Natural Philosophy" 30]. Natural philosophers needed the patronage of the masters of credit. They could warrant their schemes on the Exchange. Desaguliers, Chandos' chaplain and engineer, lectured London audiences on the dangers to which "Persons of Fortune" would be exposed if they relied on charlatans rather than on expert natural philosophers: "thus many people employ the Apothecary to save the charge of the Physician" [Stewart, "Public Lectures" 58]. But intimate alliance with the likes of Chandos made these natural philosophers obvious targets for Scriblerian ridicule and obvious collaborators with the corrupt oligarchy. An incredible place in Lagado was a high price to pay for Whig credit [Rogers, "Gulliver and the Engineers"; Thompson, *Whigs and Hunters* 178].

Natural philosophers had to distinguish themselves from manipulators of the market and the court; but they had to become manipulators too. It is important to stress the power of the new schemes, new engines, new projects which the engineers and experimenters started to promote. Larry Stewart's perceptive study "The Selling of Newton" underscores the authority won for natural philosophy through these projects. It is equally important to understand the credibility crisis which governed projects' promotion. The natural philosophical enterprise was a prospective one: why should it be trusted? The balance of this chapter is devoted to two features of Augustan culture which were used, and abused, in the debates that helped make natural philosophy credibly representative. First, the categories of "vulgar belief" and "superstition" played a key role in the construction of the natural philosophical task. They did so both as the supposed target against which reality could be contrasted and as resources to use against rivals to authority over public belief. These categories defined the boundaries inside which natural philosophical technologies could act [Burke; Roche]. It follows, second, that natural philosophy's technologies hinged on a special model of private and public space. Natural philosophers put together resources from dominant culture to make a space safe for natural knowledge production. The theater was an especially powerful cultural form in this process, at once the realm of display and illusion [Agnew chap. 4; Sennett chap. 5; Elias chap. 3]. So the chapter closes with a brief glance forward from Augustan London to the debates on theatricality and the role of the savant which characterized the end of the Enlightenment. The examination of the deluded vulgar and the deceitfully theatrical helps us see how natural philosophers tried to make themselves nature's representatives, and how they tried to disqualify others' stories.

The Transformation of Superstition

> So far are philosophers from laughing to see the astonishment of the vulgar at these experiments, that they cannot help viewing them with equal, if not greater astonishment themselves. Indeed, all the electricians of the present age can well remember the time, when, with respect to these things, they themselves would have ranked among the same ignorant, staring vulgar.
>
> Priestley, *History of Electricity,* 1767

The withdrawal of polite elites from immediate contact with plebeian culture prompted the study of and vigilance over the habits and beliefs of the vulgar [Thomas chap. 22]. The term "superstition" changed its meaning from reference to dangerous falsehood to a label for customary foolishness [Burke 241]. Witchcraft and divination, for example, moved from hostile realities to fascinating folklore. And they moved from being the care of the divines to that of the naturalists. Peter Burke comments that "it was precisely the unscientific, the marvellous, which attracted them in folktales, as it attracted historians of 'superstition' " [Burke 285]. This move must not be read as a monolithic and facile change of elite jurisdiction. The displacement gave natural philosophers a complex target and a new place to position themselves. Priestcraft and plebs allegedly agreed that "superstitious" powers were real: natural philosophers branded the clergy with the errors of their flocks, by materializing powers, bringing them under the control of experimental natural philosophy, then charging that those who still remained committed to the reality of superstitious representations were themselves deluded [Revel].

Decisions about nature's capacities were decisions rather more about the bounds of plausibility than about the validity of reference. Because the plausible and the credible were in question, the moral order of trust and fancy interacted with the social order of gentlemanliness and vulgarity. The historiographical shift from validity to plausibility allows us to understand the ways Augustans handled novel testimony. In 1726 it was reported that a Godalming woman, Mary Toft, was giving birth to litters of rabbits. The case directly connected authority, reality, and the generative powers of nature. It highlights the porosity of the highly gendered boundaries between "gentlemanly" control and "hysterical" resistance [Seligman; Hudson]. Godalming was at the center of an area exposed to Whig enclosures of common lands, under the direction of Toft's landlord, Onslow, an ally of Walpole, whom we have met as an entrepreneur of insurance "bubbles." Tenants were to be increasingly subjected to entrepreneurial management: traditional forms of "moral economy" were called in question. The customs associated with generation and fertility explicitly connected agricultural production with human growth. Toft and her community endorsed the conventional moral view that women frightened in pregnancy would give birth to monsters. Thus, for example, a draft of 1706, in which Newton contrasted apparent wonders with the powers of God, "whose Ideas work more powerfully upon matter than the Imagination of a mother works upon an embrio" [McGuire, "Force" 205]. Local men-midwives, royal surgeons, and Whig courtiers all seized upon the Toft case as a testing ground for their authority. Initially, few were minded to doubt these reports. Stories of her wonders were printed next to tales of "an illiterate Man who . . . does not understand one Syllable of Mathematicks," but had nevertheless produced a perpetual motion machine. Swift was not unique in juxtaposing Newtonian projectors and visionary lunatics [Rogers, "Gulliver and the Engineers" 14–15].

The diseases of credit were visibly infecting the public sphere. In November 1726 Toft was shifted from Godalming to a London brothel, where she could be torn away from her local culture, interrogated by eminent court officials, and broken to a confession of conspiracy. Onslow energetically collected depositions to sustain this hostile view; London patricians worked hard to distance themselves from their early endorsement. It is not the case that the elite had always been skeptical of Toft's testimony. The episode rapidly became a moment at which rival epistemological authorities—lawyers, physicians, surgeons, midwives—tested out their control. Whiston, Newton's heretical disciple, found precedents for the rabbit birth in biblical prophecy. John Arbuthnot gave his comments on Toft's conduct, initially enthusiastically, then satirically. Hogarth's notorious cartoon "Cunicularii, or The Wise Men" explicitly (and blasphemously) linked the events with the Nativity, and hence with monstrous conceptions both religious and political. The Toft episode reminds us of the significance of talk of generation and fertility and the meaning of its subjection to rival regimes of truth. Toft's rabbits were simultaneously a wondrous birth, an object of traditional appropriation by the Surrey peasantry, and the newly defined property of Onslow in the countryside and the elite surgeons in the city. In the eighteenth century, Ludmilla Jordanova tells us, "physiological processes were tools with which social events could be explored, and may therefore be said to stand in a mediating relationship to them" [90]. Because of these mediations, the contests of elite physiologies with their allegedly subordinate rivals are not to be read as the assertion of self-evident reason, but rather as engagements with wide ranges of dangerous and plausible alternatives. The truth of the wondrous birth depended on Mary Toft's credibility: and this changed with the rapid political changes of landed society and its members [Dabydeen 57–59].

Figure 16.4. Hogarth's blasphemous representation of Mary Toft and the "Wise Men of Godliman." The "rabbit getter" is identified standing behind Mary Toft. Reprinted from Hogarth, *Cunicularii,* courtesy of the Trustees of the British Museum.

The categories of popular "error" mattered throughout society. Disputes between Newtonians and Leibnizians at the Hanoverian court highlight the place of the category of "vulgar belief" in the natural philosophical quest for authority. These involved contests over the nature of power in the worlds natural and political. Newton's Royal Society colleagues argued for the reality of a Providence represented in the civil order by the monarch and demonstrated to citizens by his spokesmen, the Newtonian party. Newton announced in 1706 that "if natural Philosophy in all its Parts, by pursuing this Method, shall at length be perfected, the Bounds of Moral Philosophy will be also enlarged" [*Opticks* 405]. Divine government was best shown through managed "Phaenomena": "Metaphysical arguments are slippery and understood by few" [Schaffer, "Natural Philosophy" 4]. Newton made up a history of philosophy to justify his authority and to place the divine role of his natural philosophy. "Vulgar superstition" was a key term in this story. There had once been "primitive Christians," "those that are in the hedges and the high ways" [Manuel 112–13]. In drafts for the *Principia,* Newton stated that the Scriptures had been written for these "ordinary people who fail to abstract thought from sensible appearances"; so these texts should not be used by literalist divines to contest natural philosophy, which aimed to "free the reader from certain vulgar prejudices" and teach lessons about "absolute quantities" [*Mathematical Papers* vi, 192].

A nice example of the contingency of rival views of the "vulgar" is provided by this question of absolute and relative quantities. In his drafts on mechanics of 1685, Newton insisted that God alone could perceive the true motions of bodies. The "vulgar," by contrast, perceived only the apparent quantities rather than true measures of such terms. The contrast between divinity and vulgarity, as he reaffirmed in successive versions of the *Principia,* was also the distinction between measure and appearance, between mathematics and experience, and, ultimately, between master and servant. "The purity of mathematical and philosophical truths," he wrote portentously in book 1, must not be "defiled" by confusion with "vulgar measures." When, in the General Scholium published in 1713, he wished to account for the nature of God, he pointed out that the absolute terms used of His power were "titles which have no respect to servants" [Cohen 524–25]. In complete contrast, his critic the Tory lawyer Roger North objected to the "pertinacious prejudice" that real motions were absolute: "These I say are the opinions of the vulgar, but however Great philosophers, and chiefly Sir Is. N. think fitt to maintain them" [Stewart, "Samuel Clarke" 67]. So Newton reckoned the vulgar were relativists, and North reckoned they were absolutists. Both men also claimed they could mend the mistake. But North took a sober High Church view of vulgar capacity, insinuating that it was a commonplace illusion that bodies and motions had some autonomous existence. Priestly custodians would correct this, if they could. Against this, in Newton's history, the vulgar had been corrupted by their appointed guardians, who promoted idolatry and the wrong model of monarchy [North 11, 129–131]. Idolatry was the attribution of divine power to material subordinates, the chief superstition of contemporary culture. Real natural philosophy taught where true power lay. The "business of natural philosophy" was to show how these real powers worked, and the originally humble were lost models of how this work should be done. The contemporary elite were the corrupt targets against which this natural philosophy should fight. In the 1690s he wrote that "the human race is prone to mystery, and holds nothing quite so holy and perfect as what cannot be understood" [McGuire, "Newton on Place"].

These were good weapons to use under the court Whig regime established in London in 1714 [Shapin, "Of Gods and Kings"]. Leibniz told the Princess of Wales that Newtonian natural philosophy bred irreligious superstition, because it made the powers of God's subordinates (including monarchs) into a set of wondrous miracles fit only for popular consumption. He told others that Newtonianism revived "a more than papistical theology" and "a thoroughly scholastic philosophy," telling remarks in a regime obsessed by threats from Roman idolatry [Leibniz iii, 328]. In his exchange with Clarke, "a royal pensioner," Leibniz claimed that the "realities" of Newtonianism, such as "active principles" and "gravity," "bring us back again into the kingdom of darkness" [Alexander 189, 92]. Leibniz analogized court Whig natural philosophical stories about nonmechanical powers with folktales, and his own science with the courtly discourse of Mlle. de Scudéry: "Chimeras begin to appear again, and they are pleasing because they have something in them that is wonderful. What has happened in poetry, happens also in the philosophical world. People are grown weary of rational romances, such as were the French *Clelia* or the German *Aramène* and they are become fond again of the tales of fairies" [Alexander 93]. The British answered that the realities they represented were not "wonders and absurdities" but robust experimental phenomena designed rather to correct than to sustain superstition, and that this way "divine powers" could be securely established [Hall 314; Hacking, *Emergence of Probability:* 172–74]. Clarke reckoned that Leibniz was the true vulgarian, "appealing from reason to vulgar opinion, which philosophers should not do." Events "which the vulgar call prodigies," and which Clarke's colleagues such as the Huguenot de Moivre did their best to quantify, such as "eclipses, monstrous births, madness in men," were "the irregular and more rare effect of usual causes." Leibniz was "conspiring" to make the court Whigs look superstitious and sinister. Newtonians had the better techniques for sorting out superstitions and winning subjects to obedience [Alexander 53; Schneider].

The ascendancy of Newton's natural philosophy in Georgian culture was secure at least to the extent that it could stake its claim as a weapon against fantasy and delusion, whether of speculators, or of the lower orders, or of its political rivals. Realities were used to win an audience; illusions were abused to discredit enemies. This was not a process of effortless rationalization. It was a fragile social construct. Observers often questioned whether natural philosophy was powerful enough to heal strife or safe enough to escape fantasy itself. During an outburst of religious enthusiasm in London in 1707–8, involving revivalist rallies and pretended resurrections of the dead sponsored by refugees from French persecution, Whig natural philosophers aimed to explain away spiritual possession as a mixture of overwrought imagination and Newtonian ethereal vapours. Swift satirized these stories as no better than the enthusiasms they sought to rationalize, while the

High Churchmen recognized them as materialist fables which aimed to drive spirit from the world [Schwartz 35–37]. In similar vein, Swift joined Addison in satirizing astrology, precisely by hitching it to "vulgar" wonder-mongering [Curry; Thomas 423–24]. This satire did *not* mean that the doctrine of celestial significance vanished: in a reformed, powerful form it provided a basis for Newtonian cometography, which urged a better story about divine powers visible in the heavens. Newtonians lectured in coffeehouses about this new celestial economy of active principles, and fashionable handbooks propagated the same message [Schaffer, "Newton's Comets"]. Maupertuis observed that the Newtonian cometographers had "spoken of comets in a manner which re-establishes them in all the terror they once had." He meant this as a compliment. The Scriblerians made exactly the same point about the lecturers, but as a criticism: Newtonians' faith in their mastery of celestial powers was ludicrous and fantastical [Waff; Schaffer, "Authorized Prophets" 53; Rousseau].

Thus natural philosophers found it hard to make these representations real, that is, invulnerable to cultural criticism. After Scriblerian attacks on the modish speculations of the purveyors of theories of madness, theories of the heavens, and theories of spirits, Fielding joined in with a vicious attack on Edmond Halley's cometary theories, branding them as vulgar hysteria. Significantly, he spotted the link between this natural philosophical fantasy and court culture. On the showing of Halley's claim that the Deluge had a cometary cause, Fielding joked, "it would be extremely difficult to conceive how her Majesty and her Court could be preserved alive in such a Convulsion" [Goldgar, "Fielding" 142]. The barb was well aimed. Men like Halley and Newton were court philosophers, but for Fielding this could not legitimate their status as moral representatives. He presided as magistrate over Tyburn riots in the 1740s against surgeons who claimed criminal corpses for anatomizing. Pondering his experience, Fielding wrote that "the people of fashion seized several places to their own use, such as courts, assemblies, operas, balls &c., the people of no fashion . . . have been in constant possession of all hops, fairs, revels. So far from looking on each other as brethren in the Christian language, they seem scarce to regard each other as of the same species" [Thompson, "Patrician Society" 395; Linebaugh 91–96]. These divisions were themselves shaped by politics, and it seemed implausible to many that natural philosophers could heal such wounds with their ministrations [Isherwood 81]. Fielding's remarks usefully remind us that it was necessary for these philosophers to produce *spaces* in which their work could effectively be pursued.

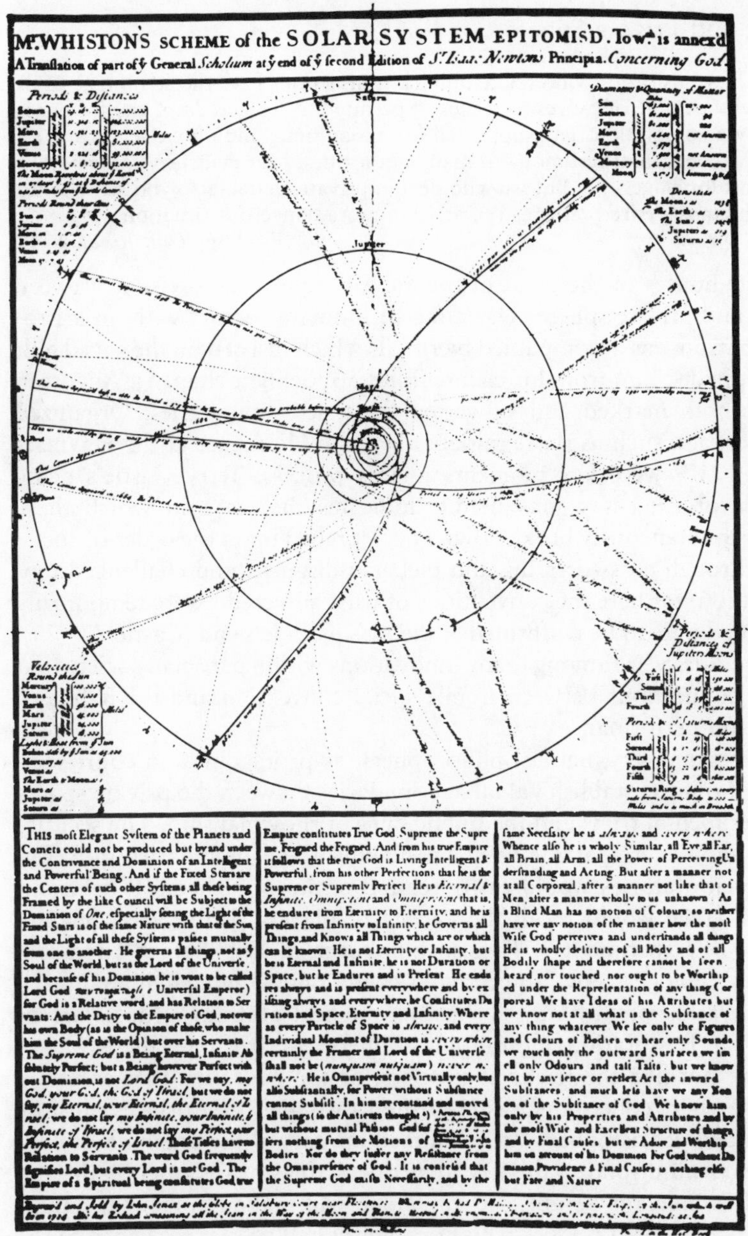

Figure 16.5. Newtonian natural philosophy displayed: William Whiston's broadside "Scheme of the Solar System" (1724). Whiston represents the heliocentric system, the planets and their satellites, and the more prominent comets. The text below is a translation of the General Scholium to the second (1713) edition of the *Principia*. Reprinted from Whiston, *Solar System* (1724).

Public and Private Spaces

> Those historians who relate publick transactions have the advantage of us who confine ourselves to scenes of private life. The credit of the former is by common notoriety supported for a long time; and public records, with the concurrent testimony of many authorities, bear evidence to their truth in future ages. . . . But we who deal in private characters, who search into the most retired recesses . . . are in a more dangerous situation.
>
> Fielding, *Tom Jones,* 1749

In the houses of the great of the ancien régime, the division between public and private spheres was effaced: intimate contact with an aristocratic patron was accompanied by rituals which insisted on the social gulf which divided him from his clients [Elias 53; Sennett chap. 5]. Augustan culture both marked and subverted these new boundaries. Organized masquerades, such as those initiated by John Heidegger at the Haymarket in 1717, were key moments in this process. Terry Castle's acute analysis of Augustan masquerade indicates the ways in which these events simultaneously broke down and yet relied upon the order of social class, through cross-dressing and plebeian disguise, and challenged representation, for here the conventions of trust and credit were temporarily suspended only to be reaffirmed at the masquerade's end [Castle 77–79]. Masquerades were among many innovations within patrician society that forged connections between fragile social convention and the habits of credit and performance.

In the same way, natural philosophers, as protagonists in court societies, set out to establish valuable boundaries between the private spaces of experimental trials and the public ones of showmanship. The security of the showmen's facts hinged on making these boundaries safe. But private laboratories would easily remind critics of alchemical delusion; and the stage would recall the deceits of players [Hannaway; Shapin, "House of Experiment"]. Thus in Edinburgh in 1724 James Thomson, Newton's eulogist, saw "some com'd from London here lately that teach natural Philosophy by way of show by the beat of drum" [M. L. Greenberg 117]. Restoration natural philosophers asserted that "the works of God are not like the tricks of jugglers, or the pageants, that entertain princes, where concealment is requisite to wonder." Yet princes must be entertained. Christopher Wren summed up part of the dilemma of concealment and display: "the key, that opens treasures is often plain and rusty, but unless it be gilt, the key alone will make no shew at court" [Boyle ii, 30; Birch i, 289]. This vocabulary had special relevance to the predicament of natural philosophers in Augustan Britain. According to Newton, the "business of natural philosophy" was explicitly histrionic: its job was to extract active principles from apparently passive matter, and thus to impress a polite audience with the dramatic lesson that divinely sustained powers operated within the world of matter. The performances in coffeehouses and lecture rooms, armed with spectacular instrumentation and bright sparks, were the realization simultaneously of the cosmology and of the proper job of natural philosophy [Schaffer, "Natural Philosophy" 3–5].

Novel phenomena of electrical fire, developed in London by Newton's lieutenants from 1705, were crafted to fit this role [Freudenthal]. The wonders of the electrical machine allegedly depended on "real" active principles, and could then be mastered and displayed before fee-paying audiences by skilled electrical philosophers. Horace Walpole commented that electricity had become "the *fashionable* cause," while Priestley, the first historian of this program, noted that "if we only consider what it is in objects that makes them capable of exciting that pleasing astonishment, which has such charms for all mankind, we shall not wonder at the eagerness with which persons of both sexes, and of every age and condition, run to see electrical experiments" [Walpole ii, 207; Priestley, *History and Present State* ii, 134–35]. Electrical natural philosophy was domesticated in salon culture [Heilbron, "G. M. Bose"]. Detailed reports of trials with fire appeared in journals and booklets, which carried stories of "phenomena, so surprising as to awaken the indolent curiosity of the public, the ladies and the people of quality, who never regard natural philosophy but when it works miracles" [Haller 194]. The creation of what was called the "vast country of Electricity" hinged upon the existence of a social space in which public and private realms overlapped. The salons and coffeehouses were private enough to allow the lecturers to master their audience and these fragile phenomena, and sustain a polite culture of mannered philosophizing; and public enough to disseminate the realities of this natural philosophy throughout the elite [Porter, "Science"]. This territory, however, was fraught with moral and practical troubles. The reference to "miracle" shows this point. It was not obviously legitimate, in Augustan Britain, to show "miracles" to a fee-paying audience. Furthermore, the "secrecy" which was essential to natural philosophical work behind the scenes, lest the shows fail, was hard to match with a project which professed openness and the importance of witnessing [Hackmann 104–5].

The threat of deceit was real. The French natural philosopher Nollet, who learnt much from Desaguliers' shows, traveled to Italy in 1749–50 to quell what he saw as an outbreak of deceitful practices in medical electricity. When he followed the rules of public natural philosophy, by banning "children, servants or people of the lower class" and dealing only with "reasonable people . . . of an age sufficient to leave nothing to

Figure 16.6a. Electrical showmanship in the 1740s. 16.6a is a representation of Benjamin Rackstrow's trial in which an electrified crown discharged around the victim's head, the so-called "beatification."

Figure 16.6b. Electrical showmanship in the 1740s. 16.6b illustrates a demonstration by Nollet in which an electrified young man, suspended by silk cords, has sparks drawn from his nose and uses his hand to make pieces of paper move. Reprinted from Rackstrow, *Miscellaneous observations* (1748); Nollet, *Essai sur l'électricité des corps* (1746).

be feared of the truth of what they might depose," he managed to expose the electrical quacks: "a great part of the electrical cures have been no other than temporary shadows which have been taken with a little too much precipitation and complaisance for realities" [Nollet 377, 383]. Nollet's remark that "I'm always fearful when I see extraordinary facts propagated with people who are poor, and who know that they'll be looked after while they have fixed upon them the attention of eminent men," and his talk of 'temporary shadows,' capture the natural philosophical dilemma: they plied their trade as theatricals in a culture which welcomed the marvellous; they were always to be suspected as charlatans in a culture which scarcely credited the stage as a place where realities could be discovered [Benguigui 186]. A wide range of early-eighteenth-century resources helped fix the difference between real and illusory performances. Children were taught of philosophical shows, Whig poets lauded the splendors of orreries, electrical machines, and air pumps, and relentless satire was directed against any who seemed to violate the properties of the private sphere on the public platform of philosophical lecturing [Waff; Secord; Jones 203–8]. For all this, "the distinction between serious instruction and popular entertainment was difficult to maintain" [Money 131]. The same conclusion has been drawn for Paris and for London: everywhere the boundaries between private and public space, between illusion and reality, were hard to define and yet indispensable to secure natural philosophical status [Isherwood 50; Altick].

Historians have often emphasized the theatricality of the Augustan political order. E. P. Thompson writes that "the credibility of the gentry as paternalists arose from the high visibility of certain of their functions and the low visibility of others." This distinction between the patricians' withdrawal from plebeian culture and their demonstrative display of power at times of crisis had "much of the studied self-consciousness of public theatre." Public shows at Tyburn, or in the coffeehouses and masquerades, took part in this cultural form [Thompson, "Patrician Society" 389]. Plebeian culture also developed what has been called the "counter-theatre" of satire and protest [Brewer 35]. In 1718 some Jacobite "bumpkins" informed their local justices that "to honour King George's Coronation day a blazing star appeared over Mr. Chetwynd's house. Their worships were wise enough to go and see this wonder, and found, to their no little disappointment, their star to end in a turnip," a vegetable often chosen to symbolize the Hanoverian monarch [Thompson, "Eighteenth-Century English Society" 159]. Confronted with Whig display and popular histrionics, pietists and Tories penned powerful attacks on the theatricality of culture. "The theatre is the epitome of Duncehood in action," comments Pat Rogers on the attitudes of the Scriblerians to the "public theatre" of the corrupt oligarchy [Rogers, *Hacks and Dunces* 69]. Divines such as the nonjuring enthusiast William Law wrote notorious assaults against the stage, and then made this polemic into a direct challenge to the legitimacy of public natural philosophy.

Law's allies in the transformation of an attack on idolatry and the theater to an attack on natural philosophy included Samuel Richardson, then Law's printer, Jacobite sympathizer and author of a pamphlet strong against the stage (1735); John Byrom, Jacobite poet and physician; and John Freke, distinguished Tory surgeon [McKillop; Bechler; Sale 126–27]. Byrom penned remarkable verses on Aaron Hill's *Art of Acting* in which he satirized a public culture obsessed by appearance and the management of style and physiognomy [Byrom 1: 255–63]. Byrom and Freke helped edit Richardson's *Clarissa,* while Richardson joined in his colleagues' assault on natural philosophical lecturing: he condemned Whiston for "showing eclipses and preaching the millennium . . . to gay people who, if they have white teeth, hear him with open mouths, though perhaps shut hearts" [Richardson 3: 318–19]. As Richardson's comment implies, these men drew the contrast between pietist, *private* experience of divinity, to which they all shared a loyalty sustained by their readings in Boehme and other visionary texts, and the corrupt *public* culture of commercial theatricals. Byrom, for example, insisted on the virtue of "enthusiasm," where this was carefully defined as private light rather than public ecstasy [2: 167–97]. This emerged most visibly in Freke's assault in 1746 upon the leading natural philosopher Benjamin Martin, instrument maker, publisher, and lecturer [Millburn]. Martin appealed to an audience well versed in the rapid commodification of natural knowledge across a wide rage of disciplines. Martin told his customers that "that which was thought to be a Miracle in *Elisha's* Time, is now but the common Amusement of the *Virtuosi*" [*Young Gentleman* 318].

The pious Tory Freke reacted with fury to comments like these. He attacked both the ontology and the culture of Martin's world. He reckoned that electrical fire was a divine power made visible here on earth solely through the disturbance of an original, moral, balance [*Treatise* 26]. So electrical showmanship was both blasphemous and crudely catchpenny, "tricks like ledgerdemain . . . performed by him whose time is little worth" [*Treatise* 137–39]. The disputes heightened conflicts between codes of gentility and of piety. They challenged the authority of the theater and the market. Divine sparks could not be shown to fee-paying audiences, nor could natural philosophers legitimately perform on stage. In response, Martin conceded that "I should be glad to have a little more Money; yet Thanks to Heaven and Friends, I have no Necessity so great as to be guilty of any *mean or ungenerous Action* for Money" [*Supplement* 28]. Above all, Martin judged Freke's pietism as no better than a Quixotic fantasy, and urged against this "knight-errant" the moral rectitude of the commercialization of natural philosophy: "Good Sir Knight, why all this Ire? . . . Do not the *Chemists,* and *Anatomists,* the *Physicians,* and *Divines* everywhere, *read lectures for money* ? Are they for this reason to be stigmatiz'd with odious names of artful *Tricksters, Cheats,* and *Ledgerdemain-men* ? If not, then why are those who give *Lectures* in *Electricity* for *Money* ?" [*Supplement* 27–28]

These were good questions: Freke was himself a prominent participant in the world of surgical display. An eminent member of the College of Surgeons, he performed Tyburn anatomies and appeared as president in Hogarth's representation of such an event, the *Reward of Cruelty* (1751) [Ireland 2:326]. Freke also figured as a colorful and eccentric authority in Fielding's *Tom Jones* (1749), where the fight with Martin was obliquely mentioned and Fielding's anti-Jacobite hostility to such as Richardson and Freke was amply stressed [book 2, chap. 4; book 4, chap. 9]. The contrast between Tory pietists and Whig lecturers was not simply a contrast between the worlds of private and public experience; it was a struggle, rather, for the right to speak on behalf of divinity and morality. Freke reckoned that the established realms of anatomy theater and law court were legitimate sites of moral knowledge, those of coffeehouse and stage not so. And he also argued that natural philosophers had somehow infringed this boundary, and that *as a result* their ontology and their epistemology had been corrupted too.

The Natural Philosopher's Paradox

> The Theatrical stage is nothing more than a representation, or, as Aristotle calls it, an imitation of what really exists. Hence, perhaps, we might fairly pay a very high compliment to those, who, by their writings or actions have been so capable of imitating life, as to have their pictures in a manner confounded with, or mistaken for the originals. But in reality, we are not so fond of paying compliments to these people, . . . and have much more pleasure in hissing and buffetting them, than in admiring their excellence.
>
> Fielding, *Tom Jones,* 1749

Comparisons between the world and the stage, such as that made so compellingly by Fielding in *Tom Jones,* remind us of the central problems of natural philosophical plausibility. In Augustan Britain charges of vulgarity and of theatricality were commonplace in natural philosophical dispute. Authority hinged on the credit vested in specific practices, such as public lecturing, laboratory experimentation, or surgical anatomy. Accuracy of reference depended on establishing prior patterns of credibility. For this reason, any epistemology which now aims to account for

Figure 16.7. John Freke presides over an anatomy in Surgeons' Hall following an execution at Tyburn. Reprinted from Hogarth, *Reward of Cruelty* (1751), courtesy of the Trustees of the British Museum.

the command exercised by natural philosophers' representations must draw on resources and genres unfamiliar to the classical tradition in philosophy of science. That tradition judges eighteenth-century developments as a pattern of rationalization. As Michel Foucault frequently pointed out, it is common for such epistemologies to counterpose reason against power. In so doing, they merely reiterate some important self-images of the Enlightened savants. This chapter has been designed to support the claim that here reason and power were co-produced: the rationale of natural philosophy included the subversion of its rivals and the empowerment of its own regime.

"Shall we investigate this kind of rationalism which seems to be specific to our modern culture and which originates in the *Aufklärung*?" Foucault asks. "I think that the word rationalization is dangerous. What we have to do is analyse specific rationalities rather than always invoking the progress of rationalization in general" ["Subject and Power" 210]. Such a specification demands a reexamination of some received epistemic disjunctions, between truth and error, between knowledge and power, between nature's reality and culture's illusions. As usual, such a reexamination involves a revision of our own discipline's canon. John Forrester makes the useful point that propositional models in epistemology have elided truth as conformity with a state of affairs in the world, and truth as conformity with what exists in the mind. The former contrasts truth and error, the latter truth with lies. The rationalist and analytical traditions have distracted our attention from credit and deceit, and sought distinctions between the work of rhetors and that of philosophers [Forrester 146; Bennington]. In Augustan culture, for example, natural philosophers plied their trade in a world of distrust and loss of credit. The theater and the market mattered to their trade because these were forums where illusion and plausibility were always tried out. Both David Hume and Adam Smith pointed out the intimate connection between the prevalence of deceit and what Hume, in his analysis of the authority of miracles, called the "strong propensity of mankind to the extraordinary and the marvellous" [Hume 529]. Both agreed that the progress of enlightenment, and the specific task of natural philosophy, was the correction of this propensity. The incredible would become the rational through the engagement of philosophers with the world of wonders: Smith argued in the 1750s that since the task of natural philosophy was "to allay this tumult of the imagination," it followed that "all the different systems of nature" had succeeded *not* because of "their agreement or inconsistency with truth and reality," but only through their ability "to sooth the imagination and to render the theatre of nature a more coherent, and therefore a more magnificent spectacle." Portentously enough, the young Smith was keen to include Newtonianism under this charge [Smith, *Essays* 46]. So an investigation of the grounds of natural philosophical authority needs to study texts on the philosophy of histrionics and performance, and to admit to the canon of philosophy of science material hitherto confined to the aesthetic and moral realms.

The most celebrated Enlightenment texts on the "truth" and "reality" of performance, Diderot's posthumously published *Paradoxe sur le comédien* (1773–78) and Rousseau's *Lettre sur les spectacles* (1758), embrace and analyze these problems of legitimacy, performance, and deceit. Diderot explicitly draws on the work of British actors, such as Garrick, and novelists, such as Richardson, to make this point. His essay attacked the arguments of an important English work on Garrick, John Hill's *The Actor* (1750 and 1755). John Hill, notorious hack, naturalist, and enemy of the Royal Society and its natural philosophical coterie, described the ways in which the master performer of Drury Lane successfully imitated truth through a spontaneous sympathy with natural passion [Woods; Tort]. Hill and his allies deployed an explicit link between the natural philosophy of fire and electricity and the aesthetics of sympathy. Garrick himself urged the necessity of a "keen sensibility that bursts at once from genius and like electric fire shoots through the veins, marrow bones and all of every spectator" [Wasserman 268; Hobson 196]. This electrical model made actors enthusiasts: Diderot reckoned, in contrast, that they were their own marionettes. The contrast recalls in detail the Scriblerian polemics about Whig naturalists, who materialized spirit, and vulgar prophets, who spiritualized their own passionate afflatus. A model of truth and illusion informed both histrionics and natural philosophy. Diderot's "paradox" was that the "sublime moments of nature," the stock-in-trade of natural philosophy lectures too, were more securely communicated by a performer the more controlled that performer's artifice [Diderot, *Paradoxe* 138]. For Diderot, performance could secure its legitimacy if it became autonomous from corrupting patronage and establish power over its audience rather than depending upon the public. This power would be best secured if all citizens, in a free society, themselves became skilled performers. Rousseau contrasted the vicious metropolitan world of illusion and deceit with a republic in which all citizens would be open to inspection: "Make the beholders the spectacle, make them actors themselves; make each of them see himself and love himself in the others so that they will all be more closely united" [Fried 221].

These claims match those Diderot made in his works on natural philosophy, notably the *Interpretation de la nature* (1753). In this remarkable outline of an ideal initiation into experimental philosophy, Diderot attacked the failings of contemporary natural philosophy. These were just its private secretiveness (Diderot charged Newton, for example, with criminal concealment) and its public histrionics (he also charged Nollet with modish rejection of electrotherapy) [*Oeuvres* 203, 215–16]. It could not teach audiences how to become philosophers because it delighted in concealment; it could not teach its audience how to become free spirits, because it was enslaved to a fashionable public. The attack on the natural philosophers was part of Diderot's Grub Street politics, well marked, as Robert Darnton points out, in his evocation of the deranged and subversive performance of *Rameau's Nephew* (1761–79) [*Literary Underground* 118–20; Pilkington 72–79]. Diderot urged that the function of courses in experimental philosophy must be to communicate just that combination of artifice and enthusiasm which he recognized in men such as Garrick or Richardson. "Does what is shown of experimental physics in public lectures suffice to obtain that kind of philosophical enthusiasm?" asked Diderot. His answer was no. "Our performers of experimental courses are a little like someone who thinks he has given a great dinner just because he has many people at his table. One should principally set out to stimulate the appetite so that many, moved by the wish to satisfy it, will pass from the condition of disciples to that of amateurs, and thence to the profession of philosophers" [Caplan 8–10; Diderot *Oeuvres* 214].

The "profession" of eighteenth-century natural philosophy found useful resources in arguments like these. Adam Smith, a strong admirer of Diderot's *Encyclopédie,* noted in the 1760s that "in opulent and commercial societies to think or to reason comes to be, like every other employment, a particular business, which is carried on by a very few people who furnish the public with all the thought and reason possessed by the vast multitudes that labour" [Smith, *Essays* 245–48; Smith, *Lectures* 574]. It was accepted that savants' powers depended on the construction of separable communities of performers. The "end of Enlightenment" is heavily marked by the career of such constructions. Masonry, for example, was a key feature of their world, at once private and theatrical, offering the promise of moral, intellectual, and political progress [Koselleck 70–97]. Diderot's account of the "délire philosophique" was also helpful. Philosophical materialists argued that the *intellectual* powers which performers needed so as to command their audience were the same as the *material* powers which their performances displayed: electrical fire and cerebral fluids were to be identified, so that the ability of the skilled natural philosopher artificially to command both nature and culture could be given a plausible basis in reality.

This was why "electrical machines" were confused with "infernal" ones, especially in the practices of mesmerists and galvanists, who spoke of "animal magnetism" and "animal electricity," and who used the mesmeric trough and the galvanic circuits as accounts of the real structure of nature [Schaffer, "Natural Philosophy" 10; Vartanian; Haslam 35]. The identification of the powers of the philosophical mind and those of the nature the philosophers represented was well illustrated in the case of

Figure 16.8. Experimental natural philosophy in performance: Joseph Wright's representation of a pneumatic experiment. Reprinted from Joseph Wright, *Experiment with a bird in the air pump*.

mesmerism: where court Whigs had been careful to announce themselves as delegates of a divine reality visible through active principles, peddlers in animal magnetism materialized these powers and, ultimately, identified them with the capacities of the performers' own bodies [Darnton, *Mesmerism*]. In the notorious reports of James Tilly Matthews in the 1790s, thought transference, political subversion, and republican anarchy are all accounted the direct consequences of a mesmeric "gang" let loose in London [Porter, Introduction]. Mesmerism's career nicely illustrates the problem of private and public space. Its masonic lodges inevitably attracted suspicion; its salon games attracted the derision of those who suspected public charlatanry. The same strictures applied to the Republican *fåetes* which followed on Rousseau's proposals for utopian revels in which all would become performers. Under the supervision of savants such as the astronomer and atheist Jéråome Lalande, the Parisian spectacles inverted the conventional direction of the gaze. Now the state could survey its own subjects: they had become the spectacle. The private world, in which conspiracy could flourish, and the stage, upon which citizens could be deluded, had both been superseded [Ozouf].

Under anti-Jacobin and conservative assault, the weaknesses of natural philosophy were condemned: it had not successfully developed a new aesthetics, but had allegedly lapsed into the old society of spectacle. Its private world had not created virtue, but reproduced subversion and delusion. No doubt this problematic suspicion of the reality of knowledge achieved in the lab remains. Witness *Frankenstein* (1818), which connects the graveyard and the attic as equally important sites of the production of the natural philosophically real but morally forbidden and (as it emerges) illusory knowledge, in noteworthy contradistinction to the virtuous privacy of the family home [Mellor; Richardson xiii]. This problem of space was crucial for the establishment of the natural philosophical role. Only with the emergence of spaces simultaneously open to inspection but closed from view, in the teaching laboratories, clinics, and "panopticons" of the nineteenth century, was this security even partly achieved [Forgan; Foucault, *Discipline and Punish* 195–228]. Just as realist epistemology depended on securing the *social* boundaries around its own enterprise, it also hinged on the impermeability of the *architecture* of science.

Conclusion: Realism's Amnesia

The period between Newtonian natural philosophy and late Enlightenment mathematical science witnessed the establishment of a defined, if fragile, community of scientists, that "enclosing community" to which Gillian Beer refers [45]. The community became vested with growing power: Foucault observes that "from the nineteenth century on, every scholar becomes a professor or director of a laboratory" [Foucault, "Power and Norm" 64]. New institutional forms such as the teaching laboratory, and new literary technologies, notably the imposition of the *passive voice* in much of scientific writing, to displace the standard autobiographical active voice, accompany this transformation. The point of this paper has been to show the resources in play in the establishment of such communities, and to show, too, that communities like this are established not by a flight from culture but by working within it. Thus the security of that community was a precise measure of the "realism" which its representations might command. They were as fragile as each other. The implication for our understanding of representation is that questions of trust and legitimacy are hard to separate from questions of adequacy and reference. We have surveyed a number of cultural resources which eighteenth-century natural philosophers used in order to make themselves secure representatives. Realism, as a claim that there are entities that exist and constrain their own representations, starts to look like a contingent resource. This is a rather familiar lesson for students of literary form. It's familiar, too, in some recent philosophical analyses of status of scientific representation. Nancy Cartwright observes that "there inevitably arises a mismatch between the abstract-theoretical representation and the concrete situations represented. The result is that abstract formulae do not describe reality but imaginary constructions. They are best judged neither true nor false of reality itself" [194].

In that case, the question is how it came to pass that natural philosophers reckoned they could speak for such a reality. Natural philosophers worked hard to make a direct access to nature count and then make it clear that they had such access. They did this by describing other sources of power as illusory. Engineers were to be distinguished from charlatans. Plebeians who claimed traditional right and custom were dismissed as superstitious. Their clerical guardians were often no better. Precision measurement, allegedly giving unique access to this nature, was held up as a privileged practice. Realism is powerful because once representatives are trusted and legitimated, the processes by which this status is achieved are obliterated. In controversy, rivals seek to recall these polemical histories. Onslow made out Toft as a cunning woman exploiting pleb credulity; Leibniz recalled the occult roots of Newtonianism; Martin pointed out the pietist delirium of Freke's Quixotic philosophy. The success of realism as an epistemology for the history of science accompanies its constitutional *amnesia*. What Steven Woolgar calls the "method of splitting and inversion," through which representations of reality are first divorced from, and then deduced from, that real, captures this thought. "Once the object is construed as pregiven, fixed, and antecedent, the involvement of the agent of representation appears merely peripheral and transitory. It is as if observers merely stumble upon a pre-existing scene" [Woolgar 68–69]. This process, it must be stressed, has a recoverable history. It is not a matter of conspiratorial, and verbal, sleight-of-hand. Controversies about rival representations, and thus about questions of credit and trust, are closed when the cultural genealogies of these representations vanish from public discourse [Shapin, "Politics of Observation"]. In this sense, realism is forgetful. It cannot easily be put to work either by representatives in conflict, or, of course, by historians of representation. The study of the history of science needs to imitate recent studies of other technologies of representation—like, for example, photography, where it has been urged that rejection of the idea that the Real is "below," "before," or "behind" the process of pictorial production must take on the "crucial relation of meaning to questions of practice and power" [Tagg 101]. The task of science would then look less like a quantification of its own realities than a disqualification of others' representations.

WORKS CITED

Agnew, J. C. *Worlds Apart: The Market and the Theater in Anglo-American Thought*, 1550–1750. Cambridge: Cambridge University Press, 1986.

Alexander, H. G., ed. *The Leibniz-Clark Correspondence*. Manchester: Manchester University Press, 1956.

Altick, R. *The Shows of London*. Cambridge: Harvard University Press, 1978.

Arbuthnot, John. *Life and Works*. Ed. G. A. Aitken. Oxford: Oxford University Press, 1892.

Bachelard, G. *La formation de l'esprit scientifique*. Paris: Vrin, 1938.

Bachelard, G. *Le rationalisme appliqué*. Paris: Presses Universitaires de France, 1949.

Barrell, J. *English Literature in History, 1730–1780: An Equal, Wide, Survey*. London: Hutchinson, 1983.

Bechler, R. " 'Tryal by what is contrary': Samuel Richardson and Christian Dialectic." In V. Grosvenor Myer, ed., *Samuel Richardson: Passion and Prudence*. London: Vision Press, 1986. 93–112.

Beer, G. "Problems of Description in the Language of Discovery." In G. Levine, ed., *One Culture*. Madison: University of Wisconsin Press, 1987. 35–58.

Benguigui, I. *Théories électriques du XVIIIe siècle: correspondance Nollet-Jallabert*. Geneva: Georg, 1984.

Bennington, G. "The Perfect Cheat: Locke and Empiricism's Rhetoric." In A. E. Benjamin, G. N. Cantor, and J. R. R. Christie, eds., *The Figural and the Literal*. Manchester: Manchester University Press, 1987. 103–23.

Bentham, Jeremy. *Works*. Ed. John Bowring. 11 vols. Edinburgh, 1838–48.

Birch, T., ed. *The History of the Royal Society*. 4 vols. London, 1756.

Blake, W. *Complete Writings*. Ed. G. Keynes. Oxford: Oxford University Press, 1966.

Boyle, Robert. *Works*. Ed. T. Birch. 6 vols. London, 1772.

Brewer, J. "Theater and Counter-Theater in Georgian Politics." *Radical History Review* 22 (1980): 7–40.

Brown, Harcourt. "From London to Lapland: Maupertuis, Johann Bernoulli I and *la terre applatie*." In C. G. S. Williams, ed., *Literature and History in the Ages of Ideas*. Columbus: Ohio University Press, 1975. 69–94.

Brunet, P. *Maupertuis*. 2 vols. Paris: Blanchard, 1929.

Buck, P. "People Who Counted: Political Arithmetic in the Eighteenth Century." *Isis* 73 (1982): 28–45.

Burke, P. *Popular Culture in Early Modern Europe*. London: Temple Smith, 1978.

Byrom, John. *Poems*. Ed. A. W. Ward. 2 vols. Manchester: Chetham Society, 1896.

Cantor, G. N. "Berkeley's *The Analyst* Revisited." *Isis* 75 (1984): 668–83.

Caplan, J. *Framed Narratives: Diderot's Genealogy of the Beholder*. Manchester: Manchester University Press, 1985.

Carswell, J. *The South Sea Bubble*. London: Cressett, 1961.

Cartwright, N. *Nature's Capacities and Their Measurement* Oxford: Clarendon, 1989.

Castle, T. *Masquerade and Civilization: The Carnivalesque in Eighteenth-Century English Culture and Fiction*. London: Methuen, 1986.
Chartier, R. *Cultural History* Cambridge: Polity, 1988.
Cohen, I. B. "Isaac Newton's *Principia,* the Scriptures and Divine Providence." In S. Morgenbesser, P. Suppes, and M. White, eds., *Philosophy, Science and Method*. New York: St. Martin's, 1969. 523–48.
Collins, H. M. *Changing Order*. Beverly Hills: Sage, 1985.
Curry, P. *Prophecy and Power*. Cambridge: Polity, 1989.
Dabydeen, D. *Hogarth, Walpole, and Commercial Britain*. London: Hansib, 1987.
Darnton, R. *The Literary Underground of the Old Regime*. Cambridge: Harvard University Press, 1982.
Darnton, R. *Mesmerism and the End of the Enlightenment in France*. Cambridge: Harvard University Press, 1968.
Daston, L. J. "The Domestication of Risk: Mathematical Probability and Insurance, 1650–1830." In L. Krüger, L. J. Daston, and M. Heidelberger, eds., *The Probabilistic Revolution*. Cambridge: MIT Press, 1987. 1: 237–60.
Daston, L. J. "Mathematical Probability and the Reasonable Man of the Eighteenth Century." In J. Dauben and V. Sexton, eds., *History and Philosophy of Science: Selected Papers*. New York: Academy of Sciences, 1983. 52–72.
Defoe, Daniel. *The Political History of the Devil*. London, 1726.
Dennis, John. *The Stage Defended*. London, 1726.
Diderot, Denis. *Oeuvres Philosophiques*. Ed. P. Vernière. Paris: Garnier, 1964.
Diderot, Denis. *Paradoxe sur le comédien*. Ed. R. Laubreaux. Paris: Flammarion, 1981.
Elias, N. *The Court Society*. Oxford: Blackwell, 1983.
Fielding, Henry. *Tom Jones* (1749). Ed. R. P. C. Mutter. Harmondsworth: Penguin, 1966.
Forgan, S. "Context, Image and Function: A Preliminary Enquiry into the Architecture of Scientific Societies'." *British Journal for the History of Science* 19 (1986): 89–114.
Forrester, J. "Lying on the Couch." In Hilary Lawson and Lisa Appignanesi, eds., *Dismantling Truth: Reality in the Postmodern World*. London: Weidenfeld & Nicolson, 1989. 145–66.
Foucault, M. *Discipline and Punish: The Birth of the Prison*. Harmondsworth: Penguin, 1977.
Foucault, M. "Power and Norm." In M. Morris and P. Patton, eds., *Michel Foucault: Power, Truth, Strategy*. Sydney: Feral Publications, 1979. 59–66.
Foucault, M. *Power/Knowledge: Selected Interviews and Other Writings 1972–1977*. Ed. C. Gordon. New York: Pantheon, 1980.
Foucault, M. "The Subject and Power." In H. L. Dreyfus and P. Rabinow, *Michel Foucault: Beyond Structuralism and Hermeneutics*. Brighton: Harvester, 1982. 208–26.
Freke, John. *An Essay to Shew the Cause of Electricity*. London, 1746.
Freke, John. *Treatise on the Nature and Properties of Fire*. London, 1752.
Freudenthal, G. "Early Electricity between Chemistry and Physics." *Historical Studies in Physical Sciences* 11 (1981): 203–29.

Fried, M. *Absorption and Theatricality: Painting and Beholder in the Age of Diderot*. Berkeley: University of California Press, 1980.

Goldgar, B. "Fielding, the Flood Makers, and Natural Philosophy." *Modern Philosophy* 8 (1982): 136–44.

Goldgar, B. *Walpole and the Wits*. Lincoln: University of Nebraska Press, 1976.

Golinski, J. "Utility and Audience in Eighteenth Century Chemistry: Case Studies of William Cullen and Joseph Priestley." *British Journal for the History of Science* 21 (1988): 1–32.

Goulemot, J. M. "Démons, merveilles, et philosophie à l'âge classique." *Annales E.S.C.* 35 (1980): 1223–50.

Greenberg, M. L. "Eighteenth-Century Poetry Represents Moments of Scientific Discovery." In S. Peterfreund, ed., *Literature and Science: Theory and Practice*. Boston: Northeastern University Press, 1990. 115–37.

Greenberg, J. "Geodesy in Paris in the 1730s." *Historical Studies in Physical Science* 13 (1983): 239–60.

Guicciardini, N. "Flowing Ducks and Vanishing Quantities." In S. Rossi, ed., *Science and Imagination in Eighteenth-Century British Culture*. Milan: Università di Milano, 1987. 231–35.

Hacking, I. *The Emergence of Probability*. Cambridge: Cambridge University Press, 1975.

Hacking, I. *Representing and Intervening*. Cambridge: Cambridge University Press, 1983.

Hackmann, W. *Electricity from Glass*. Alphen: Noordhoff, 1978.

Hall, A. R. *Philosophers at War: The Quarrel between Newton and Leibniz*. Cambridge: Cambridge University Press, 1980.

[Haller, Albrecht von]. "Historical Account of the Wonderful Discoveries Made in Germany concerning Electricity." *Gentleman's Magazine* 15 (1745): 193–97.

Hannaway, O. "Laboratory Design and the Aim of Science." *Isis* 77 (1986): 585–610.

Haslam, John. *Illustrations of Madness*. London, 1810.

Heilbron, J. L. *Elements of Early Modern Physics*. Berkeley: University of California Press, 1982.

Heilbron, J. L. "G. M. Bose: Prime Mover in the Invention of the Leyden Jar?" *Isis* 57 (1966): 264–67.

Hobson, M. *The Object of Art: The Theory of Illusion in Eighteenth-Century France*. Cambridge: Cambridge University Press, 1982.

Hudson, G. "The Politics of Credulity—The Mary Toft Case." M. Phil. diss. Wellcome Unit for History of Medicine, Cambridge University.

Hume, David. *Essays, Moral, Political and Literary* [1741–42]. London: Grant Richards, 1903.

Ireland, J. *Hogarth Illustrated*. 2 vols. London, 1791.

Isherwood, R. M. *Farce and Fantasy: Popular Entertainment in Eighteenth-Century Paris*. Paris: Oxford University Press, 1986.

Jones, W. P. *The Rhetoric of Science: A Study of Scientific Ideas and Imagery in Eighteenth-Century English Poetry*. London: Routledge, 1966.

Jordanova, L. J. "Naturalizing the Family: Literature and the Biomedical Sciences in the Late Enlightenment." In L. J. Jordanova, ed., *Languages of Nature*. London: Free Association Books, 1986. 86–116.

Ketcham, M. G. "Scientific and Poetic Imagination in James Thomson's 'Poem Sacred to the Memory of Sir Isaac Newton.'" *Philological Quarterly* 61 (1982): 33–50.

Koselleck, R. *Critique and Crisis: Enlightenment and the Pathogenesis of Modern Society.* Oxford: Berg, 1988.

Laplace, P. S. *Essai philosophique sur les probabilités*. Paris, 1814.

Latour, B. "Opening One Eye While Closing the Other: A Note on Some Religious Paintings." In G. Fyfe and J. Law, eds., *Picturing Power.* London: Routledge, 1988. 15–38.

Latour, B. "Visualisation and Cognition: Thinking with Eyes and Hands." *Knowledge and Society* 6 (1986): 1–40.

Law, William. *The Absolute Unlawfulness of the Stage Entertainment Fully Demonstrated.* London, 1726.

Leibniz, G. W. *Philosophische Schriften*. Ed. C. I. Gerhardt. 7 vols. Hildesheim: Georg Olms, 1960.

Linebaugh, P. "The Tyburn Riot against the Surgeons." In D. Hay et al., eds., *Albion's Fatal Tree*. Harmondsworth: Penguin, 1975. 65–118.

Macdonald, M. "Religion, Social Change and Psychological Healing in England." *Studies in Church History* 19 (1982): 101–26.

Manuel, F. *The Religion of Isaac Newton*. Oxford: Oxford University Press, 1974.

Marin, L. *Portrait of the King*. London: Macmillan, 1988.

Martin, Benjamin. *A Supplement [to an Essay on Electricity]*. Bath, 1746.

Martin, Benjamin. *The Young Gentleman and Lady's Philosophy.* 2d ed. 2 vols. London, 1772.

McGuire, J. E. "Force, Active Principles and Newton's Invisible Realm." *Ambix* 15 (1968): 154–208.

McGuire, J. E. "Newton on Place, Time and God." *British Journal for the History of Science* 11 (1978): 114–29.

McKeon, M. *The Origins of the English Novel*. London: Radius, 1988.

McKillop, A. D. "Richardson's Early Writings." *Journal of English and German Philology* 53 (1954): 72–75.

McManners, J. *Death and the Enlightenment*. Oxford: Oxford University Press, 1985.

Mellor, A. "*Frankenstein:* A Feminist Critique of Science." In G. Levine, ed., *One Culture*. Madison: University of Wisconsin Press, 1987. 287–312.

Merchant, C. *The Death of Nature: Women, Ecology and the Scientific Revolution* London: Wildwood House, 1980.

Millburn, J. R. *Benjamin Martin*. Leyden: Noordhoff, 1976.

Money, J. *Experience and Identity: Birmingham and the West Midlands, 1760–1800*. Manchester: Manchester University Press, 1977.

Newton, I. *Mathematical Papers*. Ed. D. T. Whiteside. 8 vols. Cambridge: Cambridge University Press, 1967–81.

Newton, I. *Opticks*. Based on 4th ed. (1730). New York: Dover, 1952.
Nicolson, M. H. *Newton Demands the Muse*. Princeton: Princeton University Press, 1946.
Nollet, J. A. "An Examination of Certain Phenomena in Electricity Published in Italy." *Philosophical Transactions* 46 (1749): 368–97.
North, Roger. *General Preface and Life of Dr. John North*. Ed. P. Millard. Toronto: University of Toronto Press, 1984.
Ozouf, M. *La fête révolutionnaire 1789–1799*. Paris: Gallimard, 1976.
Pickering, A. *Constructing Quarks*. Edinburgh: Edinburgh University Press, 1984.
Pilkington, A. E. " 'Nature' as an Ethical Norm in the Enlightenment." In L. J. Jordanova, ed., *Languages of Nature*. London: Free Association Books, 1986.
Pocock, J. G. A. *The Machiavellian Moment*. Princeton: Princeton University Press, 1975.
Pope, Alexander. *An Essay concerning the Origin of Sciences. Prose Works*, Vol. 3, ed. Rosemary Cowler. Oxford: Blackwell, 1986. 277–304.
Pope, Alexander. *The Memoirs of the Extraordinary Life, Works and Discoveries of Martinus Scriblerus*. Ed. C. Kerby-Miller. Oxford: Oxford University Press, 1988.
Porter, R. S. Introduction to John Haslam, *Illustrations of Madness*. London: Routledge, 1988. xi–lxiv.
Porter, R. S. "Medicine and the Enlightenment in Eighteenth Century England." *Bulletin of the Society for the Social History of Medicine* 25 (1979): 27–40.
Porter, R. S. "Science, Provincial Culture and Public Opinion in Enlightenment England." *British Journal of Eighteenth Century Studies* 3 (1980): 20–46.
Porter, R. S. "William Hunter: A Surgeon and a Gentleman." In W. Bynum and R. S. Porter, eds., *William Hunter and the Eighteenth-Century Medical World*. Cambridge: Cambridge University Press, 1986. 7–34.
Priestley, Joseph. *History and Present State of Electricity*. London, 1767.
Priestley, Joseph. *History and Present State of Electricity*. 3d ed. London, 1775.
Priestley, Joseph. *Theological and Miscellaneous Works*. Ed. J. T. Rutt. 25 vols. London, 1817–32.
Ramsey, M. *Professional and Popular Medicine in France, 1770–1830*. Cambridge: Cambridge University Press, 1988.
Reid, Thomas. *Works*. Ed. W. Hamilton. Edinburgh, 1846.
Revel, J. "Forms of Expertise: Intellectuals and "Popular" Culture in France, 1650–1800." In S. Kaplan, ed., *Understanding Popular Culture*. Paris: Mouton, 1984. 255–73.
Richardson, R. *Death, Dissection and the Destitute*. London: Routledge, 1987.
Roche, D. *Les républicains des lettres*. Paris: Fayard, 1988.
Rogers, P. "Gulliver and the Engineers." In *Literature and Popular Culture in Eighteenth-Century England*. Brighton: Harvester, 1985. 11–28.
Rogers, P. *Hacks and Dunces: Pope, Swift and Grub Street*. London: Methuen, 1980.
Rousseau, G. S. " 'Wicked Whiston' and the Scriblerians." *Studies in Eighteenth-Century Culture* 17 (1987): 17–44.

Sale, W. M. *Samuel Richardson: Master Printer.* Ithaca: Cornell University Press, 1950.

Schaffer, S. "Authorized Prophets: Comets and Astronomers after 1759." *Studies in Eighteenth Century Culture* 17 (1987): 45–74.

Schaffer, S. "Defoe's Natural Philosophy and the Worlds of Credit." In J. Christie and S. Shuttleworth, eds., *Nature Transfigured.* Manchester: Manchester University Press, 1989. 13–44.

Schaffer, S. "Glass Works: Newton's Prisms and the Uses of Experiment." In D. Gooding at al., eds., *The Uses of Experiment.* Cambridge: Cambridge University Press, 1989. 67–104.

Schaffer, S. "Natural Philosophy and Public Spectacle in the Eighteenth Century." *History of Science* 21 (1983): 1–43.

Schaffer, S. "Newton's Comets and the Transformation of Astrology." In P. Curry, ed., *Astrology, Science and Society.* Woodbridge: Boydell, 1987. 219–44.

Schaffer, S. "Priestley and the Politics of Spirit." In C. J. Lawrence and R. Anderson, eds., *Science, Medicine and Dissent: Joseph Priestley.* London: Wellcome Trust, 1987. 39–54.

Schneider, I. "Der Mathematiker Abraham de Moivre." *Archive for History of Exact Sciences* 5 (1968): 177–317.

Schwartz, H. *Knaves, Fools, Madmen and "that subtile effluvium": A Study of the Opposition to the French Prophets in England, 1706–1710.* Gainesville: University of Florida, 1978.

Secord, J. A. "Newton in the Nursery: Tom Telescope and the Philosophy of Tops and Balls, 1761–1838." *History of Science* 23 (1985): 127–51.

Seligman, S. A. "Mary Toft—the Rabbit Breeder." *Medical History* 5 (1961):349–60.

Sennett, R. *The Fall of Public Man.* London: Faber, 1986.

Shapin, S. "The House of Experiment in Seventeenth-Century England." *Isis* 79 (1988): 373–404.

Shapin, S. "Of Gods and Kings: Natural Philosophy and Politics in the Leibniz-Clarke Disputes." *Isis* 72 (1981): 187–215.

Shapin, S. "The Politics of Observation." In R. Wallis, ed. *On the Margins of Science.* Keele: University of Keele, 1979. 139–78.

Shapin, S. "Pump and Circumstance: Robert Boyle's Literary Technology." *Social Studies of Science* 14 (1984): 481–520.

Smith, Adam. *Essays on Philosophical Subjects.* Ed. W. P. D. Wightman and J. C. Bryce. Oxford: Clarendon Press, 1980.

Smith, Adam. *Lectures on Jurisprudence.* Ed. R. L. Meek, D. D. Raphael, and P. G. Stein. Oxford: Clarendon Press, 1978.

Stewart, L. "Public Lectures and Private Patronage in Newtonian England." *Isis* 77 (1986): 47–58.

Stewart, L. "Samuel Clarke, Newtonianism and the Factions of Post-Revolutionary England." *Journal of the History of Ideas* 42 (1981): 53–72.

Stewart, L. "The Selling of Newton: Science and Technology in Early Eighteenth-Century England." *Journal of British Studies* 25 (1986): 179–92.

Swift, Jonathan. *Gulliver's Travels*. Ed. J. Hayward. London: Nonesuch Press, 1968.

Swift, Jonathan. *A Tale of a Tub*. Ed. K. Williams. London: Dent, 1975.

Tagg, J. *The Burden of Representation: Essays on Photographies and Histories*. London: Macmillan, 1988.

Thomas, K. *Religion and the Decline of Magic*. Harmondsworth: Penguin, 1972.

Thompson, E. P. "Eighteenth Century English Society: Class Struggle without Class?" *Social History* 3 (1978): 133–65.

Thompson, E. P. "The Moral Economy of the English Crowd in the Eighteenth Century." *Past and Present* 50 (1971): 76–136.

Thompson, E. P. "Patrician Society, Plebeian Culture." *Journal of Social History* 7 (1974): 382–405.

Thompson, E. P. *Whigs and Hunters*. Harmondsworth: Penguin, 1977.

Tort, Patrick. *L'origine du Paradoxe sur le Comédien*. Paris: Vrin, 1980.

Vartanian, A. *Diderot and Descartes*. Princeton: Princeton University Press, 1953.

Vovelle, M. *La mentalité révolutionnaire*. Paris, Editions sociales, 1985.

Waff, C. "Comet Halley's First Expected Return: English Public Apprehensions 1755–58." *Journal for the History of Astronomy* 17 (1986): 1–37.

Walpole, Horace. *Letters*. Ed. P. Cunningham. 8 vols. London, 1857.

Wassermann, E. R. "The Sympathetic Imagination in Eighteenth-Century Theories of Acting." *Journal of English and Germanic Philology* 46 (1947): 265–72.

Watt, I. *The Rise of the Novel*. Harmondsworth: Penguin, 1983.

Westrum, R. "Science and Social Intelligence about Anomalies: The Case of Meteorites." *Social Studies of Science* 78 (1978): 461–93.

Williams, R. *The Country and the City*. London: Paladin, 1975.

Woods, L. *Garrick Claims the Stage: Acting as a Social Emblem in Eighteenth-Century England*. Westport: Greenwood Press, 1984.

Woolgar, S. *Science: The Very Idea*. London: Tavistock, 1988.

Contributors
Index

Contributors

Gillian Beer is Professor of English at Cambridge University and a Fellow of Girton College. She has written widely on issues concerned with science and literature. Among her books are *Darwin's Plots* (1983), *George Eliot* (1986), and *Arguing with the Past* (1989).

Paul M. Churchland is Professor of Philosophy at the University of California, San Diego. He is also a member of UCSD's Institute for Neural Computation, the Cognitive Science Faculty, and the Science Studies Faculty. He is the author of *Scientific Realism and the Plasticity of Mind* (1979), *Matter and Consciousness* (1984), and *A Neurocomputational Perspective* (1989).

Elizabeth Deeds Ermarth is Presidential Research Professor and Professor of English at the University of Maryland, Baltimore, author of various articles and three books: *Realism and Consensus* (1983), *George Eliot* (1985), and *Sequel to History: Postmodernism and the Crisis of Representational Time* (1992), and currently is writing a volume on the nineteenth-century novel for a six-volume study *The Novel in History* under the general editorship of Gillian Beer.

N. Katherine Hayles is the Carpenter Professor of English at the University of Iowa. She holds advanced degrees in chemistry and English and is president of the Society for Literature and Science. Her books include *The Cosmic Web: Scientific Models and Literary Strategies in the Twentieth Century* (1984) and *Chaos Bound: Orderly Disorder in Contemporary Literature and Science* (1990). She is currently at work on a book entitled *Virtual Bodies: Cybernetics and Contemporary Literature.*

Ludmilla Jordanova is Professor of History at the University of Essex and the author of *Lamarck* (1984) and *Sexual Visions* (1989). She edited and contributed to *Images of the Earth* (1979), *Languages of Nature* (1986), and *The Enlightenment and Its Shadows* (1990). She is currently completing a book called *Testaments of Women 1720–1780* for Oxford University Press.

George Levine Kenneth Burke Professor of English at Rutgers University, New Brunswick, is director of the Rutgers Center for the Critical Analysis of Contemporary Culture. His books include *Darwin and the Novelists* (1988) and *The Realistic Imagination* (1981). He is the editor of *One Culture: Studies in Science and Literature* (1987) and *Constructions of the Self* (199).

Paisley Livingston is Professor of English at McGill University, where he teaches philosophy and literature, critical theory, film, and cultural studies. His publications include *Ingmar Bergman and the Rituals of Art* (1982), *Literary Knowledge: Humanistic Inquiry and the Philosophy of Science* (1988), *Literature and Rationality: Ideas of Agency in Theory and Fiction* (1991), and *Models of Desire: René Girard and the Psychology of Mimesis* (1992).

J. Hillis Miller is Distinguished Professor of English and Comparative Literature at the University of California at Irvine. His recent books include *Versions of Pygmalion* (1990), *Victorian Subjects: Tropes, Parables, Performances, Theory Now and Then* (1990), and *Hawthorne and History* (1991). *Ariadne's Thread* and *Illustration*, the first on theory of narrative, the second on cultural studies and the relation of word and image, appeared in 1992.

Richard W. Miller is Professor of Philosophy at Cornell University. His writings include *Moral Differences* (1992), *Fact and Method* (1987), *Analyzing Marx* (1984), and articles in the philosophy of science, ethics, social and political philosophy, epistemology, and aesthetics.

Harriet Ritvo is Professor of History at MIT. She is the author of *The Animal Estate: The English and Other Creatures in the Victorian Age* (1987) and the co-editor of *Macropolitics of Nineteenth-Century Literature: Nationalism, Imperialism, Exoticism* (1991).

Bruce Robbins teaches English at Rutgers University, New Brunswick. He is the editor of *Intellectuals* (1990) and *The Phantom Public Sphere* (1993), and the author of *Secular Vocations: Intellectualism, Professionalism, Culture* (1993). He is on the editorial collective of *Social Text*.

Richard Rorty is University Professor of the Humanities at the University of Virginia. He has recently published *Objectivity, Relativism and Truth* and *Essays on Heidegger and Others*.

Simon Schaffer lectures in history of science at Cambridge University. He is the author, with Steven Shapin, of *Leviathan and the Air Pump* (1985) and co-editor of *The Uses of Experiment* (1989).

Robert Scholes is the Andrew W. Mellon Professor of the Humanities at Brown University. His latest books are *Protocols of Reading* (1989) and *In Search of James Joyce* (1992).

Jill Sigman is a graduate student in philosophy at the University of California, Berkeley.

Bas C. van Fraassen is Professor of Philosophy at Princeton University. His most recent book is *Quantum Mechanics: An Empiricist View* (1991).

Index

Science and Literature

A series edited by George Levine

One Culture: Essays in Science and Literature
Edited by George Levine

In Pursuit of a Scientific Culture: Science, Art, and Society in the Victorian Age
Peter Allan Dale

Sexual Visions: Images of Gender in Science and Medicine between the Eighteenth and Twentieth Centuries
Ludmilla Jordanova

Writing Biology: Texts in the Social Construction of Scientific Knowledge
Greg Myers

Gaston Bachelard, Subversive Humanist: Texts and Readings
Mary McAllester Jones

Realism and Representation: Essays on the Problem of Realism in Relation to Science, Literature, and Culture
Edited by George Levine

Science in the New Age: The Paranormal, Its Defenders and Debunkers, and American Culture
David J. Hess